STECK-VAUGHN
GED

Science

PROGRAM CONSULTANTS

Myra K. Baum
New York, New York

Sheron Lee Chic
Community School South
East Palo Alto, California

June E. Dean
Parent and Adult Education
Detroit Public Schools
Detroit, Michigan

Ruth E. Derfler, M.Ed.
State GED Chief Examiner
Massachusetts Department of
 Education
Malden, Massachusetts

Joan S. Flanery
Adult Education and Literacy
 Program
Ashland Independent Board
 of Education
Ashland, Kentucky

Michael E. Snyder, Ed.S.
Tennessee Department of
 Corrections
Pikeville, Tennessee

STECK-VAUGHN®
C O M P A N Y
ELEMENTARY • SECONDARY • ADULT • LIBRARY

ST. PHILIP'S COLLEGE LIBRARY

Staff Credits

Executive Editor:	Ellen Northcutt
Senior Editor:	Tim Collins
Design Manager:	John J. Harrison
Cover Design:	Rhonda Childress
Photo Editor:	Margie Foster

Editorial Development: McClanahan & Company, Inc.

Photography: Cover: (lightning) © Vince Streano/Tony Stone Images; (skeleton) © Howard Sochurek/The Stock Market. p.32 © Superstock; p.91 Smithsonian Institution; p.108 United States Geological Survey; p.148 © Superstock; p.178 © Focus On Sports.

ISBN 0-8114-7365-1

Copyright © 1996 Steck-Vaughn Company.

All rights reserved. No part of the material protected by this copyright may be reproduced or utilized in any form or by any means, electronic or mechanical, including photocopying, recording, or by any information storage and retrieval system, without permission in writing from the copyright owner. Requests for permission to make copies of any part of the work should be mailed to: Copyright Permissions, Steck-Vaughn Company, P.O. Box 26015, Austin, Texas 78755.

Printed in the United States of America.

Contents

To the Learner
What Is the GED Test?

You are taking a very big step toward changing your life with your decision to take the GED test. By opening this book, you are taking your second important step: preparing for the test. You may feel nervous about what is ahead, which is only natural. Relax and read the following pages to find out the answers to your questions.

The GED test, the Test of General Educational Development, is given by the GED Testing Service of the American Council on Education for adults who did not graduate from high school. When you pass the GED test, you will receive a certificate that is regarded as being equivalent to a high school diploma. Employers in private industry and government, as well as admissions officers in colleges and universities, accept the GED certificate as they would a high school diploma.

The GED test covers the same subjects people study in high school. The five subject areas are: Writing Skills, Interpreting Literature and the Arts, Social Studies, Science, and Mathematics. You will not be required to know all the information that is usually taught in high school. You will, however, be tested on your ability to read and process information. Certain U.S. states also require a test on the U.S. Constitution or on state government. Check with your local adult education center to see if your state requires such a test.

Each year hundreds of thousands of adults pass the GED test. The *Steck-Vaughn GED Series* will help you develop and refine the reading and thinking skills you need to pass the GED test.

GED Scores

After you complete the GED test, you will get a score for each section and a total score. The total score is an average of all the other scores. The highest score possible on a single test is 80. The scores needed to pass the GED test vary depending on where you live. The chart on page 2 shows the minimum state requirements. A score of *40 or 45* means that the score for each test must be 40 or more, but if one or more scores is below 40, an average of at least 45 is required. A minimum score of *35 and 45* means that the score for each test must be 35 or more and an average of at least 45 is required.

≡GED Score Requirements

Area	Minimum Score on Each Test		Minimum Average on All Five Tests
UNITED STATES			
Alabama, Alaska, Arizona, Connecticut, Georgia, Hawaii, Illinois, Indiana, Iowa, Kansas, Kentucky, Maine, Massachusetts, Michigan, Minnesota, Montana,Nevada, New Hampshire, North Carolina, Ohio, Pennsylvania, Rhode Island, South Carolina, Tennessee, Vermont, Virginia, Wyoming	35	and	45
Arkansas, California, Colorado, Delaware, District of Columbia, Florida, Idaho, Maryland, Missouri, New York, Oklahoma, Oregon, South Dakota, Utah, Washington, West Virginia	40	and	45
Louisiana, Mississippi, Nebraska, New Mexico, North Dakota, Texas	40	or	45
New Jersey (42 is required on Test 1; 40 is required on Tests 2, 3, and 4; 45 is required on Test 5; and 45 average on all 5 tests.)			
Wisconsin	40	and	50
CANADA			
Alberta, British Columbia, Manitoba, New Brunswick (English and French), Northwest Territories, Nova Scotia, Prince Edward Island, Saskatchewan, Yukon Territory	45		—
Newfoundland	40	and	45
U.S. TERRITORIES & OTHERS			
Guam, Kwajalein, Puerto Rico, Virgin Islands	35	and	45
Panama Canal Area, Palau	40	and	45
Mariana Islands, Marshall Islands, Micronesia	40	or	45
American Samoa	40		—

Note: GED score requirements change from time to time. For the most up-to-date information, check with your state or local GED director or GED testing center.

To the Learne

THE TESTS OF GENERAL EDUCATIONAL DEVELOPMENT

This chart gives you information on the content, number of items, and time limit for each test. In some places you do not have to take all sections of the test on the same day. If you want to take all the test sections in one day, the GED test will last an entire day. Check with your local adult education center for the requirements in your area.

Test	Content Areas	Number of Items	Time Limit (minutes)
Writing Skills Part I	Sentence Structure Usage Mechanics	55	75
Writing Skills Part II	Essay	1	45
Social Studies	Geography U.S. History Economics Political Science Behavioral Science	64	85
Science	Biology Earth Science Physics Chemistry	66	95
Interpreting Literature and the Arts	Popular Literature Classical Literature Commentary	45	65
Mathematics	Arithmetic Algebra Geometry	56	90

≡ Where Do You Go to Take the GED Test?

The GED test is offered year-round throughout the United States, its possessions, U.S. military bases worldwide, and in Canada. To find out when and where tests are held near you, contact the GED Hot Line at 1-800-62-MY-GED (1-800-626-9433) or one of these institutions in your area:

- An adult education center
- A continuing education center
- A local community college
- A public library
- A private business school or technical school
- The public board of education

In addition, the Hot Line and the institutions can give you information regarding necessary identification, testing fees, and writing implements. Schedules vary: some testing centers are open several days a week; others are open only on weekends.

ST. PHILIP'S COLLEGE LIBRARY

Why Should You Take the GED Test?

A GED certificate can help you in the following ways:

Employment

People without high school diplomas or GED certificates have much more difficulty changing jobs or moving up in their present companies. In many cases employers will not hire someone who does not have a high school diploma or the equivalent.

Education

If you want to enroll in a technical school, a vocational school, or an apprenticeship program, you often must have a high school diploma or the equivalent. If you want to enter a college or university, you must have a high school diploma or the equivalent.

Personal

The most important thing is how you feel about yourself. You have the unique opportunity to turn back the clock by making something happen that did not happen in the past. You can attain a GED certificate that will help you in the future and make you feel better about yourself now.

How to Prepare for the GED Test

Classes for GED preparation are available to anyone who wants to take the GED. The choice of whether to take classes is up to you; they are not required. If you prefer to study by yourself, the *Steck-Vaughn GED Series* has been prepared to guide your study. *Steck-Vaughn GED Exercise Books* are also available to give you additional practice for each test.

Most GED preparation programs offer individualized instruction and tutors who can help you identify areas in which you may need help. Many adult education centers offer free day or night classes. The classes are usually informal and allow you to work at your own pace and with other adults who also are studying for the GED. In addition to working on specific skills, you will be able to take practice GED tests (like those in this book) in order to check your progress. For information about classes available near you, contact one of the institutions in the list on page 3.

What You Need to Know to Pass
Test Three: **Science**

The GED Science Test examines your ability to understand, think about, and apply science information. You will not be tested on your knowledge of science facts. The GED Science Test takes 95 minutes and has 66 items. The items are divided into four content areas: biology, Earth science, chemistry, and physics.

Biology

About fifty percent of the test items involve biology. There may be passages and illustrations about cells, genetics, ecology, health, nutrition, disease, and the structure and functions of plants and animals, such as reproduction and photosynthesis.

Earth Science

About twenty percent of the test items involve Earth science. There may be passages and illustrations about landforms, earthquakes, volcanoes, rock formation, minerals, fossils, and Earth's history. Also covered are the atmosphere, weather, oceanography, tides, the solar system, and Earth's magnetic field.

Chemistry

About fifteen percent of the test items involve chemistry. There may be passages and illustrations about atoms, elements, molecules, chemical bonding, chemical reactions and their energy changes, radioactivity, and hydrocarbons.

Physics

About fifteen percent of the test items involve physics. There may be passages and illustrations about energy, motion, forces, work, machines, heat transfer, change of state, waves, optics, electricity, magnetism, and nuclear fission and fusion.

The test items require you to read, understand, and think about the science passages and illustrations in several different ways. To answer the items, you will be using four basic reading and thinking skills. The *Steck-Vaughn GED Science* book will train you to apply these skills.

Comprehension

You must read carefully and examine diagrams and charts closely to understand what the writer is saying. You may have to identify and restate specific information. You may be asked for the main idea of a passage. You may also be asked to identify an implication, or logical consequence, of what you have read. Although only twenty percent or fewer items on the test require *only* comprehension skills, these skills form the basis for the other reading and thinking skills.

Application

You will be asked to take information you have read and understood and look at it another way. To answer an application item, first you must understand an idea and then you must use it, or apply it, in another situation. For example, you may read that mammals are warm-blooded animals who give birth to live young. Then you may be asked whether a fish, bumblebee, or squirrel is a mammal. You will be taking general science information and applying it to specific situations.

Analysis

To analyze something means to take it apart and see how it works. When you analyze information, you break it down into smaller parts and examine the relationships among those parts. You may be asked to tell the difference between a fact that can be proved and an opinion. Sometimes you will have to identify a conclusion and the information on which the conclusion is based. At other times, you will be asked why something happened (a cause) or what is likely to happen as a result (an effect).

Evaluation

When you evaluate information, you make judgments about its accuracy. You may be asked whether certain information is true, based on what you have read. You will be asked whether certain conclusions, or generalizations, can be supported by the information provided. You will be asked to choose the best way to solve a problem.

Sample Passage and Items

The following is a sample passage with items. They are similar to actual GED Science Test items in the way they are put together and what they ask you to do. Following each item is an explanation of the skill area that the item tests as well as an explanation of the correct answer.

Some Amazonian Indians have learned to manage farm plots so that over the years the land changes gradually from cleared farmland back to tropical rain forest. The plots go through stages. In the first stage, the plot is cleared and regular crops are grown. In the second stage, certain wild trees and plants are allowed to return gradually. These wild species provide a variety of products, such as medicines and pesticides. In the third stage, the rain forest eventually reclaims the plot. Meanwhile, other plots are in different stages of use. As a result, the soil and the forest constantly renew themselves while supporting the Indians. In contrast, settlers in the Amazon have cleared millions of acres for crops or timber. After a few years of cultivation, the land wears out.

1. What happens to the farm plot during the second stage?

   (1) The land is cleared.
   (2) Only regular crops are grown.
   (3) A mix of farms crops and wild plants are grown.
   (4) Only wild plants are grown.
   (5) The rain forest takes over the plot.

Answer: **(3) A mix of farm crops and wild plants are grown.**

Explanation: This item tests your comprehension skill. You can find the information you need in the fourth sentence of the passage, which states that during the second stage, certain wild plants are allowed to return gradually. This suggests that both farm crops and wild plants are grown during this stage.

2. The Indians' method of managing farmland in the Amazon is most similar to which of the following?

   (1) grazing cattle in fields
   (2) planting a different crop each season in a field to renew the soil
   (3) using chemical pesticides
   (4) growing a single crop on a large farm
   (5) using fertilizer

Answer: **(2) planting a different crop each season in a field to renew the soil**

Explanation: This item tests your ability to apply the information you are given to another situation. First, you must understand that some Amazonian Indians manage their farmland so that the soil and forest can renew themselves. This idea is most similar to crop rotation, in which a different crop is planted each season. The other options do not involve the natural renewal of the land.

3. If the Indians kept the wild plants from returning to the farm plot, what would be the result?

   (1) More crops could be grown for years.
   (2) The wild plants would die out.
   (3) The quality of the crops would improve.
   (4) The crops would wear out the soil after a few seasons.
   (5) The rain forest would take over the plot.

Answer: (4) The crops would wear out the soil after a few seasons.

   Explanation: The item tests your ability to analyze information. In this case, you are being asked to predict the result of an action. If the Indians continued to grow crops, it is likely that the same thing that happened to large areas cleared for crops would happen to the small farm plots also. The land would wear out.

4. Which of the following conclusions is supported by the information in the passage

   (1) Large-scale clearing for farming is the best long-term use of the rain forest.
   (2) Areas of rain forest should not be used for growing crops.
   (3) The rain forest is being destroyed at a rate of millions of acres per year.
   (4) Dairy farming would be a better use of the rain forest.
   (5) Some farmers can use the rain forest without destroying it.

Answer: (5) Some farmers can use the rain forest without destroying it.

   Explanation: This item requires you to evaluate information for its accuracy. First, you must understand the passage. Then you must choose the conclusion that logically follows from the ideas in the passage. In this case, the conclusion supported by the passage is that a resource such as a rain forest can be used without being destroyed. Options (1) and (2) are clearly contradicted by the passage. Option (3) is true, but nothing in the passage proves it is true. Option (4) is not mentioned in the passage.

To help you develop your reading and thinking skills, the answer key for each item in this book has an explanation of why the correct answer is right and why the incorrect answers are wrong. By studying these explanations, you will learn strategies for understanding and thinking about science.

Test-Taking Skills

The GED Science Test is not the kind of test you can cram for. You will be tested on your grasp of critical thinking skills, not on your knowledge of specific information that you can know about beforehand. There are, however, some ways that you can improve your performance on the test.

Answering the Test Items

- Never skim the directions. Read them carefully so that you know exactly what to do. If you are unsure, ask the test-giver if the directions can be explained.

- First skim the passage or briefly look over the illustration to get a general idea of what it is about, and read the items once. Then, before answering the items, reread the passage carefully.

- Read all of the answer options carefully, even if you think you know the right answer. Some of the answers may not seem wrong at first glance, but one answer will always be better than the others.

- Answer all the items. Wrong answers will not be subtracted from your score. If you cannot find the correct answer, reduce the number of possible answers by eliminating all the answers you know are wrong. Then go back to the passage to figure out the correct answer. If you still cannot decide, make your best guess.

- Fill in your answer sheet carefully. To record your answers, mark one numbered space on the answer sheet beside the number that corresponds to the item. Mark only one answer space for each item; multiple answers will be scored as incorrect.

- Remember that the GED is a timed test. When the test begins, write down the time you have to finish. Then keep an eye on the time. Do not take a long time on any one item. Answer each item as best you can and go on. If you are spending a lot of time on one item, skip it. If you finish before time is up, go back to the items you skipped or were unsure of, and give them more thought.

- Don't change an answer unless you are certain your answer was wrong. Usually the first answer you choose is the correct one.

- If you feel you are getting nervous, stop working for a moment. Take a few deep breaths and relax. Then begin working again.

Study Skills

Study Regularly

- If you can, set aside an hour to study every day. If you do not have time every day, set up a schedule of the days you can study. Be sure to pick times when you will be the most relaxed and least likely to be bothered by outside distractions.

- Let others know your study time. Ask them to leave you alone for that period. It helps if you explain to others why this is important.

- You should be relaxed when you study, so find an area that is comfortable for you. If you cannot study at home, go to the library. Most public libraries have areas for reading and studying. If there is a college or university near you, find out if you can use its library. All libraries have dictionaries, encyclopedias, and other resources you can use if you need more information while you're studying.

Organize Your Study Materials

- Be sure to have pens, sharp pencils, and paper for any notes you might want to take.

- Keep all of your books together. If you are taking an adult education class, you probably will be able to borrow some books or other study material.

- Make a notebook or folder for each subject you are studying. Folders with pockets are useful for storing loose papers.

- Keep all of your material in one place so you do not waste time looking for it each time you study.

Read Regularly

- Read the newspaper, read magazines, read books. Read whatever appeals to you—but read! Regular, daily reading is the best way to improve your reading skills.

- Use the library to find material you like to read. Check the magazine section for publications of interest to you. Most libraries subscribe to hundreds of magazines ranging in interest from news to cars to music to sewing to sports. If you are not familiar with the library, ask a librarian for help. Get a library card so that you can check out material to use at home.

Take Notes

- Take notes on things that interest you or things that you think might be useful.

- When you take notes, do not copy the words directly from the book. Restate the information in your own words.

- Take notes any way you want. You do not have to write in full sentences as long as you can understand your notes later.

- Use outlines, charts, or diagrams to help you organize information and make it easier to learn.

- You may want to take notes in a question-and-answer form, such as: *What is the main idea? The main idea is . . .*

Improve Your Vocabulary

- As you read, do not skip a word you do not know. Instead, try to figure out what the word means. First, omit it from the sentence. Read the sentence without the word and try to put another word in its place. Is the meaning of the sentence the same?

- Make a list of unfamiliar words, look them up in the dictionary, and write down the meanings.

- Since a word may have several meanings, it is best to look up the word while you have the passage with you. Then you can try out the different meanings in the context.

- When you read the definition of a word, restate it in your own words. Use the word in a sentence or two.

- Use the Glossary at the end of this book to review the meanings of the key terms. All of the words you see in **boldface** type are defined in the Glossary. In addition, definitions of other important words are included. Use this list to review important vocabulary for the content areas you are studying.

Make a List of Subject Areas that Give You Trouble

- As you go through this book, make a note whenever you do not understand something. Then ask your teacher or another person for help. Later go back and review the topic.

Taking the Test

Before the Test

♦ If you have never been to the test center, go there the day before the test. If you drive, find out where to park. This way you won't get lost the day of the test.

♦ Prepare the things you need for the test: your admission ticket (if necessary), acceptable identification, some sharpened No. 2 pencils with erasers, a watch, glasses, a jacket or sweater (in case the room is cold), and a snack to eat during breaks.

♦ You will do your best work if you are rested and alert. So do not cram before the test. In fact, if you prepared for the test, cramming should be unnecessary. Instead, eat a meal and get a good night's sleep. If the test is early in the morning, set the alarm.

The Day of the Test

♦ Eat a good breakfast. Wear comfortable clothing. Make sure that you have all of the materials you need.

♦ Try to arrive at the test center about twenty minutes early. This allows time if, for example, there is a last-minute change of room.

♦ If you are going to be at the test center all day, you might pack a lunch. If you have to find a restaurant or if you wait a long time to be served, you may be late for the rest of the test.

Using this Book

♦ Start with the Pretest. It is identical to the real test in format and length. It will give you an idea of what the GED test is like. Then use the Pretest Correlation Chart to figure out your areas of strength and the areas you need to review. The chart will tell you exact units and page numbers to study.

♦ As you study, use a copy of the Study Record Sheet to keep track of the times and pages you study. Use the GED Cumulative Review and the Performance Analysis chart at the end of each unit to find out if you need to review any lessons before continuing.

♦ After you complete your review, use the Posttest to decide if you are ready for the real GED test. The Correlation Chart will tell you if you need additional review. Then use the Simulated Test and its Correlation Chart as a final check.

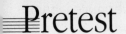

SCIENCE

Directions

The Science Pretest consists of multiple-choice questions intended to measure your understanding of general concepts in science. The questions are based on short readings that often include a graph, chart, or diagram. Study the information given, and then answer the questions that follow. Refer to the information as often as necessary in answering the questions.

You should spend no more than 95 minutes answering the 66 questions on the Science Pretest. Work carefully, but do not spend too much time on any one question. Do not skip any items. Make a reasonable guess when you are not sure of an answer. You will not be penalized for incorrect answers.

When time is up, mark the last item you finished. This will tell you whether you can finish the real GED Test in the time allowed. Then complete the test.

Record your answers to the questions on a copy of the answer sheet on page 345. Be sure that all required information is properly recorded on the answer sheet.

To record your answers, mark the numbered space on the answer sheet that corresponds to the answer you choose for each question on the test.

Example:

Which of the following is the smallest unit in a living thing?

(1) tissue
(2) organ
(3) cell
(4) muscle
(5) capillary   ① ② ● ④ ⑤

The correct answer is "cell"; therefore, answer space 3 should be marked on the answer sheet.

When you finish the test, use the Correlation Chart on page 30 to determine whether you are ready to take the real GED Test, and, if not, which skill areas need additional review.

Do not rest the point of your pencil on the answer sheet while you are considering your answer. Make no stray or unnecessary marks. If you change an answer, erase your first mark completely. Mark only one answer space for each question; multiple answers will be scored as incorrect. Do not fold or crease your answer sheet.

Adapted with permission of the American Council on Education.

Directions: Choose the best answer to each item.

Items 1 to 6 refer to the following article.

Ants are social insects. This means that they live in a group called a colony and that each ant has a job to do to help the whole group survive. Ants must live in a colony; an ant cannot survive alone.

You will find three kinds of ants in a typical colony:

1. There is one queen, who lays eggs.
2. There are winged males. The males develop from unfertilized eggs. Their role is to mate with the queen, after which they die.
3. There are workers. Most of the ants in a colony are worker ants. They are females who cannot lay eggs. Instead, they find food and sometimes fight to help the colony.

Ants are usually helpful to humans. Their underground tunneling mixes and enriches the soil. In some places ants turn more earth than earthworms. Ants spread plant seeds and feed on dead insects and other animals. Many ant species eat insects that are crop pests.

One species, the leaf-cutting ant, harms farmers' crops in Texas and Louisiana. Large leaf-cutting worker ants carry big pieces of leaves to the ant colony. There the smaller workers chop the leaves into tiny bits. The smallest worker ants transplant small pieces of fungus to the bits of leaves. The fungus then grows on the leaves, and the ants use the fungus for food.

1. All of the following activities performed by ants are helpful to humans except

    (1) enriching the soil
    (2) feeding on dead insects
    (3) cutting leaves
    (4) eating crop pests
    (5) spreading plant seeds

2. A sociobiologist studies the way living creatures behave with one another in a group. What would a sociobiologist most likely study about ants?

    (1) the diet of the ant
    (2) the anatomy of the ant
    (3) the location of the colony
    (4) the roles of the queen, winged males, and workers
    (5) the enrichment of the soil

3. In a colony there are fewer males than worker ants. Which sentence best explains this?

    (1) Since there is only one queen to be fertilized, only a few males are required.
    (2) Winged males are always away from the colony.
    (3) The formation of wings requires a specialized environment.
    (4) Winged males develop from unfertilized eggs.
    (5) After they fertilize the queen, winged males die.

4. The role of the queen ant is to produce eggs so that the colony continues. What is the most important contribution other ants make to the life of the colony?

    (1) enriching the soil
    (2) feeding other members of the colony
    (3) cutting leaves
    (4) spreading plant seeds near the colony
    (5) eating crop pests

5. Which of the following is the smallest unit that can survive?

    (1) the individual queen
    (2) the winged male
    (3) the worker
    (4) the queen and her winged males
    (5) the colony

6. Which of the following human behaviors is most similar to the behavior of the leaf-cutting worker ants?

    (1) following a political system with a king and queen
    (2) performing tasks one after another on an assembly line
    (3) raising crops
    (4) raising livestock
    (5) maintaining an army

Items 7 and 8 refer to the following map.

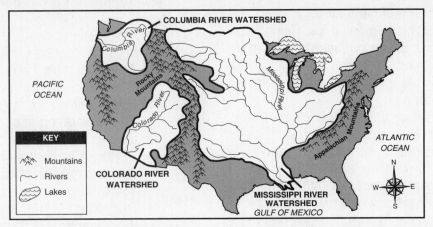

7. The area of land drained by a river is known as a watershed. Why does water in most watersheds eventually drain into an ocean?

(1) The oceans are the largest bodies of water on Earth.
(2) Each land mass is surrounded by an ocean.
(3) Water flows toward the equator.
(4) Water flows from high elevations, such as mountains, to sea level.
(5) Too much water flows into the ocean too quickly.

8. How did early explorers of the Northwest use knowledge of watersheds to know they were approaching the Pacific Ocean?

(1) They conserved water for the journey over the Rocky Mountains.
(2) They saw that the Columbia River was flowing to the west.
(3) They found the source of the Columbia River.
(4) They encountered flooding in the Columbia River watershed.
(5) They determined that the elevation of the Columbia River was too high to make it a major watershed.

Items 9 and 10 are based on the following information.

Gas is a state of matter in which the molecules of a substance fill whatever space is available. The gas laws describe what happens to the gas when pressure, volume, or temperature changes.

Boyle's law tells how the volume of a gas changes when the pressure on it changes. For example, doubling the pressure on a gas will decrease its volume by one half. If all other conditions stay the same, the volume becomes smaller as the pressure becomes greater.

Charles's law tells how the volume of a gas changes when the temperature changes. Again, if all other conditions remain the same, the volume becomes greater when the temperature is higher. For example, if the absolute temperature of a gas were doubled, its volume would double.

9. Oxygen gas is often stored under pressure in metal tanks called cylinders. What is the best reason given below for storing oxygen under pressure?

(1) Oxygen would otherwise mix with air.
(2) The oxygen can be cooled.
(3) Charles's law suggests this way is best.
(4) More oxygen will fit in the container.
(5) Pressure turns oxygen into a liquid.

10. To explain why hot-air balloons rise, you would need to know

A. Boyle's law
B. Charles's law
C. the number of molecules in the balloon

(1) A only
(2) B only
(3) C only
(4) A and B
(5) A and C

Items 11 to 14 refer to the following article.

Earth's crust is made of plates thousands of miles across and 30 or 40 miles thick. Scientists think that at one time all the continents formed a single land mass called Pangaea. Pangaea broke into huge pieces that drifted apart, forming the present continents.

Plate tectonics is the study of how plates form, move, and interact. Plates come together at three types of continually changing boundaries:

1. <u>Diverging boundaries</u> separate plates that are moving apart. These are generally located beneath the oceans. The Gulf of California is located over a diverging boundary.
2. <u>Converging boundaries</u>, located where plates are colliding, may form high mountains, deep ocean trenches, earthquakes, or volcanoes. The Himalayas are located at a converging boundary.
3. <u>Transform fault boundaries</u> occur where plates are sliding past one another. Like converging boundaries, they also cause earthquake activity. The San Andreas Fault in California is located along a transform fault boundary.

11. The formation of the Himalaya Mountains was caused by

    (1) two plates moving toward each other
    (2) two plates moving away from each other
    (3) two plates moving along each other
    (4) volcanic activity
    (5) the breakup of Pangaea

12. All of the following are related to the theory of plate tectonics <u>except</u>

    (1) patterns of volcanic activity
    (2) earthquake zones
    (3) deep ocean trenches
    (4) the locations of the continents
    (5) the rise and fall in the water level of major rivers

13. According to the theory of plate tectonics, what is true of Earth's continents?

    (1) The continents are stable in their present locations.
    (2) The continents ride on plates that move, causing new formations of land and water.
    (3) The separation of continents was caused by a rising ocean.
    (4) Earthquakes, volcanoes, and other dramatic geologic activity may stop someday.
    (5) Diverging boundaries usually occur on the continents.

14. What is likely to have caused the formation of the Andes Mountains along the west coast of South America, an area of earthquakes and volcanoes?

    (1) plates drifting apart
    (2) plates sliding past each other
    (3) two plates colliding
    (4) the lowering of sea level
    (5) the Ice Age

Items 15 and 16 are based on the graph below.

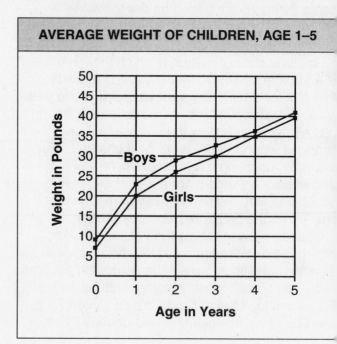

AVERAGE WEIGHT OF CHILDREN, AGE 1–5

Pretest

15. During what year do children gain the most weight?

    (1) 0–1 year
    (2) 1–2 years
    (3) 2–3 years
    (4) 3–4 years
    (5) 4–5 years

16. At age 4, Billy weighs 39 pounds. Billy's weight is

    (1) average for his age and sex
    (2) below average for his age and sex
    (3) above average for his age and sex
    (4) above average for his sex at age 5
    (5) below average for girls at age 4

Items 17 to 20 are based on the following information.

The animal kingdom is made up of thousands of species of animals. They are divided into several groups called <u>phyla</u>. Five of the phyla are described below:

1. <u>Chordata</u>. Animals have a notochord, or stiff rod of cells, as the primary skeletal support during some stage of development. Most members of this phylum are vertebrates, animals with backbones.
2. <u>Mollusca</u>. Animals have soft bodies and usually prominent shells.
3. <u>Arthropoda</u>. Animals have sectioned bodies covered by a jointed external skeleton.
4. <u>Annelida</u>. Soft-bodied, segmented animals are bilaterally symmetrical, or the same on both sides.
5. <u>Cnidaria</u>. Unsegmented animals are symmetrical around a central point and lack a true body cavity.

Each of the following animals belongs to one of the phyla described above. For each item, choose the appropriate phylum. Each phylum above <u>may</u> be used more than once in items 17 to 20.

17. The earthworm, a cylindrical segmented worm, belongs to the phylum

    (1) Chordata
    (2) Mollusca
    (3) Arthropoda
    (4) Annelida
    (5) Cnidaria

18. The clam, a soft-bodied marine animal with a shell, belongs to the phylum

    (1) Chordata
    (2) Mollusca
    (3) Arthropoda
    (4) Annelida
    (5) Cnidaria

19. A cat, an animal with a backbone, belongs to the phylum

    (1) Chordata
    (2) Mollusca
    (3) Arthropoda
    (4) Annelida
    (5) Cnidaria

20. A grasshopper, a long, slender-winged insect with an external jointed skeleton, belongs to the phylum

    (1) Chordata
    (2) Mollusca
    (3) Arthropoda
    (4) Annelida
    (5) Cnidaria

Items 21 to 25 refer to the following article.

If you drop a bar magnet into a pile of iron filings, the filings will stick to the magnet. Iron and steel and a few other metals are attracted to magnets. The force of attraction is called magnetic force. The area around a magnet where the magnetic force acts is called a magnetic field. The field is strongest at the poles, or ends, of the magnet.

Each magnet has a north and a south pole. If you hang a magnet from a string, its north pole will turn to the north. This is because Earth has a magnetic field. The magnetic north pole of Earth is located near the geographic north pole. A compass used for navigation points to the magnetic north pole and not to the geographic north pole.

Many substances that are attracted to a magnet can be magnetized, or made into a magnet. Inside these substances, groups of atoms act as tiny magnets. These groups, called magnetic domains, are usually found with their north and south poles pointing in different directions. If they can be made to line up so that their north and south poles point in the same direction, they will cause a magnetic field. The substance will be a magnet.

21. Which of the following actions could magnetize an iron bar?

    A. leaving it on top of a magnet for a few days
    B. piling iron filings on it
    C. stroking it in one direction with a magnet

(1) A only
(2) B only
(3) C only
(4) A and B
(5) A and C

22. Which of the following items would not be affected by a magnetic field?

(1) iron filings
(2) a rubber eraser
(3) a magnetic compass
(4) a horseshoe magnet
(5) a steel girder in a building

23. The magnetic needle of a compass always points to the north because

(1) compasses are used for finding direction
(2) Earth has a magnetic north pole
(3) the needle touches the north pole
(4) the magnetic domains of the needle point in different directions
(5) Earth's magnetic field is strongest at the south pole

24. Charts are available that show the difference between the geographic north pole and the magnetic north pole. These charts would be most useful for

(1) hikers on a five-mile hike
(2) a sailor navigating by the stars
(3) a sailor navigating with the use of a compass
(4) a person using a compass to find steel nails in a beam
(5) a driver deciding which direction to go on a highway

25. Suppose you cut a bar magnet in half across the middle. What will you have?

(1) one magnet with two north poles and one magnet with two south poles
(2) two magnets, each with one north pole and one south pole
(3) two magnets with only north poles
(4) two magnets with only south poles
(5) one magnet with a north and a south pole and one bar that is not a magnet

Items 26 and 27 are based on the following information.

Density is the relationship between the mass of a substance and its volume. For example, a substance of great mass and small volume is very dense. One substance can be distinguished from another if you know the density of each. The following chart shows the densities of some metals.

DENSITY OF SELECTED METALS	
Metal	Density in Grams per Cubic Centimeter
Aluminum	2.7
Iron	7.9
Copper	8.9
Lead	11.3
Mercury	13.6
Gold	19.3

26. An object will sink in a liquid if it is more dense than the liquid. Which of the following metals will sink in liquid mercury?

(1) iron
(2) copper
(3) lead
(4) gold
(5) aluminum

27. Pure gold is 24-karat gold. Since pure gold is too soft to hold its shape, jewelers almost always mix copper with gold to make jewelry. For example, 14K gold contains 14 parts of pure gold by weight to 10 parts of pure copper. Which of the following would have the greatest density?

(1) 24K gold
(2) 18K gold
(3) 14K gold
(4) 10K gold
(5) They would all have the same density.

Items 28 and 29 refer to the following chart.

FORMATION OF SEDIMENTARY ROCKS		
Agent of Formation	Type of Material in the Rock	Type of Rock Produced
Streams, winds, glaciers	Boulders, pebbles Sand Silt, clay	Conglomerate Sandstone Shale
Chemical reaction in seawater, evaporation	Dissolved minerals	Rock salt, gypsum, some limestone
Organisms	Vegetation Remains of marine animals including shells	Peat and coal Most limestone

28. Which is the best conclusion that can be drawn about the formation of limestone?

(1) It is formed only by mechanical agents such as wind, streams, and glaciers.
(2) It is formed only by chemical reactions in water.
(3) It is formed by the remains of marine animals, including shells.
(4) It is formed in the ocean.
(5) It consists of fine particles of silt.

29. Human beings often copy the methods and materials of nature. In which of the following activities do people copy nature's methods in the formation of sedimentary rock?

A. mixing concrete with pebbles
B. using mud to build an adobe house
C. obtaining salt from seawater by evaporation

(1) A only
(2) B only
(3) A and B
(4) B and C
(5) A, B, and C

Items 30 to 32 are based on the following article.

A gardener often builds a compost pile in a corner of a garden because the compost pile produces a mixture called humus. To create the compost pile, the gardener collects materials that were living, including kitchen waste (vegetable parings) and garden waste (lawn clippings and leaves). In the compost pile, microscopic organisms change this waste into humus. The gardener can then spread the humus on the soil to help plants grow well.

The most important microscopic organisms in compost are bacteria that specialize in breaking down organic matter. They thrive in temperatures up to 170°F and need air to survive. As the compost decomposes and cools, these bacteria give way to other microorganisms.

The new microorganisms include actinomycetes. These are a form of bacteria. As they become more active, they produce antibiotics, chemicals that kill the original bacteria. Protozoans are also present in compost. Their role in composting is less important than that of bacteria. Other compost organisms are fungi. They are primitive plants without chlorophyll. They are active during the final stages of composting.

30. Which microorganisms are active at the start of composting?

(1) bacteria
(2) actinomycetes
(3) protozoa
(4) fungi
(5) All of the microorganisms are active at the start of composting.

31. The removal of which of the following would have the greatest impact on the decomposition occurring in the compost pile

(1) bacteria
(2) actinomycetes
(3) protozoa
(4) fungi
(5) The impact would be the same, regardless of which are removed.

32. All of the following material would be suitable for a compost pile except

(1) manure
(2) straw
(3) lawn clippings
(4) sawdust
(5) plastic wrap

Items 33 and 34 refer to the following map.

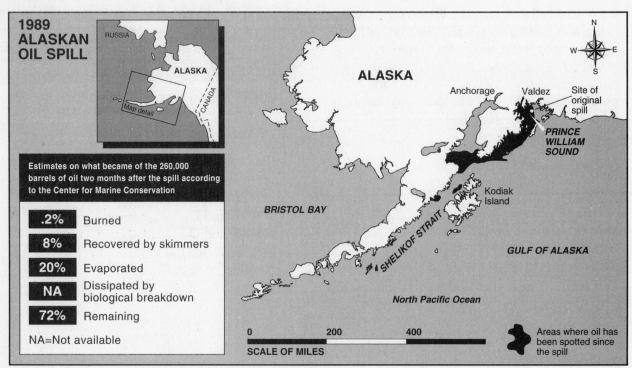

1989 ALASKAN OIL SPILL

RUSSIA
ALASKA
CANADA
Map detail

Estimates on what became of the 260,000 barrels of oil two months after the spill according to the Center for Marine Conservation

.2% Burned
8% Recovered by skimmers
20% Evaporated
NA Dissipated by biological breakdown
72% Remaining
NA=Not available

ALASKA
Anchorage   Valdez   Site of original spill
PRINCE WILLIAM SOUND
Kodiak Island
BRISTOL BAY
SHELIKOF STRAIT
GULF OF ALASKA
North Pacific Ocean

0   200   400
SCALE OF MILES

Areas where oil has been spotted since the spill

3. The map was compiled two months after the original oil spill. What is suggested by the spread of oil and the estimated amount of remaining oil?

(1) Most of the oil was cleaned up during the first two months.
(2) The oil could spread farther south and west.
(3) The oil will be cleared in four months.
(4) The ocean is able to absorb huge amounts of oil.
(5) The remaining oil will evaporate within two months.

4. An oil spill has occurred on the east coast of the United States. Based on the map, what have scientists learned that can be applied to cleaning up the new spill?

(1) The moving of barriers into position earlier will help.
(2) Skimmers should not be used.
(3) They should look into biological methods of cleaning up the oil.
(4) They will be able to clear most of the oil quickly.
(5) Evaporation will probably help clear some of the oil.

Items 35 and 36 refer to the following diagram.

HURRICANE IN NORTHERN HEMISPHERE

Path of storm— 10 miles per hour

Cloud cover

Eye

Winds— 85 miles per hour

N
W — E
S

0   Scale of Miles   350

5. Which of the following is least likely to cause serious damage to life and property in a hurricane?

(1) heavy rains
(2) flooding
(3) high winds
(4) passage of the eye
(5) All of these are likely to cause serious damage.

36. A family on the coast of Virginia took steps to protect their house from a strong hurricane. For more than ten hours, heavy rain fell and strong winds blew from the east. Then the storm quieted, and the sky cleared. What should the family do?

(1) Remove the storm protection measures because the hurricane is over.
(2) Remove the storm protection measures because the rest of the hurricane will be mild.
(3) Leave storm protection measures in place because the rain and winds will start again—this time from the other direction.
(4) Leave the storm protection measures in place because there may be another hurricane tomorrow.
(5) Resume normal activities.

Items 37 and 38 refer to the following information.

Corrosion, or rusting, is a process in which iron combines with air and water to form rust. Rust is brittle and flakes off, so fresh surfaces of the iron continue to be exposed to corrosion. Rusting can be prevented by keeping air and water from the iron surface.

37. A practical method of protecting cast-iron cookware from rusting is

(1) washing it in detergent and water
(2) not exposing it to liquids
(3) not exposing it to air
(4) oiling it to create a barrier against air and water
(5) heating it slowly

38. Plating—or coating iron with chromium, tin, nickel, or zinc—prevents rust because

(1) the rust has been permanently removed
(2) the plating metal destroys the rust
(3) the iron is mixed with the other materials
(4) the rust no longer flakes off
(5) the iron is not exposed to air and water

Items 39 and 40 refer to the following diagram.

CELL DIVISION

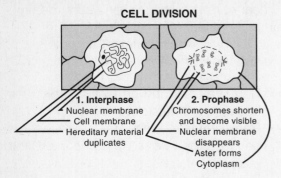

1. **Interphase**
Nuclear membrane
Cell membrane
Hereditary material
duplicates

2. **Prophase**
Chromosomes shorten
and become visible
Nuclear membrane
disappears
Aster forms
Cytoplasm

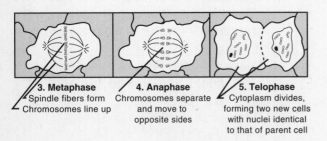

3. **Metaphase**
Spindle fibers form
Chromosomes line up

4. **Anaphase**
Chromosomes separate
and move to
opposite sides

5. **Telophase**
Cytoplasm divides,
forming two new cells
with nuclei identical
to that of parent cell

39. In cell division, one cell becomes two. Each cell must have chromosomes exactly like those of the parent cell. What step ensures that the chromosomes are the same?

(1) duplication of hereditary material (Interphase)
(2) disappearance of the nuclear membrane (Prophase)
(3) formation of the aster (Prophase)
(4) chromosomes shorten and become visible (Prophase)
(5) division of the cell material (Telophase)

40. According to the diagram, where does the material that was inside the nucleus go when the nuclear membrane disappears?

(1) It joins the cell membrane.
(2) It links to the asters.
(3) It enters the cytoplasm.
(4) It makes up the spindles.
(5) It is part of the nuclear membrane.

Items 41 and 42 refer to the following information.

Yeasts are one-celled fungi that are mixed with flour and other ingredients to make bread dough. The yeast changes some of the starches and sugars in the dough and produces alcohol and the gas carbon dioxide. When dough becomes warm, the carbon dioxide expands and causes the bread to rise. During the actual baking, the bread continues to rise until the high heat causes the yeast cells to die, and the alcohol evaporates.

41. Before baking bread, the dough is usually allowed to rise. To ensure that the dough rises, which is the best location to let it rest?

(1) in the freezer
(2) in the refrigerator
(3) in a cool spot in the kitchen
(4) in a warm spot in the kitchen
(5) in an oven heated to 450° C

42. You have probably noticed the pores, or small holes, in a slice of bread. These holes are the result of

(1) starches in the dough
(2) sugars in the dough
(3) flour in the dough
(4) salt in the dough
(5) carbon-dioxide bubbles in the dough

Energy passes through ecosystems in the form of food. In the process of photosynthesis, plants use the sun's energy to make organic material. This organic material is used as food for the plants as well as for the animals that eat plants. The feeding relationships in an ecosystem make up a food chain.

Organisms in a food chain operate at one or more levels in the chain. Producers are plants that use the sun's energy to manufacture food. Other creatures consume, or eat, the food. Primary (first-level) consumers are animals that eat plants. Secondary (second-level) consumers are animals that eat primary consumers. Tertiary (third-level) consumers are animals that eat secondary consumers. Some animals called omnivores eat plants and animals. Omnivores are at more than one consumer level. Organisms called decomposers make up the final stage in the food chain. Fungi and microorganisms break down the remains of dead plants and animals and return the components to the soil, where they are used again by plants.

Energy passes from plant to animal to animal to decomposer. Although decomposers return the remains of dead organisms to the soil, they do not return energy to the soil. Each consumer in the food chain uses up some of the energy. As a result, less energy is available to the next consumer level.

43. On an African prairie, antelopes eat grasses, and lions and cheetahs eat antelopes. Vultures eat what the cats leave. When a lion dies, vultures feed on it as well. Last, bacteria and fungi decompose what remains. In this food chain, when the vultures eat the antelopes, the vultures are functioning as

(1) producers
(2) primary consumers
(3) secondary consumers
(4) tertiary consumers
(5) decomposers

44. Which of the following is true of energy in a food chain?

(1) All the energy at one level is passed to the next level.
(2) Animals get their energy directly from the sun.
(3) There is more energy available to secondary consumers than to tertiary consumers.
(4) There is more energy available to secondary consumers than to primary consumers.
(5) Plants get their energy from the soil.

45. Some animals are classified at more than one level in the food chain because they

(1) eat many varieties of plants
(2) eat many types of insects
(3) eat only plants
(4) eat both plants and animals
(5) have different levels of energy

46. What is the original source of energy in a food chain?

(1) water
(2) the sun
(3) plants
(4) omnivores
(5) decomposers

Items 47 and 48 refer to the following diagram.

BUOYANCY

Weight of object = weight of displaced liquid (liquid pushed aside)

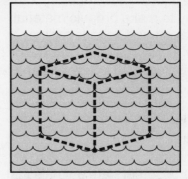

Weight of object is greater than weight of displaced liquid

47. An object will float if

(1) it displaces or pushes aside liquid
(2) its weight equals the weight of the liquid it displaces
(3) its weight is greater than the weight of the liquid it displaces
(4) its weight equals the weight of the liquid in which it is placed
(5) its weight is greater than the weight of the liquid in which it is placed

48. A solid steel cube will sink when placed in water, but a steel ship will float. Which of the following is the best explanation of why a steel ship will float?

(1) Steel is heavier than the water it displaces.
(2) Steel is lighter than the water it displaces.
(3) Steel and air are heavier than the water they displace.
(4) Steel and air are equal in weight to the water they displace.
(5) Steel and air are lighter than the water they displace.

Items 49 and 50 refer to the following diagram.

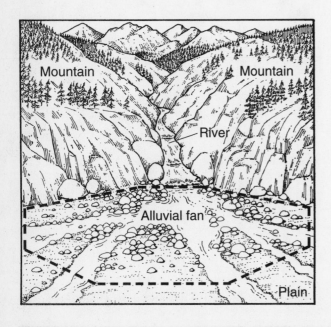

49. From the diagram you can conclude that alluvial fans

(1) are ancient land formations
(2) are formed by the action of glaciers
(3) are formed by sediment or soil carried by rivers from mountains to the plain
(4) contain rich soil that is good for agriculture
(5) occur in regions of volcanic activity

50. When the river comes out of the mountains and into the plain, it

(1) speeds up and becomes colder
(2) becomes narrower and slows down
(3) becomes narrower and speeds up
(4) spreads out and slows down
(5) goes underground

Prete

In order to be healthy, plants must take in ertain minerals from the soil. These minerals ontain the chemical elements that plants need o grow. Nitrogen is used for leaf and stem growth. Phosphorus helps strengthen roots and tems. Potassium helps prevent disease. Other elements are also needed but to a lesser extent. s plants grow, they use up the minerals in the oil. When plants are harvested, these chemicals re not returned to the soil. For this reason, ertilizers are added to the soil to restore its bility to support growing plants.

Artificial fertilizers consist of mined or nanufactured minerals that contain the missing hemicals. These are mixed in different roportions. When the composition of the soil is nalyzed, it is easy to see which chemical is nissing and to select the proper mix. Fertilizer abels show the percentages of the three major ngredients. For example, 8-12-6 means that the ertilizer contains 8 percent nitrogen, 12 percent hosphorus, and 6 percent potassium. Artificial ertilizers contain these elements in compounds hat are easy for plants to absorb.

Some people prefer to use organic or living natter, such as compost or manure, as fertilizer to eplace the missing chemicals. These natural ertilizers contain minerals in complex ompounds. Plants cannot absorb these ompounds until they have been broken down by he decay process. In addition, the exact mineral ontent of the organic matter cannot be controlled.

1. Fertilizers are added to the soil because they

   (1) replace soil worn away by erosion
   (2) restore chemicals lost in the composting process
   (3) restore chemicals used up as plants grow
   (4) help control the microorganisms in the soil
   (5) are better than manure

52. The addition of fertilizer to the soil is most similar to adding

   (1) vegetables to your diet
   (2) vitamin A to skim milk
   (3) artificial sweetener to a soft drink
   (4) fluoride to the water supply
   (5) sugar to cereal

53. On what basis could a farmer who uses organic fertilizers claim that it is better to buy these vegetables than vegetables grown using artificial fertilizers?

   (1) Organically grown vegetables use organic forms of minerals.
   (2) Organically grown vegetables use simple forms of minerals.
   (3) Organic fertilizers act on the soil in a manner more similar to nature than do chemical fertilizers.
   (4) Organic fertilizers can be more easily adjusted to achieve the correct balance of minerals than chemical fertilizers.
   (5) Organic fertilizers contain pesticides.

Items 54 to 56 are based on the following information.

Mammals are a class of animals whose females produce milk to feed their young after birth. Mammals are divided into several groups, or orders. Five of the orders are described below.

1. Carnivores are mammals that are meat-eaters.
2. Cetaceans are mammals with very large heads and tapering bodies that live entirely in the water, usually the ocean.
3. Marsupials are mammals whose females have pouches in which the young develop after birth.
4. Rodents are small mammals with a single pair of incisors, upper teeth that are used for gnawing.
5. Primates are mammals with complex brains, specialized limbs used for grasping, and eyes that can perceive depth.

54. Which of the following mammals would be of most interest to a physical anthropologist, a person who studies the evolution of humans?

(1) carnivores
(2) cetaceans
(3) marsupials
(4) rodents
(5) primates

55. The domestic cat is often valued as a mouse catcher. The domestic cat is a member of which group of mammals?

(1) carnivores
(2) cetaceans
(3) marsupials
(4) rodents
(5) primates

56. Kangaroos are mammals with powerful hind legs, long feet, and front paws used for grasping. The young kangaroo is born in an undeveloped state. It spends about six months in the mother's pouch, where it feeds on milk she produces. The key characteristic that classifies kangaroos as marsupials is

(1) powerful hind legs
(2) production of milk by the mother
(3) handlike forepaws used for grasping
(4) a pouch in which the young stay after birth
(5) two upper incisor teeth used for gnawing

Solar energy is energy from the sun. Unlike ossil fuels such as oil and coal, solar energy is a enewable resource. Fossil fuels will someday be sed up. Solar energy does not produce smoke r ash and is a clean source of energy. Fossil uels often produce smoke or ash.

One way to gather solar energy for use in a uilding is through a solar collector. A solar ollector looks like a box with a glass or plastic op. Inside the box are tubes filled with water. he sun heats the water in the tubes, and the eated water is pumped into a storage tank. rom there the hot water is piped through the uilding.

Another way to gather solar energy is to build ouses that act as solar collectors. Sunlight omes in through the windows that face the sun. Iaterials inside the house absorb and release e heat. To make sure that enough heat is tored during sunny days to warm the house on loudy days and at night, a dense material, such s stone, cement, or brick, is used to collect the nergy. The dense material is called a storage ass. At night and on sunless days, the storage ass continues to release energy into the air round it.

To convert a building so that it can use solar eat may require the redesign of windows, the reation of storage masses, and the addition of ollectors to the roof or surrounding areas.

7. What is the major reason that solar heating of homes is not widespread?

   (1) Solar heating always requires large windows.
   (2) Solar heating always requires a storage mass.
   (3) Most houses do not receive direct sunlight.
   (4) It is often difficult and expensive to convert existing houses to solar energy.
   (5) Solar heating pollutes the environment.

58. The purpose of a storage mass is to

    (1) serve as the foundation of the house
    (2) provide a decorative surface for the southern wall
    (3) heat water
    (4) store cement, stone, and brick
    (5) store reserves of energy to be used on cloudy days and at night

59. How does a storage mass provide heat to areas of the house that are not near it?

    (1) Heated air is piped into radiators throughout the house.
    (2) Heated water is piped into radiators throughout the house.
    (3) Steam is piped into radiators throughout the house.
    (4) Heated air near the storage mass creates air currents that circulate warm air throughout the house.
    (5) The storage mass generates electricity, which is used to heat the house.

60. Which of the statements listed below are included in the article as evidence of the importance of developing solar energy?

    A. The supply of fossil fuels will run out.
    B. Fossil fuels do not produce much energy.
    C. Fossil fuels are sources of pollution.
    D. Fossil fuels are imported into the United States.

    (1) A and B
    (2) B and C
    (3) A and C
    (4) A and D
    (5) A, B, and C

Items 61 to 63 are based on the following information.

The temperature at which a liquid begins to boil is called the boiling point. At the boiling point, the vapor pressure in the liquid is equal to the pressure of the atmosphere. At higher elevations, the pressure of the atmosphere decreases, and the boiling point is lowered. No matter how much more heat is applied, a liquid never gets hotter than its boiling point. It simply boils until there is no liquid left.

BOILING POINTS OF SOME LIQUIDS	
Liquid	Boiling Point at Sea Level (°C)
Chloroform ($CHCl_3$)	61.7
Ethanol (C_2H_5OH)	78.5
Water (H_2O)	100.0
Octane (C_8H_{18})	126.0

61. In New York City, which has an elevation of 0 meters, water boils at 100°C. In Denver, Colorado, at an elevation of 1,609 meters, water probably boils at

   (1) 126°C
   (2) 100°C
   (3) 95°C
   (4) 0°C
   (5) −5°C

62. At sea level, which of the following substances would boil first if they were all heated at the same rate?

   (1) chloroform
   (2) ethanol
   (3) water
   (4) octane
   (5) They would all reach the boiling point at the same time.

63. Which of the following conclusions can be supported by the information provided?

   (1) Once a liquid reaches its boiling point, its temperature increases until all the liquid evaporates.
   (2) Water has a higher boiling point than octane.
   (3) Adding salt to water raises its boiling point.
   (4) The boiling point of a liquid increases as the air pressure increases.
   (5) Chloroform is used as an anesthetic because its boiling point is lower than that of water.

Prete

Jellyfish are invertebrate animals that live in the sea. Some of these invertebrates have a two-stage life cycle. The free-swimming jellyfish mate and produce young called polyps. Polyps generally are unable to move from place to place.

The body of a jellyfish is shaped like a bell or umbrella. A clear material that looks like jelly fills the space between the top and the bottom of the bell. The jellyfish's mouth is located in the middle of the bottom surface of the bell. Tentacles grow around the edge of the bell. Jellyfish move up in the water by contracting and relaxing muscles around the edge of the bell. They drift down and depend on ocean currents and waves to move sideways.

Jellyfish usually catch their prey by using stinging cells located on the tentacles. The sting of some jellyfish can be irritating or even dangerous to humans. The sea wasp, for example, is a well-known stinger. It has a tall, rigid bell and four two-part tentacles. It lives in tropical oceans but sometimes strays as far north as Long Island Sound. The Australian variety of the sea wasp is dangerous to humans. A sting from the Australian sea wasp can be fatal.

64. When a jellyfish captures food, it swims up and then drifts down onto its prey. When does a jellyfish use its muscles during this process?

(1) when moving up
(2) when drifting down
(3) when drifting sideways
(4) when drifting up
(5) when swimming down

65. Which of the following statements is supported by the information provided?

(1) Jellyfish stings are usually fatal to humans.
(2) Jellyfish are closely related to mussels and clams.
(3) Jellyfish are concentrated in tropical oceans.
(4) Jellyfish reproduce sexually.
(5) Polyps look like jellyfish.

66. Why might a person who is standing still in the ocean be stung by a jellyfish?

(1) The waves or currents cause the jellyfish to bump into the person.
(2) The jellyfish uses its muscles to swim up to the surface.
(3) The jellyfish uses its muscles to drift down to the ocean floor.
(4) The jellyfish cannot move in shallow water.
(5) Jellyfish only sting moving creatures.

Answers are on page 257

Pretest Correlation Chart: Science

Name: _____ **Class:** _____ **Date:** _____

This chart can help you determine your strengths and weaknesses on the content and reading skill areas of the Science GED Test. Use the Answer Key on pages 257–263 to check your answers to the test. Then circle on the chart the numbers of the test items you answered correctly. Put the total number correct for each content area and skill area in each row and column. Look at the total items correct in each column and row and decide which areas are difficult for you. Use the page references to study those areas. Use a copy of the Study Record Sheet on page 31 to guide your studying.

Cognitive Skills/Content	Comprehension	Application	Analysis	Evaluation	Total Correct
Biology (*pages 32–107*)	1, **15**, 30, 45, 46, 51	6, 17, 18, 19, 20, 43, 52, 54, 55	**16**, 31, 32, **39**, **40**, 44, 56, 64, 66	2, 3, 4, 5, 53, 65	____ out of 30
Earth Science (*pages 108–147*)	11, 12, 13, 58	**8**, **29**, **34**, 36	**7**, 14, **49**, **50**, 59	**28**, **33**, **35**, 57, 60	____ out of 18
Chemistry (*pages 148–177*)	42	**27**, 37, 41, **61**	9, 10, **26**, 38, **62**	**63**	____ out of 11
Physics (*pages 178–214*)	**47**	22, 24	21, 23, 25	**48**	____ out of 7
Total Correct	____ out of 12	____ out of 19	____ out of 22	____ out of 13	Total correct: ____ out of 66

> 1–54 → You need more review.
> 55–66 → Congratulations! You're ready for the GED Test!

Boldfaced numbers indicate items based on charts, graphs, illustrations, and diagrams. For additional help, see the *Steck-Vaughn GED Science Exercise Book*.

Study Record Sheet

Name: _____   **Class:** _____   **Date:** _____

Use this chart to help you track your studies after you take the Pretest, Posttest, or Simulated Test. After each test, use the Science Correlation Charts on pages 30, 235, and 256 to help you figure out the areas you need to study. Then, make a copy of this Study Record Sheet for you to complete. In the column on the left, write the content and skill areas you want to study. Then, after each session, write the date and the pages you studied. Use the sheet to review your study habits from time to time. Are you studying regularly? Are you reviewing the material you need to cover? Do you need to schedule more frequent sessions?

Area: _____ **Pages:** _____	Pages ⟋ Date	Pages ⟋ Date	Pages ⟋ Date
Area: _____ **Pages:** _____	Pages ⟋ Date	Pages ⟋ Date	Pages ⟋ Date
Area: _____ **Pages:** _____	Pages ⟋ Date	Pages ⟋ Date	Pages ⟋ Date
Area: _____ **Pages:** _____	Pages ⟋ Date	Pages ⟋ Date	Pages ⟋ Date
Area: _____ **Pages:** _____	Pages ⟋ Date	Pages ⟋ Date	Pages ⟋ Date
Area: _____ **Pages:** _____	Pages ⟋ Date	Pages ⟋ Date	Pages ⟋ Date

Biology is the study of living organisms.

organism
a living thing

environment
the surroundings in which an organism lives

hereditary
capable of being passed from a parent to an offspring

Biology is the field of science that studies **organisms** and how they interact with one another and their **environment.** Understanding biology helps us understand ourselves and the world around us. It also helps us learn to improve the quality of life and to protect our environment.

In the first lesson of this section, you will learn about the structure of plant and animal cells. Cells are the microscopic units of which all living things are made. They take in food, carry out hundreds of chemical reactions, and reproduce. You will learn how, through the process of reproduction, cells pass on **hereditary** information from one generation to the next.

In the second lesson, you will learn how plants make their own food through the process of **photosynthesis.** You will learn how all living organisms use the process of **cellular respiration** to convert food to energy. Then you will see how these two processes are related. You will also learn how nitrogen is cycled through the **biosphere.**

The third lesson discusses theories about the origin of life and how living things evolved from small, simple organisms to the complex plants and animals we see around us today. You will learn how the environment affects the development of new **species** through the process of natural selection.

The fourth lesson explains how plants grow from a single seed and develop such features as stems, leaves, roots, and flowers. You will be introduced to the system scientists use to classify all organisms. You will learn that this system of classification is based on the idea that all living things are related to one another.

In the fifth lesson, you will learn about some of the **organ systems** of the human body. For example, you will learn how the digestive system works and how the heart pumps blood through the body. You will also learn about the glands of the body and how they regulate many of the body's functions.

The sixth lesson begins with a discussion of how scientists discovered the cause of **infectious** diseases. You will be introduced to two types of disease-causing agents, bacteria and viruses. You will learn about the structure of bacteria and viruses and how they cause diseases. At the end of the lesson, you will learn about some scientific developments used to fight infectious diseases.

The seventh lesson discusses how parent organisms pass on characteristics to their **offspring.** You will learn about the experiments that opened the field of modern **genetics.** You will also see how all genetic information is coded in each cell. You will learn about the role of the DNA molecule and about special portions of genetic molecules called genes.

In the last lesson, you will learn how organisms interact with one another and their environment in **ecosystems.** You will be introduced to factors that influence the stability of an ecosystem, including food, energy, and population density. The lesson closes with a discussion of how environmental pollution has affected all living things.

photosynthesis
the process by which plants use light energy to make food

cellular respiration
the chemical process by which living things convert food to energy for their use

biosphere
the thin layer of Earth where life exists

species
a group of similar organisms that can mate and produce fertile offspring

organ system
several organs working together to perform a function

infectious
capable of being spread from one organism to another

offspring
the direct descendants of an animal or plant

genetics
the study of inherited characteristics

ecosystem
a selected area where living and nonliving things interact

SEE ALSO: Steck-Vaughn GED Science Exercise Book, Unit 1: Biology.

Comprehension: Identifying the Main Idea

When you are studying or taking a test, you are reading to understand the material. This means you must read slowly and carefully, looking for main ideas and details.

How can you find the main ideas of a passage? First look over the passage quickly, noting how many paragraphs there are. If there are three paragraphs, you should find three main ideas.

Each paragraph is a group of sentences about a single topic, or **main idea.** The main idea of a paragraph is usually in the **topic sentence.** Often the topic sentence is the first or last sentence of the paragraph, but sometimes the topic sentence is in the middle. Wherever it is, the sentence with the main idea has a meaning general enough to cover all the points made in the paragraph. Sometimes the main idea is not stated clearly in one sentence. In that case, read the whole paragraph to find the main idea.

When you think you have found the main idea of a paragraph, look for **supporting details.** These may be reasons, proofs, examples, or particulars that add to the main idea. Sometimes the supporting details are in the form of a list.

Read the following paragraph to find the main idea and the supporting details.

A **reflex** is an automatic response to a stimulus from the environment or surroundings. For example, when you try to pick up a hot pan from the stove, the heat from the pan causes you to pull your hand away. Or, when a light is suddenly turned on in a dark room, you blink and squint against the glare. Reflexes prevent you from further injuring yourself. Because reflexes occur without your having to think about them, they are said to be automatic.

You were correct if you said the first sentence of the paragraph tells the main idea. This sentence gives a broad definition of a reflex, which is the topic of the paragraph. The second and third sentences offer examples of reflexes. The fourth sentence tells why reflexes are important. The last sentence tells why reflexes are said to be automatic.

 When identifying the main idea, look for the general idea of the entire paragraph. When identifying the supporting details, look for concepts that are more specific than the main idea.

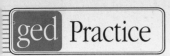

Items 1 to 5 refer to the following passage. Choose the best answer to each item.

The skin of our bodies forms a protective surface. Skin is made up of epithelial tissue, which is flat and broad. This tissue also forms a protective lining for organs, such as the stomach. The cells that make up epithelial tissue are close together. As a result, this tissue can control which substances pass through it.

Another type of human tissue is connective tissue. This tissue supports and holds together parts of the body. The cells in connective tissue are not close together. Nonliving material, such as calcium, fills the spaces between cells. Such nonliving substances give connective tissues strength. Bone and cartilage are the most familiar types of connective tissue.

1. What is the main idea of the first paragraph?

   (1) Epithelial tissue controls the passage of substances through it.
   (2) The stomach contains epithelial tissue.
   (3) Skin is a type of epithelial tissue.
   (4) The cells of epithelial tissue are close together.
   (5) Epithelial tissue forms a protective surface for parts of the body.

2. What is the main idea of the second paragraph?

   (1) Human connective tissue supports and holds together parts of the body.
   (2) Connective tissue contains nonliving material.
   (3) Bone is a familiar form of connective tissue.
   (4) Cartilage is a type of connective tissue.
   (5) Calcium is found in some connective tissue.

3. Based on the information given, which of the following statements is not true?

   (1) The function of epithelial tissue is to protect underlying tissue.
   (2) The function of connective tissue is to support and hold together the body.
   (3) It is difficult for substances to pass through epithelial tissue.
   (4) Both epithelial and connective tissue are made up of living and nonliving material.
   (5) The living cells of connective tissue are more loosely arranged than those of epithelial tissue.

4. Both paragraphs contain examples as supporting details for the main idea. Which of the following is in the form of an example?

   (1) Connective tissue contains nonliving material.
   (2) The cells of epithelial tissue are close together.
   (3) Skin is a type of epithelial tissue.
   (4) Connective tissue supports and holds together parts of the body.
   (5) Epithelial tissue controls the passage of substances through it.

5. According to the information given, which of the following is not a living material?

   (1) the protective lining of the stomach
   (2) the calcium found in bone
   (3) the epithelial tissue
   (4) the skin of our bodies
   (5) the cells of connective tissue

Answers are on page 263.

The Biology of Cells

All organisms are made up of microscopic units called <u>cells</u>. Some organisms consist of only a single cell. Other organisms are made up of many cells. Almost all cells have certain things in common, and their basic structure is similar. All cells take in food. They break down food to get energy, and then they give off waste. Cells also grow, reproduce, and die.

Most cells are divided into two general parts, the <u>nucleus</u> and the <u>cytoplasm</u>. The nucleus controls the cell's activities, and the cytoplasm carries out these activities.

The nucleus of a cell is a round body inside the cell. The three parts of the nucleus include:

1. <u>Nucleolus</u>. The nucleolus is a structure that plays a role in making protein.
2. <u>Chromatin</u>. The chromatin is the genetic material contained in the nucleus. When the cell divides, the chromatin forms chromosomes which carry the hereditary information for the cell.
3. <u>Nuclear membrane</u>. The nuclear membrane divides the nucleus from the cytoplasm.

The cytoplasm contains the other cell structures which are called <u>organelles</u>. Some organelles found in the cytoplasm include:

1. <u>Mitochondria</u>. Mitochondria are rod-shaped organelles that produce almost all the energy a cell needs. Some cells have hundreds of mitochondria.
2. <u>Endoplasmic reticulum</u>. The endoplasmic reticulum (ER) is a system of membranes running through the cytoplasm. It is thought that the ER carries materials throughout the cell.
3. <u>Ribosomes</u>. Ribosomes are tiny structures that are attached to some of the ER and scattered throughout the cytoplasm. They help make proteins.
4. <u>Vacuoles</u>. Vacuoles are storage spaces in the cytoplasm. They may contain food or water, or they may collect and excrete waste.

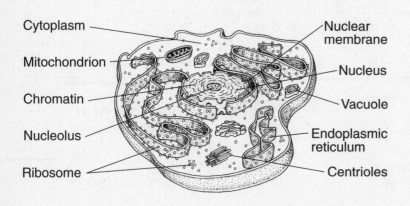

Cytoplasm

Mitochondrion

Chromatin

Nucleolus

Ribosome

Nuclear membrane

Nucleus

Vacuole

Endoplasmic reticulum

Centrioles

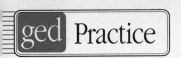
Items 1 to 6 refer to the previous passage and diagram. Choose the best answer to each item.

1. Which of the following sums up the main idea of the first paragraph?

   (1) All cells need energy to live.
   (2) Most cells have things in common and have a similar structure.
   (3) Food gives the cell energy.
   (4) The nucleus is the center of the cell.
   (5) The nucleus is an organelle.

2. Which detail most completely supports the main idea of the first paragraph?

   (1) All cells grow, reproduce, and die.
   (2) Most cells have things in common and have a similar structure.
   (3) Some organisms consist of a single cell.
   (4) The nucleus is the center of the cell.
   (5) The nucleus is an organelle.

3. What is the main idea of the second paragraph?

   (1) Most cells have a nucleus.
   (2) The nucleus controls the activities of the cell.
   (3) Most cells are divided into two basic parts.
   (4) All cells have cytoplasm.
   (5) The activities of the cell are carried out by the cytoplasm.

4. What is the main idea of the third paragraph?

   (1) The nucleus is round.
   (2) The nucleolus is part of the nucleus.
   (3) The nucleus contains a nucleolus, chromatin, and a nuclear membrane.
   (4) The nuclear membrane divides the nucleus from the cytoplasm.
   (5) Chromatin forms chromosomes during cell division.

5. Which of the following sums up the main idea of the fourth paragraph?

   (1) Cytoplasm contains all the structures inside the cell membrane except the nucleus.
   (2) Organelles are cell structures.
   (3) Mitochondria produce the energy a cell needs for its activities.
   (4) Vacuoles are storage spaces in the cytoplasm.
   (5) Cytoplasm includes the nucleus.

6. Which detail most completely supports the main idea of the fourth paragraph?

   (1) Organelles are cell structures.
   (2) Mitochondria produce most of the energy needed by a cell.
   (3) The ER is used to transport material through the cell.
   (4) A cell may contain hundreds of mitochondria.
   (5) The cytoplasm contains mitochondria, the ER, ribosomes, and vacuoles.

> **tip**
> **When identifying supporting details, watch for names, numbers, dates, and examples. Also look for key words and phrases such as *like*, *such as*, and *for instance*.**

Answers are on page 264.

Items 1 to 6 refer to the following passage and diagram. Choose the best answer to each item.

The process by which a cell divides is called mitosis. During mitosis, the chromosomes in the original cell, or parent cell, duplicate and divide into two identical sets. One set will go to each of two new cells, or daughter cells. The process of cell division (mitosis) is divided into five phases.

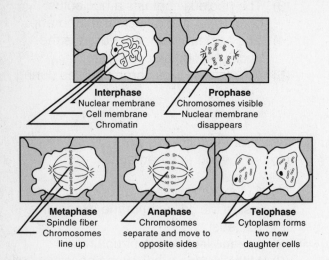

Interphase
Nuclear membrane
Cell membrane
Chromatin

Prophase
Chromosomes visible
Nuclear membrane
disappears

Metaphase
Spindle fiber
Chromosomes
line up

Anaphase
Chromosomes
separate and move to
opposite sides

Telophase
Cytoplasm forms
two new
daughter cells

During the first phase, called interphase, the chromatin (hereditary material) in the nucleus duplicates itself. This is the longest phase of mitosis.

During the second phase, called prophase, the chromatin shortens and thickens to form the chromosomes. Each chromosome is made of two identical parts that are attached at their centers. Protein fibers called spindle fibers come from opposite poles, or ends, of the cell toward the chromosomes The membrane around the nucleus disappears.

During the third phase, called metaphase, the chromosomes line up across the middle of the cell. A spindle fiber attaches to each chromosome. This is the shortest phase of mitosis.

During the fourth phase, called anaphase, the identical parts of chromosomes separate. They move toward opposite sides of the cell, pulled by the spindle fibers.

During the final phase, called telophase, the chromosomes again become threads of hereditary material (chromatin) and the spindle fibers disappear. A new membrane forms around each nucleus. After division of the nucleus is complete, the cytoplasm of the cell divides, producing two daughter cells. The two daughter cells have exactly the same hereditary material.

The two daughter cells are now in interphase. The cells grow and the chromatin duplicates itself again.

1. According to the diagram, when do the spindles first attach to the chromosomes?

   (1) interphase
   (2) prophase
   (3) metaphase
   (4) anaphase
   (5) telophase

2. What appears to be pulling the chromosomes apart during anaphase?

   (1) cell membrane
   (2) cytoplasm
   (3) nuclear membrane
   (4) nucleus
   (5) spindle fibers

3. Which phase makes sure that both daughter cells will receive all hereditary material?

   (1) interphase
   (2) prophase
   (3) metaphase
   (4) anaphase
   (5) telophase

4. What is the passage about?

   (1) In telophase, the parent cell finally forms two new cells.
   (2) Mitosis is the process by which cells divide.
   (3) Spindle fibers are important to the process of the division.
   (4) Chromosomes divide in half during mitosis.
   (5) The cytoplasm divides during mitosis.

5. According to the diagram, what do the spindle fibers seem to do in mitosis?

   (1) guide the chromosomes
   (2) produce the nucleus
   (3) form the nuclear membrane
   (4) form the hereditary material
   (5) form a cell plate

6. If the number of chromosomes in the parent cell is 46, how many chromosomes will there be in each daughter cell?

   (1) 12
   (2) 18
   (3) 23
   (4) 46
   (5) 60

Items 7 to 11 refer to the following passage.

Sexual reproductive cells are formed by a process called meiosis. This process differs from mitosis in that the resulting cells, called gametes, have half the number of chromosomes as the parent cell. Human gametes are sperm and eggs. During sexual reproduction, the two gametes combine to form a new cell called a zygote. Because the zygote contains the chromosomes from both gametes, the original number of chromosomes is restored.

Chromosomes occur in pairs. A parent cell contains a complete set of paired chromosomes. A gamete receives only one chromosome from each pair in the parent cell. Thus, a gamete has half the number of chromosomes found in the parent cell.

7. The chromosome number for human body cells is 46. What is the chromosome number for human gametes?

   (1) 12
   (2) 23
   (3) 32
   (4) 46
   (5) 48

8. The chromosome number of a cell produced by meiosis differs from the chromosome number of a cell produced by mitosis in that the cell produced by meiosis has

   (1) half the number
   (2) no chromosomes
   (3) the same number
   (4) one-fourth the number
   (5) twice the number

9. The zygote is formed during

   (1) meiosis
   (2) mitosis
   (3) sexual reproduction
   (4) cell division
   (5) gamete production

10. Some people have 47 chromosomes in their cells, rather than the usual 46. What could cause this error?

   (1) Extra hereditary material was produced during meiosis.
   (2) Some hereditary material was destroyed during sexual reproduction.
   (3) One chromosome pair did not separate properly during meiosis.
   (4) The zygote has one extra chromosome.
   (5) Three gametes, not two, combined during sexual reproduction.

11. What portion of one's chromosomes come from one's father?

   (1) 25 percent
   (2) 33 percent
   (3) 50 percent
   (4) 75 percent
   (5) 100 percent

Answers are on page 264.

Directions: Choose the <u>best answer</u> to each item.

Items 1 to 5 refer to the following information.

Plant cells have some special structures that animal cells do not have. For example, most plant cells have a cell wall surrounding the cell membrane. A cell wall is composed of several layers. The middle layer, called the middle lamella, contains the jellylike substance pectin. Primary walls on either side of the middle lamella are made of cellulose and pectin. Secondary walls form on the outside of the primary walls. These stiff walls are made of cellulose. They remain long after the cells have died.

The secondary cell walls of woody plants, such as trees and shrubs, also contain the substance lignin. This substance strengthens cell walls. About 70 percent of the cell walls in woody plants is cellulose and about 30 percent is lignin. The cell walls of woody plants contain little pectin.

Plant cells contain organelles called plastids. Chloroplasts are one kind of plastid. Chloroplasts contain the green pigment chlorophyll. Chlorophyll makes it possible for the plant to carry out photosynthesis. In photosynthesis, the plant uses energy from the sun to combine water and carbon dioxide. This process produces oxygen and sugar, which the plant uses for food.

Another kind of plastid is called a leucoplast. Leucoplasts contain enzymes that change sugar into starch. The starch is then stored in the leucoplasts.

A third kind of plastid is the chromoplast. Those structures store pigments other than chlorophyll. Chromoplasts store red, yellow, blue, and other coloring matter.

1. Which structure must a plant contain for the production of food?

   (1) sugar
   (2) nucleus
   (3) cell wall
   (4) chloroplast
   (5) leucoplast

2. What structures do plant cells have that animal cells do not?

   (1) cell wall, chloroplast, and leucoplast
   (2) cell membrane, chloroplast, and leucoplast
   (3) cell membrane, chromatin, and nucleolus
   (4) cell wall, chromatin, and nucleolus
   (5) middle lamella, pectin, and cytoplasm

3. The process of photosynthesis is responsible for which of the following?

   (1) cell division
   (2) transportation of water
   (3) absorption of nitrogen
   (4) stiffness of stems
   (5) production of sugar

4. Which cell structure is most responsible for wood retaining its stiffness after a tree dies?

   (1) the secondary cell wall
   (2) the middle lamella
   (3) the leucoplasts
   (4) the primary cell wall
   (5) the plastids

5. The cells in a rose petal would be likely to contain

   (1) many chromoplasts
   (2) many chloroplasts
   (3) many leucoplasts
   (4) a small amount of lignin
   (5) large amounts of starch

Items 6 to 10 refer to the following information.

Like all living things, trees are subject to disease, decay, and death. When a tree is wounded, fungus spores get into the wound, germinate, and send out creeping threads that attack the cell tissues. In time the tree can die unless a tree surgeon treats it.

A tree surgeon removes injured or rotted branches close to the trunk, or parent branch, so as not to leave a stub with the fungus in it. To saw off a large branch, the surgeon first undercuts it to keep the bark from tearing as the limb falls. The surgeon makes the first cut on the underside 12 to 18 inches from the trunk and continues to cut until the saw begins to bend from the pressure of the limb.

The next cut is made from above and about two inches outward from the first cut. After the limb falls, the remaining stub is removed near the trunk and the wound is treated.

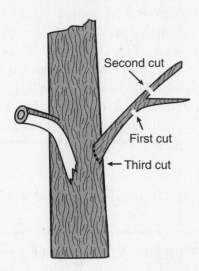

6. Why are injured or rotted branches removed from wounded trees?

   (1) to prevent the stub from showing
   (2) to prevent the bark from tearing
   (3) to prevent fungus from killing the tree
   (4) to make a clean cut
   (5) to leave a stub so that a new branch will grow

7. In the diagram, the limb on the left was not properly cut. What was the result of the improper cut?

   (1) The third cut was not necessary.
   (2) The natural swaying of the tree was prevented.
   (3) The bark was torn.
   (4) The bark grew inward and healed.
   (5) A fungus continued to grow.

8. Why is it important to remove the stub of the injured branch?

   (1) to make sure that all the fungus is removed
   (2) to prevent the bark from peeling off
   (3) to protect the underside of the branch
   (4) to make sure that another branch will grow
   (5) to prevent injury to the tree surgeon

9. Why is the first cut done on the underside of the injured limb?

   (1) because the underside is easier to reach
   (2) to keep the saw from getting stuck
   (3) to keep the bark from tearing when the limb falls
   (4) because more fungus grows on the underside
   (5) because the wound is on the underside

10. Why is a wounded tree, untreated by a tree surgeon, likely to die?

   (1) because all living things are subject to death
   (2) because fungus spores grow in wounds and eventually attack other parts of the tree
   (3) because only a tree surgeon can make the right cuts
   (4) because tree bark tears
   (5) because limbs fall

Answers are on page 265.

Comprehension: Restating Information

When you restate information, you say it in another way. Sometimes you simply use different words. At other times you may restate information with a diagram or formula. Restating information is one way to make sure you understand what you read.

There are many ways to restate information. The most common way is called **paraphrasing.** When you paraphrase, you rewrite an idea, sentence, or paragraph in your own words. When you take notes during a lecture or while reading a textbook, you are often paraphrasing the information.

Read the following paragraph and then see how the information can be restated.

The average woman gains about 24 pounds during pregnancy. About one-half of this weight is taken up by the uterus and its contents. The fetus averages 7.7 pounds, the amniotic fluid 1.8 pounds, the placenta 1.4 pounds, and the uterus 2 pounds. The remaining weight is distributed in other parts of the body. The breasts gain 0.9 pounds, weight of the blood increases by about 4 pounds, and other body fluids increase by about 2.7 pounds. The last 3.5 pounds is added body fat.

The information you have read can be restated in these words:

By the time her baby is born, the average woman has gained 24 pounds. The baby itself weighs only 7.7 pounds. Where is the other weight? The placenta accounts for 1.4 pounds and the uterus accounts for 2 pounds. About 0.9 pounds is added to the breasts and 3.5 pounds is additional body fat. Additional body fluids make up another 8.5 pounds: the weight of the blood increases by 4 pounds, the amniotic fluid makes up 1.8 pounds, and other body fluids increase by an average of 2.7 pounds.

You will notice that all the facts remain the same in the restated paragraph. The way the facts are presented, however, has changed. In addition to changes in wording, the information has been rearranged. Instead of grouping the uterus and its contents, the writer has made body fluids a group. The wording and order of the information has changed, but its meaning has not.

Now look at another way to restate information. Instead of using words, you can present information in a diagram, chart, or graph.

This bar graph has the same information as the two paragraphs. The graph makes it easy to tell at a glance where the extra weight is during pregnancy. The weight of the baby and the weight gain of each part of the mother's body are represented by bars. The higher the bar, the greater the weight gain.

There is another way to restate information. Instead of using words or diagrams, you can use formulas or math expressions. For example, you could show the various weights as a list of numbers to be added.

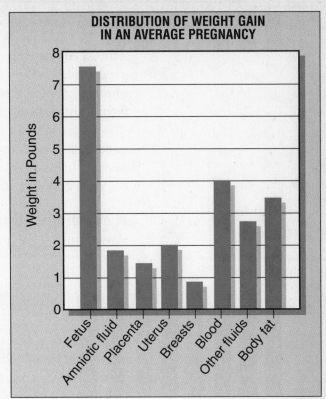

DISTRIBUTION OF WEIGHT GAIN IN AN AVERAGE PREGNANCY

 To interpret a graph, be sure to read the title and labels.

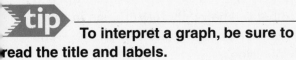 Restating Information

Items 1 and 2 refer to the following passage. Choose the best answer to each item.

Malnutrition is a poor state of health that results from an unbalanced diet. Malnutrition is often thought of as undernutrition. This problem can be caused by eating too little food or by eating too little of a particular nutrient. However, malnutrition can also be caused by overnutrition. People who eat too much food or too much of certain nutrients such as fats or vitamins also suffer from malnutrition.

1. Malnutrition is a condition in which

   (1) not enough food is eaten
   (2) too little of a specific nutrient is eaten
   (3) a person's health is affected by poor diet
   (4) a person eats too much
   (5) too much fat is eaten

2. What causes undernutrition?

   (1) not eating enough food or not eating enough of a specific nutrient
   (2) eating foods rich in fat
   (3) eating foods with very large amounts of particular vitamins
   (4) poor health
   (5) malnutrition

tip When defining terms, be certain that the definition tells exactly what the terms mean, and does not simply state a cause or a result of the term.

Answers are on page 266.

Photosynthesis

Almost all animal life depends on plants for food. Plants, however, produce their own food through a process called <u>photosynthesis</u>. In photosynthesis, green plants take water, carbon dioxide, and energy from sunlight and use these items to make sugar, oxygen, and water. The sugar is used as food and to build other substances that the plant needs, such as starches and protein. Oxygen is a by-product of photosynthesis. Plants release oxygen into the atmosphere, where animals breathe it.

Photosynthesis can be shown as a chemical equation. In the equation shown below, the arrow means <u>yields</u>.

$$\text{water} + \text{carbon dioxide} \xrightarrow[\text{chlorophyll}]{\text{light}} \text{sugar} + \text{oxygen} + \text{water}$$

This equation is a summary of all the reactions that make up photosynthesis. The diagram below shows photosynthesis in more detail. Notice that the reactions are grouped into two phases—the light reactions and the dark reactions.

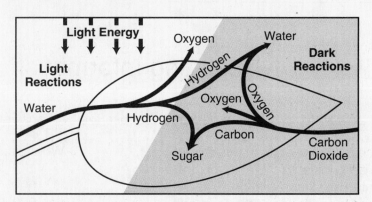

The first phase of photosynthesis is called the light reactions. The light reactions take place in sunlight. Light energy from the sun is trapped by the plant's chlorophyll, or green coloring. The chlorophyll changes light energy to chemical energy, which is used to split particles of water into hydrogen and oxygen.

The second phase of photosynthesis is called the dark reactions. Light is not needed for the dark reactions to take place. During this phase, the hydrogen produced in the light reactions combines with carbon (from carbon dioxide taken from the atmosphere) to form sugar. The rest of the hydrogen combines with oxygen to form water.

 Practice | Photosynthesis

ems 1 to 6 refer to the previous passage and diagram. Choose the best answer to each item.

1. Which substance produced in the light reactions of photosynthesis combines with the carbon found in carbon dioxide to produce sugar in the dark reactions?

   (1) oxygen
   (2) carbon
   (3) hydrogen
   (4) chlorophyll
   (5) water

2. What substance produced during photosynthesis does the plant use for food?

   (1) sugar
   (2) oxygen
   (3) water
   (4) carbon dioxide
   (5) chlorophyll

3. Which of the following restates the equation for photosynthesis?

   (1) Water plus carbon dioxide, in the presence of light and chlorophyll, yields sugar, oxygen, and water.
   (2) Water plus carbon dioxide, in the presence of chlorophyll, yields sugar, oxygen, and water.
   (3) Water plus carbon dioxide, in the presence of light and chlorophyll, yields sugar, hydrogen, and water.
   (4) Water plus oxygen, in the presence of light and chlorophyll, yields sugar, carbon dioxide, and water.
   (5) Water plus carbon dioxide, in the presence of sunlight, yields sugar, oxygen, and water.

4. Which of the following restates the main idea of the passage?

   (1) Animals eat plants for food.
   (2) Plants make their own food through photosynthesis.
   (3) Photosynthesis takes place in green plants.
   (4) Photosynthesis replaces the oxygen in the atmosphere that is used by animals.
   (5) Sunlight is needed for photosynthesis to occur.

5. Which of the following supports the statement, "The first phase of photosynthesis is called the light reactions"?

   (1) Chemical energy splits water into hydrogen and oxygen.
   (2) The plant's green coloring is called chlorophyll.
   (3) Oxygen is a by-product of photosynthesis.
   (4) Carbon dioxide is absorbed from the atmosphere.
   (5) The light reactions take place in sunlight.

6. Which of the following restates the main idea of the fourth paragraph?

   (1) Light energy from the sun is absorbed by chlorophyll.
   (2) Chlorophyll makes chemical energy from light energy.
   (3) Chemical energy splits water into hydrogen and oxygen.
   (4) The light reactions make up the first phase of photosynthesis.
   (5) Sunlight is needed for the light reactions.

Answers are on page 266.

Items 1 to 4 refer to the following passage. Choose the best answer to each item.

Cellular respiration is the process by which cells obtain the energy they need in order to function. During respiration, glucose (a kind of sugar) is broken down to release chemical energy. As a result, carbon dioxide and water are released. Many of the reactions in respiration are the opposite of those in photosynthesis, where sugar is formed from water and carbon dioxide. The equation for respiration is:

glucose + oxygen →

carbon dioxide + water + energy

There are two ways organisms obtain the oxygen they need for cellular respiration—direct and indirect respiration. Direct respiration occurs in single-celled organisms, like the amoeba. These organisms are able to exchange gases with the environment directly. This exchange takes place through cell membranes. Indirect respiration occurs in many-celled organisms where most of the body's cells are not in direct contact with the environment.

Indirect respiration can be divided into two phases. External respiration exchanges gases between the environment and the blood. Gills and lungs perform this function. Internal respiration exchanges gases between the blood and cells. The circulatory system performs this function.

1. Which organism functions with direct respiration?

   (1) human
   (2) bird
   (3) lizard
   (4) amoeba
   (5) dog

2. Which two substances would you expect to be exhaled by the lungs?

   (1) oxygen and carbon dioxide
   (2) hydrogen and oxygen
   (3) glucose and carbon dioxide
   (4) hydrogen and carbon
   (5) water vapor and carbon dioxide

3. Which two substances are the direct result of respiration?

   (1) oxygen and hydrogen
   (2) carbon dioxide and water
   (3) glucose and water
   (4) glucose and hydrogen
   (5) water and oxygen

4. How can the equation for respiration be stated in a sentence? Sugar plus oxygen

   (1) plus carbon dioxide yields water plus energy
   (2) yields carbon dioxide plus water plus energy
   (3) yields carbon dioxide plus water
   (4) yields carbon dioxide plus water plus sugar
   (5) yields carbon dioxide plus gases plus energy

> **tip** When restating information, make sure that all the original information is included. Also check that no additional information has been added.

We breathe in air through the nose or mouth. The air passes through a tube called the trachea, which runs from the back of the mouth to the lungs. The trachea divides into two bronchi, one for each lung. Each of these tubes divides, forming branches called bronchioles. The bronchioles end in small air sacs called alveoli.

The exchange of oxygen and carbon dioxide takes place at the alveoli. They are covered by a network of tiny blood vessels called capillaries. Oxygen from the air in the alveoli passes into the bloodstream. Carbon dioxide in the blood passes from the capillaries into the air in the lungs. The carbon dioxide is carried out of the body as we exhale.

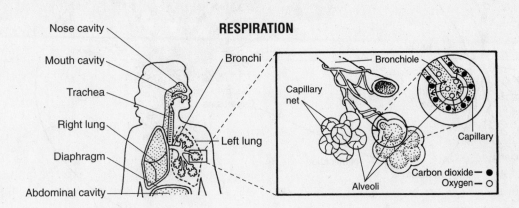

RESPIRATION

5. After inhaled air passes through the trachea, it goes through the

   (1) alveoli, bronchi, bronchioles
   (2) bronchi, bronchioles, alveoli
   (3) bronchioles, alveoli, bronchi
   (4) alveoli, bronchioles, bronchi
   (5) bronchioles, bronchi, alveoli

6. Which of the following accurately describes the air we breathe?

   (1) Inhaled air contains more carbon dioxide than exhaled air.
   (2) Inhaled air contains more oxygen than exhaled air.
   (3) Inhaled air passes directly from the trachea to the alveoli.
   (4) Exhaled air contains more oxygen than inhaled air.
   (5) Exhaled air passes through the diaphragm.

7. What is the main function of the lungs?

   (1) supporting the bronchi
   (2) warming the air we breathe
   (3) enabling the blood to absorb oxygen and release carbon dioxide
   (4) enabling the blood to absorb carbon dioxide and release water vapor
   (5) splitting water into oxygen and hydrogen

8. Most of the information in the second paragraph can also be found in the

   A. first paragraph of the passage
   B. left side of the diagram
   C. right side of the diagram

   (1) A only
   (2) B only
   (3) C only
   (4) A and B
   (5) A and C

Answers are on page 267.

Directions: Choose the best answer to each item.

Items 1 to 4 refer to the following information.

THE NITROGEN CYCLE

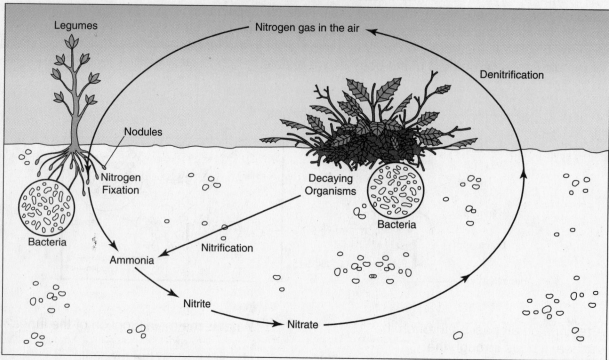

Plants and animals must have nitrogen to make proteins. Air is mostly nitrogen, but plants and animals cannot use nitrogen in gas form. Animals get nitrogen by eating plants or other animals. Plants get nitrogen from the soil. They rely on bacteria to convert nitrogen into forms that they can use.

Through a process called nitrogen fixation, certain kinds of bacteria take nitrogen from the air and combine it with other substances to make a form that plants can use. These bacteria are found only in bumps, or nodules, on the roots of plants called legumes.

Other soil bacteria take the nitrogen found in decomposing plants and animals. This nitrogen is converted to ammonia, nitrite, and nitrate in a process called nitrification. This process provides another source of nitrogen for plants.

Other bacteria return nitrogen to the atmosphere by changing nitrates into gaseous nitrogen, a process called denitrification. This nitrogen is useless to living things until nitrogen-fixing bacteria take nitrogen from the air and convert it into a form plants can use.

1. Where do plants get their nitrogen?

    (1) from other plants
    (2) directly from the atmosphere
    (3) from animals
    (4) from the soil
    (5) from protein

2. According to the information, the process of nitrogen fixation takes place

    (1) in decaying organisms
    (2) in the leaves of plants
    (3) in the roots of all plants
    (4) in the atmosphere
    (5) in nodules on the roots of legumes

3. By what process do bacteria break down the protein of decaying organisms into nitrite and nitrate compounds?

    (1) nitrogen fixation
    (2) denitrification
    (3) erosion
    (4) nitrification
    (5) ionization

4. Which process captures nitrogen from the atmosphere and turns it into forms that plants can use?

    (1) nitrification
    (2) denitrification
    (3) decomposition
    (4) nitrogen fixation
    (5) photosynthesis

Items 5 and 6 refer to the following passage and diagram.

The two main processes involved in the carbon-oxygen cycle are respiration and photosynthesis. Each of these processes produces substances used in the other process. Respiration takes place in both plants and animals. Only plants, however, are able to carry on photosynthesis. During respiration, sugar is broken down and carbon dioxide is released. During photosynthesis, water, carbon dioxide, and light energy from the sun produce oxygen, sugar, and water.

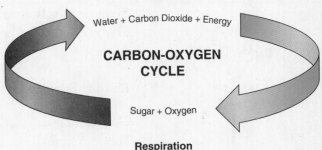

Photosynthesis

Water + Carbon Dioxide + Energy

CARBON-OXYGEN CYCLE

Sugar + Oxygen

Respiration

5. According to the diagram, what reacts with sugar during respiration to produce water, carbon dioxide, and energy?

    (1) carbon
    (2) hydrogen
    (3) oxygen
    (4) water
    (5) carbon dioxide

6. If there were no photosynthesis, the amount of oxygen in the air would

    (1) remain unchanged
    (2) increase
    (3) double
    (4) decrease
    (5) be produced by animals

Answers are on page 267.

Analysis: Cause and Effect

When you feel hungry, you probably eat. In this situation, being hungry is a cause; eating is an effect. Situations in which one thing makes another happen are called **cause and effect relationships.**

Causes and effects can be many things. They can be facts, conditions, things, events, or actions. For example, a baseball player who hits the winning home run is the cause of his or her team's victory. Too much sunlight causes sunburn. Your body's fight against an infection causes fever.

Science is full of cause and effect relationships. Scientists try to discover general laws that can predict what will result from specific causes.

Read this passage and identify the cause and effect relationships.

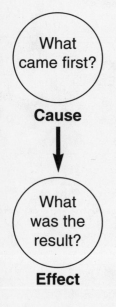

Cause

Effect

Tobacco smoke contains a poisonous chemical called nicotine. When nicotine is inhaled, it immediately causes changes in the body. It increases the heart rate and blood pressure, narrows blood vessels, and slows movements of the digestive system. Nicotine also has long-term effects. It damages the lining of the air passages in the throat and lungs.

What is the cause in this passage? Nicotine is the cause. What are the effects of nicotine? Nicotine has immediate effects, such as increased heart rate and blood pressure, narrowed blood vessels, and slowed digestive movements. It also has a long-term effect—it damages the throat and lungs.

When you read, look for cause and effect relationships. Watch for words or phrases such as cause, effect, because, as a result of, leads to, develops from, due to, thus, therefore, so, and the reason is.

Cause and effect relationships are stated very clearly in the passage about nicotine. Sometimes, however, you have to figure out a cause or effect. For example, what might be a result of damaged air passages in the lungs? The author does not say. Perhaps damaged air passages might result in breathing difficulties. Another effect might be disease of the lungs such as cancer or emphysema.

 Causes explain why things happen. Effects are what happens. Sometimes an effect will have more than one cause.

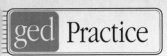

Cause and Effect

ems 1 and 2 refer to the following paragraph. Choose the best answer to each item.

Injuries, heavy bleeding, disease, and some drugs can change the way ne circulatory system works. Injuries can cause a large amount of blood o be lost. Some drugs make blood vessels expand, reducing the blood ressure in the blood vessels. When either condition happens, a person said to be "in shock." The person has low blood pressure and a weak ulse. He or she also becomes pale and may sweat heavily.

1. What causes shock?

   (1) injuries, heavy bleeding, disease, and some drugs
   (2) a weak pulse
   (3) heavy sweating
   (4) blood clots
   (5) oxygen starvation

2. What first-aid measure would help stop shock?

   (1) artificial respiration
   (2) setting a broken bone
   (3) stopping bleeding
   (4) giving a drink of water
   (5) inducing vomiting

ems 3 and 4 refer to the following diagram.

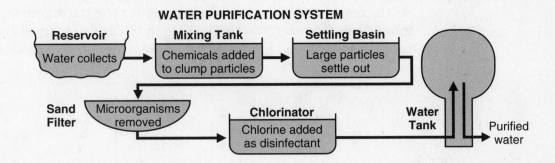

WATER PURIFICATION SYSTEM

3. What would happen if the sand filter were removed from the water purification system?

   (1) The water would contain more large particles.
   (2) The water would contain more microorganisms.
   (3) The water would contain more chlorine.
   (4) The water would contain less chlorine.
   (5) There would be no effect on the water.

4. Why is purification of drinking water necessary?

   (1) to pump water from reservoirs
   (2) to move water to water storage tanks
   (3) to conserve water supplies
   (4) to prevent the spread of harmful substances through drinking water
   (5) to prevent tooth decay

Answers are on page 268.

Evolution

Evolution means change over time. In science, the theory of evolution holds that all organisms living today have a common ancestor that evolved from the first living cells. These first cells developed about 3.5 billion years ago.

There is much evidence to support the theory of evolution. One piece of evidence is the presence of similar structures in different organisms. Called homologous structures, these body parts from different organisms have similar structures but perform different functions. For example, a whale's flipper, a human's arm, a dog's from leg, and a bird's wing are homologous structures. Each of these limbs is used in a different way. When you first look at these limbs, they appear different. But if you look closely, you will see that the bones of each limb are very similar. For this reason, they have been given the same names. The similarity of these four different limbs suggests that these four organisms evolved from a common ancestor. The differences are the result of adaptation to different environments.

Another piece of evidence that supports the theory of evolution is that the embryos of different organisms are similar. An embryo is an early stage in the development of an organism from a fertilized egg. The embryos of a fish, a bird, and a human are similar at first. For example, at one stage all of these embryos have gill slits and tail buds. As the embryos develop, the differences among the organisms become more clear. However, the similarities in the early embryos suggest that fish, birds, and humans evolved from a common ancestor.

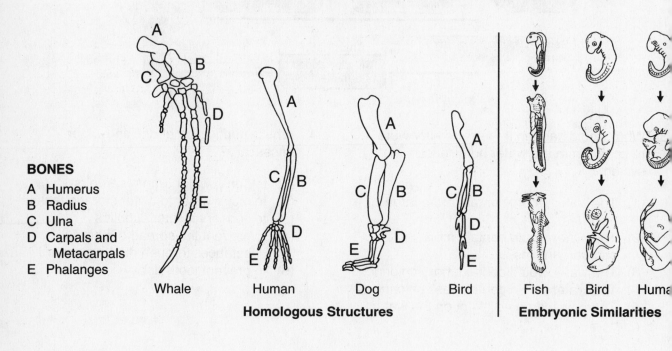

BONES

A Humerus
B Radius
C Ulna
D Carpals and
     Metacarpals
E Phalanges

Whale   Human   Dog   Bird

Homologous Structures

Fish   Bird   Human

Embryonic Similarities

ems 1 to 6 refer to the previous passage and diagram. Choose the best answer to each item.

1. According to the diagram, what is similar about the radius and ulna bones of whales, humans, dogs, and birds?

(1) They form fingerlike structures.
(2) They form footlike structures.
(3) They are positioned side by side below the humerus.
(4) They are part of an arm, leg, and wing.
(5) They are evidence of similarity among embryos.

2. What is one reason that scientists support the theory of evolution?

(1) Humans are the most highly developed organisms on Earth.
(2) Different types of organisms have homologous structures.
(3) All organisms developed 3.5 billion years ago.
(4) All embryos have gill slits and tail buds.
(5) All organisms function in the same way.

3. What caused the ancestors of whales and birds to develop into different types of animals?

(1) homologous structures
(2) similarity between embryos
(3) a common ancestor
(4) the fact that they are unrelated
(5) their evolution in different environments

4. Why does a human embryo have a tail bud?

(1) Human ancestors had tails.
(2) Fish and bird embryos have tail buds.
(3) Tails are homologous structures.
(4) Humans have evolved.
(5) The early stages of the human embryo are similar to the early stages of the fish embryo.

5. What is the main idea of the passage?

(1) Homologous structures are evidence supporting the theory of evolution.
(2) Similarity among embryos exists in organisms with a common ancestor.
(3) Birds, whales, humans, and dogs had a common ancestor.
(4) Homologous structures and similarity among embryos are evidence supporting the theory of evolution.
(5) Humans are related to birds.

6. How will the passage of a million years affect today's plant and animal species?

(1) Plants and animals will continue to evolve.
(2) Fertilization of the egg will no longer be required.
(3) Plants and animals will develop into a single life form.
(4) Animals will continue to change, but plants will remain the same.
(5) Birds and whales will become land animals.

Answers are on page 268.

Items 1 to 4 refer to the following passage. Each item describes an event that is an example of one of the steps in the theory of natural selection. Choose the answer that best matches the event described.

The key to Charles Darwin's theory of evolution is the idea of natural selection. According to Darwin, individual organisms that have traits, or characteristics, that help them live in their environment are more likely to survive and reproduce. Natural selection can be summarized in five steps.

1. Overproduction. Most organisms have many offspring. However, the environment cannot support as many organisms as are born because the resources of the environment are limited.
2. Competition. Too many offspring and limited resources cause organisms to compete for food, water, and other needs.
3. Variation. Individual organisms vary a great deal in the traits they inherit.
4. Survival. Some individuals have inherited traits that help them use the resources of the environment. These individuals are more likely to survive.
5. Reproduction. Individuals that survive pass these traits or adaptations on to their offspring.

1. In a herd of giraffes, some have longer necks than others.

   (1) overproduction
   (2) competition
   (3) variation
   (4) survival
   (5) reproduction

2. Birds that blend well with their surroundings had parents that also blended with their surroundings.

   (1) overproduction
   (2) competition
   (3) variation
   (4) survival
   (5) reproduction

3. In one season, a pine tree produces over 100 cones, each of which contains about 35 seeds.

   (1) overproduction
   (2) competition
   (3) variation
   (4) survival
   (5) reproduction

4. Only cactus plants that can store large amounts of rainwater will still be alive when the desert's next rainy season begins.

   (1) overproduction
   (2) competition
   (3) variation
   (4) survival
   (5) reproduction

tip **When reading definitions, try to think of an example of each item being defined. An example of *survival* is the cactus ability to store water.**

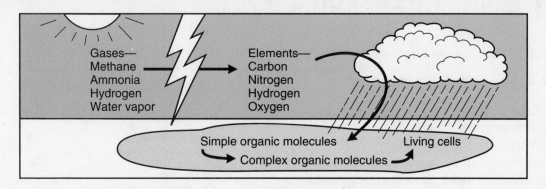

Life is thought to have first appeared on Earth about 3.5 billion years go. Many scientists believe that Earth's atmosphere was then made up ostly of ammonia, hydrogen, methane, and water vapor. These gases ontain the elements carbon, nitrogen, hydrogen, and oxygen, which are und in organic molecules. Organic molecules are the building blocks of ll living things. Organic molecules all contain carbon in combination with ne or more of the other elements.

According to one theory of the origin of life, energy from lightning or unlight helped cause chemical reactions among these molecules. As a esult, the elements carbon, nitrogen, hydrogen, and oxygen recombined o form simple organic molecules. Rain washed some of the organic olecules down from the atmosphere to Earth's surface. Here the organic olecules combined with one another. As time passed they became more omplex, and eventually the first living cells appeared.

5. What caused chemical reactions among the gas molecules of the early atmosphere?

(1) water vapor
(2) organic molecules
(3) methane
(4) rain
(5) lightning

6. Organic molecules must have existed before life could form because organic molecules

(1) make up all living things
(2) give rise to carbon
(3) provide energy
(4) make up the atmosphere
(5) produce rain

7. A current theory concerning the origin of life assumes that Earth's early atmosphere contained the gases

(1) ammonia, oxygen, and hydrogen
(2) methane, ammonia, and water vapor
(3) carbon, methane, and ammonia
(4) silicon, hydrogen, and water
(5) oxygen, hydrogen, and water

8. What element is present in all organic molecules?

(1) carbon
(2) nitrogen
(3) hydrogen
(4) oxygen
(5) all of the above

Answers are on page 269.

Directions: Choose the best answer to each item.

Items 1 to 4 refer to the following passage.

A species is a group of organisms that can mate with one another and produce fertile offspring. The development of a new species from an old one is called speciation. The result of speciation is two or more groups of organisms that can no longer reproduce with each other.

As long as the environment remains more or less the same and the entire population of a species remains isolated and together, speciation is unlikely to occur. However, environments do change and individuals do move from one place to another. In these situations, speciation is more likely to occur.

Sometimes many species evolve from one species. This kind of speciation is called adaptive radiation. Adaptive radiation occurs when small groups of individuals become separated from the rest of the population. This often happens on islands or in areas bounded by mountains. The separated populations become adapted to their separate environments. Adaptations, or traits that help individuals survive, are passed down to their offspring. Over a long period of time, each isolated group develops into a new species.

The result of adaptive radiation can be seen in Hawaii, where 28 species of silversword, a member of the sunflower family, are found. One common ancestor, probably from the Pacific coast of North America, gave rise to these different species. Each species is adapted to a different habitat ranging from sea level to mountaintops.

1. Which of the following is the most likely to contribute to speciation?

   (1) environmental changes
   (2) environmental stability
   (3) isolation of an entire species
   (4) decreased reproduction
   (5) increased population size

2. Which of the following best describes the pattern of changes that occur in species during adaptive radiation?

   (1) becoming more alike
   (2) random
   (3) becoming less alike
   (4) equal
   (5) little or no change

3. The silverswords of Hawaii are an example of

   (1) extinction
   (2) fossilization
   (3) convergent evolution
   (4) adaptive radiation
   (5) acquired traits

4. How has speciation probably affected the variety of animal and plant life?

   (1) created less variety
   (2) not affected variety
   (3) stopped the formation of new varieties
   (4) slowed the formation of new varieties
   (5) created more variety

tip

   When trying to figure out a cause and effect relationship, ask yourself if the possible cause is sufficient to produce the stated effect.

A gene is a part of a cell that determines a particular trait. A particular gene may occur in most individuals or in only a few individuals. How often a gene occurs in a population is called gene frequency. When the frequency of a particular gene increases or decreases by chance, the change in frequency is called genetic drift.

For example, suppose that a population of squirrels consists mostly of white squirrels with a few gray individuals (a). Then suppose that a waterway is constructed, and the squirrel population is divided into two isolated groups (b). The larger group still has several gray squirrels. The smaller group has only one gray squirrel. The frequency of the gene for grayness is lower in the smaller population because it has fewer gray squirrels.

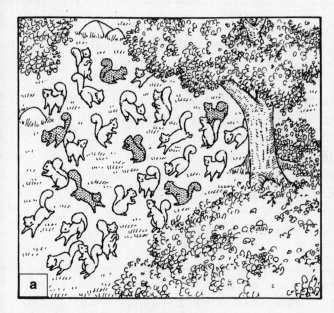 

5. Genetic drift may result from

    (1) isolation of species
    (2) speciation
    (3) adaptive radiation
    (4) chance
    (5) mating between species

6. What sort of genetic drift would be expected among the larger population of squirrels as a result of the construction of the waterway?

    (1) an increase in the gray gene's frequency
    (2) a decrease in the gray gene's frequency
    (3) an increase in the white gene's frequency
    (4) the frequency of both genes would become equal
    (5) an increase in the frequency of both genes

7. Which of the following would affect the genetic drift of the single original squirrel population in diagram (a)?

    A. Due to an increased food supply, some white squirrels increase in size.
    B. Some gray squirrels die from disease.
    C. Some white squirrels are killed.

    (1) A only
    (2) B only
    (3) C only
    (4) A and B
    (5) B and C

Answers are on page 270.

Comprehension: Identifying Implications

You have learned to look for main ideas and supporting details when you read. This helps you understand what the author is saying. Sometimes, however, the author leaves out some statements. If you think about what you read, you can figure out what is missing.

For example, suppose you read, "It was a beautiful day, and we went swimming at the beach." What can you figure out about this event that the author does not tell you? You might figure that the weather was sunny and warm. You might decide that they brought swimsuits. Can you think of anything else that is likely to be true about that trip to the beach?

When you take what is written and then figure out other things that are probably true, you are identifying **implications.** Implications are not expressed in words by the author. Rather, they are **implied** by what is written. Implications are facts that you can be reasonably sure are true because they follow from what the author wrote. They are the logical outcomes of what has actually been written.

Read this paragraph and identify some of its implications.

The thyroid gland produces a substance that helps regulate growth. One of the ingredients of this substance is the element iodine. When the body does not contain enough iodine, the thyroid gland becomes enlarged, a condition called goiter. Since seafood contains relatively large amounts of iodide, a form of iodine, goiter is not common in coastal areas where people eat a lot of seafood. Goiter is more common in mountainous and inland areas where the soil contains small amounts of iodide. In these areas, locally grown food and drinking water do not provide people with sufficient supplies of iodide.

The passage explains the relationship between a lack of iodide and the occurrence of goiter. What can we figure out from what we have read? First, the author says that people who eat a lot of seafood containing iodide usually don't get goiter. And people who live in areas where the local food and water supplies are low in iodide often do get goiter. Therefore, we can figure out that iodide must be provided in the diet to prevent goiter.

Another implication of the passage is that iodide is not evenly distributed in the foods people eat. It is easier for some groups to develop goiter because not enough iodide is present in their diets.

What does this suggest about preventing goiter? It implies that iodide could be added to some common substance that most people eat or drink in order to prevent goiter. Indeed, in the United States iodide is added to table salt for this reason.

Another implication is that goiter is not contagious—you can't catch it from someone else. As long as you have enough iodide in your diet, you will not develop goiter. Can you think of any other implications of this passage?

 To determine if an idea is implied by a passage, ask yourself if the idea is based on the facts in the passage. If it isn't, the idea is unlikely to be an implication.

 Identifying Implications

ems 1 to 4 refer to the following passage. Choose the best answer to each item.

High mountains, deserts, oceans, lakes, rivers, nd soil conditions are all geographic barriers cross which many plants and animals cannot ass. These barriers prevent many species from preading into new areas.

Sometimes a few individuals of a species are ole to cross a barrier. For example, seeds may oat from one island to another on a floating log. hese seeds could not normally survive in the cean, but by chance they are carried across the arrier. If enough individuals are transported in is way, they may establish a population in the ew area, but this is rare.

1. Which of the following statements is implied by the passage?

   (1) Frogs cannot cross lakes on floating logs.
   (2) An African zebra can easily cross the Arabian desert into Eurasia to find other grasslands.
   (3) No animal can cross the Rocky Mountains.
   (4) No animal can travel from one side of an ocean to the other.
   (5) Continents can be barriers to ocean plants and animals.

2. Which animal's spread is least affected by geographic barriers?

   (1) fish
   (2) humans
   (3) mountain goats
   (4) deer
   (5) camels

3. Which of the following would not be considered a geographic barrier?

   (1) the Atlantic Ocean
   (2) the arid soils of Death Valley
   (3) the smog-filled air above Denver
   (4) Lake Ontario
   (5) Mount Hood

4. Which of the following would allow a species to cross a barrier that it normally would not be able to cross?

   (1) whales swimming in an ocean current
   (2) a maple seed blowing in the wind
   (3) a sparrow making a nest on an ocean-going ship
   (4) a pine cone floating down a mountain stream
   (5) a snail crossing a wet sidewalk

Answers are on page 270.

Plant Growth

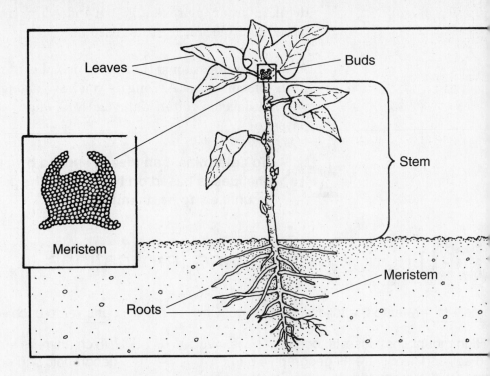

All living things grow when their cells divide, making the organism larger. In seed plants, growth occurs in specific places called meristems. During the growing season, cells in these areas divide rapidly, causing the plant to increase in size. Meristem cells are found at the tips of stems and roots.

The meristem cells of stems are found in the buds. The top bud of the stem is where the plant increases its height. Other buds on the side of the stem cause the plant to grow outward, or branch. Stem buds produce branches, flowers, and leaves.

Like stems, roots grow longer by adding cells at their tips. The meristem of a root is covered by a root cap, a layer of thick dead cells. This protects the meristem cells as the root pushes through the soil.

In woody plants, another kind of meristem cell adds to the thickness the plant. These cells form the cambium, a one-cell-thick layer in stems, branches, and roots. As the cells in the cambium layer divide, they add to the diameter of the plant.

New cells developed in the meristems eventually become different kinds of cells. Some change by becoming elongated, whereas others develop thick walls. Each cell adapts for a specific purpose, such as reproduction, support, absorption, or storage. One type of cell that develops from a meristem cell is an epidermis cell. Epidermis cells cover the plant body and help prevent water loss. Another type of cell is the vascular cell, which supports the plant and helps transport fluids through it.

Items 1 to 8 refer to the previous passage and diagram. Choose the best answer to each item.

1. Which of the following is implied by the passage?

   (1) Growth of stems does not take place between buds.
   (2) Leaves contain meristem cells.
   (3) Meristem cells in the roots are tough.
   (4) All plants have cambium.
   (5) Branches do not have cambium.

2. The fact that meristems in stems produce branches, flowers, and leaves suggests that

   (1) all meristem cells develop into the same type of structure
   (2) meristem cells become specialized as they develop
   (3) all plants have flowers
   (4) roots do not have meristem tissue
   (5) stems grow only in length

3. The immediate short-term effect of cutting off the top bud of a stem is that the

   (1) plant would stop getting taller
   (2) lower buds on the stem would stop growing
   (3) cambium cells would stop dividing
   (4) roots would branch
   (5) root caps would stop developing

4. What is the main idea of the passage?

   (1) Only living things grow by cell division.
   (2) Growth of seed plants takes place in special areas called meristems.
   (3) Roots have meristems.
   (4) Cambium is a layer of meristem cells in woody plants.
   (5) Animals and seed plants grow in similar ways.

5. The pattern of plant growth suggests that after thirty years

   (1) the bottom branch of a tree will be considerably higher than it was when it first formed
   (2) the bottom branch of a tree will be the same height above the ground as when it first formed
   (3) most new growth will take place between buds
   (4) a tree trunk will have the same diameter as after two years
   (5) a tree trunk will have a smaller diameter than after two years

6. Where can meristem cells be found in woody plants but not in most nonwoody plants?

   (1) root cap
   (2) buds at the top of the stem
   (3) buds at the sides of stems
   (4) leaves
   (5) cambium

7. If all the meristem cells in a plant were destroyed, what would most likely happen to the plant?

   (1) It would stop growing.
   (2) It would become bushy.
   (3) It would grow faster.
   (4) It would produce more leaves.
   (5) Its roots would start to branch.

8. The word apical describes the apex, or tip of a structure. Where would you expect to find apical meristems?

   (1) along stems between buds
   (2) at the ends of stems and roots
   (3) in buds on the sides of stems
   (4) in the cambium
   (5) in the leaves

Answers are on page 271.

Items 1 to 4 refer to the following information. Choose the best answer to each item.

The classification of organisms into groups is called taxonomy. Taxonomy is based on the relationships between different groups of organisms as they evolved. Biologists divide most living things into five main groups called kingdoms.

Kingdom	Characteristics	Examples
Monera	One-celled organisms Nuclear area of cell has no membrane Reproduce by cell division	Bacteria Blue-green algae
Protista	Mostly one-celled organisms Multi-celled organisms are not organized into tissues or organs Cells have an organized nucleus	Algae Protozoa Slime molds
Fungi	Mostly multi-celled organisms Not organized into tissues Cannot produce their own food	Yeasts Mildew Mold Mushrooms
Plantae	Many-celled organisms with specialized tissues and organs Cells contain chlorophyll Cell walls contain cellulose Produce food through photosynthesis	Mosses Trees Ferns Flowering Plants
Animalia	Many-celled organisms with complex tissues and organs No chlorophyll and no cell walls Food is taken into body in some way	Insects Worms Mollusks Fish Birds Mammals

1. Which organisms would be the simplest in structure and function?

   (1) bacteria
   (2) slime molds
   (3) mosses
   (4) ferns
   (5) insects

2. Which characteristic is found only in Monera?

   (1) one-celled organisms
   (2) tissues present
   (3) nuclear area has no membrane
   (4) cells produce their own food
   (5) cells contain chlorophyll

3. A goldfish has which of these characteristics

   (1) cells that lack an organized nucleus
   (2) presence of chlorophyll
   (3) absence of cell walls
   (4) produce food through photosynthesis
   (5) reproduce through cell division

4. A complex organism that cannot produce it own food is a member of which kingdom?

   (1) Monera
   (2) Protista
   (3) Fungi
   (4) Plantae
   (5) Animalia

Items 5 to 8 refer to the following passage and diagram.

Water is needed in the leaves of plants for photosynthesis to occur. But how does water from the soil reach the leaves, which may be many feet above the ground? Once water is absorbed by the roots of the plant, it passes into a type of tissue called xylem. Xylem is present in roots, stems, and leaves. In woody stems, xylem makes up most of the stem. Xylem has many long, dead cells that stand vertically next to one another, much like straws in a glass. Water passes upward through tubes made of xylem.

Phloem is the other type of tissue used for transport in plants. Phloem carries food from leaves to other parts of the plant. In woody stems, phloem is located under the outermost layer of plant tissue.

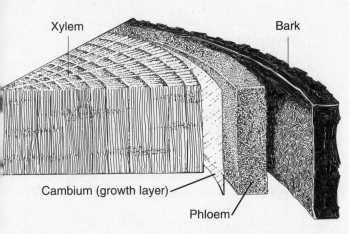

Xylem

Bark

Cambium (growth layer)

Phloem

5. What is the main source of water for most plants?

    (1) well water
    (2) rain and surface water soaking into the soil
    (3) water vapor in the atmosphere
    (4) water in the xylem tissue
    (5) irrigation systems

6. Which type of tissue carries the food produced during photosynthesis to the rest of the plant?

    (1) bark
    (2) phloem
    (3) cambium
    (4) xylem
    (5) meristem

7. What would be the immediate effect on a plant if all its xylem tissue became clogged?

    (1) Photosynthesis would slow and stop because of lack of water.
    (2) The stem would collapse.
    (3) The roots would start carrying water to the leaves.
    (4) The phloem would carry water to the leaves.
    (5) The cambium would stop growing.

8. Which type of plant tissue makes up most of the wood we use?

    (1) bark
    (2) phloem
    (3) cambium
    (4) xylem
    (5) meristem

Answers are on page 271.

Directions: Choose the <u>best answer</u> to each item.

Items 1 to 4 refer to the following information.

SEED PLANTS

Gymnosperms—Nonflowering
Exposed seeds without protective covering
Seeds do not contain stored food

Examples: Pines, junipers, yews; about
750 species

Angiosperms—Flowering
Seeds protected by pod or fleshy fruit
Seeds contain stored food for seedling
Divided into two groups

Examples: All flowering plants; about
240,000 species

Monocotyledons
Seeds have 1 cotyledon (seed leaf)
Leaves have parallel veins
Flower parts in sets of 3

Examples: Palms, grasses, lilies, irises, corn,
grain; about 40,000 species

Dicotyledons
Seeds have 2 cotyledons (seed leaves)
Leaves have netlike veins
Flower parts in sets of 4 or 5

Examples: Oaks, elms, hollies, dill, potatoes,
most beans; about 200,000 species

1. The number of species of gymnosperms compared to the number of species of angiosperms implies that

   (1) gymnosperms outnumber angiosperms
   (2) angiosperms have spread because they have advantages that gymnosperms lack
   (3) angiosperms can be found only in tropical climates
   (4) the seeds of angiosperms are less protected than the seeds of gymnosperms
   (5) gymnosperms can be found only in deserts

2. Monocotyledons differ from dicotyledons in that monocotyledons have

   (1) seeds with 1 seed leaf
   (2) seeds with 2 seed leaves
   (3) leaves with netlike veins
   (4) flower parts in sets of 4
   (5) flower parts in sets of 5

3. Since wheat belongs to the family of grasses, you would expect wheat to have

   (1) flower parts in sets of 4 or 5
   (2) flower parts in sets of 3
   (3) netlike veins
   (4) 2 cotyledons
   (5) unprotected seeds

4. Which of the following probably best explains the remarkable success of angiosperms?

   (1) They produce unprotected seeds.
   (2) They have netlike veins.
   (3) They produce protected seeds.
   (4) They produce seeds with 1 seed leaf.
   (5) They produce seeds with 2 seed leaves.

In order to germinate, or sprout, most seeds need at least three conditions: moisture, oxygen, and the correct temperature. The exact requirements vary greatly. Some seeds remain dormant for many years, waiting for the right conditions for germination. For example, the seeds of many water plants germinate underwater where there is plenty of moisture, oxygen dissolved in the water, and an even temperature. Under these conditions, however, most land plants will not germinate.

Before a seed germinates, it absorbs a lot of water, causing the seed to swell and become soft. Too much moisture will cause the growth of fungi, which may cause the seed to rot. Most seeds germinate best at a temperature between 60°F and 80°F.

While seeds are germinating, they need plenty of oxygen because of increased activity. Seeds do best in loose soil and when planted near the surface. These conditions provide a good supply of oxygen.

5. Which of the following conditions is <u>not</u> important to germination?

(1) correct temperature
(2) moisture
(3) carbon dioxide
(4) oxygen
(5) water supply

6. What is likely to be the result of planting seeds deep in the soil?

(1) Conditions for germination will improve.
(2) The seeds will not get enough water to germinate.
(3) The seeds will not get enough oxygen to germinate.
(4) The seeds will not get enough sunlight to germinate.
(5) The seeds will be too warm to germinate.

7. A maple seed can germinate on a block of ice. What is most likely to happen to the newly sprouted plant?

(1) It will take root and grow into a maple tree.
(2) It will be transported to another location.
(3) It will rot.
(4) It will grow slowly and die.
(5) It will melt.

8. Some seeds can be inactive for years and still be able to germinate. What causes them to germinate after a long period of time?

(1) Water conditions improve.
(2) Oxygen is present.
(3) Light is present.
(4) The temperature is correct.
(5) There is the correct amount of warmth, moisture, and oxygen.

9. The best title for this passage is

(1) How Seeds Germinate
(2) What Seeds Need to Germinate
(3) Soil Conditions
(4) Where Seeds Germinate
(5) The Growth of Fungi

10. The best definition for the word "dormant" as used in the first paragraph is

(1) a state of sleep
(2) not in motion
(3) resting
(4) a state of inactivity
(5) awaiting

Answers are on page 272.

Analysis: Recognizing Assumptions

People take many facts for granted when they communicate. When you read, you often must identify such facts.

Facts or ideas that are taken for granted without being explained are called unstated assumptions. You make unstated assumptions very often when you speak and write. For example, suppose you tell a friend that you got caught in a thunderstorm. You assume that your friend knows what a thunderstorm is. Therefore, you do not describe the thunder, lightning, wind, and rain. You take for granted that your friend will understand your experience.

When you read about science, you will find that there are many unstated assumptions. Writers take for granted that you know many common facts. In order to understand a passage, you must be able to identify the assumptions the writer makes.

Read this paragraph and identify some unstated assumptions.

Despite the barrier of the skin, microorganisms still manage to get inside the body. Some of them can affect the body's normal functioning and cause disease. When you get the flu or a cold, your body's functions are upset. However, this condition is temporary. You are not sick for the rest of your life. Your body has ways to get rid of the microorganisms in order for you to return to normal.

What does the writer of this paragraph take for granted and not explain?

- that microorganisms are tiny living things
- that they get into the body through the air we breathe, through the food and water we take in, and by direct contact

Were you able to identify these unstated assumptions? If so, the writer did a good job of deciding what needs to be explained and what does not.

Remember, an unstated assumption is something the writer takes for granted and does not explain. It is up to you to figure out what the unstated assumptions are.

 Both diagrams and passages may contain unstated assumptions. If you have difficulty understanding either, ask yourself: What does the illustrator or writer assume I know?

Recognizing Assumptions

Items 1 to 3 refer to the following diagram. Choose the best answer to each item.

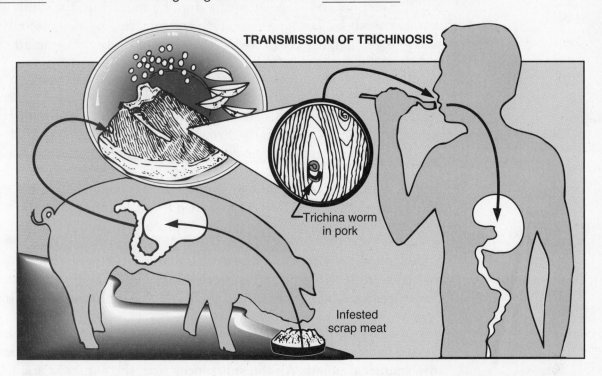

TRANSMISSION OF TRICHINOSIS

Trichina worm in pork

Infested scrap meat

1. Which of the following does the creator of the diagram assume?

    (1) that nothing can be done to prevent the transmission of trichinosis
    (2) that the reader has had trichinosis
    (3) that the reader is familiar with disease, pigs, and parasites
    (4) that the reader eats pork
    (5) that trichina occurs in the digestive system

2. Based on the information given, it is assumed that the reader already knows which of the following?

    (1) Trichinosis is a disease.
    (2) Trichinosis is spread by eating meat infested with the trichina worm.
    (3) Trichinosis is generally passed from humans to pigs.
    (4) Trichinosis can be spread from one human to another through sneezing or coughing.
    (5) Trichinosis can be prevented by washing your hands before eating.

3. Based on the information given, it is assumed that the reader already knows which of the following?

    (1) Trichinosis can be spread by eating beef, pork, or lamb.
    (2) The trichina worm is a parasite, an organism that obtains its food from another living thing.
    (3) The trichina worm can live outside the bodies of pigs and humans.
    (4) Trichinosis can be spread through contaminated water.
    (5) Trichinosis affects only adult men.

▶ **tip**

When referring to information on a diagram, think about everything you know that may relate to the topic. Apply your own knowledge as you read the new information.

Answers are on page 273.

The Human Digestive System

The human digestive system consists of a long tube called the alimentary canal. It is made up of the mouth, esophagus, stomach, small intestine, and large intestine. In a human adult, the alimentary canal is about 30 feet long. The liver and pancreas, which also have a role in digestion, are connected to the alimentary canal by small tubes.

Mouth and Esophagus. In the mouth, food is ground and moistened with saliva. Saliva contains a substance that begins to break down the starches in food. Saliva also contains mucus, which makes the food slippery enough to pass easily through the body. The tube that connects the mouth and stomach is called the esophagus.

Stomach. In the stomach, the breakdown of fats begins. Minerals are dissolved, and bacteria in food are killed by acid produced by the stomach. The stomach makes mucus to protect the lining from the acid.

Small Intestine. The small intestine is about 1 1/4 inches wide and 23 feet long. Most of the digestive process takes place here. Nutrients from digested food pass from the small intestine into the bloodstream.

Pancreas and Liver. The pancreas secretes substances that help break down proteins, starches, and fats. Bile from the liver breaks up fats into smaller droplets. All the substances from the pancreas and liver enter the small intestine by means of tubes called ducts.

Large Intestine. The undigested material from the small intestine contains a lot of water. One of the main functions of the large intestine is to absorb this water. As a result, the undigested material becomes more solid before it passes out of the body.

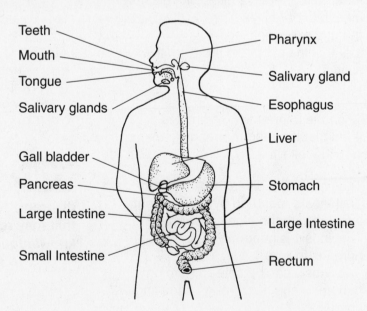

Items 1 to 8 refer to the previous passage and diagram. Choose the best answer to each item.

1. What is the purpose of the digestive system?

   (1) to move food from the mouth to the stomach
   (2) to break down food into substances the body can absorb and to get rid of wastes
   (3) to protect the lining of the organs from harmful substances swallowed with food
   (4) to protect the body against disease
   (5) to absorb oxygen from the air and release carbon dioxide

2. How is food ground up and mixed with saliva?

   (1) by contractions in the esophagus
   (2) by chemical action in the stomach
   (3) by swallowing
   (4) by absorption of water
   (5) by chewing

3. What is one of the main functions of the large intestine?

   (1) to break down proteins
   (2) to break down fats
   (3) to absorb water
   (4) to produce bile
   (5) to kill bacteria swallowed with food

4. Which organ makes up most of the length of the alimentary canal?

   (1) mouth
   (2) esophagus
   (3) stomach
   (4) small intestine
   (5) large intestine

5. Nutrients from the small intestine enter the bloodstream and go to the

   (1) large intestine
   (2) pancreas
   (3) liver
   (4) stomach
   (5) rest of the body

6. How would damage to the liver affect digestion?

   (1) Foods would not be ground up.
   (2) Proteins would not be broken down.
   (3) Starches would be changed to sugars.
   (4) Fats would not be digested properly.
   (5) Too much water would be absorbed by the large intestine.

7. What is the result of chewing and swallowing too quickly?

   (1) Food absorbs too much saliva.
   (2) Food is not ground up enough and so starches are not properly processed.
   (3) Food passes through the esophagus into the stomach.
   (4) Nutrients are not absorbed through the small intestine.
   (5) More minerals are dissolved in the stomach.

8. Through what structure does solid waste pass out of the body?

   (1) pancreas
   (2) liver
   (3) small intestine
   (4) stomach
   (5) rectum

Answers are on page 273.

Items 1 to 4 refer to the following passage and diagram. Choose the best answer to each item.

   The heart is the major organ of the circulatory system. It beats an average of 72 times a minute, pumping blood throughout the body. The right and left sides of the heart are divided by a wall called the septum. Each side is divided into two chambers. The upper chambers are called the atria, and the lower chambers are called the ventricles.

   Oxygen-poor blood from the body enters the right atrium through large veins called the venae cavae. When the atrium contracts, it forces the blood into the right ventricle. Next, the right ventricle contracts, forcing the blood into the pulmonary arteries, which carry it to the lungs. In the lungs the blood picks up oxygen. The oxygen-rich blood then flows through the pulmonary veins and back to the heart where it enters the left atrium. The left atrium contracts and forces the blood into the left ventricle. As the left ventricle contracts, it forces the blood into a large artery called the aorta. From the aorta, blood flows into a system of blood vessels that carry it throughout the body.

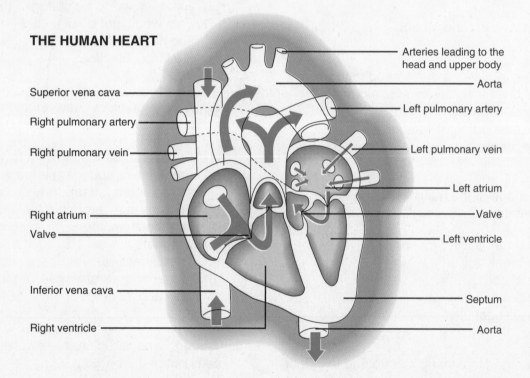

THE HUMAN HEART

1. What controls the beating of the heart?

   (1) the aorta
   (2) the venae cavae
   (3) the lungs
   (4) the brain
   (5) the intestines

2. Which chamber sends blood from the heart through the body?

   (1) the right ventricle
   (2) the right atrium
   (3) the left ventricle
   (4) the left atrium
   (5) the venae cavae

3. What would probably happen if the venae cavae became clogged?

(1) Too much blood would enter the right atrium.
(2) Too little blood would enter the right atrium.
(3) Too much blood would enter the left atrium.
(4) Too much blood would enter the lungs.
(5) Too much blood would enter the aorta.

4. What is most likely to happen if the aorta were pinched off?

(1) Too much blood would enter the left ventricle.
(2) Not enough oxygen-poor blood would enter the heart.
(3) Oxygen-poor blood would not be able to reach the lungs.
(4) The body would not get enough oxygen-rich blood.
(5) Oxygen-rich blood would enter the venae cavae.

Items 5 to 9 refer to the following passage.

Arteries carry blood away from the heart. They branch to form smaller vessels called arterioles, which enter the body's tissues and branch into capillaries. The walls of capillaries are only one cell thick. Dissolved nutrients diffuse, or spread, through the thin capillary walls into the body's cells. Waste products diffuse out of the cells and into the capillaries to be carried away. Capillaries form venules, which combine to form the large blood vessels called veins. Veins carry the blood back to the heart.

5. What is a blood vessel shaped like?

(1) a fist
(2) a pear
(3) a sphere
(4) a pyramid
(5) a tube

6. When blood vessels contract, or become narrower, what is the effect on the circulatory system?

(1) More blood circulates through the body.
(2) Less blood circulates through the body.
(3) Arteries become capillaries.
(4) Bleeding occurs.
(5) There is no effect.

7. In which of the following blood vessels would you expect waste products to be carried?

(1) veins
(2) arterioles
(3) arteries
(4) aorta
(5) heart

8. Which blood vessel carries blood from the heart to the lungs?

(1) vein
(2) venule
(3) artery
(4) capillary
(5) lymph

9. Based on the information given, it is assumed that the reader already knows which of the following?

(1) Arterioles are smaller vessels than arteries.
(2) The circulatory system has the same function as the digestive system.
(3) The heart supplies the power to move blood through the blood vessels.
(4) Venules connect to form larger blood vessels called veins.
(5) Arterioles enter body tissue and branch into capillaries.

tip   **When reading a science passage that describes a structure, try to visualize it. For example, try to "see" with your mind's eye the arteries branching into smaller and smaller arterioles.**

Answers are on page 274.

Directions: Choose the best answer to each item.

Items 1 to 6 refer to the following information.

The endocrine system is made up of glands that secrete substances called hormones. Hormones travel throughout the body but affect the functions of only some parts of the body.

Endocrine Gland	Hormone	Effect
Thyroid	Thyroxine	Controls how quickly food is converted to energy in cells
Parathyroid	Parathormone	Regulates body's use of calcium and phosphorus
Thymus	Thymosin	May affect the formation of antibodies in children
Adrenal	Adrenaline Cortisone	Prepares the body to meet emergencies Maintains salt balance
Pancreas	Insulin	Decreases level of sugar in the blood
Ovaries (female gonads)	Estrogen	Controls the development of secondary sex characteristics
Testes (male gonads)	Testosterone	Controls the development of secondary sex characteristics
Pituitary	Growth hormone Oxytocin ACTH, TSH, FSH, LH	Controls the growth of bones and muscles Causes uterine contractions in labor Regulate the secretions of the other endocrine glands

1. A person with high levels of sugar in the blood is said to have diabetes. Which hormone is lacking in a person with this condition?

   (1) thyroxine
   (2) adrenaline
   (3) insulin
   (4) oxytocin
   (5) thymosin

2. In an emergency, your heart rate and breathing quicken and you have a sudden burst of energy. Which endocrine gland causes this reaction?

   (1) adrenal
   (2) thyroid
   (3) thymus
   (4) parathyroid
   (5) pancreas

3. The body maintains its salt balance with the hormone

   (1) glucagon
   (2) cortisone
   (3) estrogen
   (4) testosterone
   (5) adrenaline

4. Which endocrine gland is different in males and females?

   (1) pituitary
   (2) gonads
   (3) adrenal
   (4) thymus
   (5) pancreas

5. A condition called <u>acromegaly</u> causes certain bones in the adult to grow larger and thicker. Which endocrine gland causes this condition?

    (1) adrenal
    (2) pancreas
    (3) thymus
    (4) thyroid
    (5) pituitary

6. How are hormones carried throughout the body?

    (1) by the digestive system
    (2) by the nerves
    (3) by the blood
    (4) by the saliva
    (5) by the skin

Items 7 to 11 refer to the following passage and diagram.

    The semicircular canals in the ear help the body to keep its balance. They contain nerve endings and a liquid. When the head moves, the liquid sloshes against the nerve endings. These nerves send a message to the brain, which interprets the position of the head. Because the three canals in the ear are positioned at right angles to one another, any change in position moves the fluid in at least one of the canals.

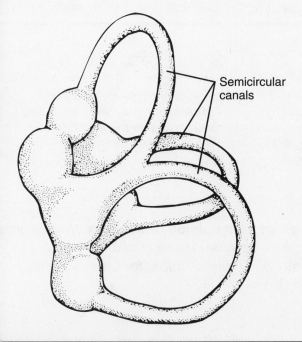

Semicircular canals

7. Where are the semicircular canals located?

    (1) in the left ear
    (2) in the right ear
    (3) in both ears
    (4) at the base of the neck
    (5) below the jaw

8. When you spin around rapidly, the fluid moves to one end of the canals. It rushes to the other side if you

    (1) slow down gradually
    (2) stop suddenly
    (3) start running
    (4) jump
    (5) keep spinning

9. What is likely to be the result of disease of the semicircular canals?

    (1) loss of hearing
    (2) damaged vision
    (3) dizziness
    (4) paralysis
    (5) poor sense of touch

10. Which condition is associated with the normal functioning of the semicircular canals?

    (1) deafness
    (2) motion sickness
    (3) measles
    (4) common cold
    (5) low blood pressure

11. The best title for this passage would be

    (1) Motion Sickness
    (2) Keeping Your Balance
    (3) The Structure of the Ear
    (4) How Nerves Send Messages
    (5) When Your Head Moves

Answers are on page 275.

Analysis: Fact or Opinion

A fact is a statement that is true. A fact can be proved. An opinion is someone's belief. An opinion may or may not be true, and it cannot be proved.

You deal with facts and opinions all the time. For example, the virus that causes AIDS is transmitted in body fluids such as blood and semen. People at high risk of contracting AIDS include drug users who share needles and people who have had infected blood transfusions. These are all facts. People who are not in a high-risk group often believe they have no chance of getting AIDS. This point of view about the risk of contracting AIDS is an opinion. It is probably not true. Even low-risk groups have some chance of getting AIDS.

Much of what you read in science is fact. However, you will also read scientists' opinions. Scientists observe things and then form an opinion, or hypothesis, to explain their observations. Then they experiment to learn if the hypothesis is correct.

Read this brief passage and distinguish the facts from the opinions.

In Lake Saima in Finland, visibility is only about six feet, even on a sunny day. How do the seals in the lake manage to catch the six pounds of fish they need to eat each day? Sight is probably useless. One possibility is echolocation—the animal version of radar. Dolphins give off pressure waves and monitor the echoes of the waves that bounce back. However, seals do not produce such waves. They do make barely audible clicks, but their ears are not good at hearing the echoes. According to one biologist, seals may be listening underwater through another type of antenna, the membranes in their whiskers.

Fact	Opinion
• Visibility is 6 feet or less. • Seals need 6 lb of fish a day. • Dolphins use echolocation. • Seals make barely audible clicks. • Seals' ears are not good at hearing echoes of clicks.	• Seals' sight is probably useless. • Echolocation may be used by seals. • Seals may use the membranes in their whiskers to listen.

When distinguishing fact from opinion, watch for certain words or phrases that signal an opinion. These might include *according to, it is possible, believe, think, feel, may, might, seem, agree,* **and** *disagree.*

Items 1 to 4 refer to the following passage. Choose the best answer to each item.

In laboratory experiments, scientists have found that animals live much longer than expected if they are fed a diet with all the necessary ingredients but with only 60 to 65 percent of the usual calories. These animals continue to appear healthy and strong after the well-fed animals in the experiment have died. For example, mice fed the special diet lived as long as 4 1/2 years. Mice who ate as much as they wanted lived an average of 3 years. The same increased life span has been shown with fish, spiders, worms, and protozoans.

A low-calorie diet may work to increase life spans only in normally short-lived creatures such as mice and insects. When food is scarce, animals become less fertile. A famine could last longer than a mouse's normal reproductive years. Such a famine could wipe out a population. Scientists think that short-lived animals may have a mechanism that helps them survive a few years of famine and still be able to reproduce. Longer-lived animals, such as monkeys and humans, are fertile for many years. Thus they may not have a mechanism to prolong life through lean years. Some scientists, however, think that restricting calories can extend the life spans of all forms of life, including humans.

1. Which of the following statements can be proved to be true?

   (1) Laboratory mice lived as long as 4 1/2 years when fed a low-calorie, nutritious diet.
   (2) Short-lived animals have a mechanism that helps them survive famine years and then reproduce.
   (3) Longer-lived animals do not have a mechanism that helps them prolong life during famine years and then reproduce.
   (4) Humans can lengthen their maximum life span by eating a reduced-calorie diet.
   (5) Given a choice, laboratory animals will eat a lower calorie diet.

2. What do different scientists believe, but have not yet proved, to be true about the effect of a reduced-calorie diet?

   A. The diet can extend the maximum life span only of short-lived animals.
   B. The diet cannot extend the maximum life span of long-lived animals.
   C. The diet can extend the maximum life span of all animals.

   (1) A only
   (2) B only
   (3) C only
   (4) A and B only
   (5) A, B, and C

3. Which of the following statements is an opinion expressed in the passage?

   (1) Mice who ate what they wanted lived 3 years on average.
   (2) You can extend your life by restricting the calories you eat.
   (3) Spiders who ate a low-calorie, nutritious diet lived longer.
   (4) A low-calorie diet increased the life spans of some short-lived animals.
   (5) Decreased calorie intake does not appear to affect the health or strength of some laboratory animals.

4. Which of the following statements is an opinion expressed in the passage?

   (1) Fish on a low-calorie diet lived longer than fish on a high-calorie diet.
   (2) Short-lived animals have a mechanism that helps them survive during a famine.
   (3) The life span of protozoans is affected by diet.
   (4) Animals become less fertile during a famine.
   (5) Monkeys are fertile for many years.

Answers are on page 275.

Disease

Diseases that can be spread from one person to another are called infectious diseases. Today, we know that infectious diseases are caused by microscopic agents called pathogens. The most common pathogens are bacteria and viruses.

Long ago, people thought that disease was caused by evil spirits that entered the body. The disease could be cured if the spirits were driven out by prayer or foul-tasting medicines. The invention of the microscope allowed scientists to see microorganisms, but over two hundred years passed before scientists started to connect microorganisms and disease. Louis Pasteur, a French scientist working in the nineteenth century, proved that yeasts cause fermentation of beet juice. He also thought that the rod-shaped organisms he found in sour juice were responsible for its souring. If such organisms could sour juice, Pasteur thought, perhaps they could also cause disease in humans.

About the same time, a German scientist named Robert Koch discovered that a specific kind of bacterium caused anthrax in sheep, cattle, and humans. While examining organs of animals that had died of anthrax, Koch found many rod-shaped bacteria in the blood vessels. He transferred some of these into the cut skin of a healthy mouse, which then developed anthrax and died. Koch found many of the same bacteria in the blood of the dead mouse.

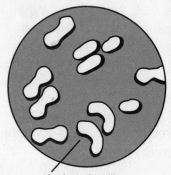

Anthrax bacillus

However, Koch was not satisfied until he could watch the bacteria multiply. He set up an experiment to grow the bacteria and infect laboratory animals. His experiments provided significant proof for Pasteur's idea that microorganisms can cause disease. Koch's procedure for studying disease-causing organisms is still used today. The steps in his method, known as Koch's postulates, are listed below.

1. Isolate the organism believed to cause the disease.
2. Grow the organism outside the animal in a sterile food medium. A group of organisms grown in this way is called a culture.
3. Produce the same disease by injecting a healthy animal with organisms from the culture.
4. Examine the sick animal and recover the organisms that caused the disease.

Most bacteria that cause disease do so by producing toxins. A toxin is a substance that keeps body cells from functioning as they normally do. For example, the disease tetanus is caused by bacteria that enter the body through deep puncture wounds. These bacteria produce a toxin that attacks nerve cells and can cause muscle contractions.

ems 1 to 7 refer to the previous passage. Choose the <u>best answer</u> to each item.

1. Before Louis Pasteur, what opinion was held about the nature of disease?

   (1) Diseases are caused by evil spirits.
   (2) Diseases are caused by microscopic agents called pathogens.
   (3) Anthrax is caused by rod-shaped bacteria.
   (4) Diseases are caused by yeast.
   (5) Diseases are caused by viruses.

2. At the time he thought of it, Pasteur's idea that microorganisms caused disease was an opinion. What contributed to this idea being accepted as fact today?

   (1) the development of foul-tasting medicines
   (2) the invention of the microscope
   (3) Pasteur's experiments with yeast and fermentation
   (4) Koch's experiments with anthrax bacteria
   (5) the discovery of microorganisms

3. Based on Koch's discovery of the microorganism that causes anthrax, what can you conclude?

   (1) All diseases are caused by microorganisms.
   (2) Improved types of yeasts would improve fermentation.
   (3) Yeast can be used to ferment juice.
   (4) Some diseases are not contagious.
   (5) The spread of anthrax can be stopped by stopping the spread of anthrax bacteria.

4. Which of the following was Pasteur's main contribution to the study of disease?

   (1) the invention of the microscope
   (2) the discovery that yeast causes fermentation
   (3) the discovery of microorganisms
   (4) the idea that microorganisms cause disease
   (5) a cure for anthrax

5. If the fourth step of Koch's postulates were not carried out during an experiment, what would be the result?

   (1) The injected animal would not get sick.
   (2) The injected animal would not die.
   (3) The cause of the disease would not be proved.
   (4) The culture would become contaminated.
   (5) The injected animal would die.

6. Why did Koch think that a specific kind of bacteria was responsible for anthrax?

   (1) Humans also get anthrax.
   (2) He found many of the bacteria in animals that had died of anthrax.
   (3) He knew that yeast causes fermentation of juice.
   (4) He knew that anthrax was highly contagious.
   (5) He was able to grow anthrax bacteria in the laboratory.

7. What is a culture?

   (1) a type of pathogen
   (2) a type of bacteria
   (3) a group of microorganisms grown in a sterile food medium
   (4) a laboratory with animal subjects
   (5) the result of fermentation

tip _____ **When answering questions about fact or opinion, look for clue words such as _think, believe,_ or _feel_ in the question and the passage.**

Answers are on page 276.

Items 1 and 2 refer to the following passage and diagram. Choose the best answer to each item.

BACTERIUM

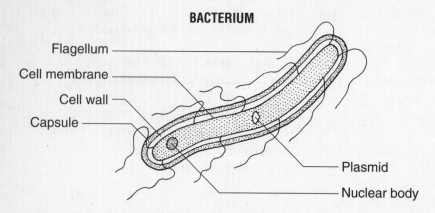

- Flagellum
- Cell membrane
- Cell wall
- Capsule
- Plasmid
- Nuclear body

Bacteria are small one-celled organisms that live almost everywhere. The largest bacteria are only about 1/65,000 centimeter across, and many are smaller. One of the ways bacteria are identified is by their shape. Bacteria shaped like spheres or circles are called cocci. Rod-shaped bacteria are called bacilli. Corkscrew-shaped or coiled bacteria are called spirilla. Some bacteria have flagella, whiplike structures that move the cell through water or other fluids.

Bacteria are surrounded by a slime layer. Some bacteria have a thick slime layer called a capsule. Bacteria that can cause serious infection usually have a capsule. Scientists think that the capsule may protect the bacteria from the body's defenses against infection.

Beneath the capsule is a stiff cell wall. Within the cell wall is a cell membrane that allows substances to pass into and out of the cell. Bacteria have a nuclear body that contains genetic material, but there is no nuclear membrane around it. Genetic material may also be found in small structures called plasmids.

To be active, bacteria need a suitable temperature, moisture, darkness, and food. Those that cause infections in humans grow best at 98.6°F, which is normal body temperature. Bacteria can remain alive but become inactive when conditions for growth are lacking. When the environment becomes favorable again, the bacteria may grow and reproduce rapidly.

1. What is the shape of the bacteria Diplococcus pneumoniae, which causes pneumonia?

    (1) rod
    (2) circular
    (3) coiled
    (4) corkscrew
    (5) whiplike

2. What is likely to happen to bacteria if the temperature of the environment drops?

    (1) They will grow rapidly.
    (2) They will reproduce rapidly.
    (3) They will become inactive.
    (4) They will cause fermentation.
    (5) They will get a disease.

A virus is made up of a single molecule of genetic material surrounded by a protein coat. The protein coat protects the genetic material of the virus from substances that could damage it.

A virus shows no signs of life as long as it is outside a living cell. It does not grow, reproduce, or perform any chemical activity necessary for life. In order to become active, a virus must invade a living cell called a host cell. Once inside the host cell, the virus transfers its own genetic material into the cell. The virus takes over all the cell's activities. The host cell is then used to duplicate the virus's own genetic material and viral protein. The duplicated materials are combined into new virus particles. Each new virus particle is exactly like the parent virus. It can leave the host cell to infect other cells and begin the cycle over again.

Most viruses can multiply only in certain kinds of cells. Some infect specific plants like potato or tobacco plants. Viruses that attack animals often attack specific tissues. Cold viruses, for example, attack the tissues that line the nose and throat. Polio viruses attack certain nerve cells in the brain and spinal cord.

3. If a virus's protein coat were destroyed, what would be the most likely outcome?

   (1) The virus would reproduce.
   (2) The virus would invade a host cell.
   (3) The viral genetic material would be damaged.
   (4) The virus would become active.
   (5) Virus particles would invade a host cell.

4. If a host cell contains virus particles, and the cell dies, the virus particles would most likely

   (1) die
   (2) be released to invade other cells
   (3) use the host cell for food
   (4) take the place of the host cell
   (5) develop protein coats

5. A virus takes over the activities of its host cell by

   (1) transferring its own genetic material into the host cell
   (2) reproducing itself in the host cell
   (3) releasing virus particles into the host cell
   (4) releasing its protein coat into the host cell
   (5) breaking down the cell's membrane

6. Scientists suspected that viruses existed before seeing them. This was possible because scientists had

   (1) identified the viral nucleus
   (2) seen viral protein coats
   (3) seen viruses
   (4) identified host cells
   (5) recognized diseases that viruses caused

7. Which of the following statements is not supported by information in the passage?

   (1) Some viruses attack tobacco cells.
   (2) Virus particles outside a host cell can't reproduce.
   (3) Virus particles occur inside and outside host cells.
   (4) Cold viruses reproduce only inside certain cells.
   (5) All viruses cause disease.

tip **When predicting the most likely** *outcome* **or** *result,* **first evaluate all choices. Eliminate any that are not logical. If you still have more than one possible answer, look for specific details that would support each choice. If you cannot find supporting details, a prediction is not valid.**

Answers are on page 276.

Directions: Choose the <u>best answer</u> to each item.

<u>Items 1 to 5</u> refer to the following passage.

In an effort to find a cure for the common cold, scientists continue learning about viruses. Rhinoviruses, the viruses that cause most colds, look like miniature planets covered with steep mountains and deep valleys. The body's immune system makes antibodies, substances that fight disease. The antibodies attach to the "mountaintops" of the viruses. However, the antibodies are easily fooled by the viruses' ability to change shape from one generation to the next. In addition, there are about 100 types of rhinoviruses, and each has mountaintops with a different shape.

Some scientists are studying the "valleys" rather than the mountains, because the valleys change less. The valleys attach to receptors on cells in the nose and throat. Several substances are being tested that will block the virus from attaching to a cell. Other scientists are trying to block the receptors on the cells' surface to keep the virus from latching on. In yet another approach, millions of synthetic copies of the human receptors are placed in the nose to act as decoys for the virus.

Most of the scientific approaches being studied do not involve destroying the virus. Instead, they involve using substances that block the virus and keep an infection from starting. However, some scientists think that it is not a good idea to prescribe a drug that might be taken by millions of healthy people simply to prevent a minor illness like a cold.

1. What do rhinoviruses look like?

    (1) decoys
    (2) comets with tails
    (3) planets with mountains and valleys
    (4) corkscrews
    (5) rods

2. Based on the information given, research scientists believe which of the following to be true, but unproved?

    (1) In the future, it may be possible to cure the common cold.
    (2) Rhinoviruses are simple pathogens.
    (3) Synthetic receptors can act as decoys for viruses.
    (4) Viruses can be destroyed with existing drugs.
    (5) About 100 types of rhinoviruses cause colds.

3. According to the passage, which of the following statements reflects an opinion some scientists have about current research on the common cold?

    (1) A drug to prevent colds may be too risky for so many people to take for such a minor illness.
    (2) Scientists will never find a cure for the common cold.
    (3) Rhinoviruses change their shape from one generation to another.
    (4) There are about 100 varieties of rhinoviruses.
    (5) Rhinoviruses attach to cells in the nasal passages.

tip ————————————————
When identifying beliefs, as opposed to facts, it is often necessary to look at what is implied in a passage, rather than what is stated.
————————————————

4. What are antibodies?

 (1) viruses
 (2) receptors on human cells
 (3) substances in the nasal passages
 (4) disease-fighting substances
 (5) drugs

5. Which of the following statements is a fact presented in the passage?

 (1) A cure for the common cold may be found soon.
 (2) It is a good idea to prescribe drugs to prevent colds.
 (3) Scientists are studying the blocking of cell receptors as a means of cold prevention.
 (4) All rhinoviruses look the same.
 (5) Most scientists think it is important to find a cure for the common cold.

Items 6 to 9 refer to the following passage.

The human body is constantly being invaded by bacteria and viruses. The immune system fights off these invaders and resists infection and disease. Certain vitamins, especially vitamin C, may help the immune system fight disease.

Linus Pauling created a stir when he proposed that large doses of vitamin C could prevent or reduce the severity of colds and flu. Other researchers have claimed that vitamin C can speed recovery from mononucleosis, viral pneumonia, and viral hepatitis. They believe that every infectious disease involves a severe loss of vitamin C throughout the body. Other experts doubt that vitamin C can be a useful treatment. They point to studies showing that vitamin C has no effect on colds after they start.

6. What do some scientists believe to be the role of vitamin C in preventing disease?

 (1) It may help the immune system.
 (2) It can cure viral pneumonia.
 (3) It can cure the flu.
 (4) It can cure a cold after it starts.
 (5) It can cure mononucleosis.

7. If vitamin C does have a significant role in helping the immune system, what should people do?

 (1) Eat a diet low in vitamin C.
 (2) Eat foods high in vitamin C.
 (3) Take huge doses of vitamin C after a disease is established.
 (4) Eat more meats and dairy products.
 (5) Do nothing special until they get sick.

8. Which of the following is presented in this passage as a fact?

 (1) Vitamin C can prevent the common cold.
 (2) Vitamin C improves the immune response.
 (3) The immune system resists invading bacteria and viruses.
 (4) The immune system cannot resist mononucleosis.
 (5) Recovery from viral pneumonia can be speeded by vitamin C.

9. What did Linus Pauling propose?

 (1) that the immune system fights disease
 (2) that the common cold can be prevented or eased with large doses of vitamin C
 (3) that mononucleosis and viral hepatitis can be cured with large doses of vitamin C
 (4) that all infectious diseases cause losses of vitamin C throughout the body
 (5) that the common cold can be cured with large doses of vitamin C

Answers are on page 277.

Evaluation: Evaluating Information

How do you decide if a statement is true or false? You apply what you know about recognizing implications, figuring out unstated assumptions, and distinguishing facts from opinions. Then you can determine whether the statement is accurate.

Suppose that you want to do your part to make a better environment. There is a lot of information in the news about things you can do to help. But how do you evaluate the information? What is really helpful and what sounds good but does not help much? A few years ago, some plastic garbage bags were advertised as degradable. Something that is degradable breaks down. So, by implication, the plastic bags would be reabsorbed into the environment. This sounded like a great idea and many people bought the bags. The unstated assumption made by advertisers was that the right conditions for degrading existed. Soon additional information became available to the consumer. The type of plastic used in the garbage bags needed sunlight to degrade. Since most trash ends up in a dark pile in a landfill, the unstated assumption was not likely to be true. The so-called degradable bags were unlikely to degrade in the landfill. Once the consumer had all the facts, the information was then evaluated differently.

When you try to evaluate the accuracy of information, ask yourself the following questions:

- Is the information based on fact or opinion?
- Does the information follow logically from the facts presented?
- Is the information based on an unstated assumption? If so, what is the assumption and is the assumption true?

The answers to these questions will help you decide whether the information is accurate or not. Remember, when answering multiple-choice test items, eliminating inaccurate choices will help you identify the correct answer.

 When deciding whether a statement is true, check to see if there are facts or evidence in the passage that support the statement. If there are facts that contradict or say the opposite of the statement, then it is likely the statement is false.

Items 1 to 4 refer to the following passage.

Choose the best answer to each item.

In medicine, infertility is defined as the inability of a couple to conceive or the inability of a woman to carry a pregnancy to a live birth. The trend toward postponing parenthood into the thirties and forties age bracket has doubled the amount of infertility in the United States over the last 20 years. Today almost 20 percent of the couples in the United States cannot have a child. Increased age contributes to problems of fertility. Difficulty producing eggs increases with a woman's age. The chance of miscarriage increases dramatically after age 35. Contrary to the myth that infertility is always the woman's problem, infertility affects both sexes equally.

1. Which of the following statements is true?

   (1) Infertility is always the woman's problem.
   (2) Most couples in their thirties and forties cannot have children.
   (3) The best time to have a child is when you are in your early twenties.
   (4) Most couples in the United States are fertile.
   (5) The chance of miscarriage decreases with increased age.

2. Given the information in the passage, which of the following statements is the most accurate?

   (1) In deciding when to have children, couples should take into account that the risk of infertility increases with age.
   (2) Age is not a factor in infertility.
   (3) People should have children when they are as young as possible.
   (4) There is no risk of infertility for couples who already have had one child.
   (5) More men than women have infertility problems.

3. Which of the following statements is a fact presented in this passage?

   (1) Couples should not postpone having children into their thirties and forties.
   (2) Infertility decreases with age.
   (3) Stress contributes to infertility.
   (4) A woman of 35 has a greater chance of miscarriage than a woman of 45.
   (5) Infertility affects both men and women.

4. Compared to a woman in her twenties, a woman in her forties is

   (1) more likely to conceive
   (2) less likely to have a miscarriage
   (3) more likely to have difficulty producing eggs
   (4) more likely to be fertile
   (5) more likely to postpone parenthood

Item 5 refers to the following passage.

About one in every 87 pregnancies produces twins. There are two kinds of twins, fraternal and identical. Fraternal twins result from the release and fertilization of more than one egg. Identical twins result from the division of the fertilized egg to form two separate embryos. Identical twins are genetically alike and always the same sex. Fraternal twins may look alike but are no more genetically alike than other siblings.

5. Given the information in the passage, which of the following statements is the most accurate?

   (1) If one twin is taller than the other, then they must be fraternal twins.
   (2) If the twins are of the same sex, then they must be identical twins.
   (3) If the twins are of different sexes, then they must be fraternal twins.
   (4) If the male twin looks alot like his twin sister, they are probably identical twins.
   (5) If both twins are good at math, they are probably identical twins.

Answers are on page 278.

Mendel and Genetics

How often have you heard someone say of a child, "She has her mother's eyes and her father's chin"? Statements like this refer to traits, or characteristics, that we inherit from our parents. The study of traits and how they are inherited is called genetics.

Gregor Mendel, an Austrian monk, has been called the father of genetics. He began his experiments in 1857. He bred pea plants because they have many traits that are easy to identify.

First, Mendel developed purebred pea plants. These plants always produced the same traits. Next, he crossed, or bred, plants with opposite traits. For example, he crossed purebred tall plants with purebred dwarf plants. He referred to this parental generation of plants as the P generation. Much to Mendel's surprise, all the plants that resulted were tall! Mendel called this F_1 generation of plants hybrids because they contained a mixture of the traits for tallness and dwarfness.

Then Mendel crossed tall hybrid plants from the F_1 generation. He found that some plants in the resulting F_2 generation were tall and some were dwarf. Each time he repeated the experiment, he found that, on average, there were three tall plants for one dwarf plant.

How did Mendel explain his results? He reasoned that the offspring inherited traits from both parents. However, some traits were more powerful than others. He called these traits dominant. The traits that did not show up in the F_1 generation he called recessive. In the F_2 generation, the plants that show the recessive trait must be plants that did not inherit any dominant trait for tallness.

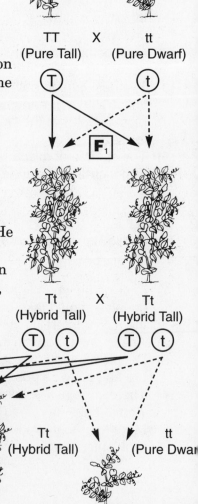

P

TT   X   tt
(Pure Tall)   (Pure Dwarf)

(T)   (t)

F_1

Tt   X   Tt
(Hybrid Tall)   (Hybrid Tall)

(T) (t)   (T) (t)

F_2

TT
(Pure Tall)

Tt
(Hybrid Tall)

Tt
(Hybrid Tall)

tt
(Pure Dwar

ems 1 to 6 refer to the previous passage and diagram. Choose the <u>best answer</u> to each item.

1. How did Mendel make sure that the results of his breeding experiments would be accurate?

   (1) He started with purebred plants.
   (2) He used hybrid plants having opposite traits.
   (3) He selected plants with several opposite traits.
   (4) He used only dwarf plants.
   (5) He used only tall plants.

2. If you cross purebred pea plants having inflated pods with purebred pea plants having wrinkled pods, all the F_1 generation will have inflated pods. Which statement about the F_1 generation is true?

   (1) The plants are all hybrids.
   (2) The plants are all purebred.
   (3) Inflated pods is a recessive trait.
   (4) Wrinkled pods is a hybrid trait.
   (5) Wrinkled pods is a dominant trait.

3. What is a dominant trait?

   (1) a trait that will appear only in purebred offspring
   (2) a trait that will appear only in hybrid offspring
   (3) a trait that will appear in some purebred and all hybrid offspring
   (4) a trait that will appear in every offspring
   (5) a trait that will disappear when bred

4. What evidence supports Mendel's conclusion that the recessive trait was carried by the F_1 generation even though none of these plants showed the recessive trait?

   (1) All of the F_1 generation plants showed the dominant characteristic.
   (2) Some of the F_2 generation plants showed the recessive trait.
   (3) Some of the F_2 generation plants showed the dominant trait.
   (4) All of the F_2 generation plants showed the recessive trait.
   (5) Some of the F_1 generation plants showed the recessive characteristic.

5. Why did Mendel use pea plants in his experiments?

   (1) They are the only type of plant that shows how genetics works.
   (2) They have characteristics that are easy to identify.
   (3) The rules of genetics apply only to plants.
   (4) They were the only plants available in Austria at that time.
   (5) They were available in dwarf varieties.

6. When two hybrid plants are bred, what is the chance that one offspring will show the recessive trait?

   (1) no chance
   (2) 1 out of 4
   (3) 2 out of 4
   (4) 3 out of 4
   (5) 4 out of 4

Answers are on page 278.

Items 1 and 2 refer to the following passage and chart. Choose the <u>best answer</u> to each item.

A gene is a portion of the genetic molecule that determines a particular trait. A plant or animal inherits half of its genes from each parent. The set of genes that a plant or animal inherits is called its <u>genotype</u>.

To depict which traits will be inherited, scientists use a Punnett square. The Punnett square below shows the crossing of pea plants with two sets of contrasting traits—tall and dwarf, and red and white flowers. The genotype of both parents is written as TtRr. Letters representing the genes from the male parent are placed across the top of the square. Letters representing the genes from the female parent are placed along the left.

Male Genes

	TR	tR	Tr	tr
TR	TTRR	TtRR	TTRr	TtRr
tR	TtRR	ttRR	TtRr	ttRr
Tr	TTRr	TtRr	TTrr	Ttrr
tr	TtRr	ttRr	Ttrr	ttrr

(Female Genes along the left)

T = tall, dominant

R = red, dominant

t = dwarf, recessive

r = white, recessive

Each square represents one possible offspring. Each offspring inherits the genes at the top of the column and the genes at the left of each row.

1. What is the offspring of crossing a female (YYTT) having dominant genes for yellow peas (Y) and dominant genes for tallness (T) with a male (yytt) having recessive genes for green peas (y) and recessive genes for dwarfness (t)?

   (1) YyTt
   (2) YYTt
   (3) Yytt
   (4) YyTT
   (5) yyTT

2. Which of the following statements is true o the offspring of a male of genotype ttrr and a female of genotype ttrr?

   (1) All offspring will inherit both dominant traits.
   (2) All offspring will inherit both recessive traits.
   (3) All offspring will inherit one dominant and one recessive trait.
   (4) Some offspring will inherit one domina and one recessive trait.
   (5) Some offspring will inherit both dominant traits.

Unit 1: Biolo

Items 3 to 6 refer to the following passage and chart.

The Punnett square shows the genotypes of offspring, but what does each offspring look like? To figure out the phenotype, or appearance, you must look at the dominant traits of each individual. For example, the phenotype of an individual with a genotype of YyIi is yellow with inflated pods. The recessive genes for green (y) and wrinkled pods (i) do not show in the individual's appearance. If there are no dominant genes for a particular trait, then the recessive trait is the phenotype. For example, an individual with genotype Yyii has a phenotype of yellow with wrinkled pods.

Male Genes

Female Genes		YI	yI	Yi	yi
	YI	YYII	YyII	YYIi	YyIi
	yI	YyII	yyII	YyIi	yyIi
	Yi	YYIi	YyIi	YYii	Yyii
	yi	YyIi	yyIi	Yyii	yyii

Y = yellow, dominant

y = green, recessive

I = inflated pods, dominant

i = wrinkled pods, recessive

3. If someone gave you a pea plant that resulted from a genetic experiment, what could you tell with greatest accuracy?

(1) the plant's phenotype
(2) the plant's genotype
(3) which recessive genes the plant has
(4) which generation the plant is from
(5) what the next generation would look like

4. According to the diagram, how many of the 16 possible offspring genotypes will be green with wrinkled pods?

(1) 8
(2) 4
(3) 3
(4) 2
(5) 1

5. How many different phenotypes are shown in the diagram?

(1) 16
(2) 5
(3) 4
(4) 3
(5) 2

6. If one of the male parent's recessive genes were changed, and the changed gene were passed on to all his offspring, this would

(1) always result in a change in the genotype of the offspring
(2) always result in a change in the phenotype of the offspring
(3) never result in a change in the genotype of the offspring
(4) never result in a change in the phenotype of the offspring
(5) have no effect on the offspring

Answers are on page 279.

Directions: Choose the best answer to each item.

Items 1 to 4 refer to the following passage and diagram.

DNA is a molecule that contains hereditary information and controls the activities of each cell. The DNA in every cell of the body bears the genetic code which determines the traits of an organism.

The structure of DNA was not known until 1953, when an American biologist, James D. Watson, and a British biophysicist, F. H. C. Crick, worked it out. They described DNA as a double helix, or spiral, made up of two strands wound around each other and connected by crosspieces. The molecule looks like a twisted ladder.

The side pieces of DNA are made of alternating units of sugar and phosphate. The rungs of the DNA ladder are composed of pairs of nitrogen bases. Adenine is always paired with thymine, and guanine is always paired with cytosine. Their positions (right and left) may vary, and their sequence along the ladder may vary. These variations in position and sequence account for the many genetic traits an organism may have.

DNA MOLECULE

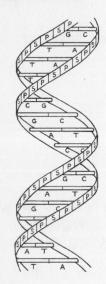

Key
A = adenine
C = cytosine
G = guanine
P = phosphate
S = sugar
T = thymine

1. Which of the following statements is always true?

   (1) Adenine is paired with cytosine.
   (2) Adenine is on the right side of the pair.
   (3) Adenine follows guanine.
   (4) Adenine is paired with thymine.
   (5) The sequence of nitrogen bases repeats itself precisely.

2. What would be the effect of straightening out the DNA molecule?

   (1) It would become shorter.
   (2) It would become longer.
   (3) It would become circular.
   (4) It would become spherical.
   (5) It would remain a helix.

3. How do offspring inherit traits from both parents?

   (1) They receive DNA from the female parent.
   (2) They receive DNA from the male parent.
   (3) The offspring create entirely new DNA.
   (4) They get some DNA from each parent.
   (5) DNA controls the activities of each cell

4. What substances make up the side pieces of DNA?

   (1) adenine and thymine
   (2) thymine and guanine
   (3) guanine and sugar
   (4) sugar and phosphate
   (5) phosphate and adenine

Scientists know more about inheritance in ower forms of life than they do in humans. One eason for this is that people have a longer life ycle. A researcher can study several enerations of insects in a few months or many enerations of bacteria in a week. At most, a esearcher can see five or six human enerations in a lifetime. The number of humans resents another problem. A single mating in a lant or simple animal may produce hundreds of ffspring. Each human family is small in omparison, and it represents a very tiny ampling of genetic possibilities. A third problem n studying human genetics is separating the ffect of heredity from the effect of environment. ince people are complex, thinking, responsive reatures, their environment influences their haracteristics.

To solve these problems, scientists who study uman genetics have a different approach. ather than tracing genetic traits through families ver time, they study the frequency of genetic aits across a large sample of the population. Vhen they know the frequency of a trait in the opulation, they can predict the probability of any iven trait appearing in offspring.

5. According to the information given, which of the following has not been established as a fact?

(1) the number of generations of bacteria in a given amount of time
(2) the relatively small number of offspring produced by two human mates
(3) the extent to which the environment influences characteristics of humans
(4) the frequency of a particular trait in a given population
(5) the life span of humans compared to that of insects and bacteria

6. Why is it difficult to study human genetics from one generation to the next?

(1) There is too much time between generations.
(2) There is too much genetic variation between generations.
(3) Environments influence people.
(4) Humans have identifiable traits.
(5) Researchers study gene frequency in large populations.

7. In order to ensure that the predictions about gene frequency in the general population are accurate, what must researchers do?

(1) use a sample consisting of one family
(2) use a sample consisting of a large and varied group of people
(3) use a sample consisting only of children
(4) use a sample consisting of several generations of one family
(5) use a sample consisting of only one ethnic group

8. Some people can taste a chemical called PTC, and others cannot. About 30 percent of the people in the United States cannot taste PTC. What is the probability that the next child born in the U.S. will not be able to taste PTC?

(1)   0
(2)   30 percent
(3)   50 percent
(4)   70 percent
(5)   100 percent

Answers are on page 279.

Analysis:
Conclusions and Supporting Statements

Understanding what you read often involves telling the difference between conclusions and supporting statements. A conclusion is a logical result or generalization. Supporting statements offer details and facts that prove the conclusion.

In science, laws, theories, and hypotheses are often conclusions. Observations, events, conditions, measurements, and other details are often supporting statements. Frequently you will be asked to explain why certain things have happened or to predict what will happen under certain circumstances. In both instances, you must be able to tell the difference between a conclusion and the information that proves the conclusion is true.

Telling the difference between conclusions and supporting statements draws on skills you have already learned. Sometimes you must distinguish a main idea (conclusion) from supporting details. Sometimes you must decide which facts support an opinion. At other times you must figure out cause and effect.

Read this brief passage and decide what is the conclusion and what are the supporting statements.

The most common water pollutants are organic materials (substances that were once living). Most organic material is attacked by bacteria and broken down into simpler substances. The greater the supply of organic matter, the larger the population of bacteria in the water, and the faster the oxygen is used up. Since all animals in a stream need oxygen, the oxygen level indicates which forms of life a polluted stream can support. Fish have the highest oxygen need. Invertebrate need less oxygen, and bacteria need still less.

What is the conclusion of this passage? From the information provided, we can conclude that polluted water cannot support certain animal life. To support this conclusion, we can point to several facts. Organic pollutants are food for bacteria, which reproduce rapidly and use up a lot of oxygen. When the oxygen level drops, fish cannot survive because they have the highest oxygen need. The invertebrate die next, and the oxygen-using bacteria die last.

 When you look for conclusions, pay attention to key words such as *for that reason, therefore, since, so,* and *thus*.

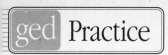

ems 1 and 2 refer to the following paragraph. Choose the best answer to each item.

Extinction, or the disappearance of a species, is a natural occurrence. All organisms are replaced sooner or later by better-adapted or newly evolved forms. However, some wild species have abruptly disappeared because humans eat or use them. The passenger pigeon and great auk were hunted to extinction during the 1800s. The buffalo was hunted almost to extinction. Today certain types of whales are likely to become extinct unless whaling nations can agree to reduce their catch.

Buffalo

Passenger pigeon

1. Which of the following statements supports the conclusion that wild animals that can be used by humans are more likely to face sudden extinction than other animals?

   (1) The passenger pigeon and great auk were hunted to extinction during the 1800s.
   (2) Extinction is a natural occurrence.
   (3) Species adapt to their environments.
   (4) Whales are no longer hunted.
   (5) All species eventually become extinct.

2. "All organisms are replaced sooner or later by better-adapted or newly evolved forms." Which conclusion does this statement support?

   (1) Whales are a protected species.
   (2) The extinction of the passenger pigeon could have been prevented.
   (3) People have no influence on which species become extinct.
   (4) Humans will eventually be replaced by another form of life.
   (5) No species lasts longer than 50 million years.

Answers are on page 280.

Ecosystems

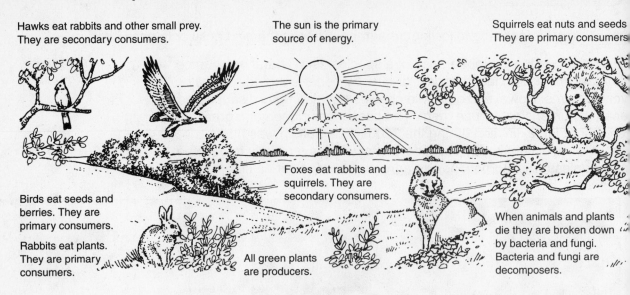

Hawks eat rabbits and other small prey. They are secondary consumers.

The sun is the primary source of energy.

Squirrels eat nuts and seeds. They are primary consumers.

Foxes eat rabbits and squirrels. They are secondary consumers.

Birds eat seeds and berries. They are primary consumers.

Rabbits eat plants. They are primary consumers.

All green plants are producers.

When animals and plants die they are broken down by bacteria and fungi. Bacteria and fungi are decomposers.

An ecosystem is a natural community in which the living and nonliving things interact. Lakes, rivers, meadows, ponds, and swamp are all ecosystems. The most important relationships in an ecosystem involve the flow of food and energy.

Food and the Ecosystem. The movement of food through a series of organisms is called a food chain. A food chain begins with producers, which in most ecosystems are green plants. Animals that eat plants are called primary consumers. Animals that eat primary consumers are called secondary consumers. Some ecosystems have tertiary consumers, which are animals that eat secondary consumers.

When plants and animals die, bacteria and fungi in the soil break them down into substances that can be used by plants. Organisms that break down plants and animals are called decomposers. Decomposers recycle the matter in an ecosystem.

Energy and the Ecosystem. The sun is the main source of energy for an ecosystem. The sun's energy enters the ecosystem through green plants, which store some of the energy. The stored energy is passed along the food chain as consumers eat producers and other consumer However, since living things use energy to carry out life processes, les and less energy is available to each level of consumer. For example, only 10 out of 1,000 units of energy are transferred from plants to primary consumers. Only 1 out of every 10 units of energy is transferred from primary consumers to secondary consumers.

Items 1 to 7 refer to the previous passage and illustration. Choose the best answer to each item.

1. Of the sentences below, which is a conclusion, not a supporting statement?

   (1) Plants produce food.
   (2) Matter in an ecosystem is being constantly recycled.
   (3) Decomposers break down dead plants and animals into substances that can be used by plants.
   (4) Secondary consumers eat primary consumers.
   (5) Primary consumers eat plants.

2. What would be the immediate result if all the primary consumers were removed from the ecosystem?

   (1) Plants would stop producing food.
   (2) Decomposers would increase their activity.
   (3) Secondary consumers would have nothing to eat.
   (4) Tertiary consumers would have more to eat.
   (5) A new source of energy would be needed.

3. Some birds eat insects as well as seeds and berries. Which of the following most accurately describes their role in the ecosystem?

   (1) producers
   (2) primary consumers
   (3) primary and secondary consumers
   (4) secondary consumers
   (5) producers and primary consumers

4. An insect that feeds on other insects that are crop pests is a

   (1) producer
   (2) primary consumer
   (3) secondary consumer
   (4) tertiary consumer
   (5) decomposer

5. Based on the information given, it is assumed that the reader already knows which of the following?

   (1) All living things are part of an ecosystem.
   (2) Only humans are not part of an ecosystem.
   (3) The sun is the main source of energy in an ecosystem.
   (4) All matter is being constantly recycled.
   (5) Squirrels are secondary consumers.

6. What is the role of decomposers in an ecosystem?

   (1) to produce food for primary consumers
   (2) to break down dead plants and animals into substances plants can use
   (3) to provide food for secondary consumers
   (4) to provide food for tertiary consumers
   (5) to provide energy

7. Which organisms are the highest-level consumers in a food chain?

   (1) hawks
   (2) seed-eating birds
   (3) rabbits
   (4) squirrels
   (5) primary consumers

Answers are on page 280.

Items 1 and 2 refer to the following passage and graph. Choose the best answer to each item.

In the year 10,000 B.C., there were about 10 million people in the world. By the year A.D. 1, that number had grown to about 300 million. The population remained fairly constant for the next 1,600 years. By the year 1650, the population had risen to only about 510 million people. During the next 200 years, however, the population more than doubled. Between 1850 and 1950, the population doubled again. The next doubling of the population took only 40 years.

Today the world's birth rate is three times higher than the death rate. The result is that the population continues to rise. The rapid increase in population is a serious problem. Overpopulated areas suffer from disease, poverty, and crime. Natural resources such as water and food are limited.

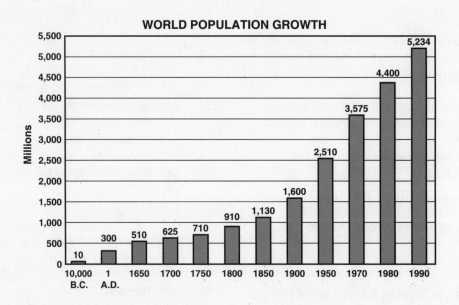

WORLD POPULATION GROWTH

1. Which of the following does not support the conclusion that world population is growing rapidly?

   (1) The birth rate is three times the death rate.
   (2) The last doubling of world population took only 40 years.
   (3) World population remained fairly stable until 1650.
   (4) Between 1900 and 1990, world population more than tripled.
   (5) Between 1950 and 1990, world population more than doubled.

2. Which factor is probably most responsible for the increased world population?

   (1) decrease in birth rate
   (2) increase in death rate
   (3) increase in disease
   (4) worse weather conditions
   (5) decrease in death rate

The number of people living in a specific area is called population density. Population density is a ratio. It is calculated by dividing the number of people living in an area by the amount of usable land available in that area. If an area's population increases, so does its population density.

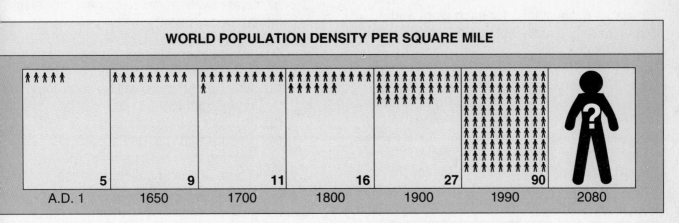

WORLD POPULATION DENSITY PER SQUARE MILE

A.D. 1	1650	1700	1800	1900	1990	2080
5	9	11	16	27	90	

3. About how many times greater was the world population density in 1990 than in 1650?

   (1) 80
   (2) 35
   (3) 10
   (4) 5
   (5) 3

4. Which of the following supports the statement, "If an area's population increases, so does its population density"?

   (1) The population density in the year A.D. 1 was about 5 people per square mile.
   (2) Population density is calculated by dividing the number of people living in an area by the amount of land available in the area.
   (3) The death rate has no effect on population density.
   (4) Population figures are estimates.
   (5) The population density in the year 1650 was 11 people per square mile.

5. According to the information in the chart, what is likely to happen to the population density by the year 2080 if all conditions remain the same?

   (1) It is likely to triple.
   (2) It is likely to decrease by one-half.
   (3) It is likely to double.
   (4) It is likely to remain the same.
   (5) It is likely to go back to the 1900 density.

6. If the birth rate and death rate remain at present levels, how can the human population density be decreased?

   (1) Increase the food supply.
   (2) Decrease the supply of fossil fuels.
   (3) Increase the amount of usable land.
   (4) Decrease the population density of selected animals.
   (5) Decrease the amount of usable land.

Answers are on page 281.

Directions: Choose the best answer to each item.

Items 1 to 5 refer to the following passage.

In stable ecosystems, for each plant and animal there is usually at least one consumer that serves to check its population growth. That is why there are usually constant numbers of plants and animals from year to year. When you take a species of plant or animal from its natural ecosystem and introduce it into another ecosystem, it might die out quickly. If it survives, the species may reproduce at an incredible rate.

How can a new species be so successful so quickly? The food relationships in an ecosystem have evolved slowly over time and they change very slowly. Just as many people are reluctant to eat an unfamiliar food, animals are unlikely to eat something they have never seen before. If there is no consumer willing to eat the new species, it will reproduce rapidly. For example, in 1859, 24 rabbits were imported from Europe to Australia, which had no rabbits. Today, Australia has well over a billion rabbits despite many efforts to control the population.

The best solution to the overpopulation of new species is prevention. However, if new organisms do overrun an area, sometimes population growth can be controlled by importing another species that will prey on the first species.

1. Which of the following caused the overpopulation of rabbits in Australia?

   (1) the importing of predators
   (2) the reluctance of people to eat rabbits
   (3) an unstable ecosystem
   (4) the overpopulation of consumers
   (5) rapid reproduction and insufficient consumers

2. What is the best way to solve the problems associated with introducing new organisms into an ecosystem?

   (1) Introduce an animal to prey on the new organism.
   (2) Ensure that there will be something the new organism will eat.
   (3) Prevent the introduction.
   (4) Ensure that the new ecosystem has nothing the new organism will eat.
   (5) There is no way to solve these problems.

3. Which of the following statements supports the conclusion that overpopulation of a new species can sometimes be controlled by the introduction of an animal that will prey on it?

   (1) The introduction of new organisms cannot always be prevented.
   (2) Rabbits were successfully wiped out in Australia.
   (3) In stable ecosystems, there is usually a least one consumer that checks another organism's population growth.
   (4) In time, the population will decrease.
   (5) The overpopulated species cannot find anything to eat.

tip When a paragraph begins with a question, the answer is frequently found in the information that follows. Be certain you know the answer before you continue reading.

4. What can you assume about the successful survival of rabbits in Australia?

    (1) an ecosystem with no food and no predators
    (2) an ecosystem with food and no predators
    (3) an ecosystem with no food and predators
    (4) an ecosystem with many meat-eating animals
    (5) an ecosystem similar to Europe's

5. Which is the best title for this passage?

    (1) Stable Ecosystems
    (2) The Introduction of Rabbits to Australia
    (3) Preventing the Introduction of New Species
    (4) The Introduction of New Species into Ecosystems
    (5) The Food Chain in a Stable Ecosystem

Items 6 to 8 refer to the following passage.

When fossil fuels such as coal, oil, and gas are burned, they release gases into the air. Three of the most common gases are:

1. Sulfur dioxide. Sulfur dioxide results from burning coal and oil that contain sulfur. When sulfur dioxide is inhaled, it usually causes choking, and, in large doses, it can be fatal. When it combines with water, it produces sulfuric acid, which can damage the eyes and lungs.
2. Nitric oxide. A by-product of burning gasoline, nitric oxide combines with oxygen in the air to form nitrogen dioxide. Nitrogen dioxide combines with water in the eyes and lungs and forms nitric acid, which can cause permanent damage.
3. Carbon monoxide. This gas is produced when fossil fuels do not burn completely. The major source of carbon monoxide is the exhaust from automobile engines. Carbon monoxide combines with the oxygen-carrying molecules in blood much faster than oxygen does. This is poisonous and can be fatal.

Sulfur dioxide and nitrogen dioxide combine with water vapor in the atmosphere to cause acid rain. Acid rain is very harmful to plant and animal life. In industrial areas, polluting gases also react in the atmosphere to produce smog, a gray or rust-colored haze. Smog can be harmful to the lungs and eyes of people and animals.

6. To prevent acid rain, the production of which of the following gases would have to be controlled?

    (1) nitric oxide and sulfur dioxide
    (2) nitric oxide and carbon monoxide
    (3) carbon monoxide and sulfur dioxide
    (4) water vapor and carbon monoxide
    (5) smog and sulfur dioxide

7. The amount of nitrogen dioxide in the atmosphere could be reduced by lowering which emissions from cars?

    (1) nitrogen dioxide
    (2) carbon monoxide
    (3) sulfur dioxide
    (4) nitric oxide
    (5) nitric acid

8. One result of the burning of fossil fuels is what is known as acid rain. Which of the following probably contributes to acid rain?

    A. sulfur dioxide
    B. nitric oxide
    C. carbon monoxide

    (1) A only
    (2) B only
    (3) C only
    (4) A and B
    (5) A and C

Answers are on page 281.

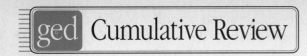

Directions: Choose the best answer to each item.

Items 1 to 5 refer to the following passage.

When disease-causing agents enter the body, white blood cells called phagocytes find them. Phagocytes surround, or engulf, microorganisms, much as an amoeba eats its food. One kind of phagocyte can enlarge to become a macrophage. Macrophages can engulf a hundred or more bacteria at one time.

Other kinds of white blood cells, called lymphocytes, produce antibodies. Antibodies are protein substances that react with specific foreign organisms in the body and make them ineffective. Lymphocytes produce many different antibodies to attack different disease organisms.

Each antibody is specific against a single disease organism. Lymphocytes do not make the antibody unless the body has been exposed to the disease organism. This exposure may be in the form of a vaccine. A vaccine contains weakened or dead disease organisms. Exposure to it causes the body to begin antibody production without making the person sick.

1. How do phagocytes destroy disease-causing organisms?

   (1) by producing antibodies
   (2) by preventing them from entering the body
   (3) by engulfing them
   (4) by splitting them
   (5) by piercing their cell walls

2. Which of the following statements is not true?

   (1) Macrophages are a kind of phagocyte.
   (2) All white bloods cells are the same.
   (3) Lymphocytes help the body fight disease.
   (4) Some white blood cells can destroy many microorganisms at a time.
   (5) Antibodies are made of protein.

3. HIV (human immunodeficiency virus), which causes AIDS, destroys certain kinds of lymphocytes. As a result, a person with HIV is likely to

   (1) have a reduced ability to fight off disease
   (2) produce an excess of antibodies
   (3) have a reduced number of phagocytes
   (4) have an excess of white blood cells
   (5) have a reduced pulse rate

4. How is being vaccinated like getting a disease?

   A. Both cause the person's lymphocytes to start making the antibodies that attack the disease organism.
   B. Both cause the person to develop the symptoms of the disease.
   C. Both cause the person to produce a large number of macrophages and phagocytes.

   (1) A only
   (2) B only
   (3) C only
   (4) A and C
   (5) A, B, and C

5. Why does the number of phagocytes and lymphocytes in the body increase during an infection?

   (1) More phagocytes and lymphocytes are needed to fight the infection.
   (2) Disease-causing microorganisms produce phagocytes and lymphocytes.
   (3) Antibodies produce more phagocytes and lymphocytes.
   (4) Red blood cells are decreasing.
   (5) The body has become immune to the infection.

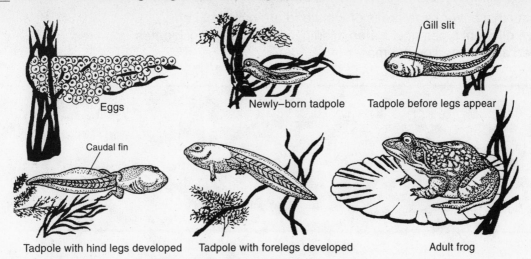

Eggs   Newly–born tadpole   Tadpole before legs appear   Gill slit

Caudal fin

Tadpole with hind legs developed   Tadpole with forelegs developed   Adult frog

The life cycle of the frog is an example of the process of metamorphosis. The word metamorphosis means change. In this process, the immature form, called a tadpole, gradually changes into an adult frog. The tadpole lives in water and breathes through gills. As it matures, the tadpole loses the gills and develops lungs. The adult frog can survive out of the water because it can breathe through its lungs.

6. Which of the following is the best title for the paragraph and diagram?

   (1) Metamorphosis in the Frog
   (2) The Structure of the Tadpole
   (3) The Life Cycle of Water-Dwelling Animals
   (4) Metamorphosis in Animals
   (5) Reproduction in Frogs

7. Which of the following statements does the author take for granted?

   (1) All animals go through metamorphosis.
   (2) All plants go through metamorphosis.
   (3) Different animal structures are suited to different types of environments.
   (4) Almost all eggs develop into adults.
   (5) Metamorphosis occurs in humans.

8. What is metamorphosis?

   (1) the process of reproduction
   (2) the process by which an immature form changes into a different adult form
   (3) the growth of any young organism into an adult
   (4) changes in an adult organism caused by aging
   (5) the process by which tadpoles absorb oxygen from water

9. Which of the following must develop before a tadpole becomes a land-dwelling adult?

   (1) arms
   (2) lungs
   (3) gills
   (4) tail
   (5) mouth

Items 10 and 11 refer to the following map and definitions.

Ecosystems that cover large areas of the world are called <u>biomes</u>.
Biomes have different types of climates, plants, and animals. Six biomes
are described and located on the map.

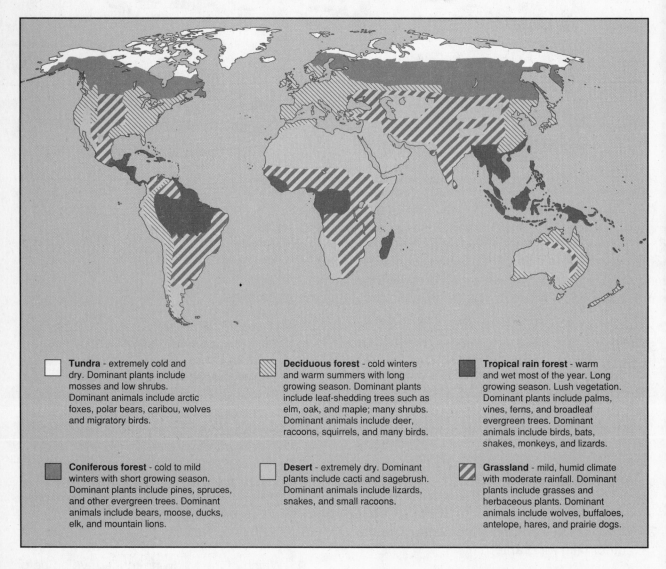

Tundra - extremely cold and
dry. Dominant plants include
mosses and low shrubs.
Dominant animals include arctic
foxes, polar bears, caribou, wolves
and migratory birds.

Deciduous forest - cold winters
and warm summers with long
growing season. Dominant plants
include leaf-shedding trees such as
elm, oak, and maple; many shrubs.
Dominant animals include deer,
racoons, squirrels, and many birds.

Tropical rain forest - warm
and wet most of the year. Long
growing season. Lush vegetation.
Dominant plants include palms,
vines, ferns, and broadleaf
evergreen trees. Dominant
animals include birds, bats,
snakes, monkeys, and lizards.

Coniferous forest - cold to mild
winters with short growing season.
Dominant plants include pines, spruces,
and other evergreen trees. Dominant
animals include bears, moose, ducks,
elk, and mountain lions.

Desert - extremely dry. Dominant
plants include cacti and sagebrush.
Dominant animals include lizards,
snakes, and small racoons.

Grassland - mild, humid climate
with moderate rainfall. Dominant
plants include grasses and
herbaceous plants. Dominant
animals include wolves, buffaloes,
antelope, hares, and prairie dogs.

10. According to the map, which kind of biome
occurs farthest north?

(1) grassland
(2) deciduous forest
(3) tundra
(4) coniferous forest
(5) desert

11. Which of the following kinds of plants would
you <u>not</u> expect to find in a tropical rain
forest?

(1) palm trees
(2) vines
(3) cacti
(4) ferns
(5) evergreen trees

THE WATER CYCLE

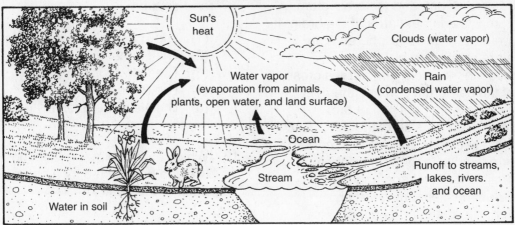

All plants and animals must have water in order to live. Cells are made mostly of water, and the chemical reactions in living things must take place in water. However, the amount of Earth's water is limited. It must be used again and again. The constant circulation of Earth's water is called the water cycle.

12. Which of the following statements is the most accurate?

   (1) Animals return water to the air only by eliminating liquid wastes.
   (2) The only water vapor in the air is found in clouds.
   (3) Plants take in water mostly by breathing.
   (4) On Earth, water is found mainly in the soil.
   (5) Water in animals' breath is returned to the air.

13. Which of the following statements supports the conclusion that water is used again and again?

   (1) Water is recirculated.
   (2) The water cycle circulates Earth's water supply.
   (3) Evaporation from the ocean returns water to the atmosphere.
   (4) Cells are composed mainly of water.
   (5) Water is needed to carry on life processes.

14. What causes water to evaporate in the water cycle?

   (1) clouds
   (2) the sun
   (3) runoff
   (4) oceans
   (5) soil

15. Which of the following statements is an opinion?

   (1) Since the supply of water is limited, it must be used again and again.
   (2) Water conservation is not useful since Earth will never run out of water.
   (3) All living organisms must have water in order to live.
   (4) The circulation of Earth's water is called the water cycle.
   (5) The chemical reactions in living things require water.

Items 16 to 19 refer to the following passage and diagram.

The human brain consists of three parts: the cerebrum, the cerebellum, and the brain stem.

The cerebrum is the largest area of the brain. It consists of two halves, or hemispheres. The hemispheres are connected by fibers and nerves. Because these fibers and nerves cross, the left half of the cerebrum controls the right side of the body, and the right half of the cerebrum controls the left side of the body. Each hemisphere also seems to specialize in certain functions. For example, the left hemisphere is largely responsible for language and logical thinking. The right hemisphere is largely responsible for artistic and perceptual expression.

The cerebellum helps the cerebrum control movement. It also coordinates information from the eyes, inner ears, and muscles to maintain balance.

The brain stem contains the medulla. This part of the brain controls the organs of the body.

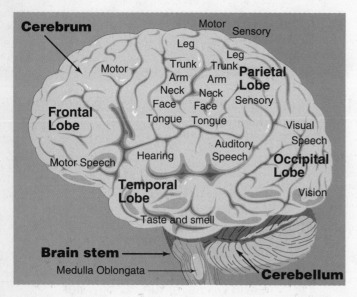

16. What would be the best title for this passage and diagram?

   (1) The Human Nervous System
   (2) The Human Brain
   (3) The Cerebrum
   (4) The Brain
   (5) The Nervous System

17. Which of the following functions is most likely to be affected by a sharp blow to the back of the head?

   (1) taste
   (2) vision
   (3) heart rate
   (4) hearing
   (5) leg movement

18. A patient has an injury to the cerebellum. What symptom is the patient most likely to show?

   (1) loss of leg movement
   (2) blurred vision
   (3) loss of hearing
   (4) speech difficulties
   (5) loss of balance

19. Which of the following statements is the most accurate?

   (1) As long as the cerebellum is functioning, motor activity will be normal.
   (2) The brain stem controls leg muscles.
   (3) Injury to the left hemisphere results in a total loss of speech.
   (4) Motor activity is controlled by the cerebrum and cerebellum.
   (5) The two hemispheres of the brain are not connected.

Unit 1: Biology

VESTIGIAL STRUCTURES

Many animals have well-developed structures that perform important functions. In other animals, a similar structure may be smaller and not have an important function. These structures are called vestigial structures. Scientists believe that vestigial structures are the remains of organs that were well-developed in ancestors of present-day organisms. Vestigial structures offer evidence to support the theory that many animals evolved from common ancestors.

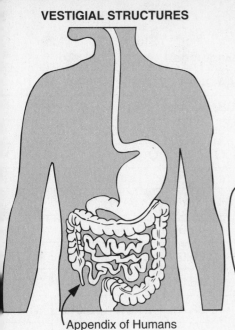

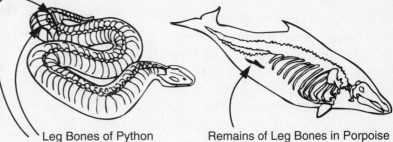

Appendix of Humans   Leg Bones of Python   Remains of Leg Bones in Porpoise

20. Which statement best summarizes the paragraph?

(1) Present-day snakes have vestigial leg bones.
(2) All animals have vestigial structures.
(3) Vestigial structures offer support for the theory of evolution.
(4) Many nonwalking animals once had functioning legs.
(5) Vestigial structures are well-developed in today's animals.

21. Based on the information given, which of the following has not been proved a scientific fact?

(1) Vestigial structures are the remains of organs that were well-developed in common ancestors.
(2) A vestigial structure may be poorly developed.
(3) Porpoises and pythons have vestigial leg bones.
(4) A vestigial structure may have no apparent function.
(5) Humans have vestigial appendixes.

22. Which of the following statements is the most accurate?

(1) The appendix of humans is a vestigial organ.
(2) Pythons once walked.
(3) The vestigial leg bones of porpoises serve an important function.
(4) Pythons and porpoises have similar skeletons.
(5) The existence of vestigial structures proves without a doubt that the theory of evolution is a fact.

23. Which statement supports the conclusion that present-day organisms evolved from common ancestors?

(1) The appendix has no apparent function in humans.
(2) Some animals have a well-developed structure, and others have a corresponding vestigial structure.
(3) Some animals have no vestigial structures.
(4) Porpoises once had legs.
(5) The leg bones of a python have no apparent function.

Items 24 to 27 refer to the following passage and charts.

There are three different genes—A, B, and O—that determine a person's blood type. Six different genotypes are possible, and they result in four different blood types, as shown in the top chart. For example, a person with blood type A may have genotype AA or AO. The type O gene is recessive, while type A and B genes are dominant. A person who inherits two dominant genes, A and B, has type AB blood.

Since a person's blood type depends on the two genes inherited from his or her parents, different populations show different frequencies of blood types. The bottom chart shows how the blood types are distributed in different population groups.

Blood Type	Genotype	Can Get Blood From	Can Give Blood To
A	AA, AO	O, A	A, AB
B	BB, BO	O, B	B, AB
AB	AB	A, B, AB, O	AB
O	OO	O	A, B, AB, O

Blood Type	A	B	AB	O
U.S.A.—White	41.0%	10.0%	4.0%	45.0%
U.S.A.—Black	26.0%	21.0%	3.7%	49.3%
Swedish	46.7%	10.3%	5.1%	37.9%
Japanese	38.4%	21.8%	8.6%	31.2%
Polynesian	60.8%	2.2%	0.5%	36.5%
Chinese	25.0%	35.0%	10.0%	30.0%
North American Indian	7.7%	1.0%	0.0%	91.3%

24. People with type O blood are sometimes called universal donors. A universal donor is someone who

   (1) can receive blood from anyone
   (2) cannot give blood to anyone
   (3) has a genotype AO
   (4) can give blood to anyone
   (5) can receive only type A blood

25. In Japan, the blood banks ran out of type AB blood. What effect would this have on blood transfusions for people there with AB blood?

   (1) They would not be able to have a blood transfusion.
   (2) They would have to get type AB blood from another country.
   (3) They could have a transfusion of type A, B, or O blood.
   (4) They could have a transfusion of type A blood only.
   (5) They could have a transfusion of type B blood only.

26. Which of the following would be the best title for the second chart?

   (1) Blood Type Frequency in Selected Population Groups
   (2) Human Blood Types
   (3) Receiving and Giving Blood
   (4) Genotypes for Each Blood Type
   (5) Blood Type Frequency in the U.S.

27. Which of the following statements is most accurate?

   (1) There are an equal number of blood types and genotypes.
   (2) The genes A, B, O, and AB determine which blood type you have.
   (3) Each individual inherits one gene for blood type from each of his or her parents.
   (4) Blood types are evenly distributed in different populations.
   (5) A person with type O blood has the genotype AO or BO.

Items 28 to 33 are based on the following passage.

Herbicides are chemicals that kill plants. When herbicides are used on crops, it is important that the herbicide kill only the weeds and not the crops. Scientists have been developing crops that are not affected by specific herbicides, enabling farmers to use herbicides to control weeds. For example, scientists have developed a strain of cotton that is resistant to the herbicide bromoxynil. When this herbicide is used, it kills weeds but not the resistant cotton plants. Other crops that have varieties resistant to certain herbicides are soybeans, tobacco, tomatoes, and sugar beets.

Some environmental groups are opposed to the development of herbicide-resistant crops. They say that these crops encourage farmers to continue to use chemicals that pollute the environment and that may be unsafe. These groups favor practices such as improved cultivation techniques and creative planting plans to make chemicals unnecessary. They prefer scientists to concentrate on developing strains of crops that are naturally resistant to disease and pests.

28. What is a herbicide-resistant crop?

(1) a variety of crop that cannot have a herbicide applied to it
(2) a variety of crop that is resistant to disease
(3) a variety of crop that is resistant to insect pests
(4) a variety of crop that is resistant to weeds
(5) a variety of crop that is not affected by particular chemical plant killers

29. Applying chemical herbicides to herbicide-resistant crops is likely to

(1) kill the crops
(2) damage the crops
(3) result in herbicides remaining on the crops after harvest
(4) kill more crop plants than weeds
(5) kill insects that are crop pests

30. Based on the information given, which of the following is not a fact?

(1) Herbicides are used to kill weeds.
(2) Tobacco and soybean varieties are resistant to certain herbicides.
(3) Bromoxynil is a chemical herbicide.
(4) Improved cultivation techniques are preferable to herbicides in controlling weeds.
(5) Scientists have developed strains of herbicide-resistant crops.

31. Based on the information given, it is assumed that the reader already knows which of the following?

(1) Herbicides are safe to use.
(2) Crops cannot be grown without herbicides.
(3) Weeds are a problem in large farming areas.
(4) All cotton plants are resistant to herbicides.
(5) Most crops are naturally resistant to pests.

32. Which of the following would not be considered a more natural way to kill unwanted weeds in fields?

A. improved cultivation techniques
B. creative planting of crops
C. new chemicals specific to certain weeds

(1) A only
(2) B only
(3) C only
(4) A and B
(5) A and C

33. The term "resistant" as used in this passage means

(1) not wanting to do something
(2) opposing
(3) striving against
(4) withstanding the effect of
(5) killing

Living things get the energy they need in different ways. Grasses get energy from sunlight through photosynthesis. Rabbits get energy by eating grasses. Foxes get energy by eating rabbits. This transfer of energy from the sun to various organisms in an ecosystem is known as a food chain. Ecosystems contain many food chains.

Organisms that make their own food are called producers. Food chains always begin with producers, like the grass shown in the diagram. Notice that the levels above the producer consist of consumers. A consumer is an organism that gets its food by eating other organisms.

FOOD CHAIN

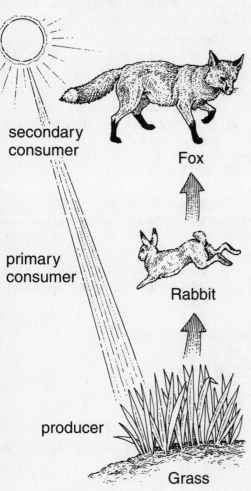

secondary consumer

Fox

primary consumer

Rabbit

producer

Grass

34. The correct order of the transfer of energy in the food chain described above, from the original source to the final consumer, is

(1) rabbit, grass, fox
(2) fox, grass, rabbit, sun
(3) grass, rabbit, fox
(4) sun, grass, fox, rabbit
(5) sun, grass, rabbit, fox

35. If a predator of the fox were added to the diagram, it would

(1) be a producer
(2) appear at the bottom of the diagram
(3) be a primary consumer
(4) appear at the top of the diagram
(5) be a secondary consumer

36. If disease killed off an ecosystem's population of rabbits, how would the food chain shown most likely be affected?

(1) A new producer would become part of the food chain.
(2) The food chain would consist of foxes feeding on grass.
(3) The amount of grass would decrease.
(4) The fox population would decrease.
(5) It would not be affected.

37. Which of the following statements is most accurate?

(1) Some food chains consist only of organisms that feed on other organisms.
(2) An organism that eats only plants cannot be a secondary consumer.
(3) Producers are organisms that get energy by eating other organisms.
(4) Consumers eat only plants.
(5) Consumers eat only animals.

Answers are on page 282.

Unit 1: Biology

Performance Analysis
Unit 1 Cumulative Review: Biology

Name: _____ Class: _____ Date: _____

Use the Answer Key on pages 282–285 to check your answers to the Unit 1 Cumulative Review: Biology. Then use the chart to figure out the skill areas in which you need additional review. Circle on the chart the numbers of the test items you answered correctly. Then go back and review the lessons for the skill areas that are difficult for you. For additional review, see the *Steck-Vaughn GED Science Exercise Book,* Unit 1: Biology.

Thinking Skill Area	Biology	Lesson(s) for Review
Comprehension	1, **6**, **8**, **9**, **10**, **16**, **20**, **24**, **26**, 28, 33, **34**	1, 2, 4
Analysis	3, 4, 5, **7**, **11**, **13**, **14**, **15**, **17**, **18**, **21**, **23**, **25**, 29, 30, 31, 32, **35**, **36**	3, 5, 6, 8
Evaluation	2, **12**, **19**, **22**, **27**, **37**	7

Boldfaced numbers indicate items based on charts, graphs, illustrations, and diagrams.

Unit 2

EARTH SCIENCE

A volcano can dramatically change Earth's surface.

Earth science is the branch of science that studies Earth and the space around Earth. Knowledge of Earth science can be useful in many ways. It helps us understand the environment in which we live.

In lesson 9 you will learn about the structure of Earth. You will also learn how Earth has changed over time. Major changes signal the beginning or end of an **era,** which is a major division of geologic time.

In lesson 10 you will learn about the air that surrounds Earth. The gases that surround Earth make up the **atmosphere.** The atmosphere, which consists of four main layers, extends from the surface of Earth into outer space.

era
*a major division of
geologic time*

atmosphere
*the layers of gases that
surround Earth*

In this lesson you will also learn about the water that covers approximately 70 percent of Earth's surface. Earth's water supply is constantly being renewed through a series of steps called the **water cycle.** You will come to understand how moisture from Earth's surface forms clouds and how this moisture eventually falls back to Earth in the form of rain, snow, sleet, or hail.

Air and water create changing weather patterns. You will discover how our weather is caused by the movement of **air masses,** which are large areas of air that have a similar temperature and humidity level throughout.

In lesson 11 you will learn about Earth's resources. You will discover that one of the world's most important resources is petroleum. Petroleum provides fuel for energy. It also provides the raw materials needed for many useful chemicals. The fact that consumers use so much petroleum, however, has presented a problem. Petroleum is a **nonrenewable resource**—that is, it cannot be replaced once it is used. Many scientists fear that the world may run out of petroleum before other resources can be found to take its place.

In lesson 12 you will learn how Earth is constantly changing. Some of these changes, such as earthquakes and volcanoes, are dramatic and dangerous. Others, such as **erosion** and **mass wasting,** can occur so slowly that many years pass before we see their effects.

water cycle
continuous movement of water from Earth's surface to the air, then back to the surface again

air mass
large body of air that has a similar temperature and humidity level throughout

nonrenewable resource
a resource that cannot be replaced once it is used

erosion
the gradual wearing away and moving of rocks, soil, and sand

mass wasting
the downhill movement of rocks and soil caused by gravity

SEE ALSO: Steck-Vaughn GED Science Exercise Book, Unit 2: Earth Science.

Earth Science Overview

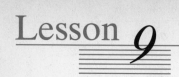

Comprehension: Identifying Implications

When you identify an implication, you figure out something that is likely to be true based on what you have read.

An implication is a fact that is not stated directly by the author. Rather, it is suggested by the author's words. For example, if you read "The oceans cover about 70 percent of Earth's surface," you would understand what the author said about oceans. But you would also be able to infer, or figure out, another fact: since Earth's surface is either water or land, about 30 percent of Earth's surface must be land.

You can increase your ability to identify implications by following three suggestions as you read.

1. Think about consequences. A consequence is an effect or result. If something happens, what is likely to happen next? If certain conditions exist, what effect does this have? If a tornado occurs, for example, damage is the likely result.
2. Use common sense. By using your common sense, you can make reasonable assumptions based on the information given. For example, if the sky is clear, you can assume that it will not rain.
3. Look for generalizations. If a statement is true in general, it must be true for specific items as well. For example, if ocean water is salty (general statement), then water from the Pacific Ocean must be salty, too (specific instance).

 To identify implications, ask yourself: *If* this statement is true, *then* what other facts follow logically from the statement?

 Identifying Implications

Items 1 and 2 refer to the following paragraph. Choose the best answer to each item.

A galaxy is a group of millions or billions of stars. The galaxy in which our sun is located is called the Milky Way. The Milky Way is a disk-shaped galaxy with two or more spiral arms that extend from the center. Our sun and the solar system are located in one of the spiral arms. It takes the sun about 225 million years to make one turn around the center of the galaxy. Measurements of the movements of different stars in the galaxy show that they move with respect to one another while turning around the center of the galaxy. Thousands of years ago, people saw the stars in slightly different patterns than the way we see stars today.

1. A star located farther from the center of the galaxy than the sun is likely to

   (1) take longer than 225 million years to make one turn around the center of the galaxy
   (2) take 225 million years to make one turn around the center of the galaxy
   (3) take fewer than 225 million years to make one turn around the galaxy
   (4) turn around the center of the galaxy first in one direction and then in the other
   (5) remain in the same place

2. In 50,000 B.C., the group of stars called the Big Dipper looked like an arrow. Today, the group looks like a cup with a long handle. What can be said about the appearance of the Big Dipper in another 50,000 years?

   (1) It will look like an arrow.
   (2) It will look like a cup with a long handle.
   (3) Its appearance will not change.
   (4) Its appearance will have changed slightly.
   (5) It will have disappeared.

> **tip**
>
> **When using information on charts, first read all the labels that explain what the information represents. Then look for the specific information you need to know.**

Items 3 and 4 refer to the following chart.

Planet	Distance from Sun In Astronomical Units*
Mercury	0.39
Venus	0.72
Earth	1.0
Mars	1.5
Jupiter	5.2
Saturn	9.2
Uranus	19.2
Neptune	30.0
Pluto	39.4

*One astronomical unit is the distance from Earth to the sun.

3. A planet that is more than one astronomical unit from the sun is

   (1) closer to the sun than Earth is
   (2) the same distance from the sun as Earth is
   (3) farther from the sun than Earth is
   (4) likely to receive more solar energy than Earth does
   (5) a planet with no moon

4. It takes the sun's light 8 minutes to reach Earth. How long does it take the sun's light to reach Neptune?

   (1) 15 seconds
   (2)   8 minutes
   (3) 24 minutes
   (4) 240 minutes
   (5) 30 hours

Answers are on page 285.

The Planet Earth

For many years, scientists have been gathering information about Earth's interior. Intense heat and high pressure make human exploration of this region impossible. Thus, most of what is known about the interior structure of Earth has been learned by studying the movement of seismic waves, or vibrations, produced by earthquakes. From this indirect evidence, scientists have concluded that Earth is made up of four different layers: the crust, the mantle, the outer core, and the inner core.

1. The <u>crust</u> is the part of Earth that is familiar to us, for it includes Earth's surface. This layer is made up of many kinds of rock. The crust ranges from about 8 kilometers thick under the oceans to about 40 kilometers thick under the continents.
2. The <u>mantle</u> lies beneath the crust. The mantle is composed of rock that contains mainly oxygen, iron, magnesium, and silicon. The temperatures in this region range from 870°C to 2,200°C and cause some of the solid rock to flow.
3. The <u>outer core</u> is below the mantle. The outer core is composed of molten iron and nickel. Temperatures in the outer core range from 2,200°C to 5,000°C.
4. The <u>inner core</u> is at the center of Earth. This region, which has a temperature of about 5,000°C, is solid iron and nickel. Although iron and nickel usually melt at this temperature, great pressure in the inner core pushes the particles together so tightly that they remain solid.

EARTH'S LAYERS

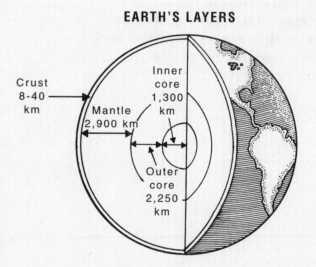

Crust 8-40 km
Mantle 2,900 km
Inner core 1,300 km
Outer core 2,250 km

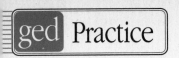

tems 1 to 7 refer to the previous passage and diagram. Choose the <u>best answer</u> to each item.

1. What is the most likely thickness of Earth's crust under Africa?

    (1)   8 kilometers
    (2)   40 kilometers
    (3) 1,300 kilometers
    (4) 2,250 kilometers
    (5) 2,900 kilometers

2. What led scientists to conclude that Earth is made up of four different layers?

    (1) direct evidence from human observation
    (2) rock samples from all four layers
    (3) unchanging seismic wave patterns
    (4) changing behavior of seismic waves as they reach each layer of Earth's interior
    (5) temperature readings from Earth's interior

3. Which layer of Earth has been explored directly by humans?

    (1) crust
    (2) mantle
    (3) outer core
    (4) inner core
    (5) all four layers

4. Like a magnet, Earth has a magnetic field. What is the most likely cause of Earth's magnetism?

    (1) high temperatures in the core
    (2) oxygen in Earth's crust
    (3) iron in the inner and outer cores
    (4) high pressure on the core
    (5) continents

5. What are seismic waves?

    (1) vibrations produced by earthquakes
    (2) light waves from the sun that penetrate Earth's surface
    (3) movements of liquid rock in Earth's mantle
    (4) deep ocean waves
    (5) volcanic eruptions

6. Based on the information given, which of the following does the author of the passage assume to be true?

    (1) It is reasonable to draw scientific conclusions from indirect evidence.
    (2) Indirect evidence is superior to human observation.
    (3) Someday humans will explore the inner core.
    (4) Earth is made of five different layers.
    (5) Each of Earth's layers is thicker than the one above it.

7. One type of seismic wave, called a secondary wave, can only travel through solids. A secondary wave traveling from Earth's surface toward its center would

    (1) travel straight through Earth
    (2) travel through the crust, mantle, and outer core and stop at the inner core
    (3) travel through the crust and mantle and stop at the outer core
    (4) travel through the crust and stop at the mantle
    (5) not be able to penetrate rocks below the surface

Answers are on page 285.

Items 1 to 5 refer to the following passage. Choose the best answer to each item.

A fossil is the evidence or remains of a living thing. Most fossils form when plants or animals die and are buried in layers of crumbled rock particles called sediments, which later harden.

The chances of an organism leaving a fossil are actually small. The soft parts of a dead organism usually decay or are eaten before a fossil can form. Fossils that do form are often incomplete. The organisms most likely to be preserved as fossils are ones that lived in or near water. There, sand and mud provide quick burial for these organisms.

Some fossils show only the mark or evidence of a living thing. Called trace fossils, these include footprints, tracks, and burrows. Much of what is known about dinosaurs has come from footprints found in rock.

Fossils can show changes in Earth's surface and climate. For example, fossils of coral found in Antarctica show that the climate of this region was once much warmer.

Fossils can also help date layers of rock. If a particular type of organism lived on Earth for only a brief period of time, the rock containing its fossil must be from approximately the same time period.

1. In a mountainous region of Canada, fossils of fish are found. Which is the most likely explanation?

   (1) The region was once much colder.
   (2) The region was once much warmer.
   (3) The region was once under water.
   (4) Fish that lived in mountain streams formed fossils.
   (5) Dead fish were taken up the mountain.

2. Which of the following would be most similar to a trace fossil?

   (1) human footprints made in concrete before it hardened
   (2) a fly trapped in concrete before it hardened
   (3) tire tracks in the sand
   (4) footprints of a deer in the snow
   (5) a leaf frozen in ice

3. If a well preserved fossil of a complete bird were discovered, it could be concluded that

   (1) the bird's soft parts were eaten
   (2) the bird was killed by a predator
   (3) there are also trace fossils made by a bird nearby
   (4) the bird lived in a wet climate
   (5) the bird was buried soon after dying

4. Which of the following is not an example of a fossil?

   (1) tracks of a snake made in mud that later hardens to mudstone
   (2) an insect trapped in sap that becomes amber
   (3) the imprint of a fern preserved in siltstone
   (4) grooves carved in rock by a glacier
   (5) a woolly mammoth frozen in ice

5. The fossil record is not used to show which of the following:

   (1) changes in Earth's surface
   (2) changes in Earth's climate
   (3) dating rock layers
   (4) establishing animal behavior
   (5) identifying extinct life forms

Scientists have developed a geologic time line to record the history of
arth. Geologic time is often described in terms of four eras.

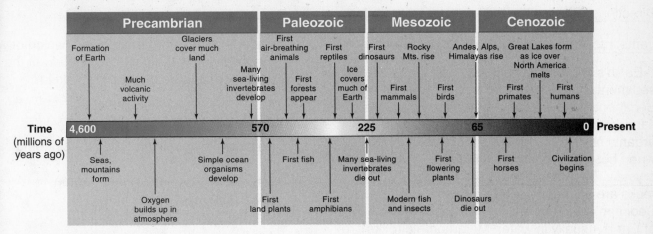

6. According to the time line, where did the first living things originate?

   (1) in the Precambrian Era
   (2) in the atmosphere
   (3) in the ocean
   (4) in the Paleozoic Era
   (5) in a swamp

7. What might have been eaten by the first fish?

   (1) flowering plants
   (2) sea-living invertebrates
   (3) insects
   (4) amphibians
   (5) land plants

8. Which of the following kinds of fossils would most likely be found in Mesozoic rocks?

   (1) only simple ocean organisms
   (2) land plants, dinosaurs, and horses
   (3) fish, land plants, and dinosaurs
   (4) primates and humans
   (5) flowering plants and primates

9. Which of the following statements is most accurate?

   (1) Human civilization has been in existence for over half the history of Earth.
   (2) Dinosaurs were the chief form of life during the Paleozoic Era.
   (3) The Great Lakes are younger than the Rocky Mountains.
   (4) Dinosaurs died out 5 million years ago.
   (5) The first life forms appeared on land.

10. For approximately how many years did dinosaurs inhabit Earth?

    (1)   160 years
    (2) 4,535 million years
    (3)   160 million years
    (4)   160 billion years
    (5)   225 million years

11. Which of the following statements cannot be directly supported by information on the time line?

    (1) All organisms evolved from the first living cells.
    (2) The Earth is about 4,600 million years old.
    (3) The Paleozoic Era came before the Mesozoic Era.
    (4) We are living in the Cenozoic Era.
    (5) Simple ocean organisms appeared during the Precambrian.

Answers are on page 286.

Directions: Choose the best answer to each item.

Items 1 to 4 refer to the following passage.

Earth's crust contains three main types of rock: sedimentary, igneous, and metamorphic. Sedimentary rocks are formed when particles of sand, mud, pieces of rock, or remains of dead organisms harden. Igneous rocks are formed when hot liquid rock, called magma, hardens into crystals. Metamorphic rocks are formed when rocks are altered by extreme heat and pressure. Sedimentary rocks are formed near the surface of Earth, usually in water. Metamorphic rocks are formed in the lower part of Earth's crust or in the upper part of the mantle.

Magma can cool and form crystals to produce igneous rock above or below the surface of Earth. Large mineral crystals form when magma cools slowly. Heat is lost very slowly beneath Earth's surface. Magma can break through Earth's crust in a volcanic eruption. It is then called lava. As lava comes in contact with the air, cooling can be very rapid. This sudden cooling leads to the formation of barely visible crystals.

1. According to the passage, which of the following could explain why igneous and metamorphic rocks form deep beneath Earth's surface?

   (1) Temperatures in Earth's interior are high.
   (2) Pressure in Earth's interior is low.
   (3) The rocks are protected from wind and weather.
   (4) Chemical reactions can occur beneath Earth's crust.
   (5) Magma hardens more quickly beneath Earth's crust.

2. Based on the information given, which of the following is the best explanation of the presence of large mineral crystals in igneous rock?

   (1) the force of a volcano
   (2) the slow cooling of molten rock below Earth's surface
   (3) the effect of air on the magma
   (4) the rapid cooling of lava
   (5) particles of sand harden

3. An igneous rock reaches Earth's surface and is broken down by weathering and erosion. The pieces of rock would then be likely to

   (1) melt and become magma
   (2) become sediments and harden into sedimentary rock
   (3) be pushed together to form a metamorphic rock
   (4) form another igneous rock
   (5) be carried into the ocean and form metamorphic rock

4. Based on the information given, which of the following statements is most accurate?

   (1) Igneous rock is always formed from metamorphic rock.
   (2) Sedimentary rock is always formed from organic material.
   (3) Sedimentary rock is always formed from particles of rock.
   (4) Metamorphic rock is always formed from igneous, sedimentary, or other metamorphic rock.
   (5) Molten rock is always found under Earth's surface.

In order to be called a mineral, a substance must have five basic properties, or characteristics.

1. It must be found naturally on Earth.
2. It must be a solid.
3. It must never have been alive.
4. It must be made of particular elements.
5. Its particles must be arranged in a definite pattern called a crystal.

Valuable minerals are often found mixed in with other rocks. Rock deposits that contain valuable minerals are called <u>ores</u>. Removing a mineral from ore involves mining the ore and then smelting it. During smelting, the ore is heated in such a way that the valuable mineral is separated from the other substances in the rock.

5. Which of the following could <u>not</u> be a mineral?

   (1) a crystalline salt
   (2) a substance formed in the mantle
   (3) a substance consisting of 18% oxygen and 82% silicon
   (4) a solid that is shiny
   (5) a rock formed from plant remains

6. Which of the following would be involved in removing iron from its ore?

   (1) adding impurities
   (2) polishing
   (3) freezing
   (4) high temperatures
   (5) strong odors

7. Which of the following is <u>not</u> a characteristic used to determine whether or not a substance is a mineral?

   (1) chemical composition
   (2) internal structure
   (3) naturally occurring as opposed to being synthetic
   (4) physical state
   (5) value

8. What is smelting?

   (1) mining the ore
   (2) identifying minerals
   (3) crystallizing noncrystalline substances
   (4) heating ore to separate a mineral
   (5) changing the properties of a mineral

9. Someone looking at a piece of granite noticed that it had been formed from tiny particles of three different colors. Another sample of granite was formed from particles of four different colors. What could lead someone to conclude that granite is <u>not</u> a mineral?

   A. Granite is manmade.
   B. Granite is made of several minerals.
   C. Granite is a mineral.

   (1) A only
   (2) B only
   (3) C only
   (4) A and B
   (5) B and C

10. Deposits of pure, crystalline sulfur have been found inside the craters of active volcanoes. What characteristics of minerals does this description include?

    A. It is made of particular elements.
    B. It is found naturally on Earth.
    C. It is a solid.

    (1) A only
    (2) A and B
    (3) A and C
    (4) B and C
    (5) A, B, and C

11. Why is a bone not a mineral?

    (1) It is not a solid.
    (2) It contains calcium.
    (3) It contains phosphorus.
    (4) It was once alive.
    (5) It is hard.

Answers are on page 287.

Application: Other Contexts

When you put your knowledge to use in new situations, you are applying ideas to another context.

Some people have jobs that involve a lot of application skills. For example, the person who tells you the weather report on television is probably a meteorologist. A meteorologist's job is to use general information about climate and weather patterns to predict the weather at a specific place and time. Another job that involves application skills is that of an engineer. An engineer applies the laws of physics or chemistry to build bridges or develop new plastics, for example. What other jobs that involve the skill of application can you think of?

When you study science, you are learning a subject that has many practical applications. The principles discovered by scientists can be applied to most areas of life. When you read about a science topic, think about how this knowledge might be used in other contexts, or situations. You can increase your ability to apply science knowledge to new situations by asking yourself:

- What is being described or explained?
- What situations might this information relate to?
- How would this information be used in those situations?

Read this brief paragraph and see how the information can be applied to other situations.

The average weather over a long period of time is called climate. One of the most important factors in climate is temperature. In general, temperature is determined by how much sunlight a location receives. The area near the equator receives the greatest amount of sunlight, while areas near the North and South Poles receive the least. Average temperature usually decreases as you move from the equator to the poles.

This information about temperature is very general. It states that the average temperature decreases as you move north and south from the equator. However, we can apply this information to specific situations. For example, we can compare two cities and decide which is likely to have the higher average temperature. Mexico City, Mexico is likely to be warmer than Toronto, Canada. New Orleans, Louisiana is warmer on average than Portland, Maine.

 tip **When applying given information to a new situation, ask yourself what you already know about the new situation. Then apply all the information to the new context.**

Items 1 to 6 refer to the following paragraph. Choose the best answer to each item.

Rocks and other materials on Earth's surface can be broken down into small bits. This process is called weathering. Over long periods of time, weathering gradually wears down natural formations. Weathering also affects structures made by humans—such as buildings.

There are two types of weathering: mechanical and chemical. An example of mechanical weathering occurs when water freezes in the cracks of rocks. The freezing water expands, causing the cracks to open wider. Chemical weathering occurs when substances in the atmosphere combine with materials on Earth and slowly change them into something else.

Organisms can cause both mechanical and chemical weathering. Roots from plants can grow into the cracks in a rock. As the roots grow, the cracks become bigger. Lichens can grow on a rock's surface. As they grow, they produce chemicals that break the rock down.

1. Which of the following is an example of chemical weathering?

   (1) acid rain wearing away limestone
   (2) potholes in streets after a cold winter
   (3) roots widening the cracks in a rock
   (4) water in a swimming pool freezing and cracking the pool walls
   (5) pipes freezing and bursting during cold weather

2. A situation similar to mechanical weathering exists when

   (1) polluted air darkens the stone trim on a building
   (2) detergent and water remove dirt from clothes
   (3) acid rain falls on uninhabited forest areas
   (4) a glass jar full of soup bursts when placed in the freezer
   (5) moss grows in shady areas under trees

3. Which of the following is an example of mechanical weathering?

   (1) A pebble falling downhill breaks as it hits the ground.
   (2) Groundwater dissolves limestone.
   (3) A car door rusts.
   (4) Water freezes in a lake.
   (5) Feldspar breaks down and combines with water to form clay.

4. Chemical weathering is most likely to occur

   (1) when two rocks collide
   (2) inside damp caves
   (3) during a sandstorm
   (4) when a glacier moves through a valley
   (5) during a drought

5. Considering what you have read about weathering, which of the following is likely to be least affected by the weathering process?

   (1) a rocky hillside
   (2) a limestone building
   (3) a sidewalk
   (4) a city street
   (5) a glass jar in a landfill

6. What is the best title for this passage?

   (1) Rocks and Other Materials
   (2) Earth's Surface
   (3) Weathering on Earth
   (4) Cold Weather and Rocks
   (5) The Effect of Lichens on Rock

Answers are on page 288.

Air and Water

The air that surrounds Earth is called the atmosphere. Earth's atmosphere provides us with a safe environment. It gives us moisture and oxygen, a comfortable temperature, and protection from the sun's ultraviolet rays.

The atmosphere contains gases necessary for the survival of all living things. Gases in the atmosphere include nitrogen, oxygen, carbon dioxide, water vapor, and argon. There are also small amounts of neon, helium, krypton, and xenon.

The atmosphere is divided into four main layers. The lowest layer is called the troposphere. This is the layer in which we live. The troposphere extends to a height of about 10 miles. As you go higher, the air becomes colder and less dense, or "thinner." For example, at an altitude of 3.5 miles, there is only half as much oxygen as there is at Earth's surface.

Above the troposphere is the stratosphere. The stratosphere extends to a height of about 30 miles. A form of oxygen called ozone is found in the stratosphere and the mesosphere. Ozone shields Earth from the sun's harmful ultraviolet rays.

Above the stratosphere is the mesosphere. The mesosphere extends to a height of about 50 miles. The temperature in the mesosphere drops to about −100°C.

The uppermost region of the atmosphere is the thermosphere. The thermosphere does not have a well-defined upper limit. It is the hottest layer of the atmosphere, with temperatures as high as 2,000°C.

LAYERS OF EARTH'S ATMOSPHERE

Troposphere = 0 to 10 mi.

Ozone Layer

Thermosphere = 50 mi. & up

10 mi. 30 mi. 50 mi.

Earth's surface

Stratosphere = 10 to 30 mi.

Mesosphere = 30 to 50 mi.

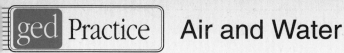
ems 1 to 7 refer to the previous information. Choose the <u>best answer</u> to each item.

1. Which of the following people would need the most protection from the sun's ultraviolet rays?

   (1) a teacher
   (2) a mountain climber
   (3) an astronaut
   (4) a commercial airline pilot
   (5) a meteorologist

2. Someone at the top of Mt. Everest, which is about 29,000 feet high, would be in the

   (1) troposphere
   (2) stratosphere
   (3) ozone layer
   (4) mesosphere
   (5) thermosphere

3. Which of the following people is likely to experience dropping temperatures and thinner air during the course of a day?

   (1) a lifeguard
   (2) a mountain climber
   (3) an airline attendant
   (4) a landscape gardener
   (5) a farmer

4. What would be the effect of destroying the ozone layer?

   (1) People would have trouble breathing.
   (2) The sun's ultraviolet rays would be reflected back into space.
   (3) More ultraviolet rays would reach Earth's surface.
   (4) The stratosphere would disappear.
   (5) There would be no effect.

5. Which of the following gases is present in the atmosphere in very small amounts?

   (1) nitrogen
   (2) oxygen
   (3) carbon dioxide
   (4) water vapor
   (5) krypton

6. Based on the information given, it is assumed that the reader already knows which of the following?

   (1) Gravity holds the atmosphere in place around Earth.
   (2) The higher up you go, the denser the atmosphere becomes.
   (3) Helium does not occur naturally in the atmosphere.
   (4) The uppermost region of the atmosphere is the thermosphere.
   (5) No human being has gone higher than the mesosphere.

7. A runner from Boston, Massachusetts, at sea level, traveled to Denver, Colorado, in the Rocky Mountains. While jogging in Denver, the runner had trouble breathing. Which of the following statements is supported by this experience?

   (1) Physical activity is more difficult in tropical weather.
   (2) The mesosphere extends to about 50 miles above Earth's surface.
   (3) The higher you go in the troposphere, the less oxygen is available.
   (4) The ozone layer protects Earth from the sun's ultraviolet rays.
   (5) The air becomes colder as you go higher in the troposphere.

Answers are on page 288.

Items 1 to 7 refer to the following passage. Choose the best answer to each item.

Changes in weather are caused by movements of air masses. An air mass has a similar temperature and humidity level throughout. An air mass may cover thousands of square miles.

Air masses are named according to where they form. There are four major types of air masses that affect the United States: maritime tropical, maritime polar, continental tropical, and continental polar. They are called maritime if they come from the sea and continental if they form over land.

A maritime tropical air mass forms over the ocean near the equator. Its air is warm and moist. In the summer it brings hot, humid weather to the United States, but in the winter it may come in contact with a cold air mass and cause rain or snow.

A maritime polar air mass forms over the Pacific Ocean in both winter and summer and over the North Atlantic Ocean in summer. It contains cool, moist air. During the summer this air mass brings fog to the western coastal states and cool weather to the eastern states. In the winter this air mass produces heavy snow and very cold temperatures.

A continental tropical air mass forms over Mexico during the summer. It brings hot, dry air to the southwestern United States.

A continental polar air mass forms over land in northern Canada. It contains cold, dry air. It brings very cold weather to the United States in winter.

1. Which of the following statements describes air masses that form over land?

   (1) They contain cold, moist air.
   (2) They contain warm, moist air.
   (3) They contain dry air.
   (4) They contain moist air.
   (5) They contain moist air in winter and dry air in summer.

2. A snowstorm in the Northern Pacific states could be caused by which of the following air masses?

   (1) maritime polar
   (2) continental tropical
   (3) continental polar
   (4) maritime polar or continental polar
   (5) continental polar or continental tropical

3. Which of the following is the best title for this passage?

   (1) Types of Air Masses
   (2) Where Air Masses Form
   (3) When Air Masses Meet
   (4) Continental Air Masses
   (5) Air and Weather

4. Air masses that form off the coast of Hawaii and over northwest Canada are likely to

   (1) be both very moist
   (2) be both very dry
   (3) cause weather changes in the contiguous 48 states
   (4) both bring warm weather to Mexico
   (5) both bring cool, dry weather to California

> **tip** When selecting a title for a passage, look for the option that best summarizes the main idea of the passage. The best title should be neither too broad nor too specific.

5. Which of the following is a false statement concerning air masses?

(1) An air mass is called maritime if it originates over water.
(2) An air mass is called continental if it originates over land.
(3) Air masses called tropical originate over tropical seas.
(4) The arrival of a new air mass can cause a change in humidity.
(5) Air masses cover a very large area.

6. A maritime tropical air mass meets a continental polar air mass over the East Coast in January. What is the weather likely to be?

(1) sunny
(2) snowy
(3) hurricane
(4) dry and cold
(5) dry and warm

7. Air masses cause changes in weather because

(1) they bring in cooler air
(2) they move large quantities of air
(3) they cover thousands of square miles
(4) they affect the temperature and humidity of the air
(5) they move from one area to another

Items 8 to 10 refer to the following diagram.

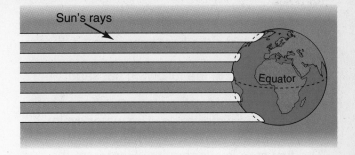

8. According to the diagram, the sun's rays

(1) strike all parts of Earth evenly
(2) are most direct at the North Pole
(3) are most direct at the South Pole
(4) are most direct in the Northern Hemisphere
(5) are most direct at the equator

9. Based on the diagram, what change should a person traveling from the middle of the Northern Hemisphere to the equator be prepared for?

(1) drier weather
(2) a greater possibility of snow
(3) cooler temperatures
(4) a greater possibility of rainy weather
(5) a greater possibility of sunburn

10. Climates near the equator are warmer than climates near the poles. Based on the diagram, which of the following statements could explain this observation?

(1) Days are longer near the equator than near the poles.
(2) The sun's rays are more concentrated near the equator than near the poles.
(3) Weather patterns produce more sunny days near the equator than near the poles.
(4) There are fewer oceans near the equator than near the poles.
(5) There is less wind near the equator than near the poles.

Answers are on page 289.

Directions: Choose the <u>best answer</u> to each item.

<u>Items 1 to 4</u> refer to the following passage.

Earth's supply of fresh water is always being renewed by the water cycle. The water cycle consists of three steps.

The first step is evaporation. Heat from the sun causes large amounts of water on the surface of Earth to change into water vapor. Much of this water comes from the oceans; the rest comes from soil, plants, and freshwater sources. The water vapor is carried by winds over land and oceans.

The next step in the cycle is condensation. Condensation is the process by which vapor turns back into liquids. This happens when warm air near the surface of Earth rises and cools. Once the air cools, it can no longer hold as much water vapor. The extra water vapor condenses into droplets that form clouds.

The final step is precipitation. When the droplets of water become too heavy to float in air, water falls in the form of rain or snow. Much of this water reaches oceans, rivers, lakes, and soil. Now this water is warmed by the sun. As some of it evaporates, the water cycle begins all over again.

1. Which of the following statements best explains why clouds form?

   (1) Water vapor in the air condenses.
   (2) Droplets of water in the air become heavy.
   (3) Droplets of water in the air evaporate.
   (4) Heat from the sun reacts with gases in the atmosphere.
   (5) Warm air above Earth reacts with cool air on the surface of Earth.

2. What is the best explanation of why the water cycle is always being renewed?

   (1) Clouds continue to release precipitation.
   (2) Oceans and rivers carry water.
   (3) Evaporation and condensation cause precipitation.
   (4) Precipitation causes condensation.
   (5) Evaporation causes condensation.

3. Which of the following series of events causes rain or snow?

   (1) Water vapor condenses and then evaporates.
   (2) Air becomes cold and then becomes warm.
   (3) Water evaporates and then condenses
   (4) Water condenses and then is carried b wind.
   (5) Warm air rises and then falls from the sky.

4. Which of the following is most similar to the water cycle?

   (1) snow falling and then melting
   (2) water running down the bathroom wall after someone takes a hot shower
   (3) plants taking in carbon dioxide and releasing oxygen
   (4) automobile engines using high-octane gasoline
   (5) letting ice cubes melt and then refreezing them

tip   **Remember, applying prior knowledge to new information can help you understand the new information more easily. As you read, think about the experiences yo have had with this topic.**

Items 5 to 8 refer to the following passage.

Approximately 70 percent of Earth's surface is covered by oceans. Ocean water makes up 97 percent of all the water on Earth. Ocean water is a mixture of gases and solids dissolved in pure water. The main solid dissolved in ocean water is sodium chloride. Sodium chloride is common table salt.

Scientists use the term salinity to describe the saltiness of ocean water. Salinity is a measure of the amount of salt for each 1,000 grams of water. Most ocean water has a salinity of between 33 and 37, meaning that between 33 and 37 grams of salt will be found in 1,000 grams of water. The ocean's salinity tends to be highest in places where there is a great deal of evaporation or little rainfall.

The sun is the major source of heat for the ocean. As a result, temperatures are highest at the surface of the ocean. Waves and currents transfer the heat downward to a depth of about 300 meters. Below 300 meters, the temperature of ocean water drops rapidly. At a depth of 1,500 meters, the temperature of the water is just a few degrees above freezing.

5. Many living things cannot use water that contains salt. According to the passage, which of the following statements must be true?

(1) About 70 percent of the water on Earth can be used to meet the needs of living things.
(2) A very small amount of the water on Earth can be used to meet the needs of many living things.
(3) Pollution has severely reduced the amount of water that can be used by living things.
(4) The amount of water than can be used by living things is steadily increasing.
(5) Lack of rainfall has decreased the amount of water available to living things.

6. About how much water on Earth is drinkable?

(1) 3 percent
(2) 33 percent
(3) 37 percent
(4) 70 percent
(5) 97 percent

7. Which of the following situations is most like the heating of ocean water?

(1) A frozen dinner placed in a microwave oven is heated evenly throughout.
(2) People sitting near a fireplace feel warm, while people sitting far from the fireplace feel chilly.
(3) Water heated on a stove begins to boil when it reaches a certain temperature.
(4) An electrical wire becomes hot when too much current flows through it.
(5) A thermos bottle keeps liquids hot for many hours on a cold day.

8. What is the approximate salinity of ocean water?

(1)   35 grams per thousand grams water
(2)   70 grams per thousand grams water
(3)   97 grams per thousand grams water
(4)   100 grams per thousand grams water
(5) 1,000 grams per thousand grams water

> **tip**   When trying to decide which situation is most like one stated in the passage, go back to the passage to make sure you understand the original situation. Then read the options and select your answer.

Answers are on page 290.

Analysis: Fact or Opinion

When you recognize that some statements are beliefs and cannot be proved, you are distinguishing opinions from facts.

In lesson 6, you learned how scientists find out if their opinions, or hypotheses, are facts. They do this by performing experiments whose results may support their ideas. Many of the facts we take for granted were once scientists' opinions.

When you read about science, you may come across opinions. You may read that scientists have different points of view about the meaning of certain facts. Sometimes the opinion is that of a scientist or another expert. Sometimes it is held by the author.

Read this brief passage, and look for opinions.

In 1979 an accident occurred at the Three Mile Island nuclear power plant. The accident caused heat to build up in the reactor vessel—the steel structure that contains the nuclear reaction and prevents the release of radiation. Fuel rods and metal pipes in the reactor vessel melted and then hardened. The steel reactor vessel showed little damage. This is important because the vessel has no backup system. If the reactor vessel fails, a nuclear reaction can melt its way through the vessel into the ground. The fact that the heavy metal reactor vessel remains intact suggests that the chance of a catastrophic nuclear power plant accident might be smaller than once thought. However, some in the nuclear power industry believe that another accident similar to that at Three Mile Island would be the last. They say that pressure from the general public would force the closing of remaining nuclear power plants.

In this paragraph, the description of the accident at Three Mile Island is factual. For example, the author states that the fuel rods melted and hardened. This is a fact that can be proved. There are also several opinions in this passage.

* The author's opinion that the chance of a catastrophic nuclear power plant accident might be smaller than once thought
* The opinion of people in the nuclear power industry that another accident would force the closing of all nuclear plants
* The opinion of the general public that nuclear power plants are dangerous

The opinions in the passage may or may not be true, but the facts can be proved to be true.

When you read, watch for words like <u>believe</u>, <u>seem</u>, <u>feel</u>, <u>think</u>, <u>agree</u>, <u>may</u>, and <u>could</u>. These words often signal an opinion rather than a fact.

 To identify a fact, look for data that have been recorded and can be checked. Data might include numerical measurements or detailed descriptions of observations.

 Fact or Opinion

ems 1 to 4 refer to the following paragraph. hoose the <u>best answer</u> to each item.

Changes in the sun's activity, such as unspots, may affect the weather. For example, ears of low sunspot activity seem to correlate /ith periods of drought in North America, as hown by rainfall records and tree rings. It is oubtful, however, that there is a direct cause nd effect relationship between sunspots and roughts. Perhaps sunspots cause some change n the atmosphere that affects the weather.

1. Which of the following is a true, provable statement?

   (1) Sunspots cause changes in the weather.
   (2) There are variations in sunspot activity.
   (3) High sunspot activity is associated with periods of drought.
   (4) Low sunspot activity is the direct cause of drought in North America.
   (5) Sunspots affect only North America.

2. Which of the following statements <u>cannot</u> be proved?

   (1) The sun is the main source of energy for Earth.
   (2) The sun's activity varies over time.
   (3) Periods of high sunspot activity seem to be followed by periods of low sunspot activity.
   (4) Sunspots affect the weather in North America.
   (5) The relationship between sunspots and weather is not completely understood.

3. According to the passage, which of the following have been used to indicate periods of drought?

   A. sunspot activity
   B. tree rings
   C. rainfall records

   (1) A only
   (2) B only
   (3) C only
   (4) A, B, and C
   (5) B and C only

4. Which of the following would support the opinion that sunspots affect the weather?

   (1) data suggesting a correlation between sunspot activity and droughts in Asia
   (2) a decrease in sunspot activity
   (3) data suggesting a correlation between sunspot activity and tides
   (4) an increase in storms in North America
   (5) data suggesting that there is no correlation between sunspots and rainfall in Africa

Answers are on page 290.

Earth's Resources

The things we need to live, such as water, food, and energy, are called resources. Sometimes resources are in short supply. In the 1970s, shipments of petroleum, or oil, to our country had been cut. All petroleum products—including gasoline—were in short supply. According to energy planners and Earth scientists, an oil shortage could occur again, and if so, it could become permanent.

Oil is a nonrenewable resource, one that cannot be replaced once it is used up. Earth scientists disagree about how much oil is left on Earth. Some say that, given our present rate of consumption, the United States will be out of oil by the year 2060. Others feel that there is enough oil to last another 300 years. All agree, however, that at some point the supply of oil will be gone.

Energy planners are trying to find ways to prevent a major oil shortage. Most believe that the best solution would be to look for a renewable resource that could be used in place of oil. A renewable resource is one that can be replaced. The most abundant renewable resource on Earth is energy from the sun. Scientists have developed solar cells that can convert sunlight into electricity. They have also developed ways to heat homes with solar energy. At present, solar energy cannot be produced at a low enough cost or on a large enough scale to meet much of our energy needs.

Another way to postpone an oil shortage is to use less oil. During the oil shortage of the 1970s, the United States passed laws to reduce the speed limit on highways and to lower the thermostats in public buildings. Citizens were shown ways to conserve energy, but lifelong habits are hard to break. Many people continue their old, energy-wasting habits.

 Practice | Earth's Resources

Items 1 to 10 refer to the previous passage. Choose the best answer to each item.

1. Which of the following statements cannot be proved?

   (1) Earth's supply of oil is limited.
   (2) The reduction of speed limits conserves energy.
   (3) There is enough oil to last 300 years.
   (4) Oil became more plentiful in the 1980s than it had been in the 1970s.
   (5) Solar energy cannot currently meet our demands for energy.

2. Based on information in the passage, which of the following statements can be proved?

   (1) Americans are wasteful of energy.
   (2) An oil shortage could easily happen again.
   (3) By the year 2060, the U.S. will be out of oil.
   (4) Solar energy is a renewable resource.
   (5) Most citizens work to conserve energy.

3. Which of the following actions would help conserve a nonrenewable resource?

   (1) driving to work instead of taking public transportation
   (2) turning off the water while brushing your teeth
   (3) driving a small, fuel-efficient car
   (4) raising shades or blinds to let in sunlight in warm weather
   (5) converting a heating system from oil to natural gas

4. Which of the following is implied by the passage?

   (1) Vehicles will eventually be powered by something other than a petroleum product.
   (2) Oil will be the best choice for home heating in 500 years.
   (3) Oil supplies will last at least 1,000 years.
   (4) If people would conserve oil, it would last forever.
   (5) Solar energy will never be inexpensive enough to use widely.

5. What would be the effect on the supply of oil if people cut down their use of it?

   (1) The supply would be used up sooner.
   (2) The supply would be used more slowly but would eventually run out.
   (3) The supply would be used more slowly and would last forever.
   (4) The supply of oil would be used up the same as it would if people did not cut down their use.
   (5) New sources of oil would be found.

6. Which of the following is a renewable resource?

   (1) oil
   (2) natural gas
   (3) coal
   (4) gasoline
   (5) solar energy

7. Which of the following statements is the most accurate?

   (1) Solar energy is an inexpensive alternative to petroleum.
   (2) A gasoline shortage is not likely to occur again.
   (3) The supply of oil will last until the year 2060.
   (4) Conserving oil will postpone the time when supplies run out.
   (5) New sources of petroleum will be found to meet our energy needs.

8. A geologist studying Earth's layers would be most interested in which of the following resources?

   (1) sunlight
   (2) ocean water
   (3) food
   (4) nuclear energy
   (5) petroleum

9. Which of the following is the best title for this passage?

   (1) Why We Have Shortages
   (2) What Are Nonrenewable Resources?
   (3) Ways to Conserve Energy
   (4) Let's Use Renewable Resources
   (5) Oil Shortages—Can They Be Avoided?

10. Which of the following uses a renewable energy resource in place of a nonrenewable energy resource?

    (1) replacing old windows in a house with modern, double-glazed windows
    (2) using windmills instead of oil-burning power plants to generate electricity
    (3) turning off lights and the television when you leave the room
    (4) replacing an old air conditioner with a newer, more efficient model
    (5) parking your car and walking into a fast-food restaurant instead of using the drive-up window

Answers are on page 291.

Items 1 to 6 refer to the following passage. Choose the best answer to each item.

The air around Earth is always moving. Moving air is called wind. Throughout history, people have used energy from the wind to move ships, turn mill wheels, and pump water.

Windmills began to appear on U.S. farms around 1860. The energy from these windmills was used to pump water out of the ground for crops and farm animals. In 1890, a windmill was invented that could generate, or make, electricity. Wind generators became very popular with American farmers.

One problem with wind generators was that they did not always work. On calm days, they could not work. On stormy days, they were often knocked down or blown apart. Because of this, most wind generators were set aside in the 1940s, when electricity from electric power plants became available to farmers.

The need to find energy sources other than fossil fuels such as coal, oil, and natural gas has sparked new interest in wind energy. In recent years, new materials and designs have been used to make several tough, efficient wind generators. These machines can adjust to changing wind conditions and withstand storms.

Energy planners do not expect wind energy ever to meet all our needs. However, they do think that the use of wind energy can help to conserve fossil fuels and reduce air pollution.

1. According to energy planners, what is the importance of wind energy?

   (1) Wind energy is a nonrenewable resource.
   (2) Wind energy can replace fossil fuels as the leading energy resource.
   (3) Wind energy was abandoned in the 1940s.
   (4) Wind energy can reduce the need for fossil fuels.
   (5) Wind energy can be used on farms.

2. Which of the following aspects of wind energy is not discussed in the passage?

   (1) how wind generators were used in the 1800s
   (2) how modern wind generators are used
   (3) the reliability of wind generators
   (4) the ability of wind energy to meet energy needs
   (5) the use of wind energy on U.S. farms

3. According to the article, modern wind generators differ from earlier wind generators in that they are

   (1) larger
   (2) less expensive
   (3) able to generate electricity
   (4) more reliable
   (5) used mainly on farms

4. According to the passage, which of the following is not mentioned as a use of wind power?

   (1) moving ships
   (2) powering factories
   (3) pumping water
   (4) making electricity
   (5) turning mill wheels

5. According to the article, what caused a new interest in wind energy?

    (1) a desire to return to a simpler lifestyle
    (2) an interest in U.S. history
    (3) a need to find more energy sources
    (4) a desire to better understand wind
    (5) an increased need for electricity on U.S. farms

6. What caused the use of most wind generators to be discontinued in the 1940s?

    (1) the need to conserve fossil fuels
    (2) the need to find energy sources other than fossil fuels
    (3) the unreliability of wind generators
    (4) an increase in storms and calm days
    (5) the invention of newer, tougher wind generators

Items 7 to 10 refer to the following passage.

One source of air pollution is the burning of coal and oil by factories and power plants. Coal and oil contain sulfur. When they are burned, sulfur is released into the atmosphere. The sulfur reacts with oxygen to form sulfur oxides. Some of these sulfur oxides combine with water in the air to form acids. Eventually these acids fall to Earth as acid rain.

Acid rain is nearly as acidic as pure lemon juice. When acid rain falls into a lake, much of the lake's plant and animal life dies. Today many lakes look clear and blue because the water is nearly empty of wildlife. Animals living near such a lake may die of starvation.

What can be done about acid rain? Factories and power plants must stop burning sulfur-containing fuels. But fuels with a low sulfur content are often expensive and hard to find.

7. The main cause of acid rain is

    (1) a lack of oxygen in the air
    (2) a lack of moisture in the air
    (3) high temperatures
    (4) the burning of certain fuels
    (5) oil released into the atmosphere

8. Based on information in the passage, which of the following statements is a fact?

    (1) Factories will stop burning coal and oil.
    (2) Research will lead to the discovery of a sulfur-free fuel.
    (3) Acid rain destroys all living things on contact.
    (4) Acid rain is formed by sulfur oxides combining with water in the air.
    (5) Dangers of acid rain are exaggerated.

9. According to the passage, some lakes look clear and blue because they have

    (1) too much oxygen
    (2) many plants and animals
    (3) had above-average rainfall
    (4) been polluted by oil
    (5) lost their wildlife as a result of acid rain

10. Based on information in the passage, which of the following statements can be assumed to be true?

    (1) Sulfur is poisonous to living things.
    (2) Plants and animals live well in water that is clear and blue.
    (3) High levels of acidity can be harmful to living things.
    (4) Plants and animals die when acid is removed from rainwater.
    (5) Plants and animals live best when sulfur is present in the air.

Answers are on page 291.

Directions: Choose the <u>best answer</u> to each item.

<u>Items 1 to 5</u> refer to the following passage.

Most of the energy we use every day comes from fossil fuels. Fossil fuels were formed in Earth millions of years ago when the remains of dead plants and animals were buried beneath layers of mud. The chief fossil fuels are coal, petroleum, and natural gas.

Coal is solid fossil fuel. It was the first fossil fuel to be used by industry. In the United States today, coal is burned mainly to produce electric power.

Petroleum, or oil, is liquid fossil fuel. Petroleum is presently the leading fuel in the United States and other industrialized nations. Raw petroleum taken from Earth is called crude oil. The refining of crude oil produces gasoline, fuel oil for home heating, kerosene, and the raw materials for plastics, synthetic fibers, and cosmetics.

Natural gas is a fossil fuel in a gaseous state. It is less dense than liquid petroleum, so it is usually found on top of oil deposits. Natural gas is a clean-burning fuel compared to coal and oil, because it produces less air pollution. Some homes use natural gas for cooking and heating.

1. Based on the passage, which of the following best describes the relationship between fossil fuels and industry?

    (1) Fossil fuels have always been of little importance to industry.
    (2) Fossil fuels were once important but are now of little importance.
    (3) Fossil fuels were once of little importance but are now important.
    (4) Fossil fuels have been and are still of great importance to industry.
    (5) Fossil fuels are of little importance now but will be of great importance in the future.

2. A shortage of petroleum would probably <u>least</u> affect the availability of which of the following products?

    (1) 100% cotton shirt
    (2) lipstick
    (3) dress made of synthetic linen
    (4) plastic kitchen utensils
    (5) high-octane gasoline

3. According to the passage, air quality would probably improve if

    (1) oil were to replace coal in the production of electric power
    (2) natural gas were to replace oil as the leading fuel
    (3) coal were to replace oil in home heating
    (4) coal were to replace natural gas in home heating
    (5) coal were to replace oil in industry

4. Which of the following phrases describes the origin of fossil fuel?

    (1) produced from chemicals in laboratories
    (2) produced from fossilized materials in laboratories
    (3) formed underground from the remains of plants and animals
    (4) formed underground from pieces of rock
    (5) produced from crude oil in oil refineries

5. Which of the following statements is <u>not</u> supported by information in the passage?

    (1) Fossils fuels are the common type of fuel used today.
    (2) Coal has been in use longer than petroleum has.
    (3) Crude oil can be broken down into many other products.
    (4) The use of natural gas does not cause pollution.
    (5) Both fuel oil and natural gas are used for heating.

During an ice age, weather becomes colder, and the ice caps and glaciers spread south and north from the poles. Earth has gone through many ice ages, the last of which ended about 10,000 years ago.

No one is certain what causes ice ages, but there are many opinions on the subject. Scientists have pointed to changes in energy output from the sun, the amount of volcanic dust in the atmosphere, Earth's magnetic field, the amount of carbon dioxide in the atmosphere, and circulation of deep ocean currents as possible causes of ice ages. A recent hypothesis links ice ages with slight but regular changes in Earth's orbit around the sun.

6. Which of the following is a fact supported by the passage?

    (1) Changes in Earth's magnetic field result in ice ages.
    (2) The circulation of deep ocean currents causes ice ages.
    (3) The last ice age ended about 10,000 years ago.
    (4) During an ice age, the amount of volcanic dust in the atmosphere is greater than usual.
    (5) Solar energy output varies, leading to ice ages.

7. If, during an ice age, glaciers hundreds of feet thick reached the middle of the United States, what would be the likely result?

    (1) People would move to the Southern Hemisphere.
    (2) People would move toward the equator.
    (3) People would remain in the northern part of the United States.
    (4) The human race would die out.
    (5) The days would become shorter.

8. What would happen to the polar ice cap in Antarctica during an ice age?

    (1) It would become thinner and smaller.
    (2) It would spread northward.
    (3) It would spread southward.
    (4) It would be warmed by increased energy from the sun.
    (5) It would stay the same.

9. Which of the following would be a good title for this passage?

    (1) Ice Ages Past and Present
    (2) The Spread of the Polar Ice Caps
    (3) What Causes an Ice Age?
    (4) The Effect of Ice Ages on Human Civilization
    (5) A New Ice Age Is on the Way

10. Which of the following might indicate the beginning of a new ice age?

    (1) an increase in temperatures worldwide
    (2) a shrinking of glaciers
    (3) a rise in sea level worldwide
    (4) a decrease in temperatures worldwide
    (5) a decrease in the size of polar ice caps

11. An increase in the amount of volcanic dust in the atmosphere might cause an ice age because

    (1) the dust would block the sun's energy, resulting in lower temperatures
    (2) volcanic dust contains ice
    (3) volcanic eruptions in coastal areas affect ocean currents
    (4) volcanic eruptions affect Earth's magnetic field
    (5) volcanic eruptions affect Earth's orbit

Answers are on page 292.

Lesson 12

Analysis: Cause and Effect

As you learned in lesson 3, a cause is something that makes something else happen. An effect is what happens as a result of a cause. When there is a long-term shortage of rain, for example, grass and other vegetation turn brown and dry. The lack of rain is a cause, and the drying out of plants is an effect.

 **You can identify a cause by asking yourself, "Why did this happen?" You can identify an effect by asking yourself, "What happened?"**

Often an effect goes on to become the cause of another effect. For example, the brown and dry vegetation—the effect of a drought—can become the cause of starvation for animals that depend on vegetation for food. An earthquake—the result of movement in the Earth's interior—sometimes goes on to become the cause of further effects such as collapsed buildings and roads.

As you read, it is important to be aware of cause and effect relationships. Watch for words and phrases such as <u>because</u>, <u>since</u>, <u>thus</u>, <u>effect</u>, <u>affect</u>, <u>result</u>, <u>occurs when</u>, <u>was caused by</u>, <u>led to</u>, and <u>due to</u>. These often signal cause and effect relationships.

ged Practice | Cause and Effect

<u>Items 1 and 2</u> refer to the following passage. Choose the <u>best answer</u> to each item.

Beaches are always changing. Sand is moved around by wind, waves, and currents. Beaches can get smaller during the winter when high storm waves carry sand from the beach out to sea. In the summer, calmer waves and currents move the sand back to the beach, making it larger.

When offshore currents slow down, they deposit sand. In this way, certain shore features are formed. Sand bars are long piles of sand that are mostly under water. If they are connected to the shore, the sand bars are called spits. Very long sand bars that are above the water line are called barrier bars or barrier islands. Barrier islands run parallel to the coast and are separated from it by a narrow body of water. During storms, barrier islands protect the coast on the mainland from the full force of wind and waves. Atlantic City, New Jersey and Miami Beach, Florida are cities built on barrier islands.

1. What would be the effect on a beach if there were several mild winters without severe storms?

   (1) The beach would get smaller.
   (2) The beach would get smaller, and then larger.
   (3) The beach would get larger.
   (4) The beach would get larger and then smaller.
   (5) The beach would remain unchanged.

2. Why are people who live on a barrier island evacuated when a hurricane is approaching?

   (1) Roads are likely to collapse.
   (2) Flooding and wind damage are likely to occur.
   (3) Telephone service may be temporarily interrupted.
   (4) Food will be in short supply.
   (5) Drinking water will be scarce.

Items 3 and 4 refer to the following diagram.

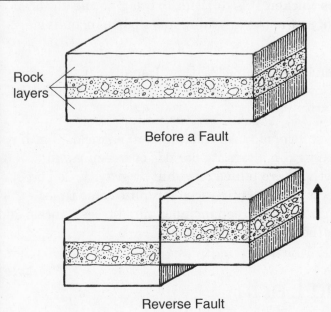

Before a Fault

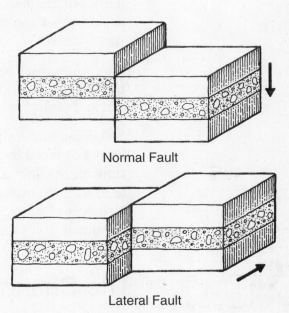

Normal Fault

Reverse Fault

Lateral Fault

3. What is the result of both normal and reverse faults?

   (1) Rocks move sideways.
   (2) A steep face of rock is exposed.
   (3) A river valley is formed.
   (4) Layers of rock are lined up.
   (5) Rock layers curve.

4. What is a likely result of normal and reverse faulting over a wide area and long time period?

   (1) formation of lakes
   (2) formation of rivers
   (3) formation of mountains
   (4) formation of level plains
   (5) formation of deserts

Answers are on page 293.

The Changing Earth

Changes in Earth's surface can be caused when the force of gravity pulls rocks and soil down mountain slopes. This is called mass wasting. Sediments that come to rest at the base of a cliff form a talus slope.

Mass wasting can occur rapidly or slowly. One type of rapid mass wasting is a landslide. During a landslide, huge quantities of soil, small stones, and large rocks tumble down a mountain. A landslide can be caused by an earthquake, volcanic eruption, or heavy rain—any natural event that weakens the supporting rock.

Another type of rapid mass wasting is a mudflow. A mudflow is usually caused by a heavy rain. As rain mixes with soil to form mud, gravity begins to pull the mud downhill. As the mud moves, it picks up more soil and becomes thicker. It is difficult to imagine the power of a mudflow—it can move just about anything in its path, including a whole house!

Slow mass wasting can occur in an earthflow. Usually caused by a heavy rain, an earthflow consists of the slow, downhill movement of soil and plant life.

Soil creep is the slowest form of mass wasting. Soil particles that have been disturbed by heavy rain, alternate periods of freezing and thawing, or animal activity are pulled downhill by gravity. Soil creep is so slow that its effects often go unnoticed for quite some time. Evidence of a long period of soil creep includes tilted trees, fences, and telephone poles along the side of a steep slope.

 Practice The Changing Earth

Items 1 to 12 refer to the previous passage. Choose the best answer to each item.

1. Which is not a cause of mass wasting?

   (1) heavy rain
   (2) animal activity
   (3) earthquakes
   (4) wind
   (5) volcanic eruptions

2. A row of tilted trees along a steep slope could be a result of

   (1) a talus slope
   (2) soil creep
   (3) a mudflow
   (4) a landslide
   (5) rapid mass wasting

3. What is the basic cause of each case of mass wasting?

   (1) heavy rain
   (2) volcanic eruption
   (3) animal activity
   (4) earthflows
   (5) gravity

▶ **tip** ── **When answering questions that include the word *not*, be certain to evaluate each choice. Then choose the one that received no support in the passage. In this type of question, the answer that is "wrong" is the correct response.**

4. Which area is likely to experience the least rapid mass wasting?

   (1) the Great Plains
   (2) the Rocky Mountains
   (3) the Allegheny Mountains
   (4) the Grand Canyon
   (5) Mt. St. Helens

5. Which of the following conditions is usually necessary in order for a mudflow to occur?

   (1) an earthquake
   (2) a volcanic eruption
   (3) heavy rain
   (4) animal activity
   (5) bare land

6. Which of the following is likely to cause the most severe property damage?

   (1) earthflow
   (2) soil creep
   (3) slow mass wasting
   (4) landslide
   (5) talus slope

7. Which of the following statements is always true?

   (1) Mass wasting is the result of earthquakes and volcanic eruptions.
   (2) Rapid mass wasting occurs only in coastal areas.
   (3) The general movement in mass wasting is from high ground to low ground.
   (4) Heavy rains are present in all cases of mass wasting.
   (5) Mountain ranges can be formed by mass wasting.

8. What is a talus slope?

   (1) a mountainside without topsoil
   (2) a mountain valley
   (3) sediments piled at the base of a cliff
   (4) a rocky outcrop on a slope
   (5) tilted landscape features

9. Which of the following is the best title for this passage?

   (1) Gravity
   (2) What is Soil Creep?
   (3) Rapid and Slow Mass Wasting
   (4) Slow Mass Wasting
   (5) Damage Caused by Mass Wasting

10. Which of the following is at the greatest risk of being damaged by a landslide?

   (1) a house at the crest of a hill
   (2) a road at the base of a steep slope
   (3) a volcano in the Cascade Mountains
   (4) a boat in a lake
   (5) a tilted tree along a river

11. Which of the following is true of an earthflow?

   (1) It is not likely to occur during a drought.
   (2) It occurs at the same rate as a mudflow.
   (3) It is an example of rapid mass wasting.
   (4) It occurs only in steep mountainous regions.
   (5) It does not result in a talus slope.

12. Which of the following is most likely to be responsible for large rocks falling onto a highway?

   (1) an earthflow
   (2) soil creep
   (3) a mudflow
   (4) rapid mass wasting
   (5) slow mass wasting

Answers are on page 293.

Items 1 and 2 refer to the following passage. Choose the best answer to each item.

An earthquake is the shaking and trembling that results from the sudden movement of rock in Earth's crust. When a strong earthquake hits a populated area, there can be tremendous destruction and hundreds of deaths.

The most common cause of earthquakes is faulting. A fault is a break in Earth's crust. During faulting, rocks along the fault begin to move. They break and slide past each other. Parts of Earth's crust may be pushed together or pulled apart. During this process, energy is released.

The point beneath Earth's surface where the rocks break and move is the focus of the earthquake. Directly above the focus, on Earth's surface, is the epicenter. The most violent shaking occurs at the epicenter.

When rocks in Earth's crust break, vibrations travel out in all directions from the focus. These vibrations are known as seismic waves. There are three main types of seismic waves.

The seismic waves that travel the fastest are called primary waves. These waves can travel through solids, liquids, and gases. Primary waves are push-pull waves. They cause pieces of rock to move back and forth in the same direction as the wave is moving.

The seismic waves that travel the next fastest are secondary waves. Secondary waves can travel through solids but not through liquids or gases. Rock pieces disturbed by secondary waves move from side to side at right angles to the direction the wave is traveling.

The slowest seismic waves are surface waves. Surface waves travel from the focus directly up to the epicenter. Surface waves cause the ground to bend and twist, sometimes causing whole buildings to collapse.

The more energy an earthquake releases, the stronger and more destructive it is. The strength of an earthquake is measured on a special scale, the Richter scale. The Richter scale measures how much energy an earthquake releases by assigning the earthquake a number from one to ten. Any number above six on the Richter scale indicates a very strong earthquake.

1. According to the passage, the strength of an earthquake is directly related to which of the following?

   (1) length of the fault
   (2) amount of energy released
   (3) speed of the seismic waves
   (4) distance from the focus to the epicenter
   (5) amount of rock broken

2. From the information given, one can conclude that

   (1) surface waves are the most destructive
   (2) primary waves are the most destructive
   (3) all seismic waves except surface waves are destructive
   (4) all seismic waves are equally destructive
   (5) seismic waves are not destructive

Erosion is the moving and wearing away of rock materials by natural causes. A dramatic cause of erosion is a glacier.

A glacier is a large mass of moving ice. Most glaciers form in mountains where snow builds up faster than it can melt. As snow falls upon snow, year after year, the snow changes into ice. When the ice becomes heavy enough, the pull of gravity causes it to move slowly down the mountain. As the glacier moves, it picks up blocks of rock. As the rocks become frozen into the bottom of the glacier, they carve away more rock. Some of this rock is left behind at the edges of the glacier.

Sometimes, after flowing down a mountain, a glacier will enter a river valley that is narrower than the glacier. As the glacier squeezes through the valley, it erodes both the floor and sides of the valley. As a result, the valley changes from a V-shaped valley to a broad U-shaped valley.

3. Which of the following is not an effect of a moving glacier?

   (1) the formation of tall mountain peaks
   (2) the movement of large and small rocks
   (3) deposits of rock
   (4) the change in shape of a valley
   (5) the carving away of rock

4. What would be the effect of several unusually long, hot summers on mountain glaciers?

   (1) Glaciers would move down the mountain more rapidly.
   (2) Glaciers would reach farther down the mountain.
   (3) The edges of the glaciers would melt, making the glaciers smaller.
   (4) The glaciers would become thicker and more dense.
   (5) The glaciers would carve river valleys into U-shapes.

5. Which of the following is not an example of erosion?

   (1) the washing away of sand by river water
   (2) the moving of pebbles by ice in a glacier
   (3) the removal of soil by wind
   (4) the breaking up of granite by a jackhammer
   (5) the moving of rock pieces downhill by gravity

6. Which is the best title for this passage?

   (1) Glaciers
   (2) Agents of Erosion
   (3) How Glaciers Form
   (4) How Glaciers Carve Valleys
   (5) Glacial Erosion

> **tip** When selecting a title for a passage, look for the option that best summarizes the main idea of the passage. The best title should be neither too broad nor too specific.

Answers are on page 294.

Directions: Choose the <u>best answer</u> to each item.

<u>Items 1 to 6</u> refer to the following article.

Deep within Earth, the rock is a hot liquid called magma. In some places, magma works its way toward Earth's surface by melting solid rock or by moving through cracks in rock. When magma reaches Earth's surface, it is called lava. The place where lava reaches Earth's surface is called a volcano.

In every volcano there is at least one opening called a vent. It is through the vent that the volcano erupts. You may think of a volcanic eruption as being a violent, dramatic event. Sometimes it is, but a volcanic eruption can also be a quiet flow of lava.

Volcanoes can be classified according to the type of eruptions that form them. There are three main types of volcanoes.

Cinder cone volcanoes are formed from explosive eruptions. Explosive eruptions are caused when lava in vents hardens into rocks. Steam and new lava build up under the rocks, causing pressure. Eventually the pressure becomes great enough to cause a violent explosion. The volcano is formed out of cinders and other rock particles that are blown into the air. A cinder cone volcano has a narrow base and steep sides.

Shield volcanoes result from quiet lava flow. The lava from shield volcanoes flows over a large area because it is thin and runny. A shield volcano, which forms after several quiet eruptions, is a gently sloping, dome-shaped mountain.

Composite volcanoes build up when explosive and quiet eruptions alternate. First an explosive eruption spews rock and cinders onto the surface. Then a quiet eruption occurs, producing a lava flow that covers the cinders and rock particles. After many alternating eruptions, a cone-shaped mountain, with a relatively wide base, is formed. Two famous composite volcanoes are Mt. Vesuvius in Italy and Mt. St. Helens in the United States.

Volcanoes are like "windows" that let us see inside Earth. By analyzing the chemical composition of lava, scientists are able to determine the chemical composition of the magma from which the lava formed.

1. Which of the following is a necessary condition for the formation of a volcano?

    (1) a violent eruption of lava
    (2) the melting of solid rock
    (3) the hardening of lava in vents
    (4) the release of cinders into the air
    (5) the movement of magma to Earth's surface

2. According to the article, the classification of volcanoes is based on which of the following?

    (1) their shape
    (2) their size
    (3) the number of vents they have
    (4) the events that cause them to form
    (5) the effect they have on the environment

3. The formation of a gently sloping, dome-shaped volcano is the result of which of the following events?

    (1) several explosive eruptions
    (2) alternating explosive and quiet eruptions
    (3) several quiet eruptions
    (4) the release of cinders into the air
    (5) the formation of steam in vents

4. Which of the following statements about lava is correct?

    (1) Lava forms cinder cone volcanoes.
    (2) Lava can be thin and runny.
    (3) Lava always flows over a wide area.
    (4) Lava produces magma.
    (5) Lava consists primarily of cinders.

5. The Hawaiian Islands are a cluster of shield volcanoes that rise above the ocean. On these islands, it is most likely that

(1) any future eruptions will be explosive
(2) when lava flows it is thin and runny
(3) the rocks are made of shells
(4) eruptions no longer occur
(5) all the mountains are steep and narrow

6. A volcano with a narrow base and steep sides most likely

(1) is not active
(2) erupts quietly
(3) is a shield volcano
(4) is Mt. St. Helens
(5) is a cinder cone volcano

---

ems 7 and 8 refer to the following information.

The dotted lines on this map show the world zones of earthquake or olcano activity. Most major earthquakes and volcanic eruptions occur long these lines.

EARTHQUAKE AND VOLCANIC ACTIVITY

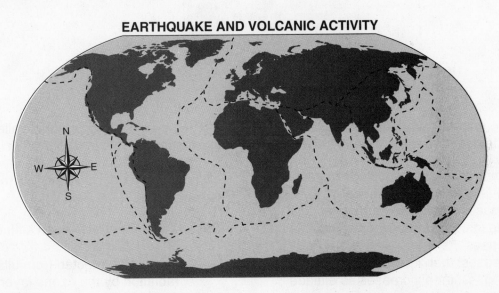

7. Which continent is generally free of major earthquakes?

(1) North America
(2) South America
(3) Asia
(4) Australia
(5) Africa

8. Which of the following areas would provide the best opportunity to study volcanic activity?

(1) northeastern Canada
(2) western South America
(3) western Africa
(4) Australia
(5) eastern South America

Answers are on page 295.

Directions: Choose the <u>best answer</u> for each item.

<u>Items 1 to 4</u> refer to the following diagram.

The diagram below shows the characteristics of the four main layers of the atmosphere.

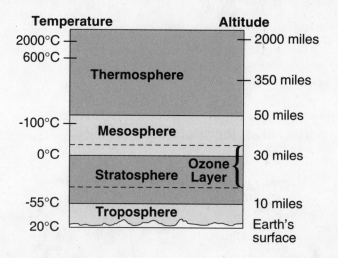

1. According to the diagram, temperature in Earth's atmosphere

   (1) remains the same as altitude increases
   (2) increases as altitude increases
   (3) decreases as altitude increases
   (4) increases, then decreases as altitude increases
   (5) decreases, then increases, then decreases, then increases as altitude increases

2. Which of the following is true of the troposphere?

   (1) It includes the ozone layer.
   (2) It is the first layer returning spacecraft encounter.
   (3) It is above the stratosphere.
   (4) It is the layer we live in.
   (5) It is thicker than the thermosphere.

3. The upper thermosphere is called the exosphere. This is where artificial satellites orbit Earth. According to the diagram, which statement must be true about these satellites?

   (1) They orbit Earth at an altitude of 62 to 124 miles.
   (2) They are protected from ultraviolet radiation by the ozone layer.
   (3) They can withstand extremely high temperatures.
   (4) They pass through thin clouds of ice.
   (5) They are used for television transmission.

4. At 50 miles above Earth's surface,

   (1) the ozone layer ends
   (2) the temperature is 600°C
   (3) the mesosphere meets the thermosphere
   (4) there are no air molecules
   (5) clouds form

Items 5 to 8 refer to the following article.

Scientists studying ice in Antarctica have discovered evidence for the theory that the amount of methane gas in the atmosphere is related to changes in Earth's climate. The scientists estimated the amount of methane in the atmosphere over a period of 160,000 years by measuring the amounts of different gases in air bubbles trapped in the polar ice. There was less methane in the atmosphere during ice ages and much more methane in the atmosphere during periods of global warming.

Other studies have shown that the amount of methane in the atmosphere nearly doubled—from 350 parts per billion during the ice ages to 650 parts per billion during warmer periods. Today, the methane level is 1,700 parts per billion. In recent years, some scientists have warned that methane can contribute to global warming because it traps heat in the atmosphere. Although the studies do not prove that increased methane levels cause Earth's temperatures to rise, they do suggest that this is possible.

5. Which of the following is <u>not</u> a fact supported by the passage?

    (1) In the ice ages, the amount of methane was about 350 parts per billion.
    (2) There is more methane in the atmosphere during periods of warming than during ice ages.
    (3) There is a relationship between the level of methane in the atmosphere and the Earth's climate.
    (4) Increased levels of methane cause global warming.
    (5) Methane levels in the atmosphere change over long periods of time.

6. Which of the following supports the conclusion that Earth may be entering a warming period?

    (1) There is methane in air bubbles trapped in polar ice.
    (2) The methane level of the atmosphere changes over a long period of time.
    (3) The methane level is much higher now than during previous warm periods.
    (4) The methane level should drop sharply over the next 100 years.
    (5) Methane levels over Antarctica are high.

7. What best describes the current scientific understanding of the relationship between methane and climate?

    (1) Higher methane levels cause Earth's climate to warm.
    (2) Lower methane levels cause Earth's climate to warm.
    (3) In periods of warmer climate, more methane is in the atmosphere.
    (4) In periods of warmer climate, less methane is in the atmosphere.
    (5) There is no relationship between the level of methane in the atmosphere and Earth's climate.

8. Which of the following is <u>not</u> true?

    (1) The present level of methane in the atmosphere is 1,700 parts per billion.
    (2) During ice ages, the level of methane in the atmosphere increases.
    (3) In periods of global warming, the level of methane in the atmosphere increases.
    (4) The Antarctica study provided measurements of methane levels in air samples from earlier periods.
    (5) The present level of methane in the atmosphere is higher than at any known period in the past.

Items 9 to 12 refer to the information below.

Over long periods of time, rocks change from one kind of rock to another. These changes occur again and again. This process is called the rock cycle.

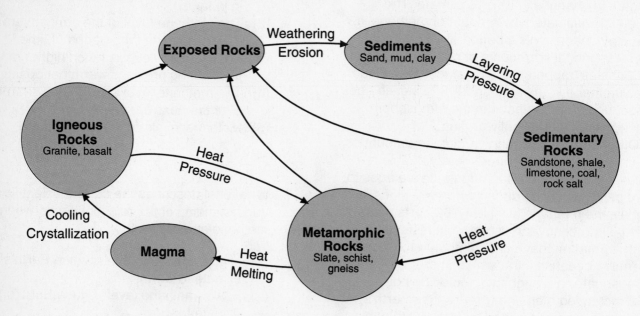

9. Which of the following statements is most accurate?

   (1) Metamorphic rocks are formed only from igneous rocks.
   (2) Sedimentary rocks are formed by heat.
   (3) Some igneous rocks are directly formed from sediments.
   (4) Weathering and erosion can affect all types of rocks.
   (5) Heat and pressure cause sedimentary rocks to form igneous rocks.

10. A hiker found a rock containing basalt. What type of rock is this likely to be?

    (1) mud, clay, or sand
    (2) sedimentary
    (3) magma
    (4) metamorphic
    (5) igneous

11. What is a good title for the information and diagram?

    (1) The Rock Cycle
    (2) The Formation of Metamorphic Rocks
    (3) Uses of Rock
    (4) The Effect of Pressure on Rocks
    (5) Erosion and Weathering of Rocks

12. What kind of rocks would you be most likely to find at a place where there had once been a river?

    A. igneous
    B. metamorphic
    C. sedimentary

    (1) A only
    (2) B only
    (3) C only
    (4) A and B only
    (5) A and C only

The oil shortages of the 1970s set off a search for new forms of energy. At the Natural Energy Laboratory of Hawaii, scientists are producing energy without burning fossil fuels and without causing pollution. They are using cold seawater.

In one process, called ocean thermal energy conversion, the difference in temperature between surface and deep seawater is used to generate electricity. In experiments conducted so far, it has taken more electricity to pump up deep seawater than the process has been able to produce. Scientists and engineers are planning to use much wider pipelines in order to pump enough seawater to produce more electricity than the process uses.

A more successful test used cold seawater for air-conditioning and industrial cooling. Cold seawater was circulated through air-conditioning systems at the lab, and the electrical costs were cut by about 75 percent.

13. Which of the following does the author consider to be true about sources of energy?

(1) Seawater will never be a practical source of energy.
(2) Solar energy is more efficient than energy from seawater.
(3) Seawater will eventually be used up.
(4) It is not wise to depend only on fossil fuels for energy.
(5) All air-conditioning systems can use cold seawater.

14. What is ocean thermal energy conversion?

(1) a process for removing salt and other minerals from seawater
(2) a process for farming sea plants and animals
(3) a process that uses the difference in temperature between warm and cold seawater to produce electricity
(4) a process to locate fossil fuel deposits under the ocean
(5) a process for air-conditioning buildings using seawater

15. In which of the following locations would using cold seawater to produce electricity be impractical?

(1) Hawaii
(2) California
(3) Florida
(4) Puerto Rico
(5) Kansas

16. Which of the following can be inferred from the article?

(1) Seawater will replace fossil fuels as the main source of energy within the next ten years.
(2) Until less electricity is used to pump up seawater than is produced by using seawater, the process will not be practical.
(3) Using fossil fuels to produce electricity costs more than using seawater.
(4) Seawater has been found to be more economical for producing electricity than for air-conditioning buildings.
(5) Using seawater to produce electricity causes a lot of pollution.

tip **When answering a question that asks you to apply information to a new context, use everything you already know about the context to help you choose the correct answer. For example, when trying to decide where using cold seawater would be impractical, use what you know about geography to figure out which states are located near the sea.**

Items 17 to 21 refer to the following diagram and passage.

EARTH'S REVOLUTION AROUND SUN

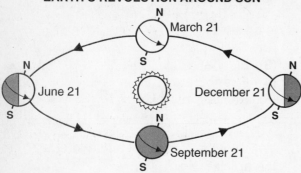

The movement of Earth around the sun is called revolution. It takes Earth 365.24 days to make one complete revolution around the sun. As it revolves, Earth also spins on its axis. This spinning is known as rotation. Earth rotates on an axis that is inclined at an angel of 23.5°.

Because Earth revolves and its axis is inclined, different parts of Earth lean toward the sun at different times of the year, resulting in seasons. When the northern hemisphere leans toward the sun, it has long periods of daylight and warm temperatures. As a result, this hemisphere gets the most energy from the sun and it experiences summer. At the same time, the southern hemisphere experiences shorter days and cooler temperatures, so it has winter. On March 21 and September 21, neither hemisphere leans toward the sun, so one hemisphere experiences spring while the other experiences autumn.

17. Which of the following is the cause of Earth's seasons?

    A. Earth's revolution
    B. Earth's rotation
    C. Earth's inclined axis

    (1) A only
    (2) B only
    (3) C only
    (4) B and C only
    (5) A and C only

18. What is rotation?

    (1) Earth's movement around the sun
    (2) the moon's movement around the Earth
    (3) the cause of the seasons
    (4) the result of the seasons
    (5) Earth's spinning on its axis

19. Which of the following is true in December?

    (1) The southern hemisphere experiences winter.
    (2) The northern hemisphere is tilted away from the sun.
    (3) Neither hemisphere leans toward the sun.
    (4) The hemispheres get the same amount of energy from the sun.
    (5) The northern hemisphere has longer days then the southern hemisphere.

20. If Earth revolved as it does now but rotated on an axis that wasn't inclined,

    (1) there would be no seasons
    (2) there would be only two seasons
    (3) half of Earth would always have night
    (4) nothing would be different
    (5) the year would be shorter

21. Which of the following is a fact presented in the passage?

    (1) It takes Earth 23.5 days to revolve around the sun.
    (2) The angle of tilt of Earth's axis is 365.24°.
    (3) Throughout the year, all parts of Earth get the same amount of the sun's energy.
    (4) Different parts of Earth get different amounts of the sun's energy at different times of the year.
    (5) The southern hemisphere experiences spring on March 21.

Answers are on page 295.

Unit 2: Earth Science

Performance Analysis
Unit 2 Cumulative Review: Earth Science

Name: _____ Class: _____ Date: _____

Use the Answer Key on pages 295–297 to check your answers to the Unit 2 Cumulative Review: Earth Science. Then use the chart to figure out the skill areas in which you need additional review. Circle on the chart the numbers of the test items you answered correctly. Then go back and review the lessons for the skill areas that are difficult for you. For additional review, see the *Steck-Vaughn GED Science Exercise Book,* Unit 2: Earth Science.

Thinking Skill Area	Earth Science	Lesson(s) for Review
Comprehension	**1**, **4**, **11**, 14, 16, **18**, **21**	1, 2, 4, 9
Application	**10**, 15, **19**, **20**	10
Analysis	**3**, 5, 6, 7, **12**, 13, **17**	3, 5, 6, 8, 11, 12
Evaluation	2, 8, **9**	7

Boldfaced numbers indicate items based on charts, graphs, illustrations, and diagrams.

CHEMISTRY

Chemistry can explain why hot air balloons fly.

Chemistry is the study of matter and changes in matter. You may think that chemistry exists only in a laboratory, but chemistry is all around you and within you. In fact, a chemical reaction within your brain enables you to understand and remember these words as you read them.

In lesson 13 you will learn about matter. **Matter** is what everything in the world is made up of. Matter can exist in any one of three common physical states — solid, liquid, or gas.

The building blocks of matter are tiny particles called **atoms.** Atoms contain three types of particles called protons, neutrons, and electrons. Atoms can form electrically charged particles called **ions.** Atoms can also bond together chemically to form molecules. A **molecule** is the smallest physical unit of a compound that still has all the properties of that compound.

matter
anything that has mass and takes up space

atom
the smallest physical unit of an element that has all the properties of that element

ion
an electrically charged atom or group of atoms

molecule
the smallest physical unit of a compound that has all the properties of that compound

In this lesson you will also learn about the elements. An **element** is the simplest of substances, for it cannot be broken down into other substances by chemical means. Scientists have listed the elements in an arrangement called the **periodic table.** As you study the periodic table, you will find out how useful it is in predicting the properties of elements.

In chemical reactions, substances are changed into new and different substances. In lesson 14 you will discover how these chemical changes take place. You will learn that during chemical reactions, bonds between atoms are broken and new bonds are formed. You will also learn that energy changes are part of chemical reactions.

In this lesson you will also learn about a familiar type of mixture called a **solution.** A solution consists of a substance called a solute dissolved in another substance called the solvent. Solutions can be made up of solids, liquids, or gases. The most familiar solutions are solid, liquid, or gas solutes dissolved in a liquid solvent.

You will also learn about an important group of chemical compounds known as acids, bases, and salts. Some of these compounds are very familiar to you. You can find an **acid** in an orange, a **base** in soap and cleaning solutions, and a **salt** right on your dinner table. And speaking of dinner, the last part of this lesson will teach you how to become a "kitchen chemist," as you learn what really happens when baking powder makes a cake rise.

In lesson 15, you will learn about **organic compounds.** These are the compounds that make up organisms. You will see that certain organic compounds, known as **hydrocarbons,** contain only the elements carbon and hydrogen. Familiar hydrocarbons include octane, found in gasoline, and propane, used as a cooking fuel.

element
a substance that cannot be broken down into simpler substances by chemical means

periodic table
an arrangement of the elements according to their properties

solution
a mixture in which one substance is dissolved in another

acid
a substance that releases hydrogen ions in a water solution

base
a substance that releases hydroxide ions in a water solution

salt
a compound that results from a chemical reaction between an acid and a base

organic compound
any compound that contains carbon

hydrocarbon
any compound made up of only carbon and hydrogen

SEE ALSO: Steck-Vaughn GED Science Exercise Book, Unit 3: Chemistry

Application: Other Contexts

When you use information you know in another situation, you are applying your knowledge in a new context.

Many of the topics you read about in science are very general. For example, you might read about the properties, or characteristics, of gases. You may read that some gases are lighter than others, such as the mixture of gases in the air. This is easier to grasp if you think about how helium-filled balloons float in the air. General science ideas are often easier to understand when you can apply them to specific examples.

Read this paragraph and see how the ideas can be applied.

When you think about anything on Earth, you must be thinking about matter or energy. Everything on Earth can be classified as matter or energy. Matter has mass and takes up space. Energy has the ability to move matter or change it.

According to the passage, everything on Earth is either matter or energy. You can apply this general idea to specific things. Think of this book. It has mass and takes up space — it must be an example of matter. Now lift up the book. To move the book, you used energy. What other specific applications of the ideas of matter and energy can you think of?

Remember, when you read about general ideas it can be helpful to apply them to specific situations. Ask yourself:

- What is being described or explained?
- What situations might this information apply to?
- How would this information be used in those situations?

 To help apply information you already know to a scientific idea, ask yourself: What characteristics are familiar to me? Do I have any experience with this idea? Then apply the answers to these questions to the new information.

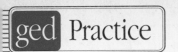

em1 refers to the following paragraph. Choose the best answer to each item.

At sea level, where the air is at standard ressure, pure water boils at 100°C. When water s heated in a closed container so that the steam annot escape, the boiling point of the water is aised above 100°C.

1. Which of the following appliances is based on the principles described above?

   (1) a microwave oven
   (2) a washing machine
   (3) a toaster
   (4) a refrigerator
   (5) a pressure cooker

Item 2 refers to the following paragraph.

Minerals dissolved in water can be removed rom water by the process of distillation. Water is added to a distilling flask and boiled. The water vapor released then passes through a cooled ube, and the condensed water flows down into a eceiving container. The minerals are left behind n the distilling flask.

2. Which of the following is an example of a use for distillation?

   (1) obtaining drinking water from ocean water
   (2) putting ice cubes in a cold drink
   (3) boiling water for tea
   (4) adding antifreeze to a car engine
   (5) bottling mineral water

tems 3 and 4 refer to the following paragraph.

Composite materials are substances that contain and have the properties of two or more different materials. Glass-reinforced plastic is one example. It consists of a plastic matrix with glass fibers embedded in it. Glass gives this composite material strength, and plastic keeps it rom being brittle.

3. An example of a composite material would be

   (1) oxygen gas
   (2) steel-belted radial tires
   (3) plastic bag
   (4) wine glass
   (5) gold ring

4. Bone consists of living cells and calcium phosphate embedded with elastic fibers. Bone is a composite material because

   (1) it is found in nature
   (2) it has the properties of two or more materials, one embedded in the other
   (3) it consists of more than one material
   (4) it contains a matrix
   (5) it is stronger than calcium phosphate or protein fibers alone

Item 5 refers to the following paragraph.

The amount of moisture in the air affects a person's comfort level. Warm or hot air can hold much more moisture than cold air. If air is cooled down, the moisture in it will begin to condense. Removing excess moisture from the air can make people feel more comfortable, especially during the summer months.

5. Which of the following takes advantage of the principle described above to provide greater comfort during summer weather?

   (1) an electric heater
   (2) an electric fan
   (3) a humidifier
   (4) a dehumidifier
   (5) an air filter

Answers are on page 297.

Matter

Matter can exist in any of three physical states. These states are solid, liquid, and gas.

- A solid is any form of matter that has a definite shape and volume. A bar of gold is an example of a solid. If you try to put a square bar of gold into a round hole, it will not fit. The gold has a definite shape. If you try to put the bar of gold into a space that is too small, it also will not fit. The bar of gold has a definite volume.
- A liquid has a definite volume, but it does not have a definite shape. If you pour a quart of milk into a gallon jug, the milk will fill only one-fourth of the jug. If you pour the same quart of milk into an eight-ounce glass, the milk will overflow. The volume of the milk does not change. However, its shape changes each time you pour it into a different container.
- A gas has neither definite shape nor definite volume. A gas will spread out to fill the volume of a container that it is placed in. You can understand this property of a gas if you think of how quickly the smell of an apple pie baking in the oven fills the whole kitchen.

Most matter can change from one state to another. If enough heat is removed from a liquid, it will freeze into a solid. Similarly, if enough heat is added to a solid, it will melt into a liquid. The temperature at which these changes of state occur is called the freezing point or melting point of substances. If enough heat is added to a liquid, the liquid will change into a gas. This process is called vaporization. When a gas is cooled enough, it changes into a liquid in a process called condensation. The temperature at which vaporization or condensation occurs is called the boiling point of a substance.

 Think about any experience you have had with these scientific ideas. Apply them to what you just read. This is applying knowledge to a new context, and it will help you answer questions on general or unfamiliar scientific ideas.

Items 1 to 8 refer to the previous passage. Choose the best answer to each item.

1. Which of the following situations would produce a change in the state of matter?

   (1) A drop of food coloring is added to a glass of water.
   (2) A container of ice cream is left on top of a hot stove.
   (3) A hole is pricked in a balloon.
   (4) A can of soup is placed on a scale.
   (5) A square block of wood is cut in half.

2. A heart-shaped cake is made by pouring cake batter into a heart-shaped mold. Which principle is illustrated by this situation?

   (1) A solid takes the shape of the container into which it is placed.
   (2) A solid has a definite shape but not a definite volume.
   (3) A liquid has a definite shape and volume.
   (4) A liquid has no definite shape.
   (5) A gas has a definite shape and volume.

3. What causes matter to change state?

   (1) the addition or removal of heat
   (2) its mass
   (3) the space it occupies
   (4) changes in volume
   (5) changes in shape

4. Which of the following is not an example of a change of state of matter?

   (1) steam condensing on a window
   (2) filling a balloon with helium
   (3) icicles melting
   (4) freezing leftover soup
   (5) boiling water until the pot is empty

5. Which of the following situations illustrates the process of condensation?

   (1) dew forming on the grass in early morning
   (2) ice cubes melting in a cold drink
   (3) rain changing to sleet
   (4) steaming vegetables
   (5) melting butter in a frying pan

6. Which of the following situations shows that gases have neither definite shape nor definite volume?

   (1) pouring a pint of orange juice into a quart container
   (2) lighting a match
   (3) adding salt to boiling water
   (4) smelling pollutants released by a nearby factory
   (5) pouring concrete into a mold

7. What are the properties that characterize a liquid?

   (1) definite shape; definite volume
   (2) definite shape; no definite volume
   (3) no definite shape; no definite volume
   (4) no definite shape; definite volume
   (5) none of the above

8. Which of the following statements is most accurate?

   (1) All matter can be found naturally in all three states.
   (2) Liquids spread out to completely fill their containers.
   (3) All matter is liquid below 100°C.
   (4) Water freezes and vaporizes at different temperatures.
   (5) Liquids melt and vaporize at different temperatures.

Answers are on page 298.

Items 1 to 5 refer to the following passage and diagram. Choose the <u>best answer</u> to each item.

All matter is made up of elements. An element is a substance that cannot be broken down into simpler substances by chemical means. Oxygen, carbon, iron, and copper are examples of elements.

Can an element be broken down into smaller and smaller pieces forever and still be an element? For example, can a piece of copper be cut into smaller and smaller pieces and still be copper? The answer is <u>no</u>. Eventually, a tiny piece would be obtained that could not be divided and still be copper. This smallest piece of an element is called an atom.

An atom is the smallest physical unit of an element that still has the properties of that element. All elements are made up of atoms. The element copper is made only of copper atoms, the element iron is made only of iron atoms, and so on.

What is an atom made of? Each atom has a small, dense core called a nucleus. The nucleus contains particles called protons, which have a positive electric charge, and neutrons, which have no charge. Moving in orbits around the nucleus are tiny, negatively charged particles called electrons. A neutron and a proton have about the same mass, which is about 1,800 times greater than the mass of an electron.

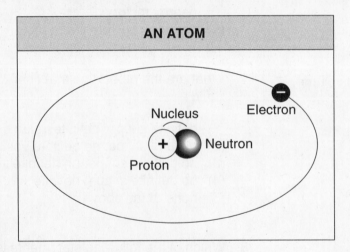

1. Which of the following statements is true of an atom of iron?

   (1) One of its electrons has the same mass as one of its protons.
   (2) Its neutrons have positive charges.
   (3) Its protons orbit the nucleus.
   (4) It is the same as an atom of copper.
   (5) It has the same properties as all other iron atoms.

2. Which of the following statements about substance X would indicate that it is <u>not</u> an element?

   (1) It breaks down when heated, producing mercury and oxygen.
   (2) It is red-orange in color.
   (3) It reacts with water to form an acid.
   (4) It is a solid at room temperature.
   (5) It can react with certain substances to form salts.

3. The total charge on an atom is zero, which means the atom is electrically neutral. Which statement explains why this is so?

   (1) The number of protons in an atom is greater than the number of electrons.
   (2) The number of protons in an atom is less than the number of electrons.
   (3) The number of protons in an atom is equal to the number of electrons.
   (4) The number of protons in an atom is equal to the number of neutrons.
   (5) The number of neutrons in an atom is equal to the number of electrons.

4. Atom X has five more protons than atom Y. Both atoms have the same mass. Which statement explains why this is so?

   (1) Atom X has more electrons than atom Y.
   (2) Atom X has fewer electrons than atom Y.
   (3) Atom X has more neutrons than atom Y.
   (4) Atom X has fewer neutrons than atom Y.
   (5) Atom X has the same number of neutrons as atom Y.

5. The structure of an atom is most similar to which of the following?

   (1) a salt crystal
   (2) a chair
   (3) an egg
   (4) the moon
   (5) the solar system

_____

ems 6 to 8 refer to the following passage.

   When two or more elements combine hemically, they form a compound. Water is a ompound because it consists of the elements xygen and hydrogen.

The smallest physical unit of a compound that still has the properties of that compound is called a molecule. A molecule is made up of two or more atoms chemically bonded together. When atoms bond together, they share or transfer electrons. If electrons are shared, the bond is said to be a covalent bond. If electrons are transferred from one atom to another, charged particles, called ions, form. A bond between two ions is said to be an ionic bond. Some atoms form bonds easily with other atoms, while some atoms hardly ever form bonds.

6. Which of the following combinations represents a compound?

   (1) two carbon atoms side-by-side in a diamond crystal
   (2) sugar and water mixed together
   (3) a hydrogen atom and a chlorine atom sharing a pair of electrons
   (4) hydrogen and nitrogen existing together in air
   (5) water and carbon dioxide mixed together in carbonated water

7. It can be inferred from the passage that atoms that do not bond easily with other atoms

   (1) have no electrons
   (2) form only ionic bonds
   (3) are present in very few compounds
   (4) are found only in water
   (5) form only covalent bonds

8. Table salt, sodium chloride, contains ionic bonds. Which of the following is true of a salt molecule?

   (1) The atoms of sodium and chloride are not bound.
   (2) Electrons are transferred from one of the atoms to another.
   (3) The sodium and chloride atoms share electrons.
   (4) Sodium and chloride do not bond easily.
   (5) The sodium atom forms bonds more easily than the chloride atom.

Answers are on page 298.

Directions: Choose the best answer to each item.

Items 1 to 4 refer to the following passage and table.

The atoms of each element are different from the atoms of every other element. What makes them different? The atoms of each element have a certain number of protons in the nucleus. The number of protons in the nucleus of an atom of an element is called its atomic number. Thus, each element has its own atomic number. The number of protons plus the number of neutrons in the atom of an element is called the atomic mass.

Scientists found that elements could be organized into groups with similar physical and chemical properties. The periodic table shows elements arranged according to their atomic number and their properties. In the horizontal

rows, called periods, the elements are arranged in order of increasing atomic number. Elements with similar properties are lined up in vertical columns called groups or families. For convenience, two subgroups are shown below the main part of the table.

Because the properties of elements vary in a regular pattern, you can tell a lot about an element by where it appears in the periodic table. For example, all the elements on the left side and in the center of the table are metals. All the elements on the right side are nonmetals. A heavy zigzag line separates the metals and nonmetals.

A Periodic Table of the Elements

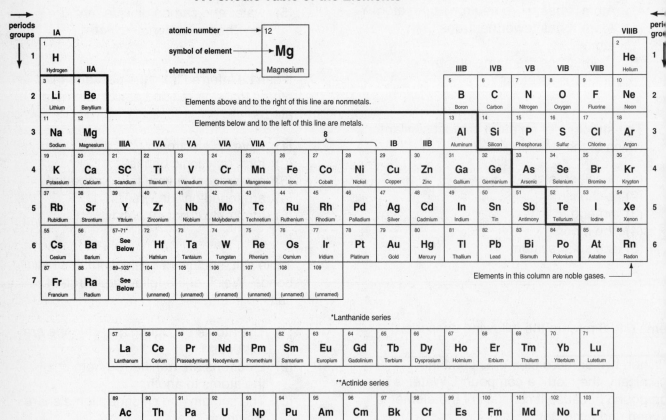

1. According to the passage, the periodic table is based on a relationship between which two factors?

   (1) atomic number and atomic size
   (2) atomic number and number of electrons
   (3) atomic number and properties
   (4) number of electrons and properties
   (5) atomic size and properties

2. According to the periodic table, which of the following groups of elements have similar properties?

   (1) sodium (Na), chlorine (Cl), hydrogen (H)
   (2) neon (Ne), argon (Ar), krypton (Kr)
   (3) lithium (Li), magnesium (Mg), sulfur (S)
   (4) oxygen (O), carbon (C), chlorine (Cl)
   (5) phosphorus (P), sulfur (S), chlorine (Cl)

3. According to the periodic table, which of the following elements would have the smallest atomic number?

   (1) zinc (Zn)
   (2) cobalt (Co)
   (3) potassium (K)
   (4) arsenic (As)
   (5) iron (Fe)

4. Which of the following statements is not supported by information in the passage?

   (1) The properties of elements vary in a regular pattern.
   (2) Elements may be classified as metals or nonmetals.
   (3) Where an element appears in the periodic table can tell you a lot about the element.
   (4) Elements in group VIB are nonmetals.
   (5) Tungsten (W) is a metal.

Items 5 to 7 refer to the following information.

Elements in the same group in the periodic table have many similar properties. Five groups of elements are described below.

- group I = very reactive metals; react violently with water
- group II = fairly reactive metals; often found in salts
- transition elements = metals, many of which can react with oxygen to form more than one compound
- group VII = very reactive nonmetals; combine with hydrogen to form acids
- group VIII = inert gases that rarely take part in chemical reactions

Each of the following questions describes an element that belongs to one of the groups listed above. Classify each element into one of the groups. More than one element may belong to the same group.

5. Element X is a silvery-gray solid that can cause an explosion when it is dropped into water.

   (1) group I
   (2) group II
   (3) transition elements
   (4) group VII
   (5) group VIII

6. Element Y combines with sulfur and oxygen to form a compound known as Epsom salts.

   (1) group I
   (2) group II
   (3) transition elements
   (4) group VII
   (5) group VIII

7. Element Z is used in light bulbs. Its presence keeps the light bulb filament from burning out quickly by not reacting with the filament.

   (1) group I
   (2) group II
   (3) transition elements
   (4) group VII
   (5) group VIII

Answers are on page 299.

Lesson 14

Evaluation: Drawing Conclusions

When you draw a conclusion, you use details and facts to prove that a broad statement is logical.

In lesson 8, you learned how to tell the difference between a conclusion and a supporting statement. A conclusion is a logical generalization. Supporting statements are details, facts, measurements, or other kinds of information that help prove that the conclusion is true.

In science, conclusions must be drawn from observable, measurable facts. When you read about a science topic, be alert for the information the author provides to prove that an idea or conclusion is correct. The information may be in the form of words, diagrams, or mathematical equations.

Read this passage and see what conclusions can be drawn based on the information that is given.

Two or more elements may either be mixed mechanically or combined chemically. If they are mixed mechanically, the result is a **mixture.** In a mixture, each element keeps its own properties. The elements may be mixed in any amount, and they may be separated from the mixture by mechanical means. Examples of mixtures are seawater, air, and mayonnaise.

If the elements are combined chemically, the result is a **compound.** In a compound, the elements lose their identity and become another substance with different properties. The elements that form a compound are always combined in the same proportions. Water is a compound formed from the elements hydrogen and oxygen.

What conclusion can we draw from this information? Can we conclude, for example, that chicken vegetable soup is a mixture? We must see if the characteristics of a mixture apply to chicken vegetable soup. Does each ingredient keep its own properties? Yes, the carrots, peas, potatoes, beans, and broth remain themselves. Can the vegetables and the broth be separated by mechanical means? Yes, a strainer can be used to remove the solids from the broth. Using the information in this passage, we can reasonably conclude that chicken vegetable soup is a mixture.

Remember, when you are asked what conclusions can be drawn from the information you are given, pay close attention to the information that is actually there. A statement may be true, yet the information you are given may not be enough to prove that it is true. Ask yourself:

1. Does this statement make sense? Is it logical and accurate?
2. If the answer is yes, then ask: What information presented here proves that this statement is true?

If there is not enough information to support a conclusion, then either the conclusion is inaccurate or there is not enough data.

 When determining whether or not a conclusion is supported by a diagram, think of the diagram as a source of facts that can be put into words. Note these facts, and then ask yourself if these facts help prove that the conclusion is true.

 Drawing Conclusions

Items 1 and 2 refer to the following passage and diagram. Choose the best answer to each item.

A chemical equation uses formulas and symbols to show what happens during a chemical reaction. In chemical reactions, the substances you start out with are called the reactants. The substances that are formed are called the products. The general form of a chemical equation is:

reactants → products

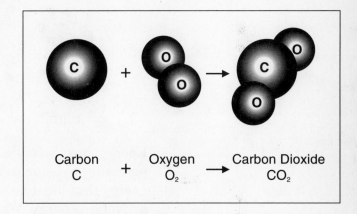

Carbon + Oxygen → Carbon Dioxide
C + O_2 → CO_2

1. Which of the following is a conclusion supported by the passage?

(1) Chemical reactions involve substances changing into other substances.
(2) Chemical reactions involve products changing into reactants.
(3) Chemical reactions involve more products than reactants.
(4) Products and reactants are always in the same state.
(5) Products can decompose to form the original reactants.

2. Which of the following conclusions about the chemical equation shown above can be supported by the information provided?

(1) C is a product of the chemical reaction.
(2) CO_2 is present in the atmosphere.
(3) CO_2 is formed when coal burns.
(4) CO_2 is a product of the chemical reaction.
(5) CO_2 is a reactant of the chemical reaction.

Answers are on page 300.

Chemical Reactions

In a chemical reaction, one or more substances change, forming one or more new substances. In some chemical reactions, molecules split apart into atoms. In other reactions, atoms join together to form molecules. In yet other reactions, atoms change places with other atoms to form new molecules.

Chemical reactions either release or absorb thermal energy. A chemical reaction that releases thermal energy is called an <u>exothermic reaction</u>. For example, when wood or oil is burned, large amounts of thermal energy are released. A chemical reaction that absorbs thermal energy is called an <u>endothermic reaction</u>. Cooking an egg is an endothermic reaction, because the egg absorbs heat energy as it changes.

EXOTHERMIC REACTION   **ENDOTHERMIC REACTION**

burning wood   cooking an egg

Energy must be added to start many reactions. The energy is necessary to begin to break the bonds in the reactant molecules. The energy that must be added to start a chemical reaction is called the <u>activation energy</u>. When you light a match to start a charcoal grill, you are supplying activation energy.

 Practice   Chemical Reactions

Items 1 to 9 refer to the previous passage. Choose the <u>best answer</u> to each item.

1. What is activation energy?

   (1) energy absorbed by a reaction
   (2) energy released by a reaction
   (3) electricity
   (4) energy needed to start a reaction
   (5) energy needed to stop a reaction

2. Which of the following is an example of an exothermic reaction?

   (1) condensing water vapor
   (2) cooking a custard
   (3) melting ice
   (4) exploding dynamite
   (5) boiling water

3. Which of the following conclusions can be supported by the information provided?

   (1) Exothermic reactions can be more useful for the energy they release than for their products.
   (2) Electricity is produced in endothermic reactions.
   (3) New chemical bonds are formed only during exothermic reactions.
   (4) Boiling water is an endothermic reaction.
   (5) Activation energy is not needed for chemical reactions.

4. Which of the following statements supports the conclusion that rusting is an exothermic reaction?

   (1) During the process of rusting, small amounts of thermal energy are released.
   (2) Activation energy produces rust.
   (3) Rusting affects only certain substances.
   (4) During rusting, metal absorbs thermal energy.
   (5) Rusting occurs in humid conditions.

5. Which of the following best describes what happens when hydrogen and oxygen combine to form water?

   (1) Molecules are breaking apart to form atoms.
   (2) Atoms are combining to form molecules.
   (3) Atoms are changing into other atoms.
   (4) Hydrogen and oxygen are undergoing a change of state.
   (5) Oxygen is a product of the reaction.

6. In the chemical reaction of photosynthesis, plants take in water and carbon dioxide and produce sugar, oxygen, and water in the presence of sunlight. What role does sunlight play in this reaction?

   (1) It is a reactant.
   (2) It is a product.
   (3) It is activation energy.
   (4) It slows the reaction.
   (5) It stops the reaction.

7. What is a chemical reaction?

   (1) a change in the state of matter
   (2) the wearing away of a substance
   (3) the change of one or more substances into a new substance with different properties
   (4) a change in the number of molecules
   (5) a change in the size of a substance

8. What is an endothermic reaction?

   (1) a reaction in which thermal energy is released
   (2) a reaction in which thermal energy is absorbed
   (3) a reaction in which energy is neither released nor absorbed
   (4) a reaction that requires activation energy to start
   (5) a reaction that changes chemical bonds

9. Which of the following is an example of a chemical reaction?

   (1) Mud hardens on a river bank.
   (2) Hydrogen combines with oxygen to form water.
   (3) Ice melts to form liquid water.
   (4) Water evaporates to form water vapor.
   (5) Rocks are ground to make gravel.

Answers are on page 300.

Items 1 to 3 refer to the following passage. Choose the best answer to each item.

A solution is a mixture in which two or more substances are dissolved in one another. Solutions can involve solids, liquids, or gases. The substance being dissolved is called the solute. The substance doing the dissolving is called the solvent. In a sugar-water solution, sugar is the solute and water is the solvent. In carbonated water, carbon dioxide is a gas solute dissolved in water, a liquid solvent.

The greatest amount of a solute that will dissolve in a given amount of solvent at a certain temperature is called solubility. Usually, solubility increases with temperature. For gases dissolved in a liquid, however, the reverse is true— solubility increases as the temperature of the solvent decreases. The rate of solution is also affected by temperature. An increase in temperature causes molecules to move and spread apart more quickly.

1. A glass of carbonated beverage left in a warm room goes flat, while a glass of the same beverage stored in the refrigerator does not. According to the information provided, which of the following statements could explain why this happens?

    (1) Water molecules evaporate more rapidly at high temperatures.
    (2) The solubility of a gas in liquid decreases as temperature increases.
    (3) Molecules move more slowly at low temperatures.
    (4) The solubility of a gas in liquid decreases as temperature decreases.
    (5) The rate of solution is slower at low temperatures than at high temperatures.

2. If two identical mixtures of salt and water are prepared and only one is stirred, the one that is stirred dissolves the salt faster. Which of the following conclusions can be supported by the information provided?

    (1) Stirring decreases the temperature of the water.
    (2) Stirring increases solubility.
    (3) Stirring increases the amount of solute
    (4) Stirring increases the amount of solvent.
    (5) Stirring causes molecules to move and spread apart more quickly.

3. Fish get the oxygen they need from oxygen gas dissolved in water. In this case, oxygen is

    (1) a solution
    (2) the solvent
    (3) a liquid
    (4) the solute
    (5) dissolved in a gas

tip   **When reading a passage, pay careful attention to the definitions it contains. For example, the definitions of solution, solvent, and solute in this passage can help you answer item 3.**

Items 4 to 8 refer to the following passage.

Three important groups of chemical compounds are acids, bases, and salts. When dissolved in water, these compounds produce ions. Ions are atoms or molecules with an electric charge. In water, acids produce hydrogen, or H^+ ions. In water, bases produce hydroxide, or OH^- ions. Citric acid is found in citrus fruits. Magnesium hydroxide is the base that is the active ingredient in many stomach remedies.

A strong acid, such as sulfuric acid, or a strong base, such as sodium hydroxide, is poisonous and can burn the skin. Yet a weak acid, such as citric acid, or a weak base, such as magnesium hydroxide, can be safely handled. The strength of an acid or base is measured on a scale called the pH scale. The pH scale ranges from 0 to 14. The number 7 is the neutral point. Substances with a pH below 7 are acidic, and substances with a pH above 7 are basic. The strongest acid would have a pH of 0, and the strongest base would have a pH of 14.

When an acid and a base combine chemically, the result is a neutral compound called a salt. Water is also a product of this reaction. A familiar salt is sodium chloride, table salt.

pH SCALE

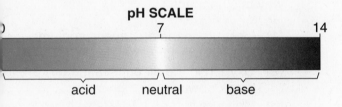

4. Which of the following statements would indicate the substance X is <u>not</u> classified as an acid?

(1) It combines chemically with certain other compounds to produce salts.
(2) It dissolves in water to produce OH^- ions.
(3) It can be poisonous if swallowed.
(4) Its pH is lower than that of water.
(5) It can be corrosive to skin.

5. An antacid relieves indigestion by neutralizing excess acid in the stomach. Based on this information, which of the following statements is true about an antacid?

(1) It contains salt.
(2) It has a low pH.
(3) It contains a base.
(4) It produces H^+ ions.
(5) It dissolves very rapidly.

6. Which of the following represents a correct ordering of substances from lowest to highest pH?

(1) magnesium hydroxide, pure water, sulfuric acid, sodium hydroxide
(2) pure water, sulfuric acid, citric acid, sodium hydroxide
(3) sulfuric acid, sodium hydroxide, citric acid, magnesium hydroxide
(4) sulfuric acid, citric acid, pure water, sodium hydroxide
(5) sodium hydroxide, pure water, citric acid, sulfuric acid

7. It can be inferred from the passage that a solution of table salt and water would have a pH of approximately

(1) 0
(2) 4
(3) 7
(4) 10
(5) 14

8. When calcium hydroxide, a base, reacts with citric acid, the reaction produces calcium citrate and water. Calcium citrate is

(1) an acid
(2) a base
(3) a compound with a pH of 6
(4) a compound with a pH of 3
(5) a salt

Answers are on page 301.

Directions: Choose the <u>best answer</u> to each item.

<u>Items 1 to 5</u> refer to the following passage.

You may not think of the kitchen as being a chemistry lab, but many chemicals can be found right on your kitchen shelf. One substance that contains several interesting chemicals is baking powder, which is used to make cake batter rise.

The principal ingredient in baking powder is sodium bicarbonate, $NaHCO_3$. When sodium bicarbonate reacts with an acid, it produces the gas carbon dioxide (CO_2) and water. When sodium bicarbonate is heated strongly, it breaks down to form carbon dioxide and sodium carbonate (Na_2CO_3). Baking powder also contains a substance that will react with water to form acids. This substance is usually a type of compound called a tartrate.

1. It can be inferred from the passage that the purpose of the tartrate in baking powder is to

   (1) provide an acid for sodium bicarbonate to react with
   (2) break down to form carbon dioxide
   (3) react with carbon dioxide
   (4) provide a salt that will make dough rise
   (5) react with water to form sodium bicarbonate

2. Sodium bicarbonate reacts with vinegar to produce carbon dioxide and water. Which of the following must be true about vinegar?

   (1) It contains sodium carbonate.
   (2) It makes bread dough rise.
   (3) It decomposes when heated.
   (4) It contains an acid.
   (5) It contains a salt.

3. The best title for the passage would be

   (1) The Chemical Formula of Baking Powder
   (2) The Chemistry of Baking Powder
   (3) What Chemicals Are in the Kitchen?
   (4) Acids in the Kitchen
   (5) Sodium Carbonate

4. When baking powder is added to cake batter, the substance that actually makes the cake rise is

   (1) salt
   (2) oxygen
   (3) water
   (4) tartrate
   (5) carbon dioxide

5. When baking powder is left uncovered in damp or humid weather, it quickly loses its effectiveness. Based on the passage, which of the following statements could explain why this happens?

   (1) Moisture in the air causes sodium bicarbonate to break down.
   (2) Oxygen in the air causes the tartrate to break down.
   (3) Moisture in the air reacts with the tartrate.
   (4) Oxygen in the air reacts with carbon dioxide.
   (5) Oxygen in the air reacts with sodium bicarbonate.

▶**tip**

When looking for an explanation of an observation, review the facts you know about the topic. Ask yourself how the facts could explain what has been observed.

Items 6 to 9 refer to the following information.

Iron (Fe) is one of the most plentiful elements on Earth, but it usually occurs combined with other elements in rock called ores. The major ore of iron is hematite (Fe_2O_3). Iron is separated from hematite in a blast furnace. Coke is burned with air, producing carbon dioxide. The carbon dioxide reacts with more coke to form carbon monoxide. Carbon monoxide removes the oxygen from the hematite, leaving the iron. The steps in the process are shown in the flow chart.

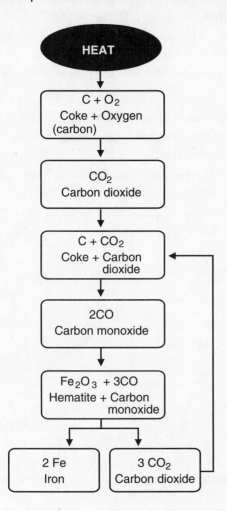

6. What substance must continually be added to the blast furnace to keep the process of separating iron going?

   (1) coke
   (2) carbon dioxide
   (3) carbon monoxide
   (4) pure iron
   (5) pure oxygen

7. According to the diagram, what substances react to form carbon monoxide?

   (1) coke and oxygen
   (2) hematite and coke
   (3) hematite and oxygen
   (4) carbon dioxide and iron
   (5) coke and carbon dioxide

8. Which of the following is a chemical reaction that occurs during the process of separating iron?

   (1) Carbon monoxide reacts with hematite.
   (2) Coke reacts with hematite.
   (3) Carbon dioxide reacts with hematite.
   (4) Carbon dioxide reacts with iron.
   (5) Carbon monoxide reacts with iron.

9. In the production of carbon dioxide described in the passage, air

   (1) provides the coke that reacts with oxygen
   (2) is a solute
   (3) is not present
   (4) reacts with Fe_2O_3
   (5) provides the oxygen that reacts with coke

Answers are on page 301.

Comprehension: Restating Information

When you restate information, you say or write that information in another way. In science, information is often restated using different words or using symbols, formulas, diagrams, and tables.

As an example, let's look at the gas methane. Methane is the main component of natural gas. You may use natural gas to heat your home or to fuel your gas stove and water heater. Besides using the word methane, you could represent this gas using the **chemical formula** CH_4. The symbols (letters) in this formula tell you what elements make up a molecule of methane. The numbers tell you how many atoms of each element there are in a molecule of methane. The formula CH_4 could be restated as "one atom of carbon (C) and four atoms of hydrogen (H)."

Another way of representing methane is as a **structural formula.** Structural formulas show the arrangement of atoms in a molecule. They do this by using lines to represent bonds that hold the atoms together. Like a chemical formula, a structural formula uses symbols to represent the elements that are present. The same symbol is repeated to show that more than one atom of that element is present. The structural formula for methane is shown below on the left.

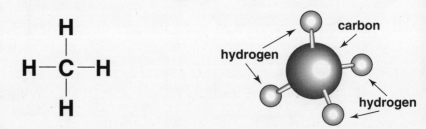

Sometimes concepts are easier to understand when they are restated as pictures in a diagram. One such way of representing methane is shown in the diagram above on the right. Here the atoms are represented as balls and the bonds that hold them together are represented as sticks.

Notice that in each way methane is represented, the facts about how many and what kinds of atoms a molecule contains remain the same. A molecule of methane always contains one atom of carbon and four atoms of hydrogen. Only the way these facts are presented (either as a chemical formula, a structural formula, or a diagram) is different.

 To identify restated information, look for key phrases that the writer has used. The phrases *in other words* and *that is* often signal that information is about to be restated.

 Restating Information

ems 1 and 2 refer to the following diagrams. Choose the best answer to each item.

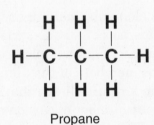

Propane

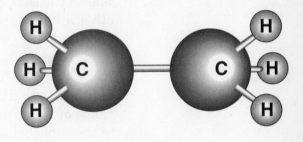

Ethane

1. Which of the following statements about a molecule of propane is supported by the diagram above?

   (1) It contains nitrogen atoms.
   (2) It is made of three atoms of carbon and three atoms of hydrogen.
   (3) It is made of three atoms of carbon and eight atoms of oxygen.
   (4) It can be represented by the formula C_3H_8.
   (5) It contains more carbon atoms than hydrogen atoms.

2. Which of the following statements about a molecule of ethane is supported by the two diagrams?

   (1) Ethane has more carbon atoms than propane.
   (2) Ethane has more hydrogen atoms than propane.
   (3) Ethane can be represented by the formula C_6H_2.
   (4) Ethane contains equal numbers of carbon and hydrogen atoms.
   (5) Ethane has fewer hydrogen atoms than propane.

 When using a diagram to answer a question, mentally restate in your own words the main idea and supporting details of the diagram before answering the question.

Answers are on page 302.

Hydrocarbons

Do you know what you have in common with trees, birds, and all living things? All living things contain carbon. Compounds that contain carbon are called <u>organic compounds</u>. A special kind of organic compound that contains only the two elements hydrogen and carbon is called a <u>hydrocarbon</u>. There are thousands of different kinds of hydrocarbons. Scientists classify these hydrocarbons into smaller subgroups called <u>series</u>.

The members of the alkane series are the most abundant of the hydrocarbons. You're probably already familiar with a number of these compounds. If you've ever been camping, you may have used propane or butane. These two gases are often sold in canisters for use in heating, camping stoves, lanterns, and lighters. The gasoline that fuels a car contains pentane, hexane, heptane, and octane. These and other alkanes are listed in the table below.

Since hydrocarbons consist of just two elements, you might think that there would be little variety in the properties of alkane series hydrocarbons. However, this is not the case. For example, look at the range of states and boiling points of the members of the alkane series in the table below. You can see from the formulas listed that each member of the series contains a different number of carbon and hydrogen atoms in its molecules. This difference in composition causes each compound to have different properties. Some members of the series are made up of molecules with more than 1,000 carbon atoms!

THE ALKANE SERIES			
Name	Formula	Physical State at Room Temperature	Boiling Point (°C)
Methane	CH_4	gas	−162
Ethane	C_2H_6	gas	−89
Propane	C_3H_8	gas	−42
Butane	C_4H_{10}	gas	−1
Pentane	C_5H_{12}	liquid	36
Hexane	C_6H_{14}	liquid	69
Heptane	C_7H_{16}	liquid	98
Octane	C_8H_{18}	liquid	126
Nonane	C_9H_{20}	liquid	151
Decane	$C_{10}H_{22}$	liquid	174
Eicosane	$C_{20}H_{42}$	solid	344

Charts often compare variable data for different items entered in the chart. Read across the tops of columns to see what is being compared. Read down the column on the left to see what items are being compared.

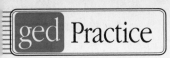

Items 1 to 8 refer to the previous information. Choose the best answer to each item.

1. Which of the following compounds is not an organic compound?

   (1) CO_2
   (2) C_2H_6
   (3) C_2H_4O
   (4) C_3H_8
   (5) H_2S

2. Which of the following compounds is not a hydrocarbon?

   (1) C_6H_{14}
   (2) CH_4
   (3) CO_2
   (4) C_2H_2
   (5) C_6H_6

3. Which of the following statements is true of members of the alkane series?

   (1) They are living things.
   (2) They are both organic compounds and hydrocarbons.
   (3) They are all liquids at room temperature.
   (4) They contain the same number of carbon atoms.
   (5) They are made up of helium atoms.

4. Which of the following conclusions can you draw from the data in the table?

   (1) Heptane boils at a lower temperature then hexane.
   (2) Butane boils at a higher temperature than ethane.
   (3) Butane melts at a lower temperature than ethane.
   (4) Eicosane contains the fewest carbon atoms.
   (5) Pentane contains fewer carbon and hydrogen atoms than butane.

5. Which of the following is true of propane?

   (1) It is sold in canisters for use in heating.
   (2) It has the formula C_2H_8.
   (3) Its molecules contain more hydrogen atoms than butane molecules contain.
   (4) It is found in the gasoline that fuels cars.
   (5) Its boiling point is 36°C.

6. If you open the valve on the fuel tank of a gas barbecue grill, the fuel that escapes is in the gaseous state. The fuel is probably

   (1) C_3H_8
   (2) octane
   (3) nonane
   (4) decane
   (5) $C_{20}H_{42}$

7. Which of the following is true of hexane?

   (1) It is a liquid at room temperature.
   (2) It has the formula $C_4H_{10.}$
   (3) Its boiling point is −162°C.
   (4) It has the formula $C_2H_{6.}$
   (5) It has more carbon atoms than hydrogen atoms.

8. Which of the following is not true of octane?

   (1) It has a boiling point of 126°C.
   (2) It is found in gasoline used for cars.
   (3) It is a gas at room temperature.
   (4) It has a higher boiling point than pentane.
   (5) Its molecules contain more carbon atoms than those of hexane.

Answers are on page 302.

Items 1 to 4 refer to the following passage. Choose the <u>best answer</u> to each item.

Although they may sound similar, alkanes and alkenes are very different hydrocarbon series. Like alkanes, members of the alkene series contain only hydrogen and carbon. However, unlike alkanes, alkenes contain double bonds in their molecules.

In alkanes, all bonds are single covalent bonds, in which one pair of electrons is shared. One bond in every alkene molecule is a double covalent bond, in which two pairs of electrons are shared.

MEMBERS OF THE ALKENE SERIES
Structural Formulas

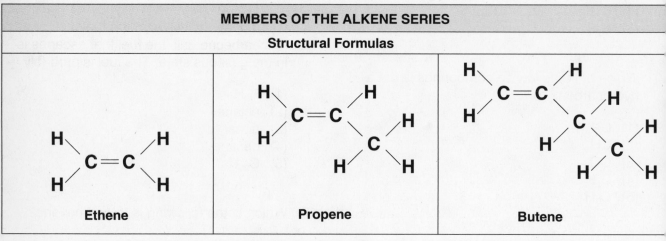

| Ethene | Propene | Butene |

= represents a double bond; − represents a single bond

1. Which of the following statements is true of both alkanes and alkenes?

   (1) They contain only single bonds.
   (2) They are not compounds.
   (3) They contain hydrogen and calcium.
   (4) They are hydrocarbons.
   (5) They contain ionic bonds.

2. Which of the following statements can be inferred from the information provided?

   (1) All alkenes contain the same number of carbon atoms.
   (2) Alkenes contain more hydrogen atoms than alkanes do.
   (3) Alkanes and alkenes contain different numbers of carbon atoms.
   (4) All alkenes contain an odd number of hydrogen atoms.
   (5) Double bonds occur only between the carbon atoms in alkenes.

3. Based on the information given, which of the following is the correct chemical formula of butene?

   (1) CH_4
   (2) C_4H_8
   (3) H_8
   (4) C_{12}
   (5) C_2H_4

4. The chemical formula of the alkane propane is C_3H_8. Based on the information in the table, it can be concluded that propane as compared to propene

   (1) has the same number of carbon and hydrogen atoms as propene
   (2) has more hydrogen atoms than propene
   (3) has more carbon atoms than propene
   (4) has fewer carbon atoms than propene
   (5) melts at a higher temperature than propene

A molecule that contains only single bonds, in which one pair of electrons is shared in each bond, is said to be saturated. In molecules that contain bonds other than single bonds, more than one pair of electrons are shared in each bond. Such molecules are said to be unsaturated. A saturated hydrocarbon contains more hydrogen than an unsaturated hydrocarbon with the same number of carbon atoms.

One example of a saturated hydrocarbon is ethane, C_2H_6. An example of an unsaturated molecule is ethene, C_2H_4. In this unsaturated hydrocarbon, two electrons of one carbon atom are paired with two electrons of another carbon atom to form a double bond.

In certain reactions, the double and triple bonds of an unsaturated hydrocarbon can be broken. Hydrogen can then be added to the molecule. A reaction in which hydrogen is added to an unsaturated hydrocarbon is called an addition reaction.

Unsaturated Hydrocarbon (Alkene)   +   Hydrogen   ➤   Saturated Hydrocarbon (Alkane)

5. Unlike a saturated molecule, an unsaturated molecule contains

(1) hydrogen atoms
(2) only single bonds
(3) shared electrons
(4) bonds other than single bonds
(5) a reduction reaction

6. Which of the following conclusions is supported by the information presented?

(1) Saturated hydrocarbons can be produced from unsaturated hydrocarbons through addition reactions.
(2) Unsaturated hydrocarbons can be produced from saturated hydrocarbons through addition reactions.
(3) In addition reactions, the number of carbon atoms present increases.
(4) Alkenes cannot be made from alkanes.
(5) Under certain conditions, hydrocarbons react with chlorine.

7. Which of the following statements is true of the addition reaction shown?

(1) The product is C_2H_6.
(2) The reactants are H_2 and C_2H_6.
(3) The product contains a double bond.
(4) One reactant is a saturated hydrocarbon.
(5) Both reactants are unsaturated hydrocarbons.

8. Which of the following is a fact presented about ethene?

(1) It is a saturated molecule.
(2) Single bonding occurs between its carbon atoms.
(3) Double bonding occurs between its carbon atoms.
(4) Its atoms contain only two electrons.
(5) It reacts to form an unsaturated molecule.

Answers are on page 303.

Directions: Choose the best answer to each item.

Items 1 to 4 refer to the following passage.

Alcohols form a large group of organic compounds. An alcohol is formed when one or more hydrogen atoms in a hydrocarbon are replaced by OH radicals. Radicals are groups of atoms that stay united during a chemical reaction, thus behaving like a single atom. The OH radical consists of an oxygen atom and a hydrogen atom bonded together.

The chemical formula of ethyl alcohol is C_2H_5OH. Ethyl alcohol is also called grain alcohol because it is most often made by fermenting grain or fruit juices. To produce ethyl alcohol, sugar is broken down by yeast, as in the following equation:

$$C_6H_{12}O_6 \rightarrow 2C_2H_5OH + 2CO_2$$

sugar   ethyl alcohol   carbon dioxide gas

1. Ethyl alcohol forms when

    (1) carbon dioxide breaks down
    (2) sugar ferments
    (3) an alcohol takes on an OH radical
    (4) grain alcohol ferments
    (5) sugar loses an OH radical

2. Which of the following statements can be inferred from the information presented?

    (1) Grain and fruit juices contain sugar.
    (2) During chemical reactions, most OH radicals break down to form oxygen and hydrogen atoms.
    (3) Fermentation is the process by which alcohols break down.
    (4) All hydrocarbons are alcohols.
    (5) Ethane contains sugar.

3. Butanol has the chemical formula C_4H_9OH. Which of the following factors alone suggests that butanol is an alcohol?

    (1) It contains four carbon atoms.
    (2) It contains hydrogen.
    (3) It contains an OH radical and the elements found in hydrocarbons.
    (4) It contains a radical.
    (5) It has the same chemical formula as the ethyl alcohol.

4. When bread dough is made, yeast, sugar, and flour are mixed and fermentation occurs. The most likely reason that the dough rises is that

    (1) yeast expands
    (2) ethyl alcohol forms as a liquid and enlarges the dough
    (3) fruit juice is added to the dough
    (4) OH radicals are present
    (5) carbon dioxide gas is given off, creating holes in the dough

Two compounds whose molecules have the ame number and kind of atoms but different rrangements of atoms are called isomers. Compare the isomers of butane shown. Although hese isomers have the same chemical formula, hey are different compounds with different roperties. For example, the straight-chain utane has a higher boiling point than the ranched-chain butane. The more carbon atoms ontained in a hydrocarbon molecule, the more somers that molecule can form.

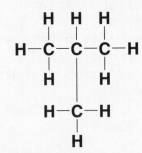

Straight Chain Butane,
C_4H_{10}

Branched Chain Butane,
C_4H_{10}

5. Which of the following is true of isomers?

   (1) They contain different numbers of atoms.
   (2) They contain different kinds of atoms.
   (3) They cannot be hydrocarbons.
   (4) They have the same properties.
   (5) They have different arrangements of atoms.

6. In the structural formula for the branched-chain isomer of butane,

   (1) all the hydrogen atoms are bonded along a straight line
   (2) all the carbon atoms are bonded along a straight line
   (3) one carbon atom branches off from the middle carbon atom
   (4) none of the carbon atoms are bonded along a straight line
   (5) the hydrogen atoms are connected to other hydrogen atoms

7. Pentane (C_5H_{12}), a member of the alkane series of hydrocarbons, has three isomers. Another member of this series, decane ($C_{10}H_{22}$), is likely to have

   (1) no isomers
   (2) a lower boiling point
   (3) more isomers
   (4) the same number of isomers
   (5) fewer isomers

8. Gasoline containing straight-chain hydrocarbons burns more quickly than gasoline containing branched-chain hydrocarbons because oxygen more easily reaches the parts of a straight-chain molecule. This, in turn, is most likely the result of

   (1) the straight-chain molecule's less compact arrangement of atoms
   (2) the branched-chain molecule's higher oxygen content
   (3) the branched-chain molecule's chemical formula
   (4) the branched-chain molecule's higher boiling point
   (5) the straight-chain molecule's higher carbon and hydrogen content

> **tip** **When information is restated in a graph or an illustration, use the graph or illustration to help you understand the information in the passage.**

Answers are on page 304.

Directions: Choose the <u>best answer</u> for each item.

<u>Items 1 to 6</u> refer to the following passage.

All atoms and molecules are constantly in motion. The motion depends upon whether the molecules are in a solid, liquid, or gas.

Molecules in a solid move the least. They only vibrate. Forces of attraction hold the molecules of a solid very tightly in place, which is why solids have both definite volume and definite shape.

The molecules in a liquid move more freely and have more energy than the molecules of a solid. Forces of attraction among liquid molecules hold them together. That is why, when you pour a liquid, it stays together.

Molecules of a gas move freely and randomly. There are almost no forces of attraction among gas molecules. A gas will escape from an open container and "disappear."

1. In a carbonated beverage you can see bubbles of gas rising to the surface. What causes these bubbles?

   (1) vibrations of gas molecules
   (2) collisions between liquid and gas molecules
   (3) gas molecules moving rapidly through less freely-moving liquid molecules
   (4) force of attraction between liquid and gas molecules
   (5) liquid molecules pushing against less freely-moving gas molecules

2. If a tank of oxygen gas began to leak, the molecules of oxygen in the tank would

   (1) move but remain in the tank
   (2) leave the tank, but stay together
   (3) not move
   (4) escape and spread apart
   (5) stop vibrating

3. Which of the following conclusions can be supported by the passage?

   (1) Large molecules move faster than small molecules.
   (2) Molecules in gases have less energy if the gas is in a small container.
   (3) You can feel the molecules vibrating when you hold a solid.
   (4) Molecules in liquids move faster than molecules in gases.
   (5) Molecules of a gas will spread out and fill any container they are in.

4. The passage discusses a relationship between which two factors?

   (1) states of matter and movement of molecules
   (2) temperature and energy of molecules
   (3) states of matter and sizes of molecules
   (4) sizes of molecules and movement of molecules
   (5) temperature and attractions between molecules

5. A block of ice is heated, and it changes into a liquid. This shows that as temperature increases,

   (1) movement of molecules decreases
   (2) movement of molecules increases
   (3) movement of molecules becomes less random
   (4) molecules collide less often
   (5) changes of state take place more slowly

6. Rocks have a definite shape because

   (1) the molecules in a solid repel each other
   (2) the molecules in gases move about freely
   (3) their molecules vibrate
   (4) forces of attraction among liquid molecules are strong
   (5) molecules in solids are held together by forces of attraction

If the numbers of protons and neutrons in the nucleus of an atom are ery different, the atom may be radioactive. A radioactive atom decays nd gives off particles until the nucleus is stable. The time needed for half he nuclei in a sample of radioactive material to decay is called its half-life. he half-life of carbon-14, for example, is 5,730 years. This means that fter 5,730 years, half the carbon-14 in a given sample will have decayed nto another substance.

HALF-LIFE OF CARBON 14

1 gram carbon-14	1/2 gram carbon-14	1/4 gram carbon-14	1/8 gram carbon-14
0 years	5,730 years	11,460 years	17,190 years

7. Using information about the half-life of radioactive substances would be of most interest to which scientist?

(1) a metallurgist looking for ways to remove metals from ores
(2) a geologist interested in estimating the age of rock samples
(3) a chemist developing new products from organic compounds
(4) an oceanographer studying wave motion
(5) a biochemist studying photosynthesis

8. Which of the following conclusions can be supported by the information provided?

(1) After 22,920 years, none of the carbon-14 will remain.
(2) After 22,920 years, 1/8 gram of carbon-14 will remain of the original 1 gram.
(3) After 22,920 years, 1/16 gram of carbon-14 will remain of the original 1 gram.
(4) Radioactive elements can be made in the laboratory.
(5) The number of electrons affects the radioactivity of an atom.

9. From the information given, which of the following reasons can cause an element to be radioactive?

(1) too many protons
(2) too many neutrons
(3) the length of its half-life
(4) an unstable nucleus
(5) particles given off by the nucleus

tip Remember, always preview an illustration or diagram before reading the text it accompanies. Then refer back to it as frequently as necessary while you read.

Items 10 to 13 refer to the following information.

Stalactites and stalagmites are column-shaped rocks that form in caves. A chemical reaction is responsible for their formation. This reaction begins as water dissolves minerals in rocks. This reaction can be modeled by mixing a solution of calcium chloride in water with a solution of sodium carbonate in water. Upon mixing, the ions Ca^{2+}, Cl^-, Na^+, and CO_3^{2-} are all present in the water.

When mixed, the Ca^{2+} and CO_3^{2-} ions join together to form a powdery white substance called calcium carbonate. This substance, whose chemical formula is $CaCO_3$, is what makes up stalactites and stalagmites. Because it is not soluble in water, it settles out of the solution, or precipitates. The precipitation of calcium carbonate is shown in the equation below.

$$CaCl_2 + Na_2CO_3 \rightarrow CaCO_3 + 2NaCl$$

This equation is read as: calcium chloride plus sodium carbonate yields calcium carbonate plus sodium chloride.

10. Why does $CaCO_3$ precipitate in the reaction shown?

    (1) Calcium reacts with water.
    (2) The solubility of $CaCO_3$ decreases after heating.
    (3) Sodium carbonate is not soluble in water.
    (4) Calcium carbonate is soluble in water.
    (5) Calcium carbonate is not soluble in water.

11. Which of the following is an unstated assumption of the passage?

    (1) Calcium carbonate is not soluble in water.
    (2) Calcium carbonate in soluble in water.
    (3) Calcium carbonate reacts with hydrochloric acid.
    (4) Calcium chloride and sodium carbonate are soluble in water.
    (5) Calcium chloride and sodium carbonate react with hydrochloric acid.

12. In the reaction shown in the information, why does sodium chloride, NaCl, not form a precipitate?

    (1) Na^+ ions and Cl^- ions do not react.
    (2) Sodium chloride is soluble in water.
    (3) There are more Na^+ ions than Cl^- ions.
    (4) The Na^+ ions become part of the precipitate that forms.
    (5) Cl^- ions do not react with $CaCO_3$.

Item 13 refers to the following passage and diagrams.

A dot diagram is frequently used to show the arrangement of electrons in the outer energy level of a atom. Most outer energy levels are complete with eight electrons. Then the atom is stable and tends not to enter into chemical reactions easily.

A dot diagram can be used to understand how atoms combine. Atoms seek to become stable. They do this by sharing electrons, loosing electrons, or gaining electrons. A dot diagram can help you predict how an atom may react with another atom.

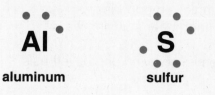

aluminum   sulfur   chlorine

neon   sodium

13. Which two atoms shown are likely to react most easily with each other?

    (1) Aluminum and sulfur
    (2) Aluminum and chlorine
    (3) Sulfur and chlorine
    (4) Sulfur and neon
    (5) Chlorine and sodium

Answers are on page 305.

Unit 3: Chemistry

Performance Analysis
Unit 3 Cumulative Review: Chemistry

Name: _____ **Class:** _____ **Date:** _____

Use the Answer Key on pages 305–306 to check your answers to the Unit 3 Cumulative Review: Chemistry. Then use the chart to figure out the skill areas in which you need additional review. Circle on the chart the numbers of the test items you answered correctly. Then go back and review the lessons for the skill areas that are difficult for you. For additional review, see the *Steck-Vaughn GED Science Exercise Book,* Unit 3: Chemistry.

Thinking Skill Area	Chemistry	Lessons for Review
Comprehension	4	1, 2, 4, 9, 15
Application	2, 6, **7**	10, 13
Analysis	1, 5, **9**, 10, 11, 12, **13**	3, 5, 6, 8, 11, 12
Evaluation	3, **8**	7, 14

Boldfaced numbers indicate items based on charts, graphs, illustrations, and diagrams.

Unit 4 PHYSICS

Physics includes the study of motion and drag.

Physics is the study of matter and energy. It is the branch of science that looks for answers to these questions: What is matter? What is energy? How are energy and matter related?

Matter makes up all the objects around us. All these objects have the potential to move, or be in **motion.** In lesson 16, you will examine motion and the terms used to describe it. One such term is **displacement.** You will learn that displacement is the distance over which an object moves and the direction in which it moves.

In lesson 16, you will also learn that objects move at different rates, or **speeds.** The speed at which an object travels is defined as how far it moves in a certain amount of time. When that object changes speed, direction, or both, it is said to accelerate.

In lesson 17 you will learn some scientific laws that describe the behavior of matter and energy. You will read about two sets of laws— Newton's laws of motion and the laws of thermodynamics.

You will learn how motion is described by Newton's first and second laws. You will discover that motion is changed by **forces.** You will also learn how machines can change the size and direction of a force to make work easier.

motion
a change in position relative to a fixed object

displacement
distance and direction traveled by an object

speed
distance traveled per unit of time

force
a push or pull acting on an object

Overview

Lesson 17 also describes the laws of **thermodynamics.** These laws explain the relationship between the energy of heat and the energy of motion. Because heat is a form of energy, it can be converted into other forms of energy. When heat is converted into the energy of motion, it is able to do work. You will discover how this takes place in the gasoline engine of an automobile.

In lesson 18 you will discover what scientists mean when they say "opposites attract," as you learn about electricity and magnetism. You will discover how electricity is related to the tiny, charged particles inside an atom. You will also find out how an **electric current** is produced and how an **electric circuit** makes the flow of current possible.

In lesson 18 you will also read about the discovery of the first magnet over 2,000 years ago. You will learn about the properties of magnets, and how an important relationship exists between electricity and magnetism.

In lesson 19 you will read about the properties of waves. A **wave** is a disturbance that transfers energy from one place to another. You will find out how a sound wave transfers energy by disturbing the molecules of the matter through which it travels. You will also learn about light waves, and how they are able to travel through space where there is no matter to carry the waves.

In lesson 19 you will also discover what happens to a light wave when it strikes a substance and bounces back, or when it passes from one material into another.

thermodynamics
the study of the relationship between heat energy and the energy of motion

electric current
the flow of electrons through a wire

electric circuit
a continuous, unbroken pathway over which electric current can flow

wave
a disturbance that travels through space or matter

SEE ALSO: Steck-Vaughn GED Science Exercise Book, Unit 4: Physics.

Lesson 16

Comprehension: Identifying the Main Idea

In science, as in all good writing, paragraphs have a definite structure. Understanding that structure can help you understand the information presented in any paragraph you read, including those about science.

Every paragraph has a main idea. The **main idea** is the general topic to which all the information in a paragraph relates. Sometimes it is explicitly stated in a single sentence, called the **topic sentence.** Sometimes the main idea is scattered through several sentences. The topic sentence may state a central proposition that the author intends to explain or discuss further. **Supporting details** explain this central proposition. They illustrate, restate, refine, and qualify the main idea with details, specific examples, facts, and figures.

Read the following paragraph to find the main idea and supporting details.

Each day you see birds fly, cars drive by, and people walk. You see objects in motion. **Motion,** also called relative motion, is a change in position relative to a fixed object. Fixed objects, or those that do not appear to move, are called **reference points.** For example, you know a bird is in motion because its position relative to a tree changes. You determine that the bird, or any object, is in motion by comparing its position to the position of a reference point, in this case a tree.

The third sentence in the paragraph is both the main idea and the topic sentence. It defines motion, which is the main topic of the entire paragraph. The other sentences are supporting details. They give further information about motion, including examples of objects in motion, a definition of reference points, and an explanation of how to tell if an object is in motion.

When trying to identify the main idea, pretend that you have to tell someone about what you have just read. Look for the most important point that you would tell someone and you'll find the main idea.

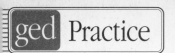
Items 1 to 4 refer to the following passage. Choose the best answer for each item.

The motion of an object doesn't look the same to everyone who sees it. How you view motion depends on your frame of reference, or your viewpoint. Think about a passenger on a train. At first, the train is standing still and the passenger is seated. To an observer standing outside the train, the passenger is not moving in relation to the train or to the train tracks. When the train begins its journey, the observer outside the train would say that the passenger is moving forward relative to the track. However, another observer sitting inside the train would say that the seated passenger is <u>not</u> moving relative to the train. This observer doesn't observe motion because the observer is moving along with the passenger and the train. The two observers have different frames of reference, so their observations of motion differ.

1. The main idea of the paragraph is

    (1) To an observer standing outside a train, a passenger is not moving in relation to the train or to the train tracks.
    (2) Frames of reference vary, depending on where you are.
    (3) How you view motion depends on your frame of reference.
    (4) Frames of reference include trains, tracks, and passengers.
    (5) Two different observers can have two different frames of reference.

2. The <u>best</u> title for this passage would be

    (1) How Reference Points and Frames of Reference Differ
    (2) Motion Depends on Your Frame of Reference
    (3) Motion
    (4) Motion on Trains
    (5) What Is a Frame of Reference?

3. Which of the following is a supporting detail of the paragraph?

    (1) Relative to the passenger, a person outside the train is moving.
    (2) Your frame of reference would include all the reference points you can see.
    (3) Your viewpoint does not affect how you observe motion.
    (4) Two observers have different frames of reference, so their observations of motion differ.
    (5) An observer sitting inside a train next to a passenger would say that the seated passenger is moving relative to the train.

4. You are in a car stopped at a red light. Suddenly you think you are rolling into the intersection but quickly realize that the car next to you has rolled backward. Which of the following <u>best</u> explains why you thought you were moving?

    (1) You can only see the other car out of the corner of your eye.
    (2) Your frame of reference is the other car which you believe to be motionless; therefore, you must be moving.
    (3) The traffic light appears to be getting closer.
    (4) Your frame of reference is momentarily confused.
    (5) Because the other car moved, you can now see the sidewalk next to you.

▶ tip

Remember, frame of reference is the same as viewpoint. What you think or observe depends on *how* you look at something.

Moving Objects

To describe the motion of an object, two of the things you might discuss are how far the object moved and where it moved. When someone asks you how far you've traveled or how much farther you have to go, they are asking about distance. Distance is the length of the path from one point to another. If, for example, you run home, the length of the path you run on is the distance you have traveled.

The dashed lines in the diagram below show the distances two people walked. The woman walked a distance of 10 meters from point A to point B. In other words, the length of the path she took was 10 meters long. The man also walked a total distance of 10 meters. Notice, however, that he took a path that started at point A but ended at point C. Although he traveled the same distance, where he traveled is different. Displacement is a measure of both the distance and the direction traveled. Displacement can be shown as an arrow between a starting point and an ending point. The solid arrows in the diagram show displacement. Any object that moves, but ends up at the same point it started from, has no displacement.

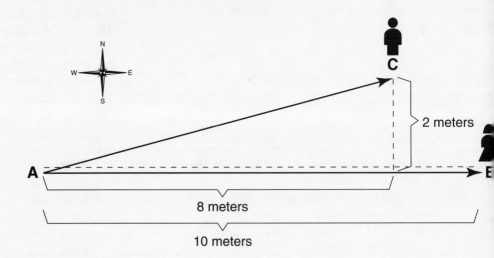

 **Practice** Moving Objects

Items 1 to 6 refer to the previous passage. Choose the best answer to each item.

1. The displacement of the woman in the diagram is

    (1) 10 meters
    (2) 20 meters
    (3) 10 meters east
    (4) the same as that of the man
    (5) 10 meters south

2. The distance traveled by the man in the diagram is

    (1) 10 meters
    (2) 20 meters
    (3) about 8 1/4 meters northeast
    (4) greater than the distance traveled by the woman
    (5) the same as his displacement

3. The distance an object travels differs from its displacement in that

   (1) only distance includes the length of the path traveled
   (2) only distance includes the direction traveled
   (3) only displacement includes the length of the path traveled
   (4) only displacement includes the direction traveled
   (5) displacement is always greater

4. Which of the following are supporting details of the second paragraph?

   A. The woman walked a distance of 10 meters.
   B. The man and the woman traveled the same distance, but they ended up in different places.
   C. Displacement is not the same as distance.

   (1) A only
   (2) A and B
   (3) B and C
   (4) A and C
   (5) A, B, and C

5. Which of the following statements is the main idea of the second paragraph?

   (1) Displacement indicates both the direction and how far an object traveled.
   (2) Distance indicates both the direction and how far an object traveled.
   (3) The dashed lines in the diagram show the distances two people walked.
   (4) Displacement can be shown as an arrow between a starting point and an ending point.
   (5) Displacement can be measured in meters

6. If a man starts at his back door, walks in circle around his back yard, and ends up at his back door, then

   (1) his distance traveled is zero
   (2) his displacement is zero
   (3) his distance traveled and displacement are both zero
   (4) his displacement is the length of his circular path
   (5) his displacement is greater than his distance

Items 7 and 8 refer to the following paragraph and diagram.

A person walks 30 meters east, then 5 meters north, then 20 meters west, and then 5 meters south.

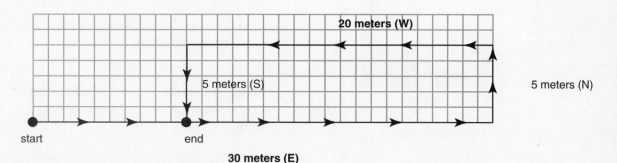

7. What is the person's displacement?

   (1) 5 meters north
   (2) 10 meters east
   (3) 15 meters north
   (4) 50 meters east
   (5) 60 meters east

8. What is the distance the person traveled?

   (1) 5 meters
   (2) 10 meters
   (3) 15 meters
   (4) 50 meters
   (5) 60 meters

Answers are on page 306.

Items 1 to 5 refer to the following passage.
Choose the <u>best answer</u> to each item.

One way to describe an object's motion is with a graph. The top graph shows the distance a car travels over the amount of time it takes the car to travel. The bottom graph shows the same car's speed over time. Speed describes how quickly an object moves.

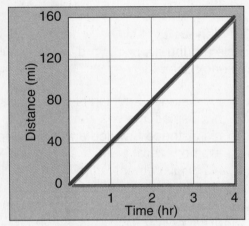

DISTANCE-TIME GRAPH

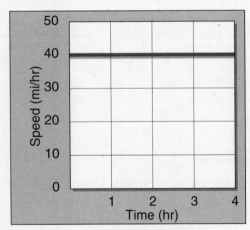

SPEED-TIME GRAPH

1. How far had the car traveled after 3 hours?

   (1)   0 miles
   (2)   40 miles
   (3)   80 miles
   (4) 120 miles
   (5)   40 miles per hour

2. Which of the following is the main idea of the paragraph?

   (1) Speed describes how quickly an object moves.
   (2) Graphs are one way to describe an object's motion.
   (3) Distance and speed describe the same thing.
   (4) The bottom graph shows a car's speed over time.
   (5) The car traveled for 4 hours.

3. Which of the following statements is true of the car's speed?

   (1) It is unrelated to time.
   (2) It is constant for 4 hours.
   (3) It begins at 0 miles per hour and ends at 40 miles per hour.
   (4) It decreases with time.
   (5) After 2 hours, it is 30 miles per hour.

4. Which of the following conclusions is supported by the information presented?

   (1) Speed never changes.
   (2) Speed is unrelated to distance.
   (3) The car covered a total distance of 160 miles in 3 hours.
   (4) The car reached its destination after 4 hours.
   (5) During the 4 hours graphed, the car made no stops.

5. How would the top graph (Distance-Time) be different if the car had stopped after 3 hours?

   (1) The line would turn down vertically after 3 hours.
   (2) The line would rise more steeply after 3 hours.
   (3) The line would end at 3 hours.
   (4) The line would become horizontal at 3 hours.
   (5) The line would rise more steeply and then turn downward after 3 hours.

Items 6 to 9 refer to the following passage.

Every time you check the speedometer in a car to see how fast you're going, you think about the speed of motion. Speed is the distance traveled per unit of time. It is calculated by dividing the distance traveled by the time spent traveling that distance. The equation for calculating speed is

$$\text{speed} = \frac{\text{distance}}{\text{time}}$$

For example, if a bowling ball rolls 10 meters in 2 seconds, the ball's speed is 10 meters divided by 2 seconds, or 5 meters per second.

Whereas speed is a measure of how fast an object moves, velocity is a measure of both how fast and in what direction an object moves. In other words, velocity describes both speed and direction. If we know that the bowling ball described above is rolling due south, then its velocity is 5 meters per second south.

6. Which of the following statements is the main idea of the first paragraph?

   (1) You think about speed when you check a car's speedometer.
   (2) Speed is the distance traveled per unit of time.
   (3) The equation used to calculate speed includes speed, velocity, and time.
   (4) A bowling ball that rolls 10 meters in 2 seconds has a speed of 5 meters per second.
   (5) Velocity describes both speed and direction.

7. Speed differs from velocity in that

   (1) only velocity describes direction
   (2) only velocity describes how fast an object moves
   (3) only speed describes direction
   (4) only speed describes how fast an object moves
   (5) only speed is connected to distance and time

8. A hiker traveling northwest covers 12 kilometers of road in 3 hours. The hiker's speed is

   (1) 12 kilometers per hour
   (2) 12 kilometers per hour northwest
   (3) 4 kilometers per hour
   (4) 4 kilometers per hour northwest
   (5) 3 kilometers per hour

9. A driver must reach a destination 400 kilometers away by 6 P.M. If she leaves at 2 P.M. and drives her car at a speed of 80 kilometers per hour, she will arrive

   (1) 1 hour early
   (2) 1/2 hour early
   (3) just in time
   (4) 2 hours late
   (5) 1 hour late

Item 10 refers to the following paragraph and map.

A driver left Smallville at 9:00 A.M., and drove south on route 70 until 11:00 A.M. Then the driver turned east on route 3, and drove the remaining distance to Center City, arriving at noon.

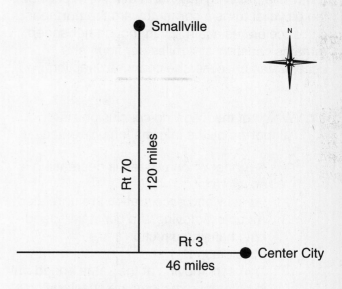

10. If velocity describes both speed and direction, what was the driver's velocity at 11:30 A.M.?

   (1) 46 miles per hour south
   (2) 46 miles per hour east
   (3) 55 miles per hour south-east
   (4) 60 miles per hour east
   (5) 60 miles per hour

Answers are on page 307.

Directions: Choose the best answer to each item.

Items 1 to 4 refer to the following passage.

When you ride a bicycle, you start out standing still and begin to pedal slowly. As you pedal faster, the bicycle moves faster. Your speed changes, and you accelerate. Acceleration is any change in speed, direction, or both; in other words, acceleration is the rate of change of velocity. Acceleration is calculated using the equation

$$\text{acceleration} = \frac{\text{final speed} - \text{original speed}}{\text{time for the change}}$$

If a bicyclist changes speed from 2 miles per hour to 4 miles per hour in 1 hour, she accelerates. Her acceleration is

$$\frac{(4 \text{ miles/hour}) - (2 \text{ miles/hour})}{1 \text{ hour}} = 2 \text{ miles/hour}^2$$

If, while traveling due north at 4 miles per hour, the bicyclist turns a corner toward the northeast, she accelerates again. Even though her speed remains constant at 4 miles per hour, she accelerates because she changes direction.

1. Which of the following conclusions is supported by the information presented?

   (1) A runner whose speed is decreasing is accelerating.
   (2) Velocity and acceleration are unrelated.
   (3) An object moving at a constant speed but changing direction is not accelerating.
   (4) Two cars moving at the same speed but in different directions are accelerating at different rates.
   (5) Acceleration always occurs at the same rate.

2. Which of the following statements is the main idea of the passage?

   (1) When you ride a bicycle, you begin to pedal slowly.
   (2) A bicyclist who changes direction accelerates.
   (3) Your speed changes as you pedal and you accelerate.
   (4) Acceleration is any change in speed, direction, or both.
   (5) Acceleration is the rate of change of velocity.

3. Which of the following moving objects is accelerating?

   A. a bird flying at a constant velocity
   B. a car making a U-turn
   C. a train increasing its speed

   (1) A only
   (2) B only
   (3) C only
   (4) A and B only
   (5) B and C only

4. Nearing the finish line, a swimmer increases his speed from 2 meters per second to 5 meters per second over 3 seconds. What is his acceleration?

   (1) 5 meters per second
   (2) 2 meters per second
   (3) 1 meter per second^2
   (4) 2 meters per second^2
   (5) 3 meters per second^2

tip **When you read a definition that uses a common word in a slightly different scientific context, make a note of how you usually use the word and what its actual scientific meaning is.**

How fast is fast motion? What you interpret to e "fast motion" versus "slow motion" probably epends on who or what you are and what you re used to. To a race car driver, anything that noves at a speed greater than 350 kilometers er hour might seem pretty fast. However, to a aterpillar, a fast pace is more likely to be a peed of 0.005 kilometers per hour! If humans alked at a caterpillar's "fast" pace, they would ever reach their destinations. A fast running peed for a human might be 25 kilometers per our. Yet for a race horse, a human pace is slow. race horse could reach a speed as great as 70 ilometers per hour, whereas a falcon can beat a ace horse with a rate of up to 160 kilometers per our. The next time you see a fast runner, nagine just how fast he or she would seem from falcon's point of view.

5. Which of the following is the main idea of the paragraph?

    (1) A fast person doesn't seem very fast to a falcon.
    (2) To a caterpillar, a fast pace is likely to be a speed of 0.005 kilometers per hour.
    (3) Animals move at different speeds.
    (4) How you view relative speed depends on the speeds you are used to.
    (5) There is always something that can move faster than you can.

6. Which of the following reflects the most likely order from fastest to slowest of typical speeds of motion?

    (1) race horse, falcon, caterpillar
    (2) falcon, race horse, human, caterpillar
    (3) caterpillar, human, race horse, falcon
    (4) falcon, race horse, caterpillar, human
    (5) human, caterpillar, falcon

7. The fastest speed a sloth can reach is about 0.8 kilometers per hour. At this speed, it could move across a field faster than

    (1) any of the animals mentioned in the passage
    (2) none of the animals mentioned in the passage
    (3) a caterpillar
    (4) a falcon
    (5) a human

8. Which of the following statements is supported by the information in the passage?

    (1) Any speed above 0.005 kilometers per hour is fast.
    (2) Any speed under 35 kilometers per hour is slow.
    (3) Race horses are faster than falcons.
    (4) There is no minimum speed above which all speeds are considered fast.
    (5) The speeds of different moving objects cannot be compared.

Item 9 refers to the following paragraph.

Newton's Third Law of Motion states that every action force causes an equal and opposite reaction force. If a moving car bumps a car stopped at a traffic light, the bumped car will move also. How far it moves depends on how hard it is hit. The moving car causes the action force. The movement of the bumped car is the reaction to that force.

9. Which of the following is a reaction force, not an action force?

    (1) hot gases leaving a rocket
    (2) wind blowing against a kite
    (3) a bat striking a ball
    (4) the backward "kick" when a soldier fires a rifle
    (5) the stroke of a swimmer against the water

Answers are on page 308.

Evaluation: Making Judgments

When you make a judgment, you choose the best alternative from a group of possibilities.

You make judgments all the time. Whenever you are faced with a problem, you think about the possible solutions, and you select the solution you decide is best. For example, suppose you have to make a weekend trip to visit your brother in a city two hundred miles away. You can take a plane, train, or bus, or you can drive your own car. If you have a limited amount of money to spend, you would have to compare the costs of these options to decide which is best.

People also make judgments about science-related matters. Scientists have to decide the best way to set up an experiment in order to get reliable results. Engineers have to decide the best way to solve problems of energy, force, and motion when designing roads, buildings and machines.

Read this passage and decide on the best way to solve a problem.

Microwaves have high heating power. In a microwave oven, microwaves are produced by a device called a magnetron located in the top or side of the oven. The beam of microwaves strikes a spinning fan located in the center of the oven. The fan reflects the microwaves in all directions. In addition, the microwaves bounce off the inner surface of the oven and are reflected in still more directions. Microwaves pass through the container holding the food and heat it throughout.

Suppose you are having trouble heating food evenly in a microwave oven. You are placing the food on the side of the oven where the magnetron is located. How can you improve the heating action? You could heat the food longer so the cool spots also heat up. This would work, but the hot spots might overheat. Another possibility is to interrupt the cooking to stir the food. That might work, but you would have to pay attention to the cooking time. Perhaps you can solve the problem by placing the food in the center of the oven. The food will cook evenly, because more microwaves will reach the food in the center of the oven than at the sides.

When you are deciding the best way to solve a problem or thinking about the advantages and disadvantages of various actions, first decide if each possibility is logical and would indeed solve the problem. Then select the solution with the most advantages.

Items 1 and 2 refer to the following passage. Choose the best answer to each item.

Climbing to the top of a mountain by the steepest slope requires a great deal of effort, or force. However, the distance that has to be covered is short. On the other hand, climbing the same mountain by the gentlest slope requires less force, but the distance to be covered is greater. In both cases, the amount of work required is the same. Work is the result of a force moving an object over a distance. This relationship can be expressed as:

work = force × distance

Work is measured in units called joules (J); force is measured in units called newtons (N), which are used to measure the pull of gravity on an object, or its weight; and distance is measured in meters. For example, the amount of work involved in lifting an object with a force of 10 newtons over a distance of 0.5 meters is

work = force × distance
5J = 10N × 0.5 meters

1. A child is asked to help clean a room by picking up one toy and putting it away. Putting away which toy would require the least work?

   (1) a truck requiring a force of 12N that goes on a shelf 0.5 meters high
   (2) a ball requiring a force of 6N that goes in a box 1 meter high
   (3) a catcher's mitt requiring a force of 8N that goes on a hook 1.5 meters high
   (4) a plastic dinosaur requiring a force of 10N that goes in a basket 1.5 meters high
   (5) a bucket of blocks requiring a force of 20N that goes on a shelf 0.1 meter high

> **tip**
> **When making judgments about a solution to a problem, look for the option with the fewest pitfalls or problems.**

2. A weight lifter wants to decrease by one-third the amount of work his arm muscle is doing when he lifts weights. Which of the following changes will accomplish this?

   (1) Triple the weight being lifted.
   (2) Reduce the distance over which the weight is lifted by one-third.
   (3) Reduce the amount of weight being lifted by two-thirds
   (4) Reduce both the weight being lifted and the distance over which it is lifted by one-third.
   (5) Triple the distance over which the weight is lifted.

Item 3 refers to the following passage.

Power is the rate at which work is done. If a 165-pound man runs up a flight of stairs that is 10 feet high, he does 1650 foot-pounds of work. If he does this in 3 seconds, his power is 550 foot-pounds per second (1650 foot-pounds per 3 seconds). This amount is equal to one horsepower.

Horsepower is used to describe the power of an engine of a motor. In cars, engines that produce more horsepower can carry a greater weight and can accelerate into traffic more easily. However, these engines use more fuel than lower-horsepower engines.

3. Which of the following conditions would be the best reason for replacing a car with one that has a more powerful engine?

   (1) You changed jobs and now drive a longer distance to work.
   (2) You want to save money on fuel.
   (3) You are moving to a place that gets a lot of snow and are concerned about driving on slippery roads.
   (4) Your new job requires you to transport heavy supplies in your car.
   (5) You are going to start driving your children to school every morning.

Answers are on page 309.

Motion

A force is a push or pull that acts on matter, causing it to speed up, slow down, or change direction. A change in the speed or direction of motion is called acceleration.

The English scientist Sir Isaac Newton formulated laws about motion. The First Law of Motion states that an object at rest tends to remain at rest, and an object in motion tends to keep moving in a straight line at the same speed, until acted upon by outside forces. For example, when you throw a ball, it eventually falls to the ground and stops rolling. It stops moving because the force of gravity has pulled it down, and the friction from the air and the ground has slowed it down. Without gravity and friction, the ball would continue moving in a straight line.

The tendency of an object to keep moving or remain at rest is called inertia. You become aware of inertia when you are riding in a car that suddenly stops. Because of inertia, you will keep moving forward until a force stops you.

Newton's Second Law of Motion states that an object will accelerate in the direction of the force that acts upon it. The mass of an object and the force that acts upon it will affect how the object accelerates. For example, a large truck requires more force than a small car to accelerate away from a stoplight at the same rate. Newton's second law can be expressed by the formula:

$$\text{force} = \text{mass} \times \text{acceleration}$$

 Practice | Motion

Items 1 to 8 refer to the previous passage. Choose the best answer to each item.

1. Which of the following designs would be best for a racing car?

   (1) small engine and lightweight body
   (2) large engine and lightweight body
   (3) small engine and heavy body
   (4) large engine and heavy body
   (5) small engine and large gas tank

2. Once a spacecraft reaches outer space, its inertia would keep it moving in a straight line at a constant speed, even if its engine is not used. What is most likely to cause the spacecraft to change direction?

   (1) running out of fuel
   (2) energy from the sun
   (3) the force of friction
   (4) the force of gravity
   (5) acceleration

3. If a force of 8 N is applied to a 2-kilogram ball, and a force of 6 N is applied to a 3-kilogram ball, how will the accelerations of the balls compare?

   (1) Both accelerations will be the same.
   (2) The acceleration of the second ball will be twice that of the first.
   (3) The acceleration of the first ball will be twice that of the second.
   (4) The acceleration of the first ball will be four times that of the second.
   (5) The acceleration of the second ball will be four times that of the first.

4. According to Newton's laws, an outside force would be required to make which of the following situations occur?

   (1) A cyclist traveling at 15 miles per hour continues to travel at the same speed in the same direction.
   (2) A person who stood through the first hour of a sold-out concert stands through the second hour.
   (3) A passenger sits on the subway while the train travels four miles in four minutes.
   (4) A rocket traveling through space continues to move in a forward direction.
   (5) A car traveling at 40 miles per hour goes around a curve at the same speed.

5. Which of the following is an example of Newton's Second Law of Motion?

   A. a pitcher throwing a fast ball
   B. a seat belt preventing a person from hitting the windshield
   C. a parked car

   (1) A only
   (2) B only
   (3) C only
   (4) A and B
   (5) B and C

6. Which of the following situations is an example of Newton's First Law of Motion?

   (1) A man finds that pushing a full wheelbarrow takes more force than pushing an empty one.
   (2) A package on the seat of a car going 60 miles per hour slides forward when the car stops suddenly.
   (3) Passengers notice that a bus rides more smoothly at 50 miles per hour than at 25 miles per hour.
   (4) A car stuck on an ice patch is able to move when a blanket is placed under the back wheels.
   (5) A football player intercepts a pass and runs in the opposite direction from which the ball was thrown.

7. Football teams use large players in the defense lines and smaller players in the backfield to run and catch passes. What is an advantage of this strategy?

   (1) Small players can accelerate quickly, while large players can apply force to stop the motion of opponents.
   (2) Large players remain at rest, while light players remain in motion.
   (3) Light players can catch passes, while large players can tackle.
   (4) Large players tend to move in a straight line, while light players can change direction easily.
   (5) The force needed to stop a large player is much greater than the force needed to stop a small one.

8. Newton's Second Law of Motion describes the relationship among which factors?

   (1) mass and acceleration
   (2) direction and force
   (3) direction, force, and acceleration
   (4) mass, force, and acceleration
   (5) mass, direction, and acceleration

Answers are on page 309.

Items 1 to 6 refer to the following paragraph and diagram. Choose the <u>best answer</u> to each item.

Energy is the ability to move matter from one place to another or to change matter from one substance to another. Energy is never used up. It just changes from one form to another. For example, you use the energy stored in your muscles to lift an object such as a pen. Some of the energy is changed into the motion of the pen. This energy is called <u>kinetic energy</u>, or the energy of motion. Some of your energy is changed into potential energy, or the energy of position. Potential energy is stored energy. The higher you lift the pen, the more potential energy you give it. Potential energy is released when matter moves. Drop the pen and its potential energy changes into kinetic energy as it falls.

1. Which of the following is an example of potential energy?

   (1) a woman jogging
   (2) a moving bicycle
   (3) a car parked on a hill
   (4) wind
   (5) a swiftly flowing stream

2. Which of the following is an example of kinetic energy?

   (1) a boy sitting still
   (2) a turning ferris wheel
   (3) a sleeping animal
   (4) a book on a table
   (5) a coat hanging in a closet

3. Which of the following statements is true about a rock that is lifted up and placed on a table?

   (1) It has no energy.
   (2) It loses energy.
   (3) It has potential energy during lifting and kinetic energy on the table.
   (4) It only has energy while it is moving.
   (5) It has kinetic energy during lifting and potential energy on the table.

4. A rolling ball stops moving. Which of the following conclusions is supported by the information in the passage?

   (1) The ball's energy is lost.
   (2) The ball's energy changes form.
   (3) The ball's potential energy becomes kinetic energy.
   (4) The matter in the ball changes to another substance.
   (5) The ball is made of energy.

5. A roller coaster ride begins as a chain slowly pulls the cars to the top of the first hill. How does the energy of the cars change during this time?

   (1) The cars gain potential energy gradually as they move higher.
   (2) The cars have the same amount of potential energy until they reach the top of the hill, and then potential energy increases.
   (3) The cars gain kinetic energy gradually as they move higher.
   (4) The cars lose kinetic energy gradually as they move higher.
   (5) The cars transfer some of their potential energy to the chain.

6. At which points during a roller coaster ride is potential energy being changed into kinetic energy?

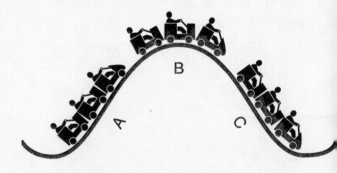

   (1) A only
   (2) B only
   (3) C only
   (4) A and B
   (5) A and C

Thermodynamics is the study of the relationship of heat energy and kinetic energy. Heat energy can be changed into other forms of energy, and other forms of energy can be changed into heat. You can feel this change when you rub your hands together briskly. Your hands begin to feel warm because the kinetic energy of rubbing them together is being changed into heat.

When one form of energy is changed into another, energy is conserved. This means that no energy is lost in the process of changing from one form to another. The conservation of energy is the first law of thermodynamics.

7. Why is the water at the bottom of Niagara Falls slightly warmer than the water at the top of the falls?

   (1) The rocks at the base of the falls give off heat energy.
   (2) More heat energy from the sun reaches the bottom of the falls.
   (3) Some of the kinetic energy of the falling water changes to heat energy when it hits the bottom of the falls.
   (4) The heat energy of the falling water changes to kinetic energy when it hits the bottom of the falls.
   (5) Heat energy is lost when water hits the bottom of the falls.

8. On a chilly day, you go out without a jacket and become cold. What is the best way to warm up?

   (1) Sit down and wrap your arms around your legs to conserve heat energy.
   (2) Lie down on the ground to conserve heat energy.
   (3) Rub your hands briskly to change kinetic energy into heat energy.
   (4) Wave your arms to change kinetic energy into heat energy.
   (5) Exercise your whole body to change kinetic energy into heat energy.

The second law of thermodynamics explains why heat moves from one object to another. If no work is done to reverse the process, heat always flows from hotter objects to colder ones. The transfer of heat from one object to another can be explained in terms of moving molecules. The molecules in hot objects have more kinetic energy and move faster than the molecules in cold objects. When two objects come in contact with each other, the higher-energy molecules in the warmer object begin to collide with the molecules in the cooler object. Energy is transferred in the process. This process shows that "coldness" is actually the absence of heat. As heat energy leaves an object, the object becomes less warm, or cold.

9. Which of the following is most similar to the action of molecules in a heated substance?

   (1) a car traveling at a steady speed in a straight line
   (2) popcorn popping
   (3) a ball rolling
   (4) Earth rotating
   (5) a truck coming to a sudden stop

10. As an ice cube in your hand melts, your hand begins to feel cold. Which of the following is a correct conclusion?

   (1) Coldness from the ice flows into your hand.
   (2) Heat leaves your hand and is absorbed by the ice.
   (3) The ice loses energy and becomes water.
   (4) Molecules in your hand gain energy from the ice.
   (5) Energy changes from one form to another as it goes from the ice to your hand.

Answers are on page 310.

Directions: Choose the best answer to each item.

Items 1 to 4 refer to the following passage.

Energy is the ability to do work. Because heat is a form of energy, it also can do work. Scientists define work as the effect of a force acting on an object, causing it to move some distance.

One way in which heat is used to do work is in a heat engine. The gasoline engine in a car is a heat engine. In a gasoline engine, hot gases move into cylinders that contain pistons. When an electric spark ignites the gases, they explode and push against the pistons. The movement of the pistons eventually transfers energy to the wheels through a series of shafts and gears. The wheels exert a force against the ground, moving the car.

Most of the energy produced by gasoline engines is wasted. Only about 12 percent of the energy provided by the fuel is used to power the car. As a result, much of the heat produced by a gasoline engine is released through the exhaust pipe into the atmosphere.

1. Which of the following is the force that begins to set a car in motion?

   (1) the burning of gasoline
   (2) the push of hot gases on a piston
   (3) the push of hot gases on shafts and gears
   (4) the push of pistons on shafts and gears
   (5) the push of the wheels against the ground

2. In a gasoline engine, hot gases power a car by

   (1) releasing oxygen
   (2) exerting pressure
   (3) transferring heat to other substances
   (4) releasing heat to the atmosphere
   (5) changing water into steam

3. According to the information provided, in which of the following situations would you be doing work?

   (1) studying for a physics test
   (2) standing in line for an hour
   (3) holding a heavy bag of groceries for an hour
   (4) pushing a grocery cart
   (5) dropping a ball out of a second-story window

4. In the same town, why is the temperature on heavily traveled streets higher than on streets with less traffic?

   (1) The heavily traveled streets absorb more sunlight than the less traveled streets.
   (2) Heat released from many cars raises the temperature of heavily-traveled streets.
   (3) The wearing away of road surfaces raises the temperature of heavily traveled streets.
   (4) Heavily traveled streets have fewer trees to provide shade.
   (5) More heat-generating industries are near heavily traveled streets.

tip **When applying information given in a passage to a new situation, make sure that the option you choose is supported by the passage. Also make sure that you used no additional information not supplied by the passage.**

Items 5 to 7 refer to the following information and diagram.

A machine is a device that helps you do work by changing the force that must be applied, the distance over which the force must be applied, or both. The amount of help a particular machine gives is called its mechanical advantage (MA). The bigger the mechanical advantage, the less force you must provide to accomplish the same amount of work.

The mechanical advantage of a machine can be found in two ways. The first way is to divide the force of the resistance (or the weight of the object to be moved) by the force of the effort. For example, if you apply 25 pounds of effort force to raise a 200-pound weight using a pulley, you can figure out that the pulley has a mechanical advantage of 8:

$$MA = \frac{\text{resistance force}}{\text{effort force}}$$

$$= \frac{200 \text{ pounds}}{25 \text{ pounds}} = 8$$

Another way to figure out mechanical advantage is to use the distances involved. Divide the effort distance by the resistance distance. The mechanical advantage of the inclined plane shown in the diagram is the length of the slope divided by its height, or 2:

$$MA = \frac{\text{effort distance}}{\text{resistance distance}}$$

$$= \frac{4 \text{ meters}}{2 \text{ meters}} = 2$$

INCLINED PLANE

Effort distance 4 m

2 m

Resistance distance

5. The pulley with the greatest mechanical advantage is the one that requires

(1) 40 pounds of effort to raise a 480-pound rock
(2) 10 pounds of effort to raise a resistance of 50 pounds
(3) 80 pounds of effort to raise an 800-pound boulder
(4) 15 pounds of effort to raise a 300-pound box
(5) 50 pounds of effort to raise a resistance of 650 pounds

6. You must raise a box four meters off the ground. Which inclined plane would give you the greatest mechanical advantage?

(1) 3 meters high and 9 meters long
(2) 4 meters high and 6 meters long
(3) 4 meters high and 8 meters long
(4) 4 meters high and 12 meters long
(5) 3 meters high and 4 meters long

7. A lever is another kind of simple machine. A lever is a bar that turns on a pivot called the fulcrum. A lever can be used to move a large rock, as shown below. If you can move a 300-pound rock by pushing down on a 6-foot long lever with a force of 25 pounds, what is the mechanical advantage of the lever?

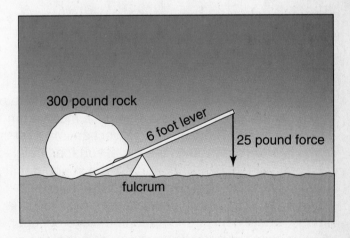

300 pound rock
6 foot lever
25 pound force
fulcrum

(1) 6
(2) 12
(3) 25
(4) 50
(5) 150

Answers are on page 311.

Lesson 18

Analysis: Cause and Effect

When you think about cause and effect, you are thinking about how one thing influences another. A cause is what makes something happen. An effect is what happens as a result of the cause.

When you flip on a light switch, you cause the lights to come on. This is a simple example of cause and effect. An obvious action, or cause, produces an obvious result, or effect.

Sometimes cause and effect relationships are not so obvious in science. In the light switch example, for instance, you can go further and think about what is really happening. When you flip the switch, you are completing an electric circuit, allowing current to flow into the bulb and produce light. That's another way to think of cause and effect in regard to turning on a light.

Now take this example further still. You can think about the nature of electricity, which you will learn about in this lesson. When you flip the switch, you are providing electrons with a path to flow through. Thus you can think about the cause and effect of one situation in many different ways.

 To identify cause and effect relationships watch for words like: *causes, thus, therefore, because, since, effect, so,* and *consequently.* Also watch for the following key phrases: *due to, leads to, develops from, the reason is, as a result,* and *what happens is.*

 Cause and Effect

Items 1 and 2 refer to the following paragraph. Choose the best answer to each item.

A photocopier works by using static electricity to produce copies of documents. Inside the photocopier is a metal drum that is given a negative charge. Lenses then project an image of the document onto the drum. Where light strikes the metal surface, the electric charge disappears. Only the dark parts of the image remain negatively charged. The copier contains a dark powder called toner, which has a positive charge. The toner is attracted to the negatively charged dark parts of the image. The toner is transferred to a piece of paper and is sealed by heat. A warm copy of the document comes out of the machine.

1. What causes the toner to form the image of the document on the drum?

    (1) The positively-charged toner is attracted to the negatively-charged areas of the drum.
    (2) The toner fills in the raised image of the document on the drum.
    (3) The document is negatively charged, and the positively-charged toner is attracted to it.
    (4) Heat from the machine causes the toner to form the image of the document.
    (5) Light from the lenses causes the image of the document to be traced on the drum.

2. The lenses failed to project an image of the document on the negatively charged drum. Rather, just light was projected. What would happen as a result?

    (1) The toner would be attracted to the drum.
    (2) The toner would be attracted to the document rather than the drum.
    (3) A grayish-black sheet of copy paper would result.
    (4) A blank sheet of copy paper would result.
    (5) An acceptable copy of the document would result.

Items 3 and 4 refer to the following information.

The friction created when objects move in air is called drag. Drag acts to slow down a moving object. The amount of drag depends on the shape of the object. Air flows more smoothly around objects with a tapered shape.

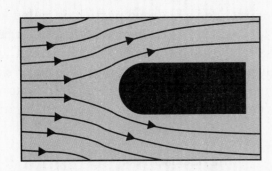

3. Which of the following would be an effect of streamlining the shape of an automobile?

    (1) increased drag
    (2) more speed for the same amount of fuel energy
    (3) less speed for the same amount of fuel energy
    (4) more speed for more fuel energy
    (5) There would be no effect.

4. Which of the following would be an effect of increasing the drag acting on a moving object?

    (1) decreased speed
    (2) increased speed
    (3) smoother movement
    (4) increased airflow
    (5) decreased friction

Answers are on page 311.

Electricity and Magnetism

Have you ever heard the saying "opposites attract"? People usually use this phrase to describe opposite personalities. But this phrase can also describe the forces in two important areas of physics—electricity and magnetism.

You may think of electricity as turning on the lights or starting an electric motor. Certainly these are important uses of electricity—but what exactly <u>is</u> electricity? Where does it come from? And how does it power the appliances that you use every day?

To answer these questions, you must first go back to the atom that you studied in lesson 13. You will recall that atoms are made up of protons, electrons, and neutrons. Protons and electrons have a property called <u>electric charge</u>. Protons are positively charged (+1) and electrons are negatively charged (–1). Neutrons have no charge—as their name implies, they are neutral (0).

The force of attraction between the positively-charged protons and the negatively-charged electrons helps hold an atom together. The structure of an atom shows the basic rule of electric charge: Unlike charges attract each other, while like charges repel each other. You can remember this rule easily if you just think of the old saying "opposites attract."

The area of force that surrounds a charged particle is called an <u>electric field</u>. The strength of an electric field depends on the distance from the charged particle—as the distance increases, the strength of the field decreases. The electric field of a charged particle exerts a force on any other charged particle. The force will be one of attraction if the particles are of unlike charge, and repulsion if the particles are of like charge.

THE HELIUM ATOM

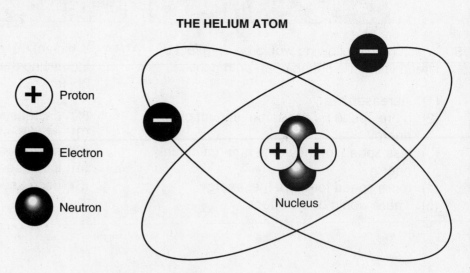

Proton

Electron

Neutron

Nucleus

Items 1 to 8 refer to the previous passage and diagram. Choose the best answer to each item.

1. A negatively-charged strip of metal is suspended from the ceiling. When another strip of metal is brought close to it, the first strip bends away. Which statement explains why this happens?

   (1) The second strip is positively charged.
   (2) The second strip is negatively charged.
   (3) The second strip contains fewer electrons than the first strip.
   (4) The second strip has a larger electric field than the first strip.
   (5) The atoms in the second strip repel the atoms in the first strip.

2. Which of the following particles always has a negative charge?

   (1) proton
   (2) neutron
   (3) electron
   (4) atom
   (5) field

3. What is an electric field?

   (1) a group of electrons
   (2) a group of protons
   (3) an area of force
   (4) a charged particle
   (5) positively charged atoms

4. Which of the following is not affected by the electric field of a charged particle?

   A. a particle with the same charge
   B. a particle with an opposite charge
   C. an uncharged particle

   (1) A only
   (2) B only
   (3) C only
   (4) A and B only
   (5) B and C only

5. Atoms and molecules with an electric charge are called ions. What is likely to happen when positively-charged ions are mixed with negatively-charged ions?

   (1) The negative and positive ions will attract each other.
   (2) The negative ions and positive ions will remain separate.
   (3) The negative ions produce a larger electric field than the positive ions.
   (4) The negative and positive ions will repel each other.
   (5) Positive ions will remain grouped together.

6. What holds an atom together?

   (1) force of gravity
   (2) chemical bonds
   (3) its nucleus
   (4) force of attraction between protons and electrons
   (5) force of attraction between neutrons and electrons

7. If an atom contains 3 protons, 4 neutrons, and 2 electrons, what is the charge on the atom?

   (1) +2
   (2) +1
   (3) 0 (neutral)
   (4) −1
   (5) −2

8. Decreasing the distance between two unlike charged particles would

   (1) decrease their electric charges
   (2) increase their electric charges
   (3) increase the flow of electricity
   (4) decrease their force of attraction
   (5) increase their force of attraction

Answers are on page 312.

Items 1 to 4 refer to the following passage. Choose the best answer to each item.

Have you ever rubbed a balloon against your sleeve and stuck it to the wall? You were able to do this because the balloon became electrically charged.

Electrons in atoms are free to move. As you rub a balloon on your sleeve, electrons from the cloth move onto the balloon. The extra electrons give the balloon a negative charge. When the balloon comes near the wall, it repels the electrons in the wall, leaving the wall positively charged. Thus, the negatively charged balloon and the positively charged wall attract each other.

The ability of electrons to move from one place to another makes electric current possible. Electric current is the flow of electrons through a wire, and it is what powers your appliances.

Electrons flow through a wire in much the same way as water flows through a hose. Just as water pressure pushes water through a hose, a source of energy pushes electrons through a wire. This source of energy is called voltage. Voltage is measured in units called volts. A battery marked "9V" supplies nine volts of energy to move electrons through a wire.

1. If you scuff your feet across a wool carpet, you may feel a shock when you touch a metal object. Which statement explains why this happens?

   (1) An electric charge builds up on the rug and then is transferred to the metal object.
   (2) Electrons from the carpet move onto your feet, causing you temporarily to have an electric charge.
   (3) Electrons flow from your feet to the carpet, causing the carpet to have an electric charge.
   (4) Electrons in the metal object are repelled by electrons on the carpet.
   (5) Scuffing across the carpet causes an increase in voltage, which then produces a shock.

2. Which of the following statements cannot be supported by the information provided?

   (1) Protons flowing onto an object cause the object to become positively charged.
   (2) Low voltage could cause a power "brownout" in a town or city.
   (3) If two balloons that had been rubbed on cloth were brought close together, they would probably repel each other.
   (4) A torn wire could cause a loss of electricity, just as a leaky hose would cause a loss of water.
   (5) Current flow increases as voltage increases.

3. Extra electrons on an electrically charged object eventually leave the object, returning it to its neutral state. A person who wishes to stick balloons to the wall as party decorations should

   (1) place the balloons on the wall just before the party begins
   (2) place the balloons far apart
   (3) place the balloons on the wall at least a day ahead of time
   (4) rub the balloons on several different types of cloth
   (5) place the balloons as close to the ceiling as possible

4. In the passage, water pressure is compared to voltage because

   (1) both provide energy to move electrons
   (2) both make possible the flow of a substance from one place to another
   (3) both are measured in units called volts
   (4) both involve the transfer of electrically charged particles
   (5) both can be used to power a battery

In order for electric current to flow, electrons must have a closed, continuous pathway over which to travel. Such a pathway is provided by an electric circuit. An electric circuit usually consists of a source of electrons, a load or resistance, and a switch connected by a wire. In the diagram the source of electrons is an eight-volt battery. The wavy lines you see are resistances. A resistance can be a light bulb, an appliance, or a motor—anything that uses or impedes the flow of electrical energy.

Electric current (I) is measured in amperes ("amps" for short). Resistance (R) is measured in ohms. Current, resistance, and voltage are related by the equation

$$V = I \times R.$$

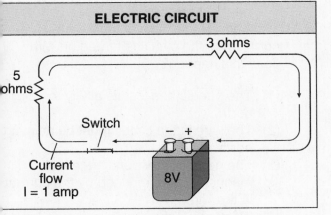

ELECTRIC CIRCUIT

5 ohms

3 ohms

Switch

Current flow
I = 1 amp

8V

5. If the voltage in the circuit above were reduced to four volts, what would be the effect on the current?

   (1) It would stay the same.
   (2) It would be cut in half.
   (3) It would double.
   (4) It would increase four times.
   (5) It would be equal to the voltage.

6. If more resistance were added to the circuit, what would be the result?

   (1) an increase in voltage
   (2) a decrease in current
   (3) an increase in current
   (4) a decrease in voltage
   (5) a greater number of electrons passing through each resistor

>tip   When evaluating a cause and effect situation, read the passage carefully to discover the relationship between the cause and its possible effects. Use definitions and equations in the passage to figure out these relationships. For example, the formula for voltage tells you that lowering the voltage would result in lowering the current (if resistance remains the same).

Answers are on page 312.

Directions: Choose the best answer to each item.

Items 1 to 4 refer to the following passage.

A magnetic field is formed around a wire conducting an electric current. This relationship between electricity and magnetism is known as electromagnetism.

Because of electromagnetism, powerful temporary magnets called electromagnets can be made by wrapping coils of wire around soft iron and passing an electric current through the wire. When the current passing through the wire is turned off, the magnet loses its magnetic properties. When the current is turned back on, the magnet regains its magnetic properties. The strength of the electromagnet depends on the number of loops of wire and the size of the current.

1. A heavy crane used at construction sites is equipped with a large electromagnet. The electromagnet will make the machine most useful for which of the following tasks?

   (1) transporting pieces of iron to distant locations
   (2) picking up pieces of scrap metal on the site and depositing them elsewhere on the site
   (3) generating electricity for the area surrounding the site
   (4) making magnets out of pieces of scrap metal found on the site
   (5) lifting objects too heavy for other types of machines on the site

tip **When reading about a situation where there is a change, ask yourself what causes the change. Also identify any result of the change.**

2. The relationship between electricity and magnetism described in the passage is best expressed by which of the following statements?

   (1) Electromagnets form magnetic fields.
   (2) Magnets cause electricity.
   (3) Wrapping wire around iron causes magnetism.
   (4) An electric current produces a magnetic field.
   (5) An electric field can be produced by an iron magnet.

3. The needle of a compass placed near the wire of an electric circuit turns away from north when the circuit is turned on. Why does this happen?

   (1) The needle has lost its ability to point north.
   (2) The wire in the circuit must be pointing north.
   (3) The needle is responding to the magnetic field produced by the current in the wire.
   (4) Electrons in the needle are repelled by electrons in the wire.
   (5) The compass needle has become an electromagnet.

4. Which hypothesis can be supported by the information given?

   (1) Magnets make electric current strong.
   (2) Electromagnets are not as strong as natural magnets.
   (3) A magnet can reverse the direction of an electric current.
   (4) The strength of an electromagnet depends upon the material used to make the magnet.
   (5) Magnetism is related to the movement of electrons.

Over 2,000 years ago, a mysterious stone was discovered that could attract bits of material containing iron. The Greeks who found this stone named it "magnetite." They had discovered an interesting property that we now call magnetism.

Magnetite is an example of a natural magnet. Most of the magnets you have probably used are artificial magnets. The simplest artificial magnet is an iron bar magnet.

If you suspend a bar magnet horizontally on a string and allow it to swing freely, one end of the magnet will always point north. This end of the magnet is called the north magnetic pole. The other end of the magnet, which points south, is called the south magnetic pole.

The area around a magnet in which magnetic forces can act is called a magnetic field. The magnetic field of a bar magnet is strongest around the poles. If a north pole of one magnet and a south pole of another magnet are brought together, they will attract each other. If two north poles or two south poles are brought together, they will repel each other. Thus the rule for magnetic poles is: Unlike poles attract each other, while like poles repel each other. Once again, "opposites attract."

5. The discovery of magnetite was important because it

   (1) made artificial magnets possible
   (2) was the first natural iron magnet
   (3) gave scientists information about the properties of iron
   (4) illustrated the property of magnetism
   (5) explained why one pole of a magnet always points north

6. The point on a bar magnet where the magnetic field is likely to be weakest is

   (1) at the north pole
   (2) at the south pole
   (3) halfway between the poles
   (4) just south of the north pole
   (5) just north of the south pole

7. The needle of a compass always points to the north. Which of the following must be true about compass needles?

   (1) Compass needles are made of magnetite.
   (2) Compass needles are made of iron.
   (3) Compass needles are magnets.
   (4) A compass needle has a north magnetic pole but no south magnetic pole.
   (5) Two compass needles will repel each other.

8. The fact that one end of a freely suspended magnet always points north suggests that

   (1) climate influences magnetism
   (2) the sun has a magnetic field
   (3) a deposit of magnetite is located north of the magnet
   (4) Earth has a magnetic field
   (5) the polar ice caps are magnetic

Item 9 refers to the following passage.

Videotape is made of a plastic material that contains tiny bits of metal. The heads that record information on the tape contain magnets. When something is recorded on a videotape, the bits of metal are arranged into specific patterns by the magnetic fields of the magnets in the heads. When you decide to record something new, the magnets in the recording heads rearrange the metal bits in the tape, and the previous recording is destroyed.

9. Which of the following care instructions is explained by this passage?

   (1) Do not leave videotapes in a hot place.
   (2) Always store videotapes in their boxes.
   (3) Do not store videotapes near metal objects.
   (4) Keep videotapes away from magnetic fields.
   (5) Always rewind videotapes after playing them.

Answers are on page 313.

Evaluation: Drawing Conclusions

When you draw a conclusion, you use examples, details, facts, and observations to prove that the conclusion is true.

You draw conclusions all the time. For example, when you look out the window to see what the weather is, you observe whether it's sunny or cloudy, windy or still. From these observations you conclude what kind of day it will be.

Scientists also draw conclusions. From measurable, observable data and from carefully designed experiments, scientists draw conclusions about the nature of the universe. If the conclusions are correct, they can be used to predict other events in the physical world.

When you read science, be on the lookout for rules, laws, principles, and equations. These are usually generalizations that can be used to evaluate specific information. For example, in an earlier lesson you learned about two of Newton's laws of motion. In answering questions about these laws, you evaluated specific events to see if they followed Newton's laws.

Thinking about conclusions also involves recognizing when conclusions are wrong. In addition, you must recognize when a conclusion is true, but it cannot be proved using the information at hand. You must examine the passage, diagram, or equation carefully to determine whether a conclusion follows logically from the information that is there.

 Drawing Conclusions

Item 1 refers to the following passage. Choose the best answer to each item.

A particle accelerator is an extremely long, narrow tunnel, either straight or circular. It is charged with powerful electric and magnetic fields. When physicists fire a tiny particle such as a proton or electron into the tunnel, the fields cause the particle to accelerate. The longer the tunnel, the greater the acceleration and energy of the particle.

Physicists can guide the particles along a path that makes them collide with each other or with another target. When the impact is great enough, the energy released as a result of the collision is converted into new particles. By studying these new particles, scientists can learn about the nature of matter.

1. Which statement can be supported by the passage?

   (1) A straight accelerator is better than a round one.
   (2) A round accelerator can achieve higher speeds than a straight one.
   (3) Higher-energy electrons are more likely to occur in an accelerator with a long tunnel than in one with a short tunnel.
   (4) Electrons move faster than protons in an accelerator.
   (5) Accelerators can produce large amounts of electricity.

Items 2 to 4 refer to the following passage.

A conductor is a substance that allows electric current to flow through it easily. Metals such as copper, gold, and aluminum are the best conductors. An insulator is any substance that resists the flow of electrons. Insulators tend to be nonmetals such as glass, plastics, porcelain, and rubber.

2. Which statement can be supported by the passage?

   (1) A silver pipe is likely to have a lower resistance than a plastic pipe.
   (2) How well a substance conducts electricity depends on its temperature.
   (3) Silver is a better insulator than plastic.
   (4) A glass tube is likely to have a lower resistance than a copper tube.
   (5) Electrons move more readily through nonmetals than through metals.

3. Which of the following would be the best use for a conductor?

   (1) as electrical wire for a lamp
   (2) as an electrical outlet cover
   (3) as shoe soles for electrical line repair persons
   (4) as a decorative base for a lamp
   (5) as the outside of a light bulb

4. Which of the following would not have a high resistance to the flow of electrons?

   (1) porcelain
   (2) aluminum
   (3) rubber
   (4) plastic
   (5) glass

Items 5 and 6 refer to the following passage.

Some materials carry electric current better than others. Resistance is a material's opposition to the flow of current. Resistance is measured in ohms. Resistance, voltage, and current are related in a formula called Ohm's Law:

$$\text{Resistance} = \frac{\text{Voltage}}{\text{Current}}$$

5. Which resistance calculation below can be supported by the passage?

   (1) 48 ohms for a lamp that uses 4 amps of current in a 12-volt circuit
   (2) 0.66 ohms for a doorbell that uses 6 amps of current in a 9-volt circuit
   (3) 24 ohms for a toaster that uses 5 amps of current in a 120-volt circuit
   (4) 40 ohms for an electric range that uses 5 amps of current in a 230-volt circuit
   (5) 7 ohms for a light bulb that uses 0.2 amps of current in a 14-volt circuit

6. Gold has a lower resistance than copper, and copper has a lower resistance than steel. The thicker the wire, the lower the resistance. Which of the following changes would not decrease the current, assuming that the voltage remains the same?

   (1) Replace a thick gold wire with a thin gold wire.
   (2) Replace a thin copper wire with a thin steel wire.
   (3) Replace a thick steel wire with a thin steel wire.
   (4) Replace a thin gold wire with a thick copper wire.
   (5) Replace a thin steel wire with a thick copper wire.

Answers are on page 314.

Waves

A wave is a disturbance that travels through space or matter. Waves transfer energy from one place to another. Some familiar types of waves include sound waves, light waves, radio waves, microwaves, and water waves. All waves, no matter what their type, have certain basic characteristics.

The amplitude of a wave is how high it rises from its rest position. When the sea is absolutely calm, the water is at its rest position. As a wave rises, the water reaches a high point, and then falls back down again. This high point is called the <u>crest</u>. The distance from the rest position to the crest is the amplitude. The greater the amplitude, the greater the energy of the wave.

The shape of a wave is created as the wave moves from its rest position to a high point, or crest, then back through the rest position to a low point. The low point of a wave is called the <u>trough</u>, and it is the same distance from the rest position as is the crest.

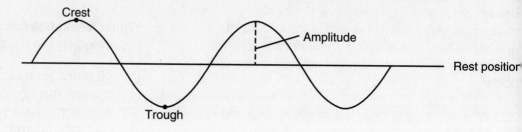

 Practice **Waves**

Items 1 to 3 refer to the previous passage and diagram. Choose the <u>best answer</u> to each item.

1. Which of the following statements <u>cannot</u> be supported by the information provided?

   (1) The amplitude of an ocean wave is equal to the distance from the rest position to the trough.
   (2) A three-foot high wave has a trough three feet deep.
   (3) The depth of the trough of a wave is double the distance from the rest position to the crest.
   (4) The higher the crest of a wave, the deeper its trough.
   (5) Crests and troughs alternate in a wave.

2. What is a wave?

   (1) a movement of water
   (2) a disturbance that travels through matter
   (3) energy in space
   (4) a disturbance that travels through space or matter
   (5) energy in space or matter

3. Which characteristic of an ocean wave would be of most interest to a surfer?

   (1) amplitude
   (2) rest position
   (3) trough
   (4) disturbance
   (5) spray

Items 4 to 8 refer to the following passage.

If you have ever watched the ocean, you have probably noticed that sometimes the waves seem to come very close together, while at other times they seem very far apart. What you were noticing was a difference in wavelength. Wavelength is the distance between the crests of two consecutive waves. Waves that appear very close together have a shorter wavelength, while those that appear far apart have a longer wavelength.

Frequency is the number of waves that pass a given point in a specific unit of time. For example, if you watched an object in the ocean bob up and down ten times in one minute, the frequency of the wave would be ten cycles per minute. In order to count one complete cycle, both a crest and a trough of the wave must pass.

If you know the wavelength and frequency of a wave, you can find its speed. If the frequency of the wave is measured in Hertz, and the wavelength is measured in meters, then the speed in meters per second is given by this equation:

$$\text{speed} = \text{wavelength} \times \text{frequency}$$

4. A wave's frequency is the relationship between

   (1) height and weight
   (2) height and distance between crests
   (3) distance between crests and amplitude
   (4) number of crests that pass a given point and unit of time
   (5) unit of time and distance

5. What is the result of decreased wavelength and frequency?

   (1) decreased speed
   (2) the same speed
   (3) increased speed
   (4) increased distance
   (5) decreased distance

6. To calculate the frequency of a wave you must

   (1) multiply wavelength times frequency
   (2) divide speed by wavelength
   (3) multiply speed times wavelength
   (4) divide wavelength by speed
   (5) multiply speed times frequency

7. What is the speed of a wave with a wavelength of 3 meters and a frequency of 6 Hertz?

   (1) 2 meters per second
   (2) 3 meters per second
   (3) 9 meters per second
   (4) 18 meters per second
   (5) 36 meters per second

8. Which of the following would be the best title for this passage?

   (1) What Causes Waves?
   (2) Parts of a Wave
   (3) Ocean Waves
   (4) Properties of Waves
   (5) Frequency and Speed

Item 9 refers to the following paragraph.

A wave traveling through water disturbs the water molecules as it passes, causing them to move in an up-and-down motion. The water molecules do not move with the wave. Once the wave passes, the water molecules become still until another disturbance occurs.

9. From the information given, what would you expect a small rowboat to do when the waves from a large motor boat strike it?

   A. drift away from its position
   B. bob up and down
   C. drift away and then return to its original position

   (1) A only
   (2) B only
   (3) C only
   (4) A and B
   (5) B and C

Answers are on page 314.

Items 1 and 2 refer to the following passage. Choose the best answer to each item.

Sounds travel as waves. For a sound wave to travel, it must have a medium, a substance capable of transmitting the wave. The medium can be a solid, a liquid, or a gas.

The wave pushes the molecules of the medium back and forth parallel to its line of motion. During one complete cycle of a sound wave, the molecules are pushed together in a compression, then spread out in a rarefaction. You can think of the wave's motion as push forward-pull back. Such waves are called longitudinal waves.

1. The motion of a longitudinal wave most resembles the motion of

   (1) an ocean wave
   (2) a pulsating rope held between two people
   (3) an accordion being played
   (4) a bouncing ball
   (5) a bicycle on a bumpy road

2. The moon has no atmosphere. Which item would be useless to take along on a trip to the moon?

   (1) a flashlight
   (2) thermal underwear
   (3) oxygen supply
   (4) cassette player with earphones
   (5) tape deck and speaker system

Items 3 to 6 refer to the following passage.

Sound waves travel best through solids, because the molecules are packed tightly together. Elastic solids, such as nickel, steel, and iron, carry sound especially well; inelastic solids, such as sound-proofing materials, carry sound less well. Liquids are second-best to solids in carrying sound, and gases are the least effective carriers of sound.

Sound travels through air at room temperature at about 1,140 feet per second. The speed of sound averages about 4,950 feet per second in water and about 19,700 feet per second in stone.

3. It can be inferred from the passage that a gas is the least effective medium for the transmission of sound waves because

   (1) its molecules are too close together
   (2) its molecules are too far apart
   (3) it is too dense
   (4) it is elastic
   (5) its temperature is too low

4. "Solid state" on audio equipment probably refers to which statement?

   (1) Sound molecules travel fastest in solids.
   (2) Solid components are more durable than other types of components.
   (3) Solids transmit sounds best.
   (4) Solids make the best amplifiers.
   (5) Solids are more elastic than gases.

5. On a very cold day, a baseball fan notices the ball in the air well before hearing the crack of the bat. Which statement offers the best explanation?

   (1) The person's ears have become stopped up by the cold.
   (2) The players are hitting the ball slower because of the cold.
   (3) Some people receive sound waves slower than other people.
   (4) The sound waves have farther to travel than usual.
   (5) Sound waves travel more slowly in cold air than in warm air.

> **tip**
> When drawing a conclusion, keep in mind all the facts presented in a passage or diagram. Then rule out any conclusions that clearly contradict these facts.

6. The expression "Put your ear to the ground" probably originated because

   (1) sound that travels through the ground will reach your ears before sound that travels through air
   (2) sound waves travel horizontally
   (3) sound waves travel faster at low altitudes than at high altitudes
   (4) some types of sounds travel only through solids
   (5) sound waves are loudest near the ground

Items 7 to 11 refer to the following passage.

Light waves are electromagnetic waves. Unlike sound waves, electromagnetic waves do not need a medium through which to travel.

Light is the part of the electromagnetic spectrum that we can see. It includes those electromagnetic waves with frequencies between 400 trillion and 750 trillion Hertz. Below these frequencies are invisible electromagnetic waves such as infrared, radio waves, microwaves, and radar. Above the frequencies of visible light are other invisible electromagnetic waves, including ultraviolet, X-rays, and gamma rays. All electromagnetic waves travel at the same speed in a given medium. The speed of light in a vacuum is 186,282 miles per second.

7. Compared to radio waves, ultraviolet waves are

   (1) visible, while radio waves are invisible
   (2) lower in energy than radio waves
   (3) lower in frequency than radio waves
   (4) higher in frequency than radio waves
   (5) of longer wavelength than radio waves

8. Which of the following statements can be disproved by the information provided?

   (1) Air is the only medium through which light can travel.
   (2) Light waves can travel through space.
   (3) Gamma rays travel just as fast as microwaves.
   (4) While sound cannot be heard on the moon, light can be seen there.
   (5) No one can see radio waves.

9. Which of the following statements is true of infrared waves?

   (1) They are produced by microwave ovens.
   (2) They travel through a vacuum at 186,282 miles per second.
   (3) They travel faster through air than X-rays.
   (4) Some have a frequency of 600 trillion Hertz.
   (5) They are not electromagnetic waves.

10. Which of the following waves has a frequency below 400 trillion Hertz?

    (1) gamma rays
    (2) light waves
    (3) ultraviolet waves
    (4) radio waves
    (5) X-rays

11. Which of the following is the best title for this passage?

    (1) Waves of the Electromagnetic Spectrum
    (2) Electromagnetism: What is It?
    (3) Light and Its Properties
    (4) Speed of Electromagnetic Waves
    (5) Frequencies of Electromagnetic Waves

Answers are on page 315.

Directions: Choose the <u>best answer</u> to each item.

<u>Items 1 and 2</u> refer to the following information.

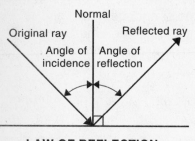

LAW OF REFLECTION

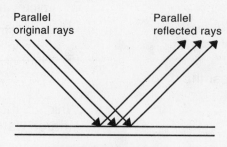

SMOOTH SURFACE

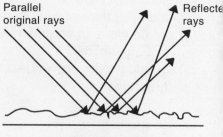

ROUGH SURFACE

When a light ray strikes a surface and bounces back, we say that it is reflected. The law of reflection states that the angle at which the original ray strikes the surface (the angle of incidence) will be equal to the angle at which the ray is reflected (angle of reflection). Both angles are measured in relation to the normal line which is at a right angle to the surface.

Because light waves travel in straight lines, they can be represented by lines that show direction, called rays. A beam of light, such as that produced by a flashlight, contains many parallel rays. If a beam of light strikes a smooth surface such as a mirror, all of the rays will be reflected parallel to one another in the same order in which they originated. If, however, a beam of light strikes a rough surface, each ray will strike the surface at a different angle of incidence, and the light will be scattered in many different directions.

1. A woman wishes to use a mirror to send a signal by flashlight to a man. The angle formed by the woman, the mirror, and the man is 60°. When the woman aims the flashlight toward the mirror, what should the angle of incidence be?

   (1)   60°
   (2)   15°
   (3)   30°
   (4)   90°
   (5)   120°

2. Dust and other foreign particles in the atmosphere scatter light. An airport control tower located near a city with polluted air would find that its light signals

   (1)   appear sharper and clearer than usual
   (2)   travel longer distances than usual
   (3)   take longer to reach their destinations than usual
   (4)   appear fuzzy and blurred
   (5)   are all reflected at the same angle

Items 3 to 7 refer to the following passage and diagram.

Where do the colors of the rainbow come from? Seven colors are seen in a rainbow: red, orange, yellow, green, blue, indigo, and violet. Each color is made up of electromagnetic waves of a different wavelength. Violet has the shortest wavelength, and red has the longest wavelength. When all the colors are mixed together, you see white light, which is colorless.

A rainbow occurs when white light passes through drops of water in the air and is separated into its different colors. The water bends, or refracts, the white light. Then each separated color reflects off the inner surface of the drop. As the light leaves the drop, each wavelength is refracted further. The light waves of different colors now are bent at different angles and are separated into the colors of the rainbow.

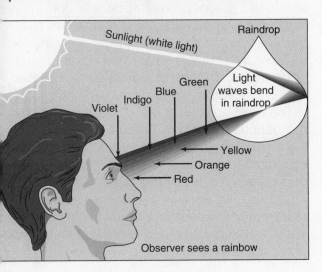

Observer sees a rainbow

3. What is white light?

(1) one of the colors of visible light
(2) one of the colors of the rainbow
(3) the absence of color
(4) a mix of all the visible colors
(5) a type of rainbow

tip When reading a passage that has a diagram with it, preview the diagram before you begin to read. Then refer back to it whenever necessary. Usually the diagram is included to help you understand the passage.

4. Scientists estimate that people can see about 17,000 different colors. What causes these colors?

(1) Each rainbow has different colors.
(2) The order of colors in the rainbow is always the same.
(3) There are 17,000 different mixtures of the colors in white light.
(4) White light is invisible.
(5) The colors are mixtures of black and the seven colors of the rainbow.

5. As white light passes through a drop of water, violet light is bent the most of all the colors of light. Which of the following conclusions is supported by the information in the passage and diagram?

(1) Green light is bent the least.
(2) Orange light is slowed down to the same speed as red light.
(3) Red light is bent the least.
(4) Yellow light is bent to the same angle as blue light.
(5) Indigo light is bent the least.

6. Rainbows are seen because

(1) red light has the shortest wavelength and violet light has the longest wavelength
(2) red light has the longest wavelength and violet light has the shortest wavelength
(3) light bends, or refracts, water
(4) colors of light get mixed together to form white light in water drops
(5) sunlight bends and separates when it passes through water drops

7. Which of the following statements is not supported by the passage and diagram?

(1) Reflection does not bend light waves.
(2) The formation of rainbows is due to refraction only.
(3) The wavelength of each color of light is refracted differently.
(4) Orange light and blue light have different wavelengths.
(5) The amount a light wave refracts depends on its wavelength.

Answers are on page 316.

Directions: Choose the best answer to each item.

Items 1 and 2 refer to the following passage.

Atoms of the same element with different numbers of neutrons are called isotopes. Isotopes that have unstable nuclei are radioactive. Radioactive isotopes can change into other isotopes or elements by a spontaneous process known as radioactive decay. In radioactive decay, the unstable nucleus of a radioactive atom breaks down until it becomes the stable nucleus of another isotope, (of the same element) or of a different element. For example, an atom of uranium may go through 13 changes until it becomes a stable atom of lead.

As it breaks down, an atom gives off radiation. There are three types of radiation. Alpha radiation consists of two positively-charged protons and two neutrons released together in what is known as an alpha particle. Beta radiation consists of negatively-charged beta particles that are actually electrons. Gamma radiation is made up of high-energy electromagnetic waves called gamma rays.

Some radioactive elements undergo alpha decay, while others undergo beta decay. Both alpha and beta decay are nearly always accompanied by the release of gamma rays. Of the three types of radiation, gamma rays are the most harmful. With tremendous penetrating power, gamma rays have the ability to destroy the cells of living things.

1. According to the passage, an atom of a radioactive element does all of the following except

   (1) release energy
   (2) increase in size
   (3) change its identity
   (4) release subatomic particles
   (5) give off gamma rays

2. Which of the following would be most useful in separating alpha particles from beta particles?

   (1) a microscope
   (2) an electric field
   (3) a powerful lamp
   (4) a mirror
   (5) a block of lead

Items 3 and 4 refer to the following passage.

Large amounts of energy are released by atoms in a process called nuclear fission. Nuclear fission is the splitting of an atomic nucleus into two smaller, approximately equal-sized nuclei. Nuclear fission can occur naturally or be forced. The first sustained and controlled fission reaction was engineered in 1942.

The rapid splitting of many nuclei is called a nuclear chain reaction. This process produces the energy generated at a nuclear power plant. uncontrolled, a chain reaction can result in a nuclear explosion. For this reason, fission reactions take place in a device called a nuclear reactor. The purpose of a reactor is to control the speed of the reaction and to prevent the escape of radioactive materials.

3. Which of the following statements about nuclear fission is not true?

   (1) It occurs spontaneously in nature.
   (2) It releases energy and matter.
   (3) It can be controlled.
   (4) It involves changes in the nucleus of an atom.
   (5) It never took place before the twentieth century.

4. What would be the most likely long-term effect of an accident at a nuclear power plant?

(1) a nuclear explosion
(2) contaminating the environment
(3) speeding up of the nuclear chain reaction
(4) stopping of the nuclear chain reaction
(5) There would be no long-term effect.

---

ems 5 and 6 refer to the following diagrams.

SERIES CIRCUIT

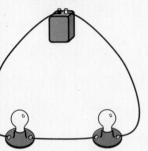

PARALLEL CIRCUIT

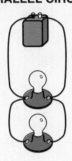

A series circuit has only one path for the electric current. When the circuit is broken, the current stops.

In a parallel circuit, the current flows in two or more separate paths. If the current in one path stops, it still flows in the other branches.

5. Which of the following is likely to use a series circuit?

(1) the wiring for a house
(2) a string of decorating lights
(3) heavy duty transmission lines
(4) the wiring in a car
(5) the wiring for several computers in an office

6. One light bulb in a kitchen circuit burns out, but the other lights still work. Which statement supports the conclusion that the kitchen uses a parallel circuit?

(1) The current has stopped in the entire circuit.
(2) The current continues in all but one path of the circuit.
(3) The current was automatically shut off by a fuse.
(4) The burned-out light bulb was on its own series circuit.
(5) A power shortage caused the light to go out.

tip **Read questions carefully to find important qualifying statements. Use these statements to eliminate wrong options. For example, in item 4 the words *long-term* can help you eliminate three options which are not long-term effects.**

Answers are on page 317.

Performance Analysis
Unit 4 Cumulative Review: Physics

Name: _____   **Class:** _____   **Date:** _____

Use the Answer Key on page 317 to check your answers to the Unit 4 Cumulative Review: Physics
Then use the chart to figure out the skill areas in which you need additional review. Circle on the
chart the numbers of the test items you answered correctly. Then go back and review the lessons
for the skill areas that are difficult for you. For additional review, see the *Steck-Vaughn GED
Science Exercise Book,* Unit 4: Physics.

Thinking Skill Areas	Physics	Lessons for Review
Comprehension	1	1, 2, 4, 9, 15, 16
Application	**5**	10, 13
Analysis	4, **6**	3, 5, 6, 8, 11, 12, 18
Evaluation	2, 3	7, 14, 17, 19

Boldfaced numbers indicate items based on charts, graphs, illustrations, and diagrams.

SCIENCE

Directions

The Science Posttest consists of multiple-choice questions intended to measure your understanding of general concepts in science. The questions are based on short readings that often include a graph, chart, or diagram. Study the information given, and then answer the questions that follow. Refer to the information as often as necessary in answering the questions.

You should spend no more than 95 minutes answering the 66 questions on the Science Posttest. Work carefully, but do not spend too much time on any one question. Do not skip any items. Make a reasonable guess when you are not sure of an answer. You will not be penalized for incorrect answers.

When time is up, mark the last item you finished. This will tell you whether you can finish the real GED Test in the time allowed. Then complete the test.

Record your answers to the questions on a copy of the answer sheet on page 345. Be sure that all required information is properly recorded on the answer sheet.

To record your answers, mark the numbered space on the answer sheet that corresponds to the answer you choose for each question on the test.

Example:

Which of the following is the smallest unit in a living thing?

(1) tissue
(2) organ
(3) cell
(4) muscle
(5) capillary

The correct answer is "cell"; therefore, answer space 3 should be marked on the answer sheet.

Do not rest the point of your pencil on the answer sheet while you are considering your answer. Make no stray or unnecessary marks. If you change an answer, erase your first mark completely. Mark only one answer space for each question; multiple answers will be scored as incorrect. Do not fold or crease your answer sheet.

When you finish the test, use the Correlation Chart on page 235 to determine whether you are ready to take the real GED Test, and, if not, which skill areas need additional review.

Adapted with permission of the American Council of Education.

Directions: Choose the best answer to each item.

Items 1 and 2 refer to the following map.

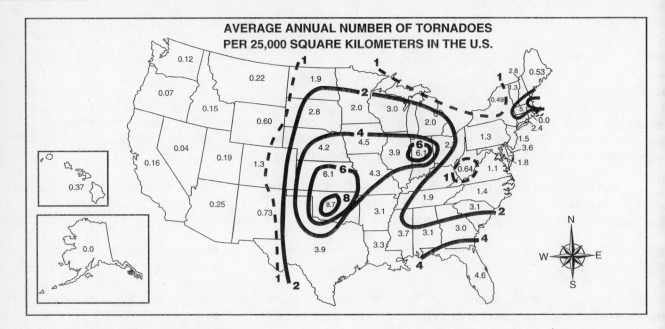

AVERAGE ANNUAL NUMBER OF TORNADOES PER 25,000 SQUARE KILOMETERS IN THE U.S.

1. According to the map, tornadoes in the United States can be found most often

   (1) in the mountains
   (2) in coastal areas
   (3) in the North
   (4) in large, flat areas
   (5) over the ocean

2. A person with a fear of tornadoes would be happiest living in

   (1) New England
   (2) Florida
   (3) Texas
   (4) the Midwest
   (5) Alaska

Items 3 and 4 refer to the following information.

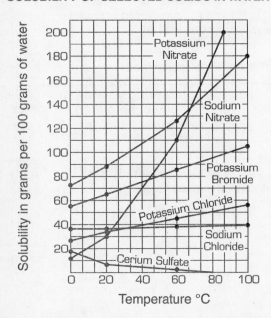

SOLUBILITY OF SELECTED SOLIDS IN WATER

3. The term solubility means the ability to dissolve. The solubilities of some substances change if the water temperature changes. The solid whose solubility changes most as the temperature of water changes is

   (1) potassium nitrate
   (2) potassium bromide
   (3) potassium chloride
   (4) sodium chloride
   (5) sodium nitrate

4. Many people think that increasing the temperature of the water will increase the solubility of any solid. Which line on the graph disproves this idea?

   (1) potassium nitrate
   (2) potassium bromide
   (3) potassium chloride
   (4) cerium sulfate
   (5) sodium nitrate

Many insects have a wormlike stage called a arva before becoming adults. The screwworm is ne larva of a fly that lays its eggs in the open ores of cattle and other animals. Hundreds of vorms can develop in a single sore and kill the ost animal. In warm climates, the screwworm loes millions of dollars of damage each year.

Controlling the screwworm has long been a roblem. Chemical control using insecticides ould kill the insects. However, applying nsecticides to individual animals is too xpensive. A biological control method was first ied in 1958 on the island of Curaçao in the Vest Indies. Large numbers of sterile male flies aised in laboratories were released on the sland. The theory was that if there were more terile males that could not fertilize female flies han fertile males, many females would mate vith the sterile males. Since the females mate nly once, most of the eggs would not be ertilized. The number of young produced would ventually reach zero.

The Curaçao project was successful, and crewworm flies were eliminated from the island. Since then, sterile-male release has been used o control the screwworm in the southwestern Jnited States. However, the screwworm also ves in Mexico, where it is not well controlled. herefore, release of sterile males must be ontinued along the border.

5. According to the article, which method of controlling screwworms continues to be used today?

   (1) spraying insecticides
   (2) treating wounded cattle
   (3) sterilizing the males in the wild
   (4) releasing laboratory-bred sterile males
   (5) sterilizing the eggs laid by the females

6. Why was the decision made to try to control screwworm damage on cows in Curaçao by biological rather than chemical methods?

   (1) Chemical insecticides were hard to obtain.
   (2) Treating cattle individually with chemical insecticides was too expensive.
   (3) The chemical methods were less effective than biological control.
   (4) Biological methods do not harm the environment.
   (5) Biological methods can be easily developed by individual farmers.

7. Which of the following is an unstated assumption made by the author of this article?

   A. A change in the ecology of an area is permissible if the results can be helpful.
   B. Getting rid of an agricultural pest has more advantages than disadvantages.
   C. Chemical pesticides may be suitable for other insect-control problems.

   (1) A only
   (2) B only
   (3) C only
   (4) A and B only
   (5) A, B, and C

8. Based on the article, you can conclude that biological control

   (1) works best on insect populations that cover a wide geographical area
   (2) works best on isolated insect populations
   (3) is always better than chemical insecticides
   (4) does not work because insects evolve different ways of reproducing
   (5) is more expensive than chemical pesticides in the long run

9. Another type of biological control is to release males that have been exposed to radiation. The sperm of these males carry deadly genetic defects. In such a situation, you would expect that the population would

(1) die out in one generation because none of the eggs would be fertilized
(2) die out in several generations because most of the eggs would not be fertilized
(3) decrease in several generations because many fertilized eggs would be seriously defective and would die
(4) stay the same because the females would continue to mate
(5) increase because more eggs would be fertilized

10. Which of the following is most similar to the sterile-male release method of controlling insects?

(1) releasing chemical insecticides in areas such as swamps
(2) spaying animals to prevent their reproduction
(3) introducing predators to feed on the pest
(4) introducing viruses or bacteria that are harmful to the pest
(5) setting traps for animal pests such as rats and mice

Items 11 and 12 refer to the following information.

A blood pressure reading is made up of two numbers such as 125/85. The first number is the greatest pressure exerted by the blood in the arteries when the heart beats. This is called the systolic pressure. The second number is the lowest pressure of the blood in the arteries. This is called the diastolic pressure. The chart shows how blood pressure varies as the heart beats, forcing blood through the arteries. Three beats would have occurred in the period shown.

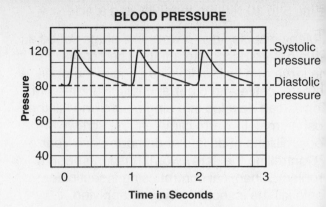

BLOOD PRESSURE

11. What is the blood pressure reading of the patient whose blood pressure is charted above?

(1) 120/80
(2) 80/120
(3) 130/90
(4) 90/130
(5) 1.5

12. What is the effect of the pumping action of the heart on blood pressure?

(1) When the heart pumps, blood pressure goes down.
(2) When the heart pumps, blood pressure goes up.
(3) When the heart pumps, blood pressure remains the same.
(4) When the heart relaxes, blood pressure goes up.
(5) When the heart relaxes, blood pressure remains the same.

Earthquakes start deep in Earth's crust. The oint where an earthquake starts is called its ocus. From the focus, energy moves outward in ll directions, causing the ground to vibrate. hese vibrations are called seismic waves.

In 1935, the American scientist Charles F. ichter developed a scale that measures the mplitude, or amount of back-and-forth novement, of the seismic waves at the focus of n earthquake. On the Richter scale, the mplitude of seismic waves increases ten times etween each whole number. For example, an arthquake that measures 5 has waves with an mplitude ten times greater than one that neasures 4.

The amount of energy released by an arthquake can be calculated from its Richter cale rating. Earthquakes that measure 4.5 or reater can cause serious damage if they occur populated areas. Earthquakes that measure or greater are considered severe. The famous 906 San Francisco earthquake measured .3, and the 1989 San Francisco earthquake neasured 7.1.

The Mercalli scale is also related to arthquakes. This scale uses Roman numerals rate earthquakes according to their effects on particular place where the quake is felt. For xample, an earthquake felt only by scientific nonitors would have a rating of I. An earthquake nat destroyed all the buildings in a wide area ould have the highest rating of XII. Since the ffects of an earthquake differ from place to lace, the Mercalli scale ratings in each place an differ.

3. What does the Richter scale measure?

   (1) the amplitude of seismic waves on Earth's surface during an earthquake
   (2) the amplitude of seismic waves at the focus of an earthquake
   (3) the direction of seismic waves in an earthquake
   (4) the amount of damage done by an earthquake
   (5) the distance between the focus of an earthquake and Earth's surface

14. The Mercalli scale measures

   (1) the amplitude of seismic waves on Earth's surface during an earthquake
   (2) the amplitude of seismic waves at the focus of an earthquake
   (3) the effect of an earthquake on the area precisely over the focus
   (4) the effects of an earthquake on a particular place
   (5) the seismic wave direction in an earthquake

15. Seismologists estimated an earthquake as 6 on the Richter scale. Later, they checked their data and gave the earthquake a rating of 7. What caused them to revise the Richter scale rating? Their data showed that the earthquake

   (1) was not considered severe
   (2) had 10 times smaller amplitude than they had first estimated
   (3) had 10 times greater amplitude than they had first estimated
   (4) had 100 times smaller amplitude than they had first estimated
   (5) had 100 times greater amplitude than they had first estimated

16. An earthquake whose focus was located near San Jose, California was rated VII on the Mercalli scale. In nearby Oakland, the earthquake was rated V on the Mercalli scale. Why were the two Mercalli ratings different?

   (1) The Mercalli scale measures amplitude of seismic waves at the focus of the earthquake.
   (2) The Mercalli scale measures amplitude of seismic waves at various points affected by the earthquake.
   (3) Earthquakes have two Mercalli ratings.
   (4) The earthquake caused less damage in Oakland than in San Jose, so the Mercalli rating in Oakland was lower.
   (5) The earthquake caused more damage in Oakland than in San Jose, so the Mercalli rating in Oakland was lower.

Items 17 to 20 refer to the following chart.

EMERGENCY ACTION FOR POISONING	
Type of Poison	**First Aid***
Inhaled poison	Provide fresh air. If victim is not breathing, begin artificial respiration.
Poison on the skin	Remove contaminated clothing. Flood skin with water for 10 minutes. Wash gently with soap and rinse.
Poison in the eye	Flood eye with lukewarm water. Repeat for 15 minutes.
Swallowed poison	Medicine: Call for advice. Chemical or household products: Unless victim is unconscious, convulsing, or cannot swallow, give milk or water. Then call for advice on whether to induce vomiting

*After emergency first-aid actions, call the poison control center, a hospital, or a doctor.

17. A three-year-old girl ate the contents of a bottle of children's aspirin tablets. What is the first thing her caregiver should do?

    (1) Flood with water.
    (2) Induce vomiting.
    (3) Give milk.
    (4) Give water.
    (5) Call the poison control center.

18. Because of a malfunction in the exhaust system of his car, a man was overcome by breathing carbon monoxide gas when he started the car in a closed garage. What emergency action should the person who finds him take first?

    (1) Open the doors and windows.
    (2) Flood the skin with water.
    (3) Call the poison control center.
    (4) Induce vomiting.
    (5) Give artificial respiration.

19. A gardener working in her shed spilled a solution of insecticide, and it splashed on her blue jeans. She continued to mix the chemical. Then her vision started to blur and her head began to ache. What should she have done immediately after the accident?

    (1) opened the doors and windows
    (2) removed her blue jeans
    (3) called the poison control center
    (4) applied an ointment
    (5) washed with soap and rinsed with wat

20. A man who got some poison in his eye wa given emergency first aid by a friend. After about 15 minutes of having his eye flooded with water, the man started to feel better. What should the friend do now?

    (1) Continue flooding the eye with water.
    (2) Flood the eye with a solution of baking soda and water.
    (3) Apply a bandage to the eye.
    (4) Call the poison control center.
    (5) Do nothing.

220

Items 21 to 25 refer to the following article.

The path taken by an electric current is called a circuit. For electricity to flow, the circuit must be complete. In a flashlight, the electric current flows from one end of a battery through a wire to the bulb. From the bulb, the current returns along another wire to the other end of the battery. A switch is a device that enables you to break or complete the circuit, thereby stopping or restarting the flow of electric current.

Batteries used in toys and portable radios are called dry cells. These batteries are a common source of electric current for objects that must be portable. Dry cell batteries produce electricity by chemical reaction. This chemical reaction increases whenever the circuit is complete. When the circuit is broken, the current stops flowing and the chemical action continues, only more slowly. When the supply of chemicals is used up, the dry cell battery is dead.

A storage battery is often used to power larger devices. Chemical reaction is also the source of electric current in the storage battery. As long as the circuit is complete, the chemical reaction continues at an increased rate. When the chemicals are used up, the production of current stops. A storage battery does not need to be thrown away; its chemicals can be restored by recharging it with electric current from an outside source.

21. You pick up a flashlight that uses dry cell batteries and press the switch. Nothing happens. From your observations, which of the following is a valid conclusion?

   A. The chemical reaction in the batteries has increased.
   B. The chemicals in the batteries may have been used up.
   C. Storage batteries are better than dry cell batteries.

(1) A only
(2) B only
(3) C only
(4) A and B only
(5) B and C only

22. A portable CD player stopped working. When its batteries were recharged, it worked again. Why did recharging help?

(1) The chemical reaction continued at a reduced rate when the circuit was broken, and the chemicals were used up.
(2) The chemical reaction continued at a steady rate when the circuit was broken, and the chemicals were used up.
(3) An outside electric current restored the chemicals in the battery so that they could produce current again.
(4) The CD player needed to be plugged in to operate.
(5) The batteries were new.

23. A boy left his toy flashlight on, but the father told him to turn it off. Why did the father think it should be off?

(1) The battery produces the same amount of current whether the light is on or off.
(2) The battery can produce electric current as long as it is being recharged.
(3) The life of the battery is the same whether the flashlight is left on or off.
(4) The life of the battery is shorter when the flashlight is left on.
(5) The battery will not wear out when the flashlight is left off.

24. Which of the following items is best suited for getting electric current from a dry cell battery?

(1) a washing machine
(2) a car
(3) a motorized wheelchair
(4) a toy truck
(5) a doorbell

25. You need a large amount of electric current to start a car's engine. A car's internal combustion engine uses a large storage battery to produce this current. It does not take all this current to keep the car running. In fact, the battery is constantly being recharged while the car's engine is running. As a result, batteries do not have to be plugged into an electric outlet for recharging. Which of the following is a conclusion from this information?

(1) A car battery is not powerful enough to provide electric current to start the motor.
(2) Car batteries frequently need to be jump-started.
(3) The car's engine generates electricity that recharges the battery as the car runs.
(4) A car battery does not need external recharging for the first 25,000 miles.
(5) A car battery does not need external recharging for the first 100,000 miles.

Item 26 refers to the following diagram.

EARTH'S REVOLUTION AROUND SUN

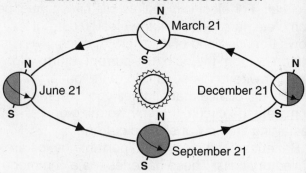

26. At the same time as Earth revolves around the sun, it rotates on its tilted axis. Which of the following conclusions can be supported by the diagram?

(1) High tides occur when Earth is closest to the sun.
(2) High tides occur when Earth is closest to the moon.
(3) On June 21, the Northern Hemisphere is tilted toward the sun.
(4) On June 21, the Northern Hemisphere is tilted away from the sun.
(5) On June 21, all parts of Earth have days and nights of equal length.

Posttes

27. A freighter is scheduled to make the trip from New York to Liverpool, England in eight days. The trip back to New York is scheduled to take nine days. What accounts for the difference in the two trips?

   (1) Liverpool's time zone is six hours ahead of New York's time zone.
   (2) The ocean currents in the North Atlantic flow from west to east.
   (3) The ocean currents in the North Atlantic flow from east to west.
   (4) The ocean currents in the South Atlantic flow from east to west.
   (5) The ocean currents in the South Atlantic flow from west to east.

Items 28 and 29 refer to the following information.

   Matter is anything that has mass and takes up space. Matter is found in three different states—solid, liquid, and gas.

1. A solid such as iron has a definite shape and takes up a definite amount of space.
2. A liquid such as milk does not have a definite shape since it can be poured. It takes up a definite amount of space.
3. A gas such as air has no definite shape and does not take up a definite amount of space. It expands to fill whatever space is available.

   Most matter can exist in any one of the three states and can change from one state to another through changes in temperature.

28. Which of the following is an example of a single form of matter in three different states?

   (1) lump of sugar, grains of sugar, sugar syrup
   (2) rock salt, salt crystals, salt water
   (3) ice, water, water vapor
   (4) glass, broken glass, molten glass
   (5) dry ice, carbon dioxide, carbonated beverage with carbon-dioxide bubbles

29. What causes a form of matter to change from one state to another?

   (1) changes in chemical makeup
   (2) changes in position
   (3) changes in color
   (4) changes in amount of heat
   (5) changes in hardness

Nearly a third of colds are caused by rhinoviruses. These viruses can survive for up to three hours outside the body—on skin, certain fabrics, and hard materials such as stainless steel and wood. Often people infect themselves. For example, a person picks up the live viruses from a contaminated surface. Later when the person rubs the nose or eyes, the viruses are transferred to the mucous membranes in the nose—a cold virus's favorite spot. Shaking hands, opening a door, and picking up a toy are frequent infection routes—more frequent than sneezes, coughs, and kisses.

To prevent a cold, experts advise you to keep your hands away from your eyes and nose and to wash your hands frequently with hot water and soap. You should also clean contaminated objects and use disposable tissues. To stop the spread of viruses that are airborne, cover a cough or a sneeze. Teaching all these methods to children is especially important. Children have the most colds and share the most viruses.

30. Why should objects contaminated with cold viruses be washed?

   (1) The viruses can ruin the objects.
   (2) The viruses survive indefinitely on objects.
   (3) A person with a cold may touch them.
   (4) Another person may pick up the viruses by touching the objects.
   (5) Even after the cold viruses die, they can infect someone.

31. Which of the following ways to avoid catching a cold is not based on scientific fact?

   (1) Wash hands often with soap and water
   (2) Keep hands away from eyes and nose.
   (3) Clean contaminated objects.
   (4) Cover sneezes.
   (5) Avoid going out in the rain.

32. What is the effect of touching your eyes or nose with unwashed hands that have touched contaminated objects?

   (1) Your face gets soiled.
   (2) Rhinoviruses may be transferred from your hands to the mucous membranes in your nose.
   (3) Rhinoviruses die when they come in contact with your skin.
   (4) Airborne germs come in contact with the mucous membranes in your nose.
   (5) There is no effect.

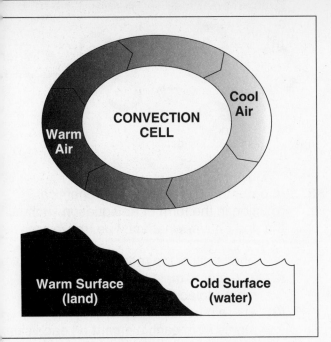

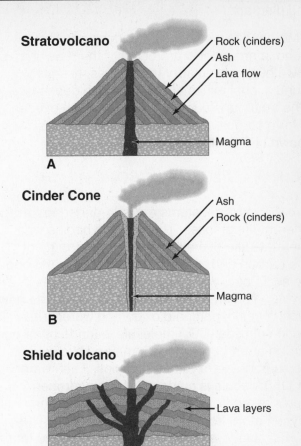

33. The convection cell in the diagram is an area of the atmosphere in which air movement is caused by variations in temperature. Which of the following conclusions is best supported by the diagram?

   (1) Warm air rises and cool air sinks.
   (2) Warm air sinks and cool air rises.
   (3) Warm air pushes cold air upward.
   (4) The temperature of Earth's surface has no effect on air movement.
   (5) Convection cells occur only where land meets water.

34. According to the diagram, in which direction should you face to keep the wind out of your eyes at this particular beach and at this time?

   (1) Face the water.
   (2) Face inland.
   (3) Have your left side to the water.
   (4) Have your right side to the water.
   (5) Face in any direction.

35. Mt. St. Helens erupted in 1980, spewing forth rock, cinders, ashes, and lava over a wide area. Mt. St. Helens is

   (1) a stratovolcano
   (2) a cinder cone
   (3) a shield volcano
   (4) a magma volcano
   (5) an extinct volcano

36. Which of the following conclusions is best supported by the diagram of volcanoes?

   (1) Volcanoes are steep mountains.
   (2) Volcanic eruptions are always rapid and explosive.
   (3) Volcanoes are mountains built from deposits of lava, rock, cinders, or ashes.
   (4) Volcanoes are most likely to occur along the boundaries of Earth's tectonic plates.
   (5) Volcanoes may lie dormant for years between eruptions.

Items 37 and 38 refer to the following information and diagram.

Methane is a colorless, odorless gas that is found in nature. It is a product of the breaking down of organic matter in marshes. It is also found in coal mines and natural gas deposits. When methane burns, it combines with oxygen to form carbon dioxide and water vapor, as shown in the following equation:

$$CH_4 + 2O_2 \rightarrow CO_2 + 2H_2O$$

In the reaction, atoms are rearranged to form different substances. The reaction begins with one molecule of methane (CH_4)—made up of one carbon and four hydrogen atoms—and one molecule of oxygen (O_2)—made up of two oxygen atoms. These recombine to form the new substances of carbon dioxide and water. The carbon dioxide (CO_2) molecule is made up of one carbon atom from the methane and two oxygen atoms from the oxygen molecules. Each water (H_2O) molecule is made up of two hydrogen atoms taken from the methane and another oxygen atom from the oxygen molecules. The atoms have formed new molecules, but the total number of each kind of atom remains the same. For example, there are four hydrogen atoms at the beginning of the reaction and four at the end.

The reaction of methane and oxygen can be hazardous to humans; the quantities of the gases and the speed of the reaction must be carefully controlled.

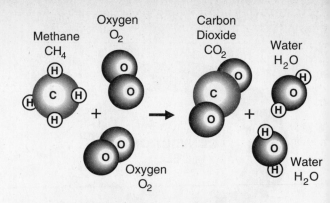

37. In order to write or express a chemical reaction in the form of an equation such as the one above, what must be true?

(1) The result of the reaction must be a gas.
(2) The atoms must be made of one or more molecules.
(3) There must be an equal number of atoms from each element on each side of the equation.
(4) The same molecules must appear on each side of the equation.
(5) Each molecule in the equation must be either divided or multiplied by two.

38. The chemical reaction shown in the diagram is hazardous. It is most dangerous to people in

(1) natural gas deposits deep within Earth
(2) marshes
(3) mines
(4) laboratories
(5) factories where other chemicals are made

THE HUMAN EYE

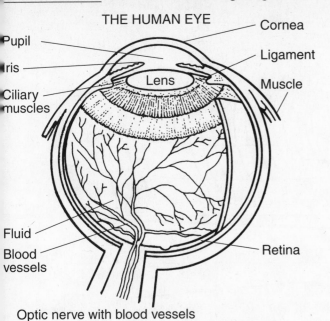

Optic nerve with blood vessels

Items 41 and 42 refer to the following information.

One way matter can change is through a chemical reaction. When matter undergoes a chemical change, the old substances are replaced by new substances with new properties, or characteristics. The energy needed to start a chemical reaction is called activation energy. Once they have started, some chemical reactions release heat energy. These are called exothermic reactions. Other chemical reactions absorb energy. These are called endothermic reactions.

39. The lens in the human eye must change shape in order for the eye to focus. What part of the eye is in the best position to control the lens shape?

(1) the retina
(2) the cornea
(3) the ciliary muscles
(4) the pupil
(5) the optic nerve

40. Light enters the eye through the pupil. The iris is the colored area around the pupil that makes the pupil larger or smaller. What is the effect of the adjustments made by the iris?

(1) The pupil changes color.
(2) The eye has a blind spot.
(3) The amount of light entering the eye is changed.
(4) The cornea bulges.
(5) The ability to see color is changed.

41. Lighter fluid is poured on charcoal in a barbecue grill, and a match is used to light the coals. In this chemical reaction, the lit match is

(1) a property of the reaction
(2) an endothermic reaction
(3) a physical change
(4) the resulting form of matter
(5) the source of activation energy

42. What is an endothermic reaction?

(1) a chemical reaction in which the properties of matter change
(2) a chemical reaction in which heat energy is released
(3) a chemical reaction in which heat energy is absorbed
(4) the application of energy to start a reaction
(5) a reaction that does not need activation energy to start

Items 43 and 44 refer to the following information.

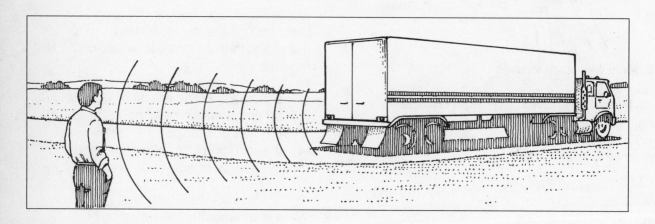

The Doppler effect describes the apparent changes that take place in waves, such as sound waves, as a result of the movement of the source or receiver of the waves. If the source of a sound and the receiver are moving closer together, the frequency seems to increase and the sound seems higher to the receiver. If the sound and the receiver are moving apart, the frequency seems to decrease and the sound seems lower.

43. Why does a truck's engine sound different when it is moving toward you and away from you?

   (1) The truck's engine makes more noise when it is moving toward the listener.
   (2) The truck's engine makes a higher-pitched sound when it is moving toward the listener.
   (3) To the listener, the frequency of the sound waves seems to change.
   (4) The driver has shifted gears.
   (5) To the listener, the engine sounds the same at all times.

44. Which of the following conclusions can be supported by the information given?

   (1) The Doppler effect works only with sound waves.
   (2) The Doppler effect can be used to determine whether a source of sound is moving away from or toward someone.
   (3) The Doppler effect works only when the source of sound is close.
   (4) The Doppler effect is a change in the actual frequency of sound waves as they are sent by the source.
   (5) The Doppler effect is used to overcome interference from other sources of sound.

Posttest

Items 45 to 48 refer to the following article.

Cholesterol is a fatty material that is made by our bodies and provided by our diets. Cholesterol helps produce cell membranes and is part of many key hormones. When the body cannot use all its cholesterol, much of the excess builds up on artery walls. Over the years, the arteries become narrower, resulting in a condition called atherosclerosis. Blood clots can form in clogged arteries. When this happens in the arteries of the heart, the flow of blood to the heart is blocked, and a heart attack occurs.

Until recently, the relationship between cholesterol and heart disease was not clear. Then 3,800 men with high cholesterol levels were studied. They were given a drug that lowers cholesterol and then were monitored. For every 1 percent decrease in the cholesterol level, there was a 2 to 3 percent decrease in the number of heart attacks and sudden deaths. Other studies confirmed these results.

Cholesterol levels can usually be lowered without drugs by reducing the amount of fat in the diet. The main sources of cholesterol are saturated fats, which the body converts to cholesterol. Saturated fats generally come from animal products. Some plant foods, such as coconut oil, palm oil, and chocolate, also contain saturated fats.

45. A person who is trying to lower his or her cholesterol level should eat less of which of the following foods?

(1) fruit
(2) vegetables
(3) steak
(4) bread
(5) sweetened juices

46. The effect of excess cholesterol in the body is that it

(1) lodges in the heart
(2) attacks the cell membranes of the heart
(3) builds up on the artery walls and can block the flow of blood to the heart
(4) causes uneven beating of the heart
(5) lowers the blood's ability to carry oxygen

47. Atherosclerosis is a condition in which

(1) the arteries become rigid
(2) the arteries become clogged
(3) the arteries become perforated
(4) heart tissue dies when it is deprived of oxygen
(5) heart tissue becomes less elastic

48. Which type of fat is the main source of cholesterol in our diets?

(1) unsaturated fat
(2) saturated fat
(3) polyunsaturated fat
(4) monounsaturated fat
(5) essential fatty acids

Items 49 to 52 refer to the following article.

The basic particles of matter—atoms and molecules—are always moving. Random motion of particles is present in solids, liquids, and gases. The energy of this movement is called kinetic energy. When a substance is heated, the kinetic energy increases, and the atoms and molecules move faster and farther apart. The volume of the substance usually increases. When a substance is cooled, it loses kinetic energy, and its volume usually decreases.

For example, the mercury in a thermometer expands when the thermometer is warmed. The more the thermometer is heated, the more it expands, and the higher the mercury rises. When the temperature decreases, the mercury contracts and moves down the thermometer.

Different substances expand by different amounts when heated. Engineers must account for these differences when designing buildings, roads, and other structures. Steel bridges, for example, have special structures at each end to allow for expansion in warm weather. Concrete bridges have expansion joints between slabs. These joints prevent the concrete from buckling when it expands.

Water behaves unlike most other substances. When it cools and freezes, it does not contract; it expands.

49. Which of the following can be concluded from the information provided?

(1) All substances expand when heated and contract when cooled.
(2) All substances contract when heated and expand when cooled.
(3) Most substances expand when heated and contract when cooled.
(4) Most substances contract when heated and expand when cooled.
(5) Most substances do not change volume when heated or cooled.

50. Why does mercury rise in a thermometer when the temperature increases?

(1) Mercury is a liquid.
(2) Mercury expands when heated.
(3) Mercury contracts when heated.
(4) Heat replaces mercury at the base of the thermometer.
(5) The glass tube of the thermometer contracts, forcing the mercury upward.

51. Given the behavior of matter when heated and cooled, which of the following would be likely to happen?

A. Telephone wires sag in the summertime.
B. A glass breaks when boiling water is poured into it.
C. Soup contracts when frozen.

(1) A only
(2) B only
(3) C only
(4) A and B only
(5) A, B, and C

52. When enough thermal energy is added, substances change from solids to liquids and then to gases. What can be concluded about the molecules and atoms in solids, liquids, and gases?

(1) The molecules and atoms of gases are the farthest apart and the most mobile.
(2) The molecules and atoms of liquids are the farthest apart and the most mobile.
(3) The molecules and atoms of solids are the farthest apart and the most mobile.
(4) The molecules and atoms of matter behave in the same way in solid, liquid, and gas forms.
(5) The molecules and atoms of a solid do not move.

Items 53 and 54 refer to the following diagram.

LAYERS OF EARTH

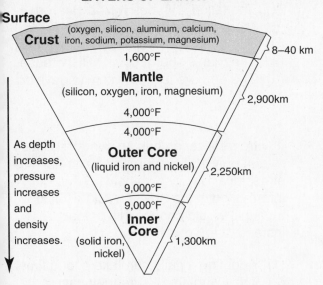

Surface

Crust (oxygen, silicon, aluminum, calcium, iron, sodium, potassium, magnesium)
8–40 km
1,600°F

Mantle
(silicon, oxygen, iron, magnesium)
2,900km
4,000°F
4,000°F

Outer Core
(liquid iron and nickel)
2,250km
9,000°F
9,000°F

Inner Core
(solid iron, nickel)
1,300km

As depth increases, pressure increases and density increases.

53. Using information about the moon's motion and distance from Earth, scientists have calculated that the average density of Earth is more than 5 grams per cubic centimeter. However, the density of rocks in Earth's crust alone is less than 3 grams per cubic centimeter. What statement would help explain the difference between Earth's average density and the density of the crust alone?

(1) Earth's interior is composed of material much more dense than the crust.
(2) Earth's interior is composed of material much less dense than the crust.
(3) The gravitational pull of the moon causes the crust material to be less dense.
(4) The gravitational pull of the sun causes the crust to be less dense.
(5) The lower density of the oceans was left out of the calculations.

54. The temperature of the inner core of Earth is hot enough to melt iron and nickel. However, iron and nickel are solid at the core. What factor in the diagram could be used to explain this?

(1) the presence in the core of other substances with high melting points
(2) the magnetic field of Earth
(3) the gravitational pull of the sun
(4) the great pressure on the inner core
(5) the chemical composition of the mantle

Items 55 and 56 refer to the following information.

A lack of vitamin C weakens some body tissues and can result in a disease called scurvy. Many foods contain little or no vitamin C. However, large amounts of vitamin C are found in citrus fruits, tomatoes, and members of the mustard family. The mustard family includes mustard greens, cabbage, broccoli, and kohlrabi. Stored or cooked food may contain less vitamin C than fresh food.

55. What foods are not good sources of vitamin C?

(1) dairy products
(2) citrus fruits
(3) mustard greens
(4) tomatoes
(5) red cabbage

56. A person concerned with getting the most vitamin C should eat which of the following foods?

(1) peas
(2) dried fruit
(3) cooked mustard greens
(4) a banana
(5) a fresh orange

Items 57 to 60 refer to the following article.

Test-tube conception, or in vitro fertilization, is a procedure for fertilizing eggs outside a woman's reproductive system. Although fertilization occurs outside the body, the egg and sperm are taken from the parents, and the child is genetically their own.

In a healthy female reproductive system, the fallopian tube transports an egg from the ovary, where the egg is produced, to the uterus. In some women, the tubes are blocked, and eggs cannot reach the uterus. If these women are otherwise healthy, they are prime candidates for in vitro fertilization.

Early in the woman's menstrual cycle, she can take fertility drugs to ensure that several eggs are produced. Without these drugs, only one egg would be produced. The eggs are surgically removed just before they are ready to be released by the ovaries. Each egg is placed in a culture dish, kept warm, and allowed to mature. Meanwhile, the man's sperm is processed. Each egg is then mixed with 100,000 to 200,000 of the processed sperm and allowed to incubate. After 12 hours, each egg is examined under a microscope to see if it has been fertilized. Usually 75 to 90 percent of the eggs will be fertilized.

One of the fertilized eggs is allowed to develop into an embryo. When it has grown into four or eight cells, the embryo is placed in the woman's uterus, and she is given hormones that help the uterus accept the egg. To succeed, the development of the embryo must be perfectly timed with developments in the uterus. Embryo transfer succeeds only about 20 percent of the time in any given cycle. During the next 12 to 16 weeks, almost half of the embryos that are transferred are lost by miscarriage. Ultimately, the couple has only a 10 percent chance that in vitro fertilization will result in the birth of a baby.

57. Why is it important to give fertility drugs early in the woman's menstrual cycle?

   (1) The fallopian tubes will be cleared.
   (2) More than one egg will be produced.
   (3) The couple will conceive on their own.
   (4) The man's sperm count will increase.
   (5) The embryo is more likely to develop normally.

58. In vitro fertilization has an overall success rate of only 10 percent, and it can be stressful and very expensive. What information in the article would explain why a couple would choose this procedure instead of adoption?

   (1) Adopting a child can take a long time.
   (2) They want to be sure they have a healthy child.
   (3) They want a child who is genetically their own.
   (4) Adoption agencies tend to reject infertile couples.
   (5) There are not enough children available for adoption.

59. What causes the high failure rate of transferring the embryo into the uterus?

   (1) Many eggs are not fertilized.
   (2) The sperm are defective.
   (3) Many culture dishes are contaminated.
   (4) The sperm are improperly processed.
   (5) The timing of embryo development and uterus development is off.

60. Which of the following conditions would make a woman a likely candidate for in vitro fertilization?

   (1) pelvic inflammatory disease
   (2) non-functioning ovaries
   (3) two damaged fallopian tubes
   (4) a surgically removed uterus
   (5) one damaged fallopian tube

ems 61 to 63 refer to the following information
nd diagrams.

A molecule of water, or H₂O, contains two hydro-
en atoms and one oxygen atom. The atoms are
rranged at an angle, not on a straight line.

WATER MOLECULE H₂O

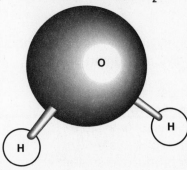

The shape of the water molecule causes it to
e polar. This means that one end of the
nolecule has a positive charge while the other
nd has a negative charge. As a result, a
ydrogen atom in one molecule is attracted to an
xygen atom in another molecule. This attraction
s called a hydrogen bond. Groups of water
nolecules are connected by hydrogen bonds.

HYDROGEN BONDS ←→

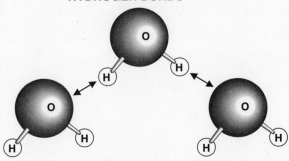

Groups of water molecules look like the
diagram below.

WATER

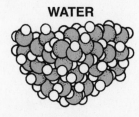

When water freezes, the hydrogen bonds
become less flexible. They hold the molecules in
a pattern that has more space between the
molecules than there is in water in its liquid form.

ICE

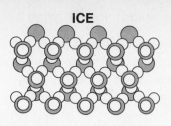

61. A glass jar full of water cracks when the
    water inside freezes. Why?

    (1) Ice takes up more space than an equal
        mass of water.
    (2) Individual water molecules increase in
        size as the temperature drops.
    (3) Glass expands when it becomes cold.
    (4) Ice has sharp edges that damage the
        glass.
    (5) Hydrogen gas is liberated, causing the
        jar to explode.

62. A liquid will boil when heat breaks the bonds
    between molecules in the liquid. What
    causes the boiling point of water to be so
    high compared to substances of similar size
    and mass?

    (1) Water is a pure substance.
    (2) Many other substances can dissolve in
        water.
    (3) The groups of molecules in water are
        tightly bound together and must absorb
        much heat energy before they break
        apart.
    (4) Water molecules are not attracted to
        one another.
    (5) Oxygen atoms do not absorb heat.

63. Which of the following conclusions can be
    drawn from the information provided?

    (1) Water is very stable; that is, it does not
        break down easily into hydrogen and
        oxygen.
    (2) There are more molecules in 1 cubic
        centimeter of water than in 1 cubic
        centimeter of ice.
    (3) Ice is denser than water.
    (4) Water is found in all living things.
    (5) Water is transparent and odorless.

Items 64 to 66 refer to the following information.

The human body contains many types of tissues and organs. These function as parts of various systems. Five of the systems are the following:

1. Muscular system. Moving skeletal and body parts such as the stomach and heart.
2. Digestive system. Eating, digesting, and absorbing foods; eliminating some wastes.
3. Circulatory system. Transporting nutrients, waste, oxygen, heat, carbon dioxide, hormones, and other substances.
4. Nervous system. Receiving stimuli from the environment, sending and interpreting data, controlling actions of other body parts.
5. Reproductive system. Producing sex cells for the continuation of the species.

64. The blood, which carries substances around the body, is part of which system?

(1) muscular system
(2) digestive system
(3) circulatory system
(4) nervous system
(5) reproductive system

65. With which system are eyes and ears most closely associated?

(1) muscular system
(2) digestive system
(3) circulatory system
(4) nervous system
(5) reproductive system

66. Which system is not vital to the survival of an individual human being?

(1) muscular system
(2) digestive system
(3) circulatory system
(4) nervous system
(5) reproductive system

Answers are on page 317

Posttes

Posttest Correlation Chart: Science

Name: _____ **Class:** _____ **Date:** _____

This chart can help you determine your strengths and weaknesses on the content and reading skill areas of the Science GED Test. Use the Answer Key on pages 317–324 to check your answers to the test. Then circle on the chart the numbers of the test items you answered correctly. Put the total number correct for each content area and skill area in each row and column. Look at the total items correct in each column and row and decide which areas are difficult for you. Use the page references to study those areas. Use a copy of the Study Record Sheet on page 31 to guide your studying.

Content	Cognitive Skills/ Comprehension	Application	Analysis	Evaluation	Total Correct
Biology (pages 32–107)	5, **11**, 30, 47, 48, 55	10, **17, 18, 19, 20**, 45, 56, 64, 65	7, **12**, 31, 32, **39, 40**, 46, 57, 59, 60, 66	6, 8, 9, 58	_____ out of 30
Earth Science (pages 108–147)	13, 14	**2, 27, 34, 35**	1, 15, 16, **53, 54**	**26, 33, 36**	_____ out of 14
Chemistry (pages 148–177)	**3**, 42, 50	28, **38**, 41, **61**	29, **37, 62**	4, 49, 51, 52, **63**	_____ out of 15
Physics (pages 178–214)	**43**	22, 24	21, 23, 25	**44**	_____ out of 7
Total Correct	____ out of 12	____ out of 19	____ out of 22	____ out of 13	Total correct: ____ out of 66

1–54 → You need more review.
55–66 → Congratulations! You're ready for the GED Test!

Boldfaced numbers indicate items based on charts, graphs, illustrations, and diagrams. For additional help, see the *Steck-Vaughn GED Science Exercise Book*.

≡Simulated Test

SCIENCE

Directions

The Science Simulated test consists of multiple-choice questions intended to measure your understanding of general concepts in science. The questions are based on short readings that often include a graph, chart, or diagram. Study the information given, and then answer the questions that follow. Refer to the information as often as necessary in answering the questions.

You should spend no more than 95 minutes answering the 66 questions on the Science Simulated Test. Work carefully, but do not spend too much time on any one question. Do not skip any items. Make a reasonable guess when you are not sure of an answer. You will not be penalized for incorrect answers.

When time is up, mark the last item you finished. This will tell you whether you can finish the real GED Test in the time allowed. Then complete the test.

Record your answers to the questions on a copy of the answer sheet on page 345. Be sure that all required information is properly recorded on the answer sheet.

To record your answers, mark the numbered space on the answer sheet that corresponds to the answer you choose for each question on the test.

Example:

Which of the following is the smallest unit in a living thing?

(1) tissue
(2) organ
(3) cell
(4) muscle
(5) capillary

The correct answer is "cell"; therefore, answer space 3 should be marked on the answer sheet.

Do not rest the point of your pencil on the answer sheet while you are considering your answer. Make no stray or unnecessary marks. If you change an answer, erase your first mark completely. Mark only one answer space for each question; multiple answers will be scored as incorrect. Do not fold or crease your answer sheet.

When you finish the test, use the Correlation Chart on page 256 to determine whether you are ready to take the real GED Test, and, if not, which skill areas need additional review.

Adapted with permission of the American Council of Education.

Items 1 and 2 refer to the following map.

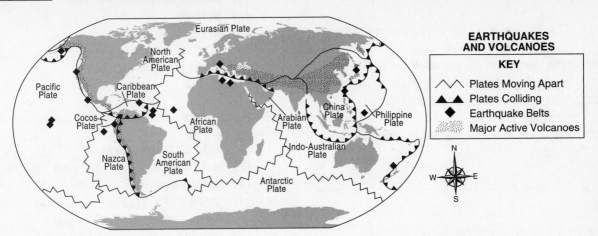

1. Large sections of Earth's crust that move slowly across Earth's surface are called plates. When two plates collide, one of the effects is the

   (1) formation of large ocean areas
   (2) creation of islands
   (3) formation of continents
   (4) formation of volcanoes
   (5) creation of rivers

2. Which of the following areas would provide a good opportunity for studying volcanoes and earthquakes?

   (1) northern Europe
   (2) southern Africa
   (3) Australia
   (4) eastern North America
   (5) western South America

Items 3 and 4 refer to the following information.

The density of a substance is its mass per unit of volume. The density of a gas is expressed in grams per liter.

DENSITY OF GASES	
Gas	Density (grams per liter)
Air	1.29
Hydrogen	0.09
Nitrogen	1.25
Oxygen	1.43
Carbon dioxide	1.98
Sulfur dioxide	2.93

3. The specific gravity of a gas is the ratio of its density to the density of air. For example, the specific gravity of oxygen is expressed as:

$$\frac{1.43}{1.29} = 1.11$$

This means that oxygen is 1.11 times as dense as air. Which of the following gases has the highest specific gravity?

   (1) hydrogen
   (2) nitrogen
   (3) oxygen
   (4) carbon dioxide
   (5) sulfur dioxide

4. Nitrogen makes up almost 80 percent of the air. Which of the following is a result of this fact?

    (1) The densities of air and nitrogen are similar.
    (2) Nitrogen is more dense than air.
    (3) Nitrogen is more dense than hydrogen.
    (4) Sulfur dioxide is less dense than nitrogen.
    (5) Nitrogen is more dense than carbon dioxide.

Items 5 to 10 refer to the following article.

Many kinds of ladybird beetles, or ladybugs, spend their time hunting insects to eat. They favor aphids and scale insects. Ladybugs can clean these harmful insects off plants, leaving the plants with energy to grow. Ladybugs have ample supplies of foul-tasting substances that repel insect-eating birds. Thus, ladybugs can spend the day in plain sight while hunting for insects.

The ladybug's appetite for harmful insects has been put to good use by farmers. An Australian variety of ladybug was imported into California to help control another Australian insect, the cottony cushion scale. This pest was accidentally introduced into America, and it quickly became a major pest in citrus orchards. The Australian ladybugs lay their eggs next to the eggs of the scale insect in citrus trees and other plants. Since a female lady bug lays about a thousand eggs and each hatchling eats about three thousand young scale insects, the benefits to citrus trees are enormous.

Ladybugs hunt until late fall when the cold limits their food supply. Then they take shelter in large groups until the spring. During the sheltering period, ladybugs can be collected in boxes and kept chilled until the spring. Then they can be sold to gardeners and farmers and released into the environment.

5. When do ladybugs hunt?

    (1) twenty-four hours a day
    (2) at night
    (3) at dawn and dusk
    (4) from spring to fall
    (5) during the winter

6. An unstated assumption of the author is tha

    (1) ladybugs are hunters
    (2) ladybugs are not active all year round
    (3) most ladybugs are harmful to plants
    (4) there are varieties of ladybugs that fee on different types of insects
    (5) ladybugs are a type of beetle

7. People's attitudes toward the ladybug have been affected by the insect's

    (1) spots
    (2) ability to repel birds
    (3) habit of sheltering during the winter
    (4) care for its young
    (5) ability to hunt other insects that feed or valuable plants

8. Which of the following conclusions is supported by the information in the article?

    (1) All varieties of ladybugs are hunters.
    (2) Female ladybugs do not provide food for their young.
    (3) Many ladybugs are beneficial to humans.
    (4) Ladybugs have a life expectancy of les than two months.
    (5) Ladybugs mate for life.

Simulated Tes

9. The winter behavior of ladybugs is most similar to

    (1) frogs burying themselves in pond bottoms for the winter
    (2) the migration of monarch butterflies south for the winter
    (3) hares turning white in winter and brown in summer
    (4) trees shedding leaves in the fall
    (5) animals growing thicker fur for the winter

10. Suppose your rosebushes are being damaged by aphids. You release some ladybugs in your garden, but two days later, the ladybugs are gone. Based on the article, which of the following statements could explain what happened?

    A. The ladybugs ran out of food and flew away to find more food.
    B. Ladybugs eat insects only on citrus trees.
    C. The ladybugs were eaten by birds.

    (1) A only
    (2) B only
    (3) C only
    (4) A and B
    (5) A and C

Items 11 and 12 refer to the following chart.

PULSE RATE AFTER ONE MINUTE OF EXERCISE			
Subject's Physical Condition	Pulse Rate (beats per minute)		
	Light Exercise	Moderate Exercise	Heavy Exercise
Excellent	66	73	82
Very good	78	85	96
Average	90	98	111
Below average	102	107	126
Poor	114	120	142

11. After one minute of moderate exercise, the pulse rate of a person in average physical condition is faster than the pulse rate of a person in

    (1) below average condition after one minute of moderate exercise
    (2) below average condition after one minute of light exercise
    (3) very good condition after one minute of heavy exercise
    (4) average condition after one minute of heavy exercise
    (5) poor condition after one minute of light exercise

12. Which of the following statements is supported by the information in the chart?

    (1) The pulse rate increases with additional minutes of exercise.
    (2) People in poor physical condition should not do heavy exercise.
    (3) As the pulse rate rises during exercise, so does the number of breaths per minute.
    (4) For people in excellent physical condition, the pulse rate increases from light to moderate exercise and decreases from moderate to heavy exercise.
    (5) There is a greater difference in the pulse rate between moderate and heavy exercise than between light and moderate exercise.

Tides are the alternate rise and fall of the sea level in oceans. They are caused primarily by the moon's gravitational pull. The sun's gravitational pull also contributes to the tides. At any one time, there are two high tides—one on the side of Earth facing the moon and one on the opposite side. The average time between high tides at any one location is 12 hours and 25 minutes.

The typical difference in sea level between high and low tides is two feet in the open ocean. Near the coast, the difference can be much greater. The greatest difference between high and low tides occurs in the Bay of Fundy in eastern Canada, where the sea level changes by 40 feet.

As the tides change, currents flow to redistribute the ocean's water. Near the coast, the direction of the current changes every 6 1/4 hours. The current first flows toward the shore in what is called a flood current. Then the current flows away from the shore in what is called an ebb current.

13. What is the primary cause of tides on Earth?

(1) ocean currents
(2) the gravitational pull of the sun
(3) the gravitational pull of the moon
(4) the positions of the planets relative to Earth
(5) the rotation of Earth

14. In the middle of the ocean, what is the usual change in sea level between high and low tides?

(1) 2 feet
(2) 6 feet
(3) 12 feet
(4) 25 feet
(5) 40 feet

15. What is a flood current?

(1) an ocean current that carries warm water from the tropics to higher latitudes
(2) an undertow
(3) a tide that floods low-lying coastal areas
(4) a current that carries water away from the shore
(5) a current that carries water toward the shore

16. When the moon, Earth, and sun are in a straight line, tides are higher than usual. What is the most likely cause of this?

(1) The sun's gravitational pull is added to that of the moon, which increases the height of the tides.
(2) The moon is in a position in which its gravitational pull is weaker.
(3) The positions of the three bodies cause an increase in rainfall, thereby raising the sea level.
(4) The positions of the three bodies cause an increase in the amount of polar ice melting, thereby raising the sea level.
(5) Tides are higher during the spring.

People who recover from an infectious disease may become immune to that disease. This immunity may last for the rest of the person's life. The immunity is caused by the formation of antibodies to fight the disease. Antibodies act to protect the body from disease-causing agents by recognizing marker proteins called antigens. Vaccines are specially prepared antigens that stimulate the body's production of antibodies without causing disease. There is a time lag before vaccines take effect, but then the immunity is generally long-term. Antiserums provide immediate short-term protection by giving the patient antibodies produced by another animal.

COMMON IMMUNIZATIONS		
Disease	Type of Immunization	Immunity Period
Diptheria	Vaccine Antiserum	5 to 10 years 2 to 3 months
Measles	Vaccine Antiserum	Over 10 years A few weeks
Mumps	Vaccine	Probably life
Poliomyelitis	Vaccine	Unknown
Tetanus	Vaccine Antiserum	5 to 10 years A few weeks

17. A thirty-year-old man cut his foot on a rusty nail. He received his last tetanus vaccination when he was twenty-seven years old. What immunization, if any, should he receive?

(1) tetanus vaccine
(2) tetanus antiserum
(3) tetanus vaccine followed by antiserum in a few weeks
(4) tetanus antiserum after he recovers
(5) none

18. A person traveling abroad was exposed to diphtheria. He was unsure of the date of his last diphtheria immunization. What immunization, if any, should he receive?

(1) diphtheria vaccine
(2) diphtheria antiserum
(3) diphtheria vaccine followed by antiserum in two months
(4) diphtheria antiserum after he recovers
(5) none

19. There was an epidemic of measles in a town, and a woman was concerned about getting sick. She had had measles (rubella) as a child many years before. What immunization, if any, should she receive?

(1) measles vaccine
(2) measles antiserum
(3) measles vaccine followed by measles antiserum
(4) measles antiserum after she becomes ill
(5) none, natural immunity now present

20. Infants are commonly immunized against diphtheria and tetanus at 2, 4, 6, and 18 months. At that point, their bodies are mature enough to maintain long-term immunity. At what approximate age would another immunization against diphtheria and tetanus be necessary?

(1) 2 years
(2) when they enter school
(3) when they graduate from high school
(4) 21 years
(5) Another immunization is not necessary.

Items 21 to 25 refer to the following article.

Sound waves are produced by rapid back-and-forth movements called vibrations. The vibrations cause disturbances in the particles of matter near them. The particles bump into one another and transmit the sound waves over distance. Because sound waves need particles of matter to transmit the disturbance caused by vibration, sound waves cannot travel through outer space.

Two factors that influence the speed of sound waves are the matter through which they travel and the temperature. Matter with particles more tightly packed, such as a solid, transmits sounds the fastest. Matter with particles loosely packed, such as a gas, transmits sound waves more slowly. In general, the higher the temperature, the faster sound travels through a given medium. The higher the temperature, the faster the particles of matter move, and the faster they bump into one another, transmitting sound waves.

Light waves, however, are produced by electric and magnetic forces. Light waves differ from sound waves in that they can travel through outer space as well as through matter. Light waves travel faster than sound waves. The speed of sound waves in air at 32°F is 1,085 feet per second. The speed of light is 186,282 miles per second.

21. Why do sound waves travel faster through solids than through gases?

(1) Gases are farther from the source of the vibration.
(2) Particles of solids are tightly packed and transmit disturbances quickly.
(3) Particles of gases are loosely packed and transmit disturbances quickly.
(4) Gases are empty space and do not transmit sound waves.
(5) Solids are warmer than gases.

22. Which of the following situations is an example of the differing speeds of sound and light?

(1) seeing lightning before hearing thunder
(2) watching the light show at a night club
(3) looking at neon signs
(4) the time it takes for sunlight to reach the Earth
(5) flying faster than sound in supersonic jets

23. Which of the following conclusions is supported by the article?

(1) The ground transmits sound faster than the air.
(2) The air transmits sound faster than the ground.
(3) Light waves travel more slowly than sound waves.
(4) Light waves travel only through solids, liquids, and gases.
(5) Light travels only through liquids and gases.

4. Which of the following situations is an
    example of sound traveling faster through a
    solid than through a gas?

    (1) a thunderclap sounding louder
        overhead than it sounds two miles away
    (2) the playing of a musical instrument
    (3) the sound of a siren when an
        ambulance approaches and then
        moves away
    (4) a hunter hearing hoofbeats by putting
        an ear to the ground
    (5) a person cupping his or her ear to hear
        better

25. Which of the following supports the
    generalization that light waves travel
    through outer space?

    (1) the reflection of light off a mirror
    (2) the passage of light through glass
    (3) our ability to see the sun and stars
    (4) our ability to see through water
    (5) our ability to see through air

Item 26 refers to the following diagram.

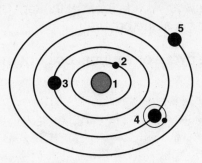

KEY
1 = Sun
2 = Mercury
3 = Venus
4 = Earth and Moon
5 = Mars

26. Which of the following conclusions can be
    drawn from the diagram?

    (1) Mars travels around the sun in less time
        than Earth does.
    (2) The rotation of the planets causes day
        and night.
    (3) Mercury is the planet closest to the sun.
    (4) Earth is the only planet with significant
        amounts of water.
    (5) The moon is always closer to the sun
        than Earth is.

Item 27 refers to the following diagrams.

The newest rock layer is at the top; the oldest rock layer is at the bottom.

LIFE CYCLE OF FAULT-BLOCK MOUNTAINS

1. Folding

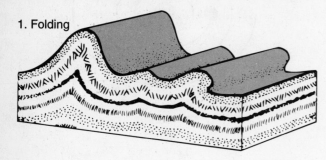

2. Faulting

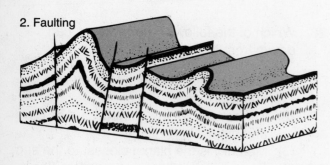

3. Erosion

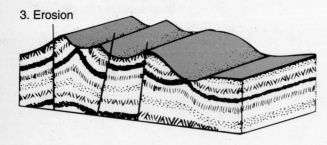

27. Older buried rock layers become exposed during

    (1) folding only
    (2) faulting only
    (3) erosion only
    (4) folding and faulting
    (5) faulting and erosion

Items 28 and 29 refer to the following chart.

RADIOACTIVE SUBSTANCES AND THEIR USES	
Substance	**Use**
Carbon 14	Estimating age of material that was once living
Arsenic 74	Finding brain tumors
Cobalt	Radiation treatment for cancer
	Tracing leaks or blockages in pipelines
Iodine 131	Treatment of thyroid gland problems
Radium	Radiation treatment for cancer
Uranium 235	Production of energy in nuclear reactors
	Atomic weapons

28. If a scientist were interested in determining the dating of a human bone from an ancient civilization, what radioactive substance could the scientist use?

    (1) carbon 14
    (2) arsenic 74
    (3) cobalt
    (4) iodine 131
    (5) radium

29. Which of the following conclusions can be drawn from the information in the chart?

    (1) All radioactive substances are expensive.
    (2) Uranium 235 is used only for production of weapons.
    (3) Radioactive substances are always beneficial to humans.
    (4) Radioactive substances have many uses.
    (5) Radioactive substances can be produced by humans.

Simulated Test

ems 30 to 32 refer to the following article.

Tumors grow from our own cells. Some tumors re malignant—cancers that are likely to cause eath if untreated. Cancer cells are harmful ecause they grow abnormally and rapidly. They se up nutrients and starve normal cells. Malignant tumors can grow large, causing ressure that interferes with circulation. As ne cancer grows, it may spread throughout ne body.

What causes cancer? A variety of chemical nd physical agents can start cancer. These iclude chemicals in plastics, cigarette smoke, nd asbestos. Radiation can also cause cancer. 'ertain viruses have been shown to cause ancer in animals. Some researchers think that ancer cells may form but stay inactive for a while. Cancer cells become active only if the ody's immune system—which defends against isease—breaks down. Some recognized ancer-causing agents are known to suppress ne immune system. People who have had rgan transplants take drugs that suppress the nmune system, and they show a higher number f cancers.

0. What are malignant tumors?

(1) cancerous growths that may cause death if untreated
(2) cancerous growths that are suppressed by the immune system
(3) harmless growths that can be removed surgically
(4) harmless growths that are a side effect of organ transplants
(5) the major cause of cancer

31. Which of the following practices would be most likely to cause cancer?

(1) eating a vegetarian diet
(2) not exercising
(3) avoiding foods with chemical additives
(4) being exposed to a high level of radiation
(5) drinking water from a remote mountain stream

32. Which of the following statements supports the theory that breakdowns in the body's immune system contribute to the growth of cancers?

(1) Smoking has been linked with lung cancer.
(2) High doses of radiation can cause cancer.
(3) Some cancer-causing agents are chemical agents.
(4) Some cancer-causing agents suppress the immune system.
(5) Cancer cells may suppress the immune system.

Items 33 and 34 refer to the following passage and diagrams.

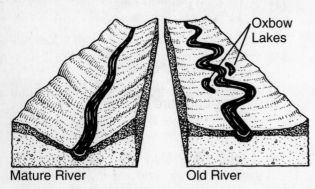

Mature River   Old River

The diagrams show a river at different stages of its life cycle. During the millions of years between the two stages, the river valley became wider and the river slower. It now winds in S curves called meanders.

33. What best accounts for the widening of the river valley?

(1) annual melting of winter snow
(2) earthquakes
(3) tides
(4) windstorms
(5) erosion by the river

34. Which of the following generalizations is supported by the diagrams?

(1) All rivers drain into an ocean.
(2) Oxbow lakes are found near old rivers.
(3) Flooding is caused by mature rivers.
(4) The valley of an old river is generally steep.
(5) Waterfalls are features of old rivers.

Items 35 and 36 refer to the following diagram.

LAYERS OF EARTH'S ATMOSPHERE

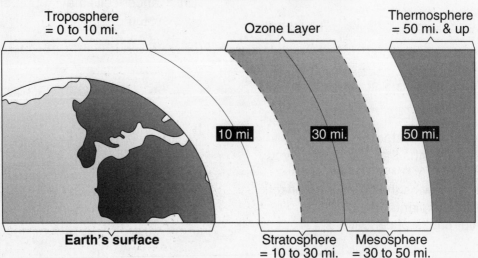

35. As the distance from Earth's surface increases, Earth's gravitational pull decreases. In addition, the air becomes less dense. Gradually the air thins until the atmosphere merges with the near-emptiness of space. In which layer of the atmosphere would a spacecraft operate most efficiently?

(1) troposphere
(2) stratosphere
(3) ozone layer
(4) mesosphere
(5) thermosphere

36. Which of the following generalizations is supported by the diagram?

(1) The ozone layer is part of both the stratosphere and the mesosphere.
(2) The ozone layer is part of both the mesosphere and the thermosphere.
(3) The troposphere extends to a height of 30 miles.
(4) The total height of the atmosphere is 50 miles.
(5) Breathing is difficult in the lower troposphere.

Simulated Te

Items 37 and 38 refer to the following information.

All matter is composed of basic substances called elements. An element is a substance that cannot be broken down into simpler substances by chemical reactions. Some common elements are iron, carbon, and oxygen. The smallest particle of an element that still has the properties of that element is called an atom. The smallest particle of the element iron is an iron atom, and a sample of the element iron contains only iron atoms.

When two or more different elements react chemically, a compound is produced. For example, iron oxide, or rust, is a compound made when iron and oxygen react together.

37. Often, when hydrogen and oxygen combine, water is formed. What is water?

(1) an atom
(2) an element
(3) part of an atom
(4) energy
(5) a compound

38. Which of the following is an unstated assumption by the author?

(1) Elements can be broken down into simpler substances by methods other than chemical reactions.
(2) All compounds are made of some combination of the elements iron and oxygen.
(3) Compounds are usually solids.
(4) Elements have at least two different types of atoms.
(5) Compounds are more interesting than elements.

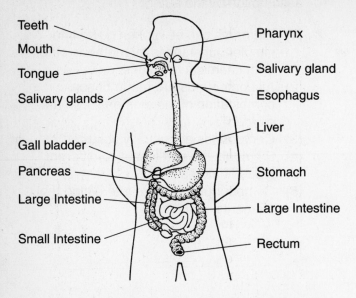

Teeth
Mouth
Tongue
Salivary glands
Gall bladder
Pancreas
Large Intestine
Small Intestine

Pharynx
Salivary gland
Esophagus
Liver
Stomach
Large Intestine
Rectum

39. The entire digestive system consists of a long main tube called the alimentary canal. The liver and pancreas are connected to the alimentary canal by small tubes. The alimentary canal ends at the

  (1) liver
  (2) pancreas
  (3) rectum
  (4) large intestine
  (5) small intestine

40. The stomach produces an acid that helps digest food. Heartburn is a painful feeling in the chest caused by stomach acids irritating the

  (1) salivary glands
  (2) esophagus
  (3) large intestine
  (4) small intestine
  (5) rectum

Items 41 and 42 refer to the following information.

Carbon monoxide is a gas produced by coal stoves, furnaces, or gas appliances when they do not get enough air. It is present in the exhaust of internal combustion engines, such as the one in cars and lawn mowers.

Carbon monoxide is a deadly poison. Since it is colorless, odorless, and tasteless, it is very difficult to detect. Victims of carbon monoxide poisoning become drowsy and then unconscious. Death can occur in minutes.

41. Which of the following actions is likely to be dangerous?

  (1) operating a well-vented coal furnace
  (2) mowing the lawn
  (3) using a properly installed gas stove
  (4) running a car engine in a closed garage
  (5) using a barbecue grill outdoors

42. What is the first symptom of carbon-monoxide poisoning?

  (1) a bad taste
  (2) convulsions
  (3) choking
  (4) unconsciousness
  (5) drowsiness

Items 43 and 44 refer to the following information.

SINGLE FIXED PULLEY

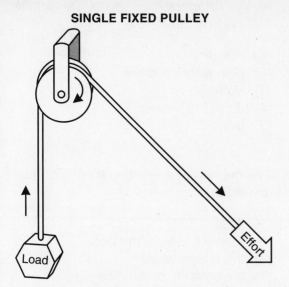

In an ideal pulley, the effort required to pull the rope is equal to the weight of the load.

43. When you pull down on the rope of a single pulley, what happens?

(1) The load remains stationary.
(2) The load moves downward.
(3) The load moves upward.
(4) The rope moves, but the pulley wheel does not turn.
(5) The pulley wheel turns, but the rope does not move.

44. Which of the following conclusions is supported by the diagram?

(1) A single, fixed pulley changes the direction in which force must be exerted.
(2) A single, fixed pulley does not change the direction in which force must be exerted, but it decreases the force required.
(3) A single, fixed pulley does not make it easier to lift a very heavy object.
(4) The distance in which the rope is pulled is half as long as the distance in which the load is lifted.
(5) The distance in which the rope is pulled is twice as long as the distance in which the load is lifted.

Items 45 to 48 refer to the following article.

Pathogens are microorganisms that cause disease. To spread disease, a pathogen must leave the body of its host and enter another body. Many pathogens enter the body through a specific route. For instance, pathogens that cause respiratory diseases usually enter through the nose.

The manner in which a pathogen travels from one person to another is related to where the pathogen lives in the host. For example, an intestinal pathogen is likely to be found in the host's feces. Respiratory pathogens can be spread by droplets sneezed or coughed into the air. Such droplets may also be carried on objects. Body fluids, such as saliva, pus, mucus, and urine carry pathogens outside their hosts. Some pathogens that live in the blood are spread by bloodsucking insects such as mosquitoes.

45. A pathogen carried by droplets coughed or sneezed into the air is likely to infect the

(1) respiratory system
(2) intestines
(3) urinary system
(4) blood
(5) respiratory system and urinary system

46. You can prevent the spread of some pathogens by frequently washing your hands. With which pathogens is this effective?

A. respiratory pathogens
B. intestinal pathogens
C. pathogens in the blood

(1) A only
(2) B only
(3) C only
(4) A and B
(5) A and C

47. Malaria is a disease spread from one person to another through the bite of a female *Anopheles* mosquito. This implies that malaria affects the

(1) blood
(2) respiratory system
(3) skeleton
(4) digestive system
(5) brain

48. The method of spreading a pathogen is related to

(1) its size
(2) where it lives in the body
(3) the temperature
(4) the severity of the disease
(5) the weight of the body

Simulated Tes

Electric currents flowing through wires produce eas of magnetic force called electromagnetic lds. These electromagnetic fields are similar to e magnetic fields produced by magnets. The ronger the electric current, the stronger is the ectromagnetic field surrounding it.

Very strong currents produce very strong lds. The force of a strong field can be felt everal yards away from the wire. For example, orescent lamps held below a 161,000-volt ansmission line light up without being plugged to an electric circuit. Many transmission lines e even more powerful.

Wires are not the only producers of ectromagnetic fields. All electric appliances oduce fields. Appliances with motors, such as air dryers and washing machines, produce ronger fields than appliances without motors, ich as lights and toasters.

Scientists are starting to question the effect of ectromagnetic fields on our health. People ing near power lines have long complained of eadaches, fatigue, memory loss, and more ness than usual. There also seem to be more ises of particular types of cancer among eople exposed to strong electromagnetic fields. though the evidence is inconclusive, it raises ome serious public health questions.

9. If high-power transmission lines that carry electricity from generating plants to homes and businesses are proved to be health hazards, what would be a likely solution to this problem?

   (1) Move all transmission lines to areas where few people live.
   (2) Move people away from high-power transmission lines.
   (3) Switch to another source of power for everyday use.
   (4) Cover the lines with material that blocks the electromagnetic fields.
   (5) Install small generators in each home and business.

50. A person who wishes to be cautious about exposure to electromagnetic fields should

   (1) use fluorescent rather than regular light bulbs
   (2) stop using magnets
   (3) be careful when plugging in and unplugging appliances
   (4) repair broken appliances immediately
   (5) avoid living near a high-voltage power line

51. Based on the information in the article, which of the following statements is not a logical conclusion?

   (1) A vacuum cleaner generates a more powerful electromagnetic field than a 25-watt light bulb.
   (2) People living near high-voltage power lines may be at greater risk for certain types of cancer than people not living near such lines.
   (3) Using an electric blanket causes cancer.
   (4) A 700,000-volt transmission line will light up unplugged fluorescent lamps held below it.
   (5) A 200,000-volt transmission line produces a stronger electromagnetic field than household wiring.

52. Which of the following statements has not yet been proved?

   (1) Electric currents produce electromagnetic fields.
   (2) The stronger the electric current, the stronger is the electromagnetic field.
   (3) Electromagnetic fields cause health problems.
   (4) Electromagnetic fields are regions of force similar to magnetic fields produced by magnets.
   (5) The electromagnetic field produced by a high-voltage power line is strong enough to light an unplugged fluorescent lamp.

Items 53 and 54 refer to the following diagram.

AIR POLLUTANTS FROM SMOKESTACKS

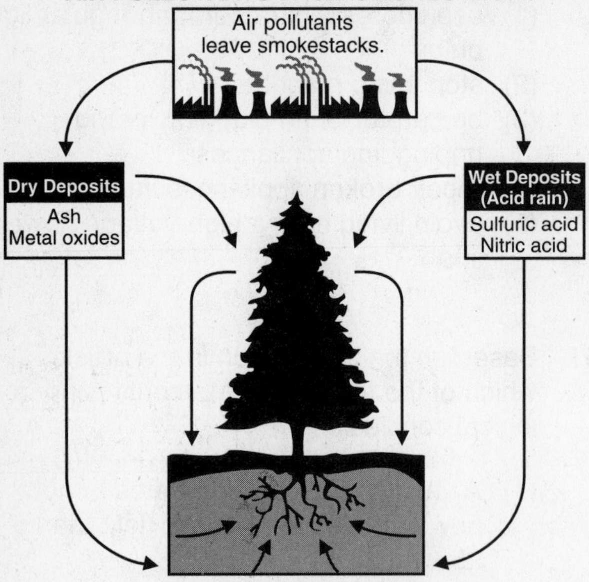

Acidified soil and water leach plant nutrients out of the soil. Heavy metals accumulate in harmful quantities.

53. What causes the air pollutants emitted by smokestacks to become wet deposits?

    (1) industrial processes
    (2) antipollution devices
    (3) petroleum
    (4) oceans
    (5) water vapor in the air

54. What is the eventual effect of dry deposits and acid rain on plant life?

    (1) The plants thrive on the heavy metals accumulating in the soil.
    (2) The root systems are strengthened because of the extra nutrients in the soil.
    (3) The leaves and stems are harmed, but the root systems remain unaffected.
    (4) The plants are weakened by the lack of nutrients and harmed by the accumulation of heavy metals.
    (5) There is no effect on plant life.

Items 55 and 56 refer to the following information.

About 8 percent of men and 0.5 percent of women are color-blind; that is, they have trouble distinguishing colors. Most color-blind people cannot distinguish red from green. Completely color-blind people see only black, white, and shades of gray; this condition is extremely rare.

55. The fact that many more men than women are color-blind implies that

    (1) color is less important to men than to women
    (2) color blindness is an illness
    (3) color blindness is related to whether a person is male or female
    (4) color blindness is associated with poor vision
    (5) color blindness is a harmless visual defect

56. If a man cannot distinguish red from green, for what occupation would he be unsuitable?

    (1) auto mechanic
    (2) computer operator
    (3) salesperson
    (4) railroad engineer
    (5) plumber

Simulated Te

Acquired immune deficiency syndrome (AIDS) is a disease that destroys the body's ability to protect itself from infection. It is an infection caused by the human immunodeficiency virus (HIV). The AIDS virus is transmitted in semen, vaginal secretions, and blood. The groups most at risk for contracting the disease are homosexual men, intravenous drug users, and their sex partners and their babies. Also at risk are people who received transfusions before blood supplies were screened for HIV.

This disease progresses slowly. During the first stage of AIDS, when the body is exposed to HIV, the person may or may not have flu-like symptoms. Within two months, antibodies to protect against HIV are produced. During the second stage, the virus is not active and the person feels fine. The second stage can last for years. In the third stage, swelling of the lymph nodes occurs, but the person is still relatively healthy. During the fourth stage, symptoms gradually appear. AIDS-related infections, tumors, and neurological diseases attack the body, eventually resulting in death.

Presently there is no way to destroy HIV once it is in the body. However, the spread of the virus can be prevented by "safer sex" techniques such as using condoms. The spread of AIDS can also be prevented by not sharing drug needles.

57. What causes AIDS?

    (1) taking drugs intravenously
    (2) engaging in homosexual activity
    (3) receiving a blood transfusion
    (4) HIV
    (5) antibodies

58. What causes the production of HIV antibodies?

    (1) exposure to HIV
    (2) blood transfusions
    (3) tumors
    (4) swelling of the lymph nodes
    (5) neurological diseases

59. Which of the following generalizations is supported by the information in the article?

    (1) The spread of AIDS is limited to the present high-risk groups.
    (2) A cure for AIDS will soon be found.
    (3) A person with HIV can infect others without being aware of it.
    (4) People who recover from AIDS are immune to HIV.
    (5) Only men get AIDS.

60. What effect on the general population will the spread of AIDS have?

    (1) Fewer people will use intravenous drugs.
    (2) Blood transfusions will no longer be given.
    (3) The disease will continue to spread into previously low-risk groups.
    (4) The disease will become less serious as it spreads.
    (5) There will be no effect on the general population.

Items 61 to 63 refer to the following chart.

FOOD ADDITIVES		
Type	**Examples**	**Possible Effects**
Preservatives	Salt Vinegar Sugar Nitrates	High blood pressure Irritation of the stomach Tooth decay, obesity Cancer

Colorings and
flavorings
	Chlorophyll,
	Carotene
	
	Synthetic
	chemicals
	Monosodium
	glutamate
		Food may appear
		  more nutritional
		  than it actually is.
		Cancer
		
		Allergic reactions

Texturizers	Pectin Gelatin Glycerol monostearate	Unknown

Supplementary
vitamins and
minerals
	Iron
	Vitamins A,
	  B complex,
	  C, D, etc.
	Iodide
		Both deficiencies
		  and excesses of
		  minerals and
		  vitamins can cause
		  disease.

61. An example of a food that contains preservatives is

    (1) enriched flour
    (2) homogenized milk
    (3) pickles
    (4) monosodium glutamate
    (5) iodized salt

62. What food additive can give a misleading appearance to food?

    (1) yellow food coloring in commercially-prepared baked goods that are made without eggs.
    (2) iron in breakfast cereal
    (3) pectin in jelly
    (4) vitamin B in white bread
    (5) vitamin D in milk

63. Why are food additives so important?

    A. They enable food to be transported long distances and to be stored for long periods of time without spoiling.
    B. They provide important minerals and vitamins.
    C. Most food additives cause disease.

    (1) A only
    (2) B only
    (3) C only
    (4) A and B
    (5) B and C

Simulated Tes

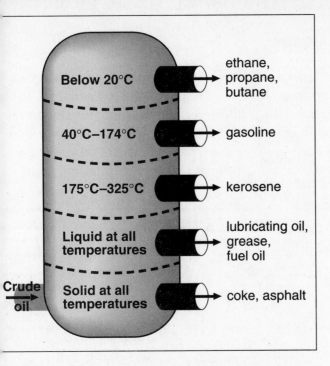

In a process called fractional distillation, crude oil is pumped into a tower where it is heated. Different petroleum products are produced through evaporation and condensation at different temperatures.

64. Which of the following statements is supported by the information provided?

(1) Asphalt is a liquid produced during fractional distillation.
(2) Coke is used to make grease.
(3) Kerosene boils at a higher temperature than gasoline.
(4) Burning petroleum fuels creates air pollution.
(5) Crude oil can be used without processing.

65. What causes the substances to separate during fractional distillation?

(1) the force of gravity
(2) the pressure of more crude oil entering the tower
(3) a series of finer and finer filters at each stage of the tower
(4) the pipes carrying the substances away from the tower
(5) the different temperatures at different heights in the tower

66. Which of the following statements is supported by the information in the diagram?

(1) The temperature remains constant throughout the tower.
(2) The higher the location in the tower, the higher is the temperature.
(3) The higher the location in the tower, the lower is the temperature.
(4) All substances produced by fractional distillation boil and then condense in the tower.
(5) All substances produced by fractional distillation condense and then boil in the tower.

Answers are on page 324.

Simulated Test Correlation Chart: Science

Name: _____   **Class:** _____   **Date:** _____

This chart can help you determine your strengths and weaknesses on the content and reading skill areas of the Science GED Test. Use the Answer Key on pages 324–330 to check your answers to the test. Then circle on the chart the numbers of the test items you answered correctly. Put the total number correct for each content area and skill area in each row and column. Look at the total items correct in each column and row and decide which areas are difficult for you. Use the page references to study those areas. Use a copy of the Study Record Sheet on page 31 to guide your studying.

Content	Cognitive Skills/ Comprehension	Application	Analysis	Evaluation	Total Correct
Biology (pages 32–107)	5, **11**, 30, 45, 48	9, **17, 18, 19, 20, 40**, 47, 56, **61, 62**	6, 31, 32, **39**, 46, 55, 57, 58, 60, **63**	7, 8, 10, **12**, 59	_____ out of 30
Earth Science (pages 108–147)	13, 14, 15, **36**	**2**, 27, 35	1, 16, **26, 33, 53, 54**	34	_____ out of 14
Chemistry (pages 148–177)	42	**28**, 37, 41	**3, 4**, 38, **65**	**29, 64, 66**	_____ out of 11
Physics (pages 178–214)	**43**	22, 24, 50	21, 25	23, **44**, 49, 51, 52	_____ out of 11
Total Correct	___ out of 11	___ out of 19	___ out of 22	___ out of 14	Total correct: ___ out of 66

1–54 → You need more review.
55–66 → Congratulations!
You're ready for the GED Test!

Boldfaced numbers indicate items based on charts, graphs, illustrations, and diagrams.
For additional help, see the *Steck-Vaughn GED Science Exercise Book*.

Answers and Explanations

1. **(3) cutting leaves** (Comprehension)
    According to the article, leaf-cutting ants
    harm crops in Texas and Louisiana. The other
    activities of ants in options (1), (2), (4), and (5)
    help make food for humans. These are
    described in the third paragraph of the article.

2. **(4) the roles of the queen, winged males,
    and workers** (Evaluation) Each type of ant
    has a specific role to play in the colony. This
    would most interest a sociobiologist. Options
    (1), (2), (3), and (5) describe only physical
    aspects of ant life, not the way ants act in a
    group.

3. **(1) Since there is only one queen to be
    fertilized, only a few males are required.**
    (Evaluation) Since each colony has only one
    queen, only a few winged males are needed to
    mate with her, whereas many workers are
    needed to find food. Options (2) and (3) are not
    related to the number of males that belong to
    a colony. Options (4) and (5) are true, but they
    are not the reason the colony has more
    workers than males.

4. **(2) feeding other members of the colony**
    (Evaluation) This is the primary job of worker
    ants. Options (1), (4), and (5) describe effects
    of ant activities that might benefit farmers.
    Option (3) describes an activity, cutting leaves,
    that can benefit one kind of ant, the leaf-
    cutter. In the article cutting leaves is viewed
    mainly as a problem for farmers.

5. **(5) the colony** (Evaluation) Only a colony can
    survive for any length of time. Options (1), (2),
    and (3) are individual types of ants that
    cannot survive on their own. Option (4) is the
    reproductive unit of the colony, but it cannot
    survive without the help of the worker ants.

6. **(2) performing tasks one after another on
    an assembly line** (Application) In assembly
    line work, each worker performs a task in the
    manufacture of a product. This is most like the
    behavior of the leaf-cutting worker ants that
    divide the labor according to size. Option (1) is
    not correct because ants do not have political
    systems. Options (3) and (4) are similar to the

function of one kind of leaf-cutting worker, not
to all leaf-cutting ants. Option (5) is incorrect
because the main job of the workers is to feed
the colony, not fight for it.

7. **(4) Water flows from high elevations,
    such as mountains, to sea level.** (Analysis)
    The map shows that the watershed areas are
    bounded by mountainous areas, which are
    higher than sea level. Water flows downward.
    Options (1) and (2) are true but do not tell why
    rivers flow in a certain direction. Options (3)
    and (5) are untrue.

8. **(2) They saw that the Columbia River
    was flowing to the west.** (Application) After
    they crossed the Rocky Mountains, explorers
    saw that water was flowing toward the west,
    not the southeast. This change suggested that
    water was flowing to a western ocean, the
    Pacific. Option (1) would not tell the explorers
    anything. Option (5) is not true. Options (3)
    and (4) would not tell the explorers about the
    location of the nearest ocean.

9. **(4) More oxygen will fit in the container.**
    (Analysis) According to Boyle's law, the
    volume of a gas becomes smaller as the
    pressure increases. This means that more
    oxygen can be stored in a cylinder if the
    oxygen is under pressure. Option (1) is not
    true. If the oxygen is contained in the
    cylinder, it will not mix with the air. Option
    (2) may be true, but it does not explain why
    oxygen is pressurized. Option (3) is incorrect
    because it mentions Charles's law, which
    discusses only questions of temperature, not
    pressure. Option (5) is incorrect because there
    is also no reason given in the passage to
    suggest that liquefying the gas would be
    helpful in storing it.

10. **(2) B only** (Analysis) Because changes in
    temperature involve Charles's law (Statement
    A) and not Boyle's law (Statement B), options
    (1), (4), and (5) are incorrect. Option (3) is
    incorrect because knowing the number of
    molecules inside the balloon (Statement C)
    will not explain why the balloon rises, nor will
    this number change as the balloon rises.

11. **(1) two plates moving toward each other**
(Comprehension) The article states that the
Himalayas were formed as a result of two
plates converging, or colliding. Options (2) and
(3) describe plate movements other than
collision. Option (4), volcanic activity, may
have accompanied the formation but did not
cause it. Option (5) involves the separation of
plates, not the formation of mountains.

12. **(5) the rise and fall in the water level of
major rivers** (Comprehension) Option (5) has
to do with changes on the surface of the land.
Plate tectonics is concerned with the deeper
movements of Earth's crust, not the surface.
Options (1), (2), (3), and (4) involve other
events associated with plate tectonics.

13. **(2) The continents ride on plates that
move, causing new formations of land and
water.** (Comprehension) Option (2) indicates
that the movement of plates is changing the
location of continents and oceans. Option (1) is
incorrect because plate movement will continue
moving land masses. Option (3) is incorrect
because the separation of continents happened
when the land mass, Pangaea, broke into huge
pieces. Option (4) implies that plate movement
has stopped, which is incorrect. Option (5) is
false because diverging boundaries are usually
beneath the oceans.

14. **(3) two plates colliding** (Analysis) The
collision of plates causes earthquakes,
volcanic activity, and the formation of high
mountains. Mountain formation does not
happen in options (1) and (2). Options (4) and
(5) only indirectly relate to the study of
Earth's plates.

15. **(1) 0–1 year** (Comprehension) Children gain
about 14 pounds from birth to their first
birthday. The largest gain is indicated by the
steepest slope on the graph. Between 1 and 2
years, they gain about 6 pounds, option (2).
Between 2 and 3 years, they gain about 4
pounds, option (3). Between 3 and 4 years,
they gain about 4 pounds, option (4). Between
4 and 5 years, they gain about 4 pounds,
option (5).

16. **(3) above average for his age and sex**
(Analysis) At 39 pounds, Billy weighs about
2 1/2 pounds more than the average boy his
age, who weighs about 36 1/2 pounds. Options
(1) and (2) are incorrect because Billy weighs
more than the average four-year-old boy.
Option (4) is incorrect because Billy weighs

less than the average five-year-old boy, who
weighs about 41 pounds. Option (5) is
incorrect because Billy weighs more than the
average four-year-old girl, who weighs about
35 pounds.

17. **(4) Annelida** (Application) The earthworm
belongs to the phylum Annelida, which
consists of soft-bodied, segmented animals
that are bilaterally symmetrical, or the same
on both sides. Option (1) is incorrect because
the earthworm does not have a notochord.
Option (2) is incorrect because Mollusca are
not segmented and the earthworm does not
have a shell. Option (3) is incorrect because
earthworms are not covered by an external
skeleton. Option (5) is incorrect because
Cnidarians are not segmented.

18. **(2) Mollusca** (Application) A clam has a soft
body and a hard shell, which is characteristic
of animals of the phylum Mollusca. Option (1)
is incorrect because the clam does not have a
notochord. Option (3) is incorrect because the
clam does not have a jointed external
skeleton. Option (4) is incorrect because a
clam has a shell, which members of the
phylum Annelida do not have. Option (5) is
incorrect because clams are not symmetrical
around a central point.

19. **(1) Chordata** (Application) The phylum
Chordata is the only one that has animals
with backbones as members. All the other
options are phyla whose members are
invertebrates, animals without backbones.

20. **(3) Arthropoda** (Application) The
grasshopper, an insect, belongs to the phylum
Arthropoda, along with other animals having
external jointed skeletons. None of the other
phyla contain animals with external jointed
skeletons.

21. **(5) A and C** (Analysis) Leaving the iron bar in
contact with a magnet (Statement A) and
stroking the bar with a magnet (Statement C)
would have the same effect. The poles of the
magnetic domains would line up and produce
a magnet. Thus, options (1) and (3) are only
partly correct. Options (2) and (4) are incorrect
because iron filings are attracted to a magnet,
but they cannot make an object into a magnet
(Statement B).

22. **(2) a rubber eraser** (Application) The article
mentions that objects containing iron and steel
are affected by magnets. Options (1), (3), (4),

and (5) all contain iron or steel. Options (3) and (4) describe two kinds of magnets which are affected by magnetic fields. Option (5), the steel girder, is large and may not visibly shift but would be affected by magnetism. A magnet would certainly stick to it!

23. **(2) Earth has a magnetic north pole** (Analysis) Earth, with a magnetic north pole, causes the suspended compass needle to point north. Option (1) is a result of the compass's behavior, not a cause. Option (3) is not true. Option (4) is incorrect because if the domains pointed in different directions, the needle would not be a magnet. Option (5) is not true because one pole is not stronger than another.

24. **(3) a sailor navigating with the use of a compass** (Application) This person might be directed off course by the difference between the two poles. The hikers in option (1) are traveling only a short distance and the driver in option (5) has only two directions to choose from. These people would not be led off course by the difference. Option (2) is incorrect because this sailor is not affected by the magnetic poles. Option (4) is incorrect because the compass will point to the nails, not to the north pole.

25. **(2) two magnets, each with one north pole and one south pole** (Analysis) The article states that each magnet has a north and a south pole. This statement makes options (1), (3), and (4) untrue. Option (5) makes no sense; if the domains are lined up in one half of the magnet, they will also be lined up in the other half.

26. **(4) gold** (Analysis) Gold is the only metal listed with a density greater than that of liquid mercury. Therefore, it is the only one that will sink in liquid mercury. Options (1), (2), (3), and (5) have densities less than that of liquid mercury, and they will float in it.

27. **(1) 24K gold** (Application) Pure gold has a density of 19.3. This is greater than the densities of the mixtures of gold and copper represented by options (2), (3), and (4), because 24-karat gold has the highest ratio of gold to copper. Option (5) is incorrect because the different karats each contain a different proportion of gold to copper, making their densities different.

28. **(4) It is formed in the ocean.** (Evaluation) The chart shows that limestone is formed by chemical reaction in water and from the remains of marine animals. Both of these methods of formation occur in the ocean. Option (1) is the method of formation for conglomerates, sandstones, and shales, not limestone. Options (2) and (3) are each only partially correct. Option (5) is incorrect because silt makes up shale, not limestone.

29. **(5) A, B, and C** (Application) People use methods and materials similar to those that form sedimentary rocks in all three cases described. Concrete, with its pebbles (Statement A), is similar to conglomerate. Constructing an adobe house of mud (Statement B) is similar to the formation of rock (shale) out of clay. Formation of rock salt by evaporation of seawater (Statement C) is the same process found in nature. Options (1), (2), (3), and (4) do not include all the methods and are therefore incorrect.

30. **(1) bacteria** (Comprehension) Bacteria start the decomposition process and are later replaced by other microorganisms. Options (2), (3), and (4) are microorganisms active in the later stages of composting. Option (5) is incorrect because each organism is active at a different time.

31. **(1) bacteria** (Analysis) The bacteria do most of the initial decomposition of the organic matter; their removal would, in effect, stop the composting process. Options (2), (3), (4), and (5) would have a lesser impact; therefore, option (1) is correct.

32. **(5) plastic wrap** (Analysis) Plastic wrap is the only material listed that is not living. Options (1), (2), (3), and (4) are all from living plants or animals and so are incorrect.

33. **(2) The oil could spread farther south and west.** (Evaluation) The spread of the oil over a vast area of ocean and coast suggests that cleanup efforts will take a long time. Option (3) is incorrect because the map shows a southwestward movement of oil, and there is not enough information to conclude that this spread has stopped. Option (1) is incorrect because the oil spread during the first two months and was not contained. Option (4) is incorrect because the oil is not easily absorbed by the ocean, but floats on top. Option (5) is incorrect because the amount estimated to

have evaporated during the first two months is only 20 percent. If an equal amount were to evaporate during the next two months, more than half the oil would still remain.

34. **(5) Evaporation will probably help clear some of the oil.** (Application) According to the map, 20 percent of the oil in the Alaskan spill evaporated. Option (1) mentions barriers, but the map does not show how barriers were or were not used. Option (2) suggests that skimmers should not be used, but the map shows that they were useful in the Alaskan accident. According to the map, information about biological dissipation is not available, so you cannot use the map to argue for option (3). Option (4) is contradicted by the map; in Alaska, most of the oil was not cleared in two months.

35. **(4) passage of the eye** (Evaluation) The eye is a calm area in the middle of the hurricane. The eye is not likely to cause damage. Options (1), (2), (3), and (5) are incorrect because rain, flooding, and wind are all likely to cause serious damage.

36. **(3) Leave storm protection measures in place because the rain and winds will start again—this time from the other direction.** (Application) The family is experiencing the lull in the storm caused by the passage of the eye over them. When the eye passes, the rain and winds resume, only from the opposite direction, or in this case the west. Option (1) is incorrect because the hurricane has not passed; if the winds had been from the west, they could have concluded that the hurricane was over when the storm ended. Option (2) is based on an assumption that may not be true, so removing the storm protection measures does not make sense. Option (4) is incorrect because hurricanes are storms of such vast size that two of them would probably not occur within a space of two days. Option (5) is incorrect because the hurricane is not over.

37. **(4) oiling it to create a barrier against air and water** (Application) Oiling the cookware provides an air- and water-resistant barrier to protect the iron from rusting. Option (1) is incorrect because water will cause the iron to rust. Options (2) and (3) are incorrect because they offer only partial protection, and they are impractical when considering cooking utensils. Option (5) does not suggest a way to keep air and water away from the iron.

38. **(5) the iron is not exposed to air and water** (Analysis) Plating iron with a rust-resistant metal protects the surface from contact with air and water, and thus protects it from corrosion. Options (1) and (2) are incorrect because plating is described as a coating process, not a removal process. Option (3) is incorrect because the iron is plated with a layer of metal; it is not mixed with another metal. Option (4) is incorrect because it says nothing about how rust is prevented from forming.

39. **(1) duplication of hereditary material (Interphase)** (Analysis) The division of hereditary material into two sets of chromosomes ensures that each new cell has the same chromosomes as the parent cell. (See Interphase in the cell division diagram.) Options (2), (3), (4), and (5) are aspects of the cell-division process, but they are not the direct cause of each new cell receiving a complete set of chromosomes from the parent.

40. **(3) It enters the cytoplasm.** (Analysis) The nuclear material goes into the cytoplasm, the cell material outside the nucleus. This is shown in the prophase stage. Option (1) is incorrect because the cell membrane functions as a protective surface for the cell contents. Options (2) and (4) are cell structures with other functions. Option (5) is incorrect because the nuclear membrane disappears at this stage.

41. **(4) in a warm spot in the kitchen** (Application) Warmth is needed for yeast action and expansion of the carbon dioxide gas. Options (1), (2), and (3) are all cool or cold places, so they would stop or slow the action of the yeast. Option (5) is incorrect because overheating the dough kills the yeast.

42. **(5) carbon-dioxide bubbles in the dough** (Comprehension) The pores, or small holes, in bread are formed by trapped bubbles of carbon dioxide gas. Options (1), (2), (3), and (4) are all solids that do not create pores.

43. **(3) secondary consumers** (Application) The vultures are eating a primary consumer when they eat the antelope, so they are functioning as secondary consumers. Option (1) is incorrect because only plants are producers. Option (2) is incorrect because the vultures are not eating plants. Although vultures are acting as tertiary consumers, option (4), when they are eating the lion, they are acting as

Answers and Explanations

secondary consumers when they are eating the antelope. Option (5) is incorrect because it applies to microorganisms that decompose organic matter.

44. **(3) There is more energy available to secondary consumers than to tertiary consumers.** (Analysis) The article states that each consumer uses some energy, so less energy is available to the next level consumer. Thus, there is more energy available to secondary consumers than to tertiary consumers. This same information shows options (1) and (4) to be incorrect. Options (2) and (5) are not true. Animals get their energy from plants, either directly or indirectly, and plants get their energy from the sun.

45. **(4) eat both plants and animals** (Comprehension) Such animals can be classified at various levels in the food chain because they eat a variety of foods at different levels. Animals such as those described in options (1) and (3) exist, but such animals would be classified only as primary consumers. Animals such as those described in option (2) would be classified as secondary consumers. Option (5) has nothing to do with food chains.

46. **(2) the sun** (Comprehension) This is the basic source of energy for the food chain because the sun is used by plants to manufacture food. There is no support for Option (1). Options (3), (4), and (5) are incorrect because they all get their energy, directly or indirectly, from the sun.

47. **(2) its weight equals the weight of the liquid it displaces** (Comprehension) According to the diagram, the cube floats when its weight is the same as the weight of the liquid it pushes aside, or displaces. Option (1) is incorrect because objects that sink also displace water. Option (3) is incorrect because, if the weight of the object is greater than that of the displaced liquid, the object sinks as shown in the second diagram. Options (4) and (5) are incorrect because the total weight of the liquid does not matter. What is important is the weight of the object in relation to the weight of the liquid pushed aside.

48. **(4) Steel and air are equal in weight to the water they displace.** (Evaluation) Steel ships float because they are not made of solid steel, but of steel and air (hollow parts of the ship). Thus, they weigh less than an equal

volume of solid steel, which would sink. Although option (1) is true, it is not correct because ships contain air as well as steel. Option (2) is not true since steel sinks. Option (3) is not true since steel ships float. Option (5) is not true since floating objects are equal in weight to the liquid they displace, not lighter.

49. **(3) are formed by sediment or soil carried by rivers from mountains to the plain** (Analysis) The diagram shows the river emerging from the mountain range and dividing into many little channels. The slowdown of the river's flow causes it to deposit the sediment it carries. Option (1) is incorrect because nothing in the diagram indicates whether the formation is new or old. Option (2) is incorrect because the diagram indicates the presence of a river, not a glacier. Options (4) and (5) cannot be assumed from the information given.

50. **(4) spreads out and slows down** (Analysis) The diagram shows the river spreading out and dividing into channels. The action of the river suddenly flowing into a flat area from the mountains causes the flow to spread out and slow. None of the other options is supported by the picture. Option (1) is incorrect because the speed of the water slows when the river reaches a flat area. The temperature is not shown. Options (2) and (3) are incorrect because the river becomes wider, not narrower. Option (5) is incorrect because nothing in the picture indicates that the stream goes underground.

51. **(3) restore chemicals used up as plants grow** (Comprehension) The first paragraph of the article indicates that this is the purpose of using fertilizer. Option (1) is incorrect because fertilizer does not replace soil. Option (2) is incorrect and untrue. Minerals are not lost in the composting process. Option (4) is incorrect because the article does not mention microorganisms in the soil. Option (5) is incorrect because manure is a form of fertilizer.

52. **(2) vitamin A to skim milk** (Application) When fat is removed from milk to produce skim milk most of the vitamin A content is lost. Vitamin A is added to replace it, and its addition is listed on the milk carton. Option (1) is too general to be correct. Option (3) is similar to adding fertilizer to soil, but the sweetener has no nutritional value. Fertilizer

adds nutritional value to the soil. Option (4) is also similar to adding fertilizer to soil, except that the fluoride does not replace something lost in the water. The water is just a convenient place to put fluoride for human consumption. Option (5) is simply a matter of taste. Most cereals contain natural sugars.

53. **(3) Organic fertilizers act on the soil in a manner more similar to nature than do chemical fertilizers.** (Evaluation) Since the action of compost and manure imitates the process of decay in nature, the farmer can claim that this crop is produced naturally and is therefore better for the environment. Option (1) is untrue since the article states that minerals are not used by the plants until they have decayed into a simpler form. Option (2) is true but is incorrect because the article states that plants use simple forms from both natural and artificial fertilizers. Option (4) is not true. Option (5) is also untrue; neither kind of fertilizer contains pesticides.

54. **(5) primates** (Application) Humans are members of the group of mammals called primates. Thus, knowing something about primates would be important to a physical anthropologist. Options (1), (2), (3), and (4) are incorrect because these groups are not closely related to humans. Option (1) includes animals such as lions and wolves. Option (2) includes marine mammals such as whales and dolphins. Option (3) includes the opossum and the kangaroo. Option (4) includes mice, squirrels, and rats.

55. **(1) carnivores** (Application) As meat-eaters, cats are members of the carnivore group, as are their relatives, tigers and lions. They are not cetaceans, option (2), because they are not ocean-dwellers. They are not marsupials, option (3), because the females do not have pouches. They are not rodents, option (4), because they do not have specialized upper teeth for gnawing. And they are not primates, option (5), because they do not have specialized limbs for grasping (such as thumbs) or complex brains.

56. **(4) a pouch in which the young stay after birth** (Analysis) The pouch is listed as the key characteristic that separates marsupials from other types of mammals. Option (1) is a characteristic of kangaroos, not of all marsupials. Option (2) is the characteristic that makes kangaroos members of the larger group, mammals. Option (3) would suggest a

relationship to the primates, who also have the ability to grasp. However, the kangaroo does not have a highly complex brain or eyes that can perceive depth, so the kangaroo is no a primate. Option (5) is incorrect because kangaroos do not have the two specialized upper incisor teeth of the rodent.

57. **(4) It is often difficult and expensive to convert existing houses to solar energy.** (Evaluation) The redesigning of windows and addition of solar collectors can be very expensive. Options (1) and (2) are incorrect because solar heating does not always involve these designs. Option (3) is not true in most areas. Option (5) is not true since solar energy is a very clean source of energy.

58. **(5) store reserves of energy to be used on cloudy days and at night** (Comprehension) The density of the materials used allows for the absorption and the gradual release of stored energy. Options (1), (2), and (4) are not purposes of a storage mass. Solar collectors— not storage masses—are generally used to heat water, option (3).

59. **(4) Heated air near the storage mass creates air currents that circulate warm air throughout the house.** (Analysis) Since warm air rises, a pattern of air flow is established in a well-designed solar house. Options (1), (2), and (3) are incorrect because houses that receive all their heat by means of solar energy do not have radiators throughout the house. Option (5) is incorrect because the storage mass generates radiant energy, or heat, not electrical energy.

60. **(3) A and C** (Evaluation) The article supports the idea that fossil fuels will run out and that they are sources of pollution (Statements A and C). Statement B is not true. Although statement D is true, it is not mentioned in the article. Any option—(1), (2), (4), and (5)—that includes B or D is incorrect.

61. **(3) 95°C** (Application) Since the boiling point of a liquid decreases with a drop in air pressure, the boiling point of water in Denver must be less than the boiling point of water in New York. This is so because Denver, at a higher elevation than New York, has a lower atmospheric pressure. Option (1) is incorrect because it is a higher temperature than the boiling point of water in New York, which is 100°C. Option (2) is incorrect because the boiling point of water will differ at different

elevations. The boiling point of water at sea level is 100°C. Options (4) and (5) are incorrect because they are the freezing and below-freezing temperatures of water.

62. **(1) chloroform** (Analysis) According to the chart, chloroform would boil first because it has the lowest boiling point, 61.7°C. Options (2), (3), and (4) are incorrect because it would take longer to heat these liquids to their boiling points than it would take to heat chloroform. Option (5) is not true, since the liquids have different boiling points. Therefore, the liquids will start to boil at different times.

63. **(4) The boiling point of a liquid increases as the air pressure increases.** (Evaluation) The information provided indicates a direct relationship between air pressure and the boiling points of liquids. In other words, as one increases, so does the other. Option (1) is incorrect because the passage indicates that once the boiling point is reached, the liquid does not get any hotter. It just boils until it evaporates. Option (2) is incorrect because the boiling point of water, 100°C, is lower than that of octane, 126°C, as is indicated in the chart. Option (3) is true but is not supported by the information provided. The passage and the chart do not deal with the effect on the liquid's boiling point of adding other substances. It is therefore incorrect. No information is given to support or disprove option (5). Although the boiling point of chloroform is lower than that of water, this fact does not necessarily have any bearing on the use of chloroform in anesthesia.

64. **(1) when moving up** (Analysis) The article states a jellyfish uses its muscles to move up in the water. Options (2) and (5) are not possible because when the jellyfish moves down to capture food, it drifts and does not use its muscles. Option (3) is not possible because jellyfish do not use their muscles to drift sideways. Option (4) is not possible because jellyfish swim up when capturing food.

65. **(4) Jellyfish reproduce sexually.** (Evaluation) The article states in the first paragraph that jellyfish mate and produce polyps. Sexual reproduction is another term for mating. Option (1) is not supported by the information provided, which is that jellyfish stings can be irritating and sometimes fatal. Option (2) is not true since mussels and clams

are not mentioned and they are not closely related to jellyfish. Option (3) is incorrect because the article states only that sea wasps, a type of jellyfish, are usually found in tropical oceans. Option (5) may or may not be true; however there is not enough information to determine this.

66. **(1) The waves or currents cause the jellyfish to bump into the person.** (Analysis) Of the options provided, only the current will cause the jellyfish to bump into a person who is standing still. The vertical motion described in options (2) and (3) will not cause the jellyfish to move toward the person. Options (4) and (5) are not supported by the information in the article.

UNIT 1: BIOLOGY
Lesson 1
GED Practice: Identifying the Main Idea (Page 35)

1. **(5) Epithelial tissue forms a protective surface for parts of the body.** (Comprehension) Option (5) is the main idea because it describes, in general, the function of epithelial tissue. The other statements are more specific. Option (1) tells something epithelial tissue does. Options (2) and (3) are examples of epithelial tissue. Option (4) describes a detail about epithelial tissue.

2. **(1) Human connective tissue supports and holds together parts of the body.** (Comprehension) This is a general statement about the purpose of connective tissue, the main idea of the second paragraph. Option (2) describes a detail about connective tissue. Options (3) and (4) are examples of connective tissue. Option (5) contains an example of the nonliving materials found in connective tissue.

3. **(4) Both epithelial and connective tissue are made up of living and nonliving material.** (Comprehension) Nonliving tissue is mentioned only in relationship to connective tissue. Options (1) and (2) are incorrect because the function of the two types of tissue is correct as stated. The first paragraph implies that epithelial tissue's close cells keep out undesirable substances, so option (3) is incorrect. Option (5) is stated in the second paragraph so it is an incorrect choice.

4. **(3) Skin is a type of epithelial tissue.** (Comprehension) This is an example. The other options are incorrect. Options (1), (2),

and (5) provide details describing tissues. Option (4) is the main idea of the second paragraph.

5. **(2) the calcium found in bone** (Comprehension) The second paragraph mentions calcium as a nonliving material found in connective tissue. Bone is a type of connective tissue. All other options are living and are mentioned in the passage.

GED Practice: The Biology of Cells (Page 37)

1. **(2) Most cells have things in common and have a similar structure.** (Comprehension) This is a statement of the main idea of the paragraph. Options (1) and (3) are true but do not state the main idea. Options (4) and (5) name structures that most cells have in common.

2. **(1) All cells grow, reproduce, and die.** (Comprehension) Option (1) gives details that all cells have in common. Option (2) is incorrect because it is the main idea, not a detail. Option (3) refers only to some cells. Options (4) and (5) are structures that cells have in common, so each only partly supports the main idea.

3. **(3) Most cells are divided into two basic parts.** (Comprehension) Option (3) is the main idea of the paragraph. Although options (1), (2), (4), and (5) are all true, they give specific information about option (3) and thus are supporting details.

4. **(3) The nucleus contains a nucleolus, chromatin, and a nuclear membrane.** (Comprehension) Option (3), which simply names the parts of the nucleus, is the main idea. Note that this is an implicit main idea; the paragraph does not contain a topic sentence. Options (1), (2), (4), and (5) provide details about the nucleus and its parts.

5. **(1) Cytoplasm contains all the structures inside the cell membrane except the nucleus.** (Comprehension) Option (1) states the main idea of the paragraph. It is about cytoplasm and the structures in it. Options (2), (3), and (4) are incorrect because they give specific information about the parts of the cytoplasm. Option (5) states the opposite of the main idea.

6. **(5) The cytoplasm contains mitochondria, the ER, ribosomes, and vacuoles.**

(Comprehension) In naming several parts of the cytoplasm, option (5) supports the main idea, that the cytoplasm contains all the cell structures except the nucleus. Option (1) is a definition of organelles. Options (2), (3), and (4) are true, but they are specific details about various parts of the cytoplasm.

GED Review: Lesson 1 (Pages 38–39)

1. **(3) metaphase** (Comprehension) Spindle fibers first appear in the diagram representing metaphase. During interphase, option (1), the spindles have not yet appeared. In prophase, option (2), the spindles are forming. During the last two phases, options (4) and (5), the spindles are already contracting and disappearing.

2. **(5) spindle fibers** (Comprehension) By examining the diagram, you can see that the spindle fibers are the only structures attached to the chromosomes. Therefore, they must be pulling the chromosomes apart. Option (1) remains in one place and does not change its appearance. Option (2) has no way to pull the chromosomes apart. Options (3) and (4) are not seen during anaphase.

3. **(1) interphase** (Comprehension) According to the passage, the hereditary material that makes up the chromosomes is duplicated during the first phase, or interphase. The already duplicated chromosomes are present during each of the other phases, options (2), (3), (4), and (5).

4. **(2) Mitosis is the process by which cells divide.** (Comprehension) The paragraph describes the process of mitosis, which is mentioned only in option (2). Options (1), (3), (4), and (5) are all true, but they describe only specific aspects of mitosis.

5. **(1) guide the chromosomes** (Comprehension) By examining the diagram and reading the passage, you can see that the spindle fibers guide the chromosomes toward the opposite sides of the cell. They could not produce the nucleus, option (2), or form the nuclear membrane, option (3), since these structures reappear in the daughter cells after the spindle fibers have disappeared. The hereditary material, option (4), has already become chromosomes. There is no cell plate, option (5), mentioned in the passage.

Answers and Explanations

6. **(4) 46** (Comprehension) According to the passage, each daughter cell will have the same number of chromosomes as the parent cell, 46 chromosomes. Options (1), (2), (3), and (5) are incorrect because they are numbers other than 46.

7. **(2) 23** (Application) According to the passage, a gamete has half the number of chromosomes found in a parent cell. Since the cells have 46 chromosomes, the gametes have half that number, or 23. Options (1), (3), (4), and (5) are incorrect because they are numbers other than 23.

8. **(1) half the number** (Comprehension) The number of chromosomes resulting from meiosis is half that of the parent cell. Options (2), (3), (4), and (5) are incorrect because they are values other than half.

9. **(3) sexual reproduction** (Comprehension) During sexual reproduction two gametes combine to form a zygote. Options (1) and (2) are incorrect because both are types of cell division that do not produce a zygote. Option (4) is incorrect because a zygote forms during the union, not division, of cells. During gamete production a cell with 23 chromosomes is formed, so option (5) is incorrect.

10. **(3) One chromosome pair did not separate properly during meiosis.** (Application) If one pair of chromosomes fails to separate during meiosis, one gamete will have an extra chromosome and one will be missing a chromosome. If the gamete with the extra chromosome combines with a normal human gamete, the zygote will have 47—not 46—chromosomes. Option (1) is incorrect because meiosis moves chromosomes to new cells, but no hereditary material is produced. Option (2) is incorrect because sexual reproduction does not destroy hereditary material. While option (4) is a true statement, it does not explain what caused this condition. If three gametes combined, option (5), the result would be 69 chromosomes, not 47.

11. **(3) 50 percent** (Comprehension) If one chromosome from each pair comes from each parent, then each parent contributes 50 percent of an individual's chromosomes.

1. **(4) chloroplast** (Comprehension) Photosynthesis cannot take place without chlorophyll, which is stored in the chloroplast. Option (1) is the food manufactured in the chloroplast. Option (2) is the part of the cell that controls the cell's activities. Option (3) provides stiffness to the cell. Option (5) changes the sugar produced by photosynthesis in the chloroplast into starch.

2. **(1) cell wall, chloroplast, and leucoplast** (Comprehension) The first paragraph states that the cell wall is a structure in plant cells, not animal cells; the third and fourth paragraphs describe chloroplasts and leucoplasts, two kinds of plastids, organelles found only in plant cells. Option (2) is incorrect because the cell membrane is found in both plants and animals. Option (3) is incorrect because the cell membrane, chromatin, and nucleolus are found in the cells of both plants and animals. Option (4) is incorrect because the chromatin and nucleolus are found in the cells of both plants and animals. Option (5) is incorrect because cytoplasm is found in both plants and animals.

3. **(5) production of sugar** (Comprehension) According to the passage, the products of photosynthesis are sugar and oxygen. Option (1) is controlled by the nucleus of the cell. Options (2), (3), and (4) have nothing to do with photosynthesis and are not mentioned in the passage.

4. **(1) the secondary cell wall** (Comprehension) This layer is made stiff by cellulose and often remains after the cell has died. The middle lamella, option (2), is made up of pectin, a jellylike substance, which would not make wood stiff. Options (3) and (5) are organelles that have nothing to do with cell stiffness. The primary cell wall, option (4), is made up of cellulose and pectin and would not be stiff enough to maintain wood's hard structure, especially after the tree has died.

5. **(1) many chromoplasts** (Application) Rose petals contain pigments, which are stored in chromoplasts. Flower petals are not green, so they do not have chloroplasts, option (2). Flower petals do not store food, so they do not contain leucoplasts, option (3), or starch, option (5). Flower petals are not woody, so they do not contain lignin, option (4).

6. **(3) to prevent fungus from killing the tree** (Comprehension) If the injured branch is not removed, the fungus will spread, eventually killing the tree. Option (1) has nothing to do with injured branches. Options (2) and (4) are incorrect because they are not the reason the branch is being removed. Option (5) is not true, since stubs are not left when branches are properly removed.

7. **(3) The bark was torn.** (Comprehension) The diagram shows that the bark was torn, so option (3) is the only possible answer. Options (1), (2), (4), and (5) are not results that can be seen in the diagram.

8. **(1) to make sure that all the fungus is removed** (Comprehension) The stub is removed so that the fungus will not spread to other branches or the trunk. Options (2) and (3) are not the reasons for removing the stub. Options (4) and (5) are not true.

9. **(3) to keep the bark from tearing when the limb falls** (Comprehension) When the limb breaks away, the cut in the limb keeps the bark from being torn from the branch or trunk. Option (1) is incorrect because ease in cutting is not mentioned in the passage. Option (2) is incorrect because the saw getting stuck is not mentioned. Option (4) is incorrect because the passage describes fungus getting into the wound, not growing on the tree's underside. Option (5) is incorrect because the cut is made on the underside regardless of where the wound occurs.

10. **(2) because fungus spores grow in wounds and eventually attack other parts of the tree** (Analysis) According to the passage, fungus spores may get into a tree's wound, infecting the tree with disease. The implication is that treatment can save the tree. As all living things are subject to death, option (1) is not the reason. Option (3) is true but does not explain why a wounded tree may die. Although options (4) and (5) describe events that do occur, these events are not causes for a tree dying.

Lesson 2
GED Practice: Restating Information (Page 43)
1. **(3) a person's health is affected by poor diet** (Comprehension) The paragraph states that malnutrition is a poor state of health that can result from overeating as well as undereating. Options (1), (2), (4), and (5) define malnutrition as either overeating or undereating. Therefore, they are not complete definitions of malnutrition.

2. **(1) not eating enough food or not eating enough of a specific nutrient** (Comprehension) Undernutrition can be a matter of not getting enough food, or it can be a matter of a nutrient deficiency. Options (2) and (3) are incorrect because they are causes of overnutrition. Option (4) is incorrect because poor health is described as a result of undernutrition, not a cause. Option (5) is incorrect because undernutrition is a form of malnutrition; malnutrition does not cause undernutrition.

GED Practice: Photosynthesis (Page 45)
1. **(3) hydrogen** (Comprehension) The fifth paragraph states that hydrogen produced in the light reactions combines with carbon to form sugar in the dark reactions. Options (1), (2), (4), and (5) are incorrect because they are substances other than hydrogen.

2. **(1) sugar** (Comprehension) The first paragraph states that sugar is used as food and to build other substances such as starches and proteins that the plant needs. The other products of photosynthesis are waste materials, options (2) and (3). Option (4), carbon dioxide, is not a product of photosynthesis. Neither is chlorophyll, option (5).

3. **(1) Water plus carbon dioxide, in the presence of light and chlorophyll, yields sugar, oxygen, and water.** (Comprehension) This is the only statement that includes all the reacting substances and products shown in the equation. Option (2) is incorrect because it leaves out light. Option (3) is incorrect because hydrogen is not a product of photosynthesis. Option (4) is incorrect because oxygen is not used in photosynthesis; it is a product of photosynthesis. Option (5) is incorrect because it leaves out chlorophyll.

4. **(2) Plants make their own food through photosynthesis.** (Comprehension) The passage describes how photosynthesis works. Although options (1), (3), (4), and (5) are true statements, they are not the main idea of the passage. They are all supporting details.

5. **(5) The light reactions take place in sunlight.** (Comprehension) This statement explains why the light reactions are called light reactions. Options (1), (2), (3), and (4) are all true, but they do not support the statement in the question.

6. **(4) The light reactions make up the first phase of photosynthesis.** (Comprehension) This restates the topic sentence of the fourth paragraph, the sentence that gives the general idea of the paragraph. Options (1), (2), (3), and (5) are supporting details that explain the first phase of photosynthesis.

GED Review: Lesson 2 (Pages 46–47)

1. **(4) amoeba** (Comprehension) Direct respiration occurs in single-celled organisms. Indirect respiration occurs in most many-celled organisms. Option (4) is the only single-celled organism listed. Options (1), (2), (3), and (5) are incorrect because they all are many-celled organisms.

2. **(5) water vapor and carbon dioxide** (Comprehension) Since water and carbon dioxide are the result of respiration, it follows that carbon dioxide and water vapor would be exhaled. In option (1), oxygen is not a result of respiration. In option (2), neither hydrogen nor oxygen is the result of respiration. In option (3), sugar is not a result of respiration. In option (4), neither hydrogen nor carbon is the result of respiration.

3. **(2) carbon dioxide and water** (Comprehension) According to the equation, carbon dioxide and water are the only two substances that result from respiration. Options (1), (3), (4), and (5) are incorrect because neither hydrogen, glucose, nor oxygen is a direct result of respiration.

4. **(2) yields carbon dioxide plus water plus energy** (Comprehension) This restates the respiration equation. Option (1) is incorrect because carbon dioxide is a product of respiration. Option (3) is incorrect because it leaves out energy. Option (4) is incorrect because sugar is not a result of respiration. Option (5) is incorrect because respiration yields carbon dioxide and water, not "gases."

5. **(2) bronchi, bronchioles, alveoli** (Comprehension) According to the passage and the diagram, the air we inhale passes through the trachea, bronchi, and bronchioles before arriving at the alveoli. Options (1), (3), (4),

and (5) are incorrect because the structures are listed in the wrong order.

6. **(2) Inhaled air contains more oxygen than exhaled air.** (Comprehension) Since oxygen in the air is absorbed into the bloodstream in the alveoli, the air that is left to exhale contains less oxygen. Option (1) is incorrect because there is more carbon dioxide in exhaled air. Option (3) is incorrect because inhaled air must go through the bronchi and bronchioles before reaching the alveoli. Option (4) is incorrect because inhaled air contains more oxygen. Option (5) is incorrect because no air passes through the diaphragm.

7. **(3) enabling the blood to absorb oxygen and release carbon dioxide** (Comprehension) The main function of the lungs, as described in the passage, is to exchange oxygen in inhaled air and replace it with carbon dioxide in exhaled air. Its main function is not to support the bronchi, option (1), or to warm the air, option (2). It does not absorb carbon dioxide, option (4), nor does it split water into oxygen and hydrogen, option (5).

8. **(3) C only** (Comprehension) The right side of the diagram, Statement C, shows a close-up of the exchange in the lungs of oxygen and carbon dioxide, which is the topic of the second paragraph. Options (1) and (5) are incorrect because the first paragraph, Statement A, describes how air gets into the alveoli, not what happens there. Options (2) and (4) are incorrect because the left side of the diagram, Statement B, shows the path of air into the lungs, not the exchange of oxygen and carbon dioxide.

GED Mini-Test: Lesson 2 (Pages 48–49)

1. **(4) from the soil** (Comprehension) It is stated in the first paragraph that plants get nitrogen from the soil. Therefore, options (1), (2), (3), and (5) are incorrect because they are sources other than soil.

2. **(5) in nodules on the roots of legumes** (Comprehension) The diagram and the second paragraph show that nitrogen fixation takes place in the nodules on roots. Options (1), (2), (3), and (4) are incorrect because they are locations other than in nodules of legumes.

3. **(4) nitrification** (Comprehension) Nitrification is the process by which nitrogen is made available to plants by the breakdown

of decaying organisms. Options (1) and (2) name other nitrogen conversion processes. Options (3) and (5) are processes that have nothing to do with the nitrogen cycle.

4. **(4) nitrogen fixation** (Comprehension) The diagram shows that option (4), nitrogen fixation, is the process that converts nitrogen from the atmosphere to forms that plants can use. Option (1) is how nitrogen from decomposing matter is put back into the soil. Option (2) is the release of nitrogen back into the air. Option (3) is the breakdown of animal and plant matter. Option (5) is not part of the nitrogen cycle.

5. **(3) oxygen** (Comprehension) Oxygen reacts with sugar to produce water, carbon dioxide, and energy. Therefore, options (1), (2), (4), and (5) are all incorrect.

6. **(4) decrease** (Analysis) Photosynthesis provides most of the oxygen for the oxygen-carbon cycle. Without it, the amount of oxygen in the air would decrease. Options (1), (2), and (3) are incorrect because animals would continue to take in oxygen, thus depleting the supply of oxygen in the air. As a result, the supply couldn't remain unchanged, increase or double. Option (5) is incorrect because animals do not produce oxygen.

Lesson 3
GED Practice: Cause and Effect (Page 51)
1. **(1) injuries, heavy bleeding, disease, and some drugs** (Comprehension) In the first sentence of the passage, these conditions are said to interfere with the circulation of the blood, which is what happens with shock. Options (2) and (3) are symptoms of shock, not causes. Options (4) and (5) are not mentioned in the passage.

2. **(3) stopping bleeding** (Analysis) Since one of the causes of shock is a loss of blood, stopping blood loss would help stop shock. Options (1), (2), (4), and (5) are incorrect because they are first-aid measures that do not affect the circulatory system and therefore would not be helpful.

3. **(2) The water would contain more microorganisms.** (Analysis) According to the diagram, the purpose of the sand filter is to remove microorganisms from the water. If the sand filter were removed, the result would be more microorganisms left in the water. Since

this result would occur, option (5) cannot be correct. Option (1) is a result of removing the settling basin. Option (3) is a result of adding more chlorine. Option (4) is a result of removing the chlorinator.

4. **(4) to prevent the spread of harmful substances through drinking water** (Analysis) The diagram shows that water purification removes unwanted material, such as microorganisms, from the water supply. The effect of purification is that people do not drink such materials along with the water. Options (1) and (2) involve the movement of water, not water purification. Option (3) is incorrect because conservation has nothing to do with water purification. Option (5) involves adding a chemical, fluoride, to the water. This is not a step in purifying water.

GED Practice: Evolution (Page 53)
1. **(3) They are positioned side by side below the humerus.** (Comprehension) The diagram shows that in all four animals the radius and ulna are next to each other just below the humerus. They are not part of the fingers, option (1), or the feet, option (2). Option (4) is incorrect because it lists homologous structures in different organisms. Option (5) is incorrect because the diagram does not show the bones of embryos.

2. **(2) Different types of organisms have homologous structures.** (Analysis) This fact is one piece of evidence that supports the theory of evolution. Option (1) may be true, but it does not offer support for the theory of evolution. Option (3) is not true; organisms have evolved gradually over time. Option (4) is incorrect because the passage states that fish, bird, and human embryos have gill slits and tail buds, but it does not say all embryos have these structures. Option (5) is not true.

3. **(5) their evolution in different environments** (Analysis) Differences in structure between whales and birds are the result of one species evolving in the ocean and the other evolving in the air. Options (1) and (2) are incorrect because homologous structures and similarity between embryos are a result of evolution, not a cause. Option (3) is true but does not explain why whales and birds developed differently. According to the passage, option (4) is not true, so it could not explain why whales and birds are different.

4. **(1) Human ancestors had tails.** (Analysis) The presence of a tail bud indicates that at one time the ancestors of humans had tails. Options (2), (4), and (5) are true, but they are incorrect because they do not explain why human embryos have tail buds. Option (3) may be true of some organisms, but not humans, since humans have no tails.

5. **(4) Homologous structures and similarity among embryos are evidence supporting the theory of evolution.** (Comprehension) The passage is about facts that support the idea that organisms have developed over time from a common ancestor. Options (1) and (2) are each only partly correct, since they mention only one of the sources of evidence. Options (3) and (5) are true, but they are supporting details, not the main idea.

6. **(1) Plants and animals will continue to evolve.** (Analysis) Evolution is an ongoing process; it will not stop with today's organisms. Options (2), (3), and (5) are specific events that are unlikely and cannot be predicted based on the passage. Option (4) is not true; both plants and animals will continue to change.

GED Review: Lesson 3 (Pages 54–55)

1. **(3) variation** (Application) The differences in the necks of giraffes are variations within a species. Options (1) and (5) are incorrect because the statement about giraffes says nothing about reproduction. Option (2) is incorrect because the statement does not describe any competition among giraffes. Option (4) is incorrect because the survival value of having a longer neck is not included in the statement.

2. **(5) reproduction** (Application) The parent birds passed on their coloration trait to their offspring. Option (1) is incorrect; the statement does not mention how many baby birds there were. Option (2) is incorrect; the statement does not refer to any competition between these birds and any other birds. Option (3) is incorrect; the statement does not describe any differences among the birds. While it can be assumed that their coloration helped the birds survive, it is not part of the statement, so option (4) is incorrect.

3. **(1) overproduction** (Application) In one season, a single pine tree produces enough seeds to start a forest of "offspring." Thus, this statement reflects production of too many "offspring." Option (2) is incorrect because the statement doesn't mention competition for food, water, etc. among the seeds. Option (3) is incorrect since no mention is made about variation among the seeds produced. Option (4) is incorrect because the statement doesn't mention the survival rate of the seeds. Option (5) is incorrect since there is no mention of the seeds growing, reproducing, and passing traits on to their offspring.

4. **(4) survival** (Application) Only plants that can store water will survive between rainy periods. Option (1) is incorrect because the cactus is storing water, not producing offspring. Option (2) is incorrect because, although competition for water exists in the desert, it is not described here. Option (3) is incorrect because, although there is variation in the ability of plants to store water, the point being made in the statement is that only certain cactus plants survive. Option (5) is incorrect because the statement does not mention reproduction.

5. **(5) lightning** (Analysis) Energy from lightning was a cause of the chemical reactions among gas molecules in the early atmosphere. Options (1) and (3) are incorrect because these gases were present in the atmosphere, not causes of chemical reactions. Option (2) was a result of the recombining of elements, not a cause. Option (4) did not cause chemical reactions.

6. **(1) make up all living things** (Analysis) According to the passage, organic molecules are the building blocks of all living things. Therefore, organic molecules had to exist before living things could evolve. Organic molecules do not give rise to carbon, option (2); carbon is part of any organic molecule. Energy, option (3), was obtained from other sources before life emerged. Organic molecules do not make up the atmosphere, option (4); many kinds of gases do. Option (5) is not true, since organic molecules don't produce rain.

7. **(2) methane, ammonia, and water vapor** (Comprehension) According to the passage, Earth's atmosphere was composed of ammonia, hydrogen, methane, and water vapor. Option (2) contains three of these gases. Options (1) and (5) are incorrect because they include oxygen. Option (3) is incorrect because it includes carbon. Option (4) is incorrect because it includes silicon.

8. **(1) carbon** (Comprehension) According to the passage, carbon is present in combination with one or more of the other elements listed. Carbon is therefore found in all organic molecules. Options (2), (3), and (4) are incorrect because they are elements other than carbon. Option (5) is incorrect because not all organic molecules contain all these elements.

GED Mini-Test: Lesson 3 (Pages 56–57)

1. **(1) environmental changes** (Analysis) According to the passage, environmental changes are one of the things that contribute to speciation. Options (2) and (3) do not contribute to speciation. Options (4) and (5) have little effect on speciation and are not mentioned in the passage.

2. **(3) becoming less alike** (Analysis) During adaptive radiation, species change and become less alike. Option (1) is the opposite of what happens. Random differences, option (2), are not a factor in adaptive radiation. Option (4) is incorrect because equal changes in population would not create different species. Option (5) is incorrect because the result of adaptive radiation is always a change of some kind.

3. **(4) adaptive radiation** (Comprehension) The passage uses the development of many species of silversword in Hawaii as a classic example of adaptive radiation. With option (1) there would be no silversword. Option (2) is incorrect because the passage says nothing about fossils. Option (3) is not mentioned and is the opposite result of adaptive radiation. Option (5) is not mentioned in the passage and does not affect adaptive radiation.

4. **(5) created more variety** (Analysis) Speciation allows new species of organisms to evolve, creating more variety. Option (1) would be the result if no speciation occurred. Options (2) and (3) are incorrect since more variety occurred. Option (4) is incorrect because speciation adds more variety.

5. **(4) chance** (Comprehension) Chance variation of the gene frequency within a population is genetic drift. Options (1), (2), and (3) describe ways that new species develop. Option (5) is incorrect because mating between species is rare and not related to genetic drift.

6. **(1) an increase in the gray gene's frequency** (Analysis) Since the larger group of squirrels now has more gray squirrels in proportion to the number of white squirrels than before, the frequency of the gray gene is increased. Options (2), (3), (4), and (5) are incorrect because they do not describe the new proportion of gray to white squirrels.

7. **(5) B and C** (Analysis) The loss of part of the population by chance affects genetic drift. Both Statement B, death by disease, and Statement C, removal by predators, would result in the loss of part of the population. Options (1) and (4) are incorrect because a change in an animal's size, Statement A, would not affect genetic drift. Options (2) and (3) are incorrect because each includes only one of the two causes of population loss.

Lesson 4
GED Practice: Identifying Implications (Page 59)

1. **(5) Continents can be barriers to ocean plants and animals.** (Comprehension) The passage mentions various types of geographic barriers and indicates that they prevent many types of plants and animals from spreading. The example of continents acting as a barrier to ocean life is the same type of situation. Options (1), (2), (3), and (4) are not true: these geographic features are not barriers to all animals.

2. **(2) humans** (Comprehension) Humans have spread into all types of areas because they have created ways to overcome geographic barriers. Options (1), (3), (4), and (5) are incorrect because these animals are all restricted by the limits of their normal habitats.

3. **(3) the smog-filled air above Denver** (Application) Air is not a geographic barrier. Options (1), (2), (4), and (5) are all examples of geographic barriers mentioned in the passage.

4. **(3) a sparrow making a nest on an ocean-going ship** (Analysis) Sparrows cannot fly across an ocean. If they nest on a ship, they might be carried a long distance. The other choices are ways species normally move from place to place, and do not represent crossing a barrier.

1. **(1) Growth of stems does not take place between buds.** (Comprehension) The passage states that growth takes place at the buds; it implies that growth does not take place between buds. Option (2) is incorrect; the passage says nothing about growth of leaves. Option (3) is not true; meristem cells are delicate, so plants form root caps to protect them. Option (4) is not true, the passage states that woody plants have cambium. Option (5) is not true; the passage states that cambium is present in stems, branches, and roots.

2. **(2) meristem cells become specialized as they develop** (Comprehension) Meristems develop into all three structures, so they must take on the characteristics of each during growth. Option (1) is contradicted by the passage. Options (3) and (4) are not true. Option (5) is not true of woody stems.

3. **(1) plant would stop getting taller** (Analysis) Since growth from the top bud is upward growth, the effect of cutting off the top bud would be to stop upward growth, at least for a while. Cutting off the top bud would not have the effects listed in options (2), (3), (4), and (5). None of these options is stated or implied in the passage.

4. **(2) Growth of seed plants takes place in special areas called meristems.** (Comprehension) This is the general topic, or main idea, of the passage. Options (1), (3), and (4) are details in the passage. Option (5) is incorrect because animals are not mentioned in the passage.

5. **(2) the bottom branch of a tree will be the same height above the ground as when it first formed** (Comprehension) Since upward growth of a seed plant is from the top of the stem only, once branches grow along the stem, they will stay at the same height above the ground. Option (1) is not true since the tree grows from the top of the stem. Option (3) is not true since there is no growth between buds. Options (4) and (5) are not true since after thirty years the cambium cells will have added to the thickness of the trunk.

6. **(5) cambium** (Comprehension) The passage states that cambium is found in woody plants and implies that it is not found in most nonwoody plants. Options (1) and (4) are incorrect because these structures do not contain meristem cells. Options (2) and (3) are incorrect because these structures are found in both woody and nonwoody plants.

7. **(1) It would stop growing.** (Analysis) Since meristem cells form the growth regions of a plant, their destruction would stop all growth. Options (2), (3), (4), and (5) all could not happen without meristem cells.

8. **(2) at the ends of stems and roots** (Analysis) The word apical describes the tip, or end, of stems and roots. Option (1) is incorrect because there is no meristem between buds. Options (3) and (4) refer to meristem cells that are not at the tips of structures. Option (5) is incorrect because there is no meristem in leaves.

GED Review: Lesson 4 (Pages 62–63)

1. **(1) bacteria** (Comprehension) Bacteria, members of the kingdom Monera, are the simplest since they are all one-celled and lack a membrane around the nucleus. Option (2) is incorrect because slime molds, members of the kingdom Protista, are a little more complex; they may have more than one cell. Options (3), (4), and (5) are members of more complex kingdoms; their cells are organized into specialized tissues and organs.

2. **(3) nuclear area has no membrane** (Comprehension) According to the chart, of the five options, this is the only characteristic that is found only in the kingdom Monera. Option (1) is incorrect because other organisms, not only Monera, can be one celled. Options (2), (4), and (5) are characteristics of kingdoms other than Monera.

3. **(3) absence of cell walls** (Comprehension) Since a goldfish is a type of fish, it can be classified as a member of the kingdom Animalia. The only characteristic of animals presented in the five options is the absence of cell walls. Options (1), (2), (4), and (5) are not characteristics of Animalia.

4. **(5) Animalia** (Comprehension) According to the chart, animals take food into their bodies. This implies that they cannot produce their own food. Animals are complex, being made up of tissues and organs. Options (1), (2), (3), and (4) are kingdoms whose members either are not complex or can produce their own food.

5. **(2) rain and surface water soaking into the soil** (Comprehension) Since the passage states that the plant absorbs water from the soil into the roots, it follows that most of the water a plant gets is from rain and surface water that has soaked into the soil. Options (1) and (5) are incorrect because very few plants depend on wells or irrigation systems for water. Option (3) is incorrect because the passage says that water is absorbed by the roots. Option (4) is incorrect because xylem only carries the water; it is not a source of water.

6. **(2) phloem** (Comprehension) The last paragraph of the passage describes the function of phloem, which is to carry food from the leaves to the rest of the plant. Therefore, options (1), (3), (4), and (5) are incorrect because they are tissues other than phloem.

7. **(1) Photosynthesis would slow and stop because of lack of water.** (Analysis) Clogging the xylem would have the effect of stopping the water flow to the leaves, where photosynthesis takes place. Since water is one of the ingredients of photosynthesis, it would slow and stop. Options (2) and (5) are incorrect because they would not happen right away. There is no evidence given to support options (3) and (4).

8. **(4) xylem** (Comprehension) By studying the diagram, you can see that the main part of the trunk of the tree is xylem tissue. Option (1) is incorrect because bark is trimmed from wood and not often used. When the bark is trimmed, it is likely that some phloem, option (2), and cambium, option (3) are also trimmed. Meristem, option (5), is not mentioned in the passage.

GED Mini-Test: Lesson 4 (Pages 64–65)
1. **(2) angiosperms have spread because they have advantages that gymnosperms lack** (Comprehension) The dramatic difference in the number of species of gymnosperms and angiosperms implies that the more numerous type of plant has characteristics that allow adaptation to many environments. These advantages have caused the spread of angiosperms. Option (1) is incorrect; the reverse is true. Options (3) and (5) are not true; both types of plants are found in a variety of environments. Option (4) is not true because angiosperms have protective coverings for their seeds.

2. **(1) seeds with 1 seed leaf** (Comprehension) The information indicates that seeds with 1 seed leaf are a distinguishing characteristic of monocotyledons. Options (2), (3), (4), and (5) are incorrect because they are characteristics of dicotyledons.

3. **(2) flower parts in sets of 3** (Comprehension) Since wheat is a grass, and grasses are monocotyledons, it follows that wheat flowers have flower parts in sets of 3. Options (1), (3), and (4) are characteristics of dicotyledons. Option (5) is a characteristic of gymnosperms.

4. **(3) They produce protected seeds.** (Analysis) The fact that the seeds are protected means that more of them survive to become seedlings and mature plants. This contributed to the success of the angiosperms. Option (1) is not a characteristic of angiosperms. Each of options (2), (4), and (5) is a characteristic of a subgroup of angiosperms, but they do not contribute directly to the success of these plants.

5. **(3) carbon dioxide** (Comprehension) The passage states that the correct temperature, moisture, and oxygen are necessary for germination. This implies that other conditions, such as carbon dioxide, are not important. Options (1), (2), and (4) are incorrect because they are important to germination. Option (5) is another way to say moisture.

6. **(3) The seeds will not get enough oxygen to germinate.** (Analysis) The passage indicates that seeds are planted near the surface to ensure a good oxygen supply. Therefore the result of deep planting would be to decrease the supply of oxygen. Option (1) is incorrect because conditions do not improve with deep planting. Temperature and water are less affected by the depth of the seed, so options (2) and (5) are incorrect. Sunlight is not always necessary for germination, so option (4) is incorrect.

7. **(4) It will grow slowly and die.** (Comprehension) Although a maple seed can germinate under poor conditions, this does not imply it can also grow successfully to maturity. Option (1) is incorrect because a maple tree cannot grow in ice. Option (2) may happen, but it is not the most likely outcome.

Option (3) is unlikely since rotting usually happens under warm conditions with too much moisture. While the ice may melt, plants do not melt, so option (5) is not true.

8. **(5) There is the correct amount of warmth, moisture, and oxygen.** (Analysis) The passage states that three conditions must be met. Therefore, some seeds must stay inactive until all of these conditions for growth are correct as stated in option (5). Options (1), (2), and (4) each name only one of the three conditions necessary for germination. Option (3) is not always necessary for germination.

9. **(2) What Seeds Need to Germinate** (Comprehension) This title summarizes the information in the passage. Option (1) is incorrect because the passage does not tell how seeds germinate, only what conditions are necessary. Option (3) is too vague and is about a totally different topic. Options (4) and (5) address only a portion of the information given so they are incorrect.

10. **(4) a state of inactivity** (Analysis) Dormant seeds are inactive. Options (1), (3), and (5) are not the best choices because seeds do not "sleep," "rest," or "await." These are activities of animals. Option (2) is incorrect because it implies that later the seeds are in motion.

Lesson 5
GED Practice: Recognizing Assumptions (Page 67)

1. **(3) that the reader is familiar with disease, pigs, and parasites** (Analysis) Since the diagram shows the transmission of the disease trichinosis by the parasite trichina from a pig to a human, the reader needs to be familiar with disease, pigs, and parasites to understand the diagram. Option (1) is not true. Options (2) and (4) are incorrect because the reader doesn't need to have had the disease or eat pork in order to understand the diagram. Option (5) is true, but since it is clearly shown in the diagram, it cannot be called an unstated assumption.

2. **(1) Trichinosis is a disease.** (Analysis) The infection of humans by trichina worms causes a disease called trichinosis. The diagram shows how this disease is transmitted, but does not state that it is a disease. Option (2) is true, but since it is clearly shown in the diagram, it cannot be called an unstated assumption. Option (3) is the opposite of what the diagram shows. Option (4) is not true; trichinosis does not affect the respiratory

system and is not spread by coughing and sneezing. Option (5) is not true; since the trichina worms are inside the meat, washing your hands will not prevent the spread of trichinosis.

3. **(2) The trichina worm is a parasite, an organism that obtains its food from another living thing.** (Analysis) The diagram shows that the trichina worm lives in other animals. Such an organism is called a parasite. Option (1) is not true; the diagram does not indicate that trichinosis can be caught from beef or lamb. Options (3), (4), and (5) are not true.

GED Practice: The Human Digestive System (Page 69)

1. **(2) to break down food into substances the body can absorb and to get rid of wastes** (Analysis) Although the passage discusses how the digestive system works, the general purpose is never stated. The purpose of the digestive system is an unstated assumption. Option (1) is true but is only part of the digestive system's function. Option (3) is not true. Option (4) is one function of the stomach. Option (5) is the function of the respiratory system, not the digestive system.

2. **(5) by chewing** (Analysis) Although the passage does not state this, we can assume that chewing is the process by which food is ground up and mixed with saliva. Since saliva is present in the mouth, options (1) and (2) are incorrect. Swallowing, option (3), is the way food is passed through the esophagus and into the stomach. Option (4) has nothing to do with grinding up food.

3. **(3) to absorb water** (Comprehension) In the paragraph about the large intestine, it is stated that one of the main functions of the large intestine is to absorb water. Options (1), (2), (4), and (5) are functions of other parts of the digestive system.

4. **(4) small intestine** (Comprehension) The passage states that the alimentary canal is about 30 feet long. Since the small intestine is about 23 feet long, it makes up most of the length of the alimentary canal. If you look at the diagram, you will see that the other organs are much shorter than the small intestine. Options (1), (2), (3), and (5) are incorrect because they are body parts other than the small intestine.

5. **(5) rest of the body** (Comprehension) Since nutrients pass into the blood and the blood travels throughout the body, the nutrients are carried throughout the body. Options (1), (2), (3), and (4) are therefore only partly correct.

6. **(4) Fats would not be digested properly.** (Analysis) The function of bile is to break down fats into small droplets. This process would be disrupted if anything were wrong with the liver. Options (1), (2), (3), and (5) are not functions of the liver.

7. **(2) Food is not ground up enough and so starches are not properly processed.** (Analysis) The mouth's function is to grind and moisten the food and to begin the breakdown of starch. If food does not spend enough time in the mouth, the result is that it is not properly processed. Option (1) is the opposite of what happens when you swallow too quickly. Option (3) is true whether or not food is chewed properly. Options (4) and (5) are not part of the action of the mouth.

8. **(5) rectum** (Comprehension) The diagram shows that the large intestine empties into the rectum, which is the passage out of the body. Options (1), (2), (3), and (4) are incorrect because they are internal organs that are not close to a body opening.

GED Review: Lesson 5 (Pages 70–71)
1. **(4) the brain** (Analysis) That the brain controls the beating of the heart, as it controls all body activities, is an unstated assumption of the passage. Options (1), (2), (3), and (5) are incorrect since they are body parts with functions not associated with controlling activities of other organs.

2. **(3) the left ventricle** (Comprehension) The left ventricle forces blood into the aorta, which leads to blood vessels throughout the body. Option (1) sends oxygen-poor blood to the lungs. Option (2) collects oxygen-poor blood from the body. Option (4) receives oxygen-rich blood from the lungs. Option (5) is a pair of blood vessels, not one of the chambers of the heart.

3. **(2) Too little blood would enter the right atrium.** (Analysis) Since the venae cavae bring blood from the body to the right atrium, a clogged vena cava would slow the rate of blood entering the right atrium. Option (1) states the opposite. Options (3) and (4) are incorrect because the venae cavae do not connect with the left atrium or the lungs. The slowed flow of blood to the right atrium would also slow, not increase, the flow of blood to the aorta, so option (5) is incorrect.

4. **(4) The body would not get enough oxygen-rich blood.** (Analysis) Since the aorta sends oxygen-rich blood throughout the body, if it were pinched off, this flow of blood would be reduced. Option (1) is incorrect because blood doesn't enter the left ventricle through the aorta. Option (2) is incorrect because oxygen-poor blood enters the heart through the venae cavae, not the aorta. Option (3) is incorrect because oxygen-poor blood passes to the lungs through the pulmonary arteries, not the aorta. Option (5) is incorrect because oxygen-rich blood does not enter the venae cavae.

5. **(5) a tube** (Analysis) Blood vessels carry liquid blood throughout the body and are shaped like tubes of various thicknesses. Options (1), (2), (3), and (4) are incorrect because they are closed shapes and not suitable for carrying liquids around the body.

6. **(2) Less blood circulates through the body.** (Analysis) If the vessels become narrower, they carry less blood. Option (1) is the opposite of what would take place. Option (3) is not possible. Option (4) occurs when there are breaks in the blood vessels. Option (5) is incorrect because there is an effect.

7. **(1) veins** (Comprehension) According to the paragraph, waste products are carried away from the body's tissues, and veins carry blood from the tissues back to the heart. Options (2), (3), and (4) all refer to blood vessels that carry blood away from the heart, not back to it. Option (5) is not a blood vessel.

8. **(3) artery** (Comprehension) According to the paragraph, arteries carry blood away from the heart. Options (1) and (2) refer to blood vessels that carry blood toward the heart. Option (4) connects arteries and veins. Option (5) refers to a part of the circulatory system that does not carry blood.

9. **(3) The heart supplies the power to move blood through the blood vessels.** (Analysis) The passage gives information about the types and functions of blood vessels assuming that the reader knows that the heart pumps the blood through them. Options (1), (2), (4), and (5) are true but are stated in the passage.

1. **(3) insulin** (Comprehension) According to the chart, insulin secreted by the pancreas lowers the level of sugar in the blood. Therefore, if the blood has a high level of sugar, adequate amounts of insulin must be lacking. Options (1), (2), (4) and (5) are incorrect because they name other hormones, which have different functions.

2. **(1) adrenal** (Analysis) According to the chart, adrenaline secreted by the adrenal glands prepares the body for emergencies. The reactions stated in the question are reactions to emergency situations and are caused by adrenaline. Options (2), (3), (4), and (5) are incorrect because they name other endocrine glands.

3. **(2) cortisone** (Comprehension) According to the chart, cortisone is the hormone that maintains the body's salt balance. Option (1) is not mentioned in the chart. Options (3) and (4) are sex hormones. Option (5) is the hormone secreted in emergencies.

4. **(2) gonads** (Comprehension) According to the chart, the gonads are different in males and females. Options (1), (3), (4), and (5) are incorrect because they name other endocrine glands that are the same in both males and females.

5. **(5) pituitary** (Analysis) According to the chart, the growth hormone produced by the pituitary gland controls the growth and development of bones and muscles. Extra growth in some bones, therefore, is probably the effect of the growth hormone produced by the pituitary gland. Options (1), (2), (3), and (4) are incorrect because they name other endocrine glands that have functions different from the one described in the question.

6. **(3) by the blood** (Analysis) The blood is the only option mentioned that can carry substances to all organs of the body. Options (1), (2), (4), and (5) are incorrect because they have other functions.

7. **(3) in both ears** (Analysis) Although the passage says the canals are in "the ear," you can assume that the canals are present in both ears, because the human body is the same on both sides. Options (1) and (2) are only partly correct. Options (4) and (5) are not true.

8. **(2) stop suddenly** (Analysis) Stopping suddenly causes the fluid to slosh quickly to the other side. Option (1) is incorrect because if you slowed gradually, the fluid would move gradually. Option (3) is incorrect because the fluid would move back if you moved forward. Option (4) is incorrect because jumping would cause the fluid to move up and down. Option (5) would keep the fluid at one end of the canals.

9. **(3) dizziness** (Analysis) The semicircular canals help keep the body's balance, and when the body seems unbalanced you feel dizzy. Options (1), (2), (4), and (5) are incorrect because they are not related to balance.

10. **(2) motion sickness** (Analysis) Motion sickness can result from continuous rhythmic motion (as in a car), which moves the fluid in the semicircular canals. Options (1), (3), (4), and (5) are incorrect because they are not related to the semicircular canals.

11. **(2) Keeping Your Balance** (Comprehension) The passage describes how the semicircular canals help the body keep its balance. Options (1) and (5) are not mentioned. Option (3) implies that the passage is about all parts of the ear, which it is not. How the nerves of the semicircular canals send messages, option (4), is mentioned only as a detail.

Lesson 6
GED Practice: Fact or Opinion (Page 75)

1. **(1) Laboratory mice lived as long as 4 1/2 years when fed a low-calorie, nutritious diet.** (Analysis) Option (1) is the only fact; it describes the result of an experiment. Options (2), (3), and (4) are all opinions, or hypotheses, that scientists have formed about the results of experiments and their application to other forms of life. Option (5) is not discussed in the passage. It may be someone's opinion, but no data is given to support it.

2. **(5) A, B, and C** (Analysis) These options, even though they may be opposites of one another, are all held by some scientists interested in this research. The second paragraph of the passage describes the different ideas the scientists have suggested to explain the results and importance of the experiments and those ideas include Statements A, B, and C. Options (1), (2), (3), and (4) are incorrect because they do not include A, B, and C.

3. **(2) You can extend your life by restricting the calories you eat.** (Analysis) Option (2) is the only opinion; scientists believe but haven't proved that restricting calories can extend the life spans of humans. Options (1), (3), (4), and (5) are incorrect because they are facts confirmed by experiments.

4. **(2) Short-lived animals have a mechanism that helps them survive during a famine.** (Analysis) Option (2) is the only opinion. The passage says that scientists think this is true. Options (1), (3), (4), and (5) are all facts given in the passage.

GED Practice: Disease (Page 77)

1. **(1) Diseases are caused by evil spirits.** (Analysis) The relationship between microorganisms and disease had not yet been proved, so all views about disease were opinions. Options (2) and (3) are incorrect because they were discovered during Pasteur's time. Options (4) and (5) are incorrect because they were not known until after Pasteur's time.

2. **(4) Koch's experiments with anthrax bacteria** (Analysis) Koch's experiments proved that a specific kind of bacteria was the cause of anthrax. This fact supported Pasteur's idea. Option (1) has nothing to do with the cause of disease. Options (2) and (5) happened before Pasteur's time. Option (3), the yeast experiments, did not help prove the cause of disease.

3. **(5) The spread of anthrax can be stopped by stopping the spread of anthrax bacteria.** (Comprehension) Since a specific organism causes the disease in animals, if you can prevent the organism from getting into another animal, you can stop the spread of the disease. Option (1) is not true; some diseases such as cancer are not caused by microorganisms. Options (2) and (3) are incorrect because fermentation is not a disease. Option (4) is true but does not follow from Koch's discovery of the anthrax bacteria, since anthrax is contagious.

4. **(4) the idea that microorganisms cause disease** (Comprehension) This idea forms the basis of all later discoveries about infectious diseases. Options (1), (3), and (5) are not contributions of Pasteur. Option (2) is one of Pasteur's contributions, but it is not directly related to the study of disease.

5. **(3) The cause of the disease would not be proved.** (Analysis) Since the fourth step of Koch's postulates involves confirming that the pathogens are indeed present in the diseased animal, leaving out this step means you cannot prove that the disease was caused by the pathogens. Option (1) is not true. Options (2) and (5) would be possible even without step 4 of the postulates. Option (4) is not true.

6. **(2) He found many of the bacteria in animals that had died of anthrax.** (Comprehension) Finding bacteria while examining the organs of the dead animals is what led Koch to think that the bacteria might be the cause of anthrax. Options (1), (4), and (5) are true but are not reasons for thinking anthrax is caused by a specific microorganism. Option (3) is incorrect because fermentation is not related to anthrax.

7. **(3) a group of microorganisms grown in a sterile food medium** (Comprehension) According to the passage, a culture is organisms grown in the laboratory on a sterile food medium. Options (1), (2), (4), and (5) are incorrect, since they do not describe the condition of growth in a sterile food medium.

GED Review: Lesson 6 (Pages 78–79)

1. **(2) circular** (Comprehension) The clue to the answer is in the word Diplococcus, which indicates that the bacteria is a type of coccus, or circular-shaped bacteria. The other options refer to bacilli, option (1); spirilla, options (3) and (4); and the shape of the flagella, option (5).

2. **(3) They will become inactive.** (Analysis) A suitable temperature is one of the conditions bacteria need in order to grow and reproduce. When the temperature drops, they are likely to stop growing and reproducing, and they become inactive. Options (1) and (2) are incorrect because they describe what bacteria do under good conditions. Options (4) and (5) are not related to drops in temperature.

3. **(3) The viral genetic material would be damaged.** (Analysis) Since the protein coat protects the genetic material, if the protein coat were destroyed, the genetic material could be damaged. Options (1) and (4) are incorrect because neither can happen until a virus invades a host cell. Options (2) and (5) would be impossible once the virus had lost its protein coat.

4. **(2) be released to invade other cells** (Analysis) The most likely answer to the question is that the virus particles would be released to invade other cells. Although viruses are inactive outside of host cells, there is no reason to suspect they would die, option (1), because the passage states that virus particles <u>can</u> leave the host cell. Viruses do not take in food, option (3). Virus particles could not accomplish option (4) since they cannot function by themselves. Viruses already have protein coats, option (5).

5. **(1) transferring its own genetic material into the host cell** (Comprehension) The passage states that this is how a virus takes over the activities of a host cell. Options (2), (3), and (4) cannot happen until the virus has already taken over the cell's activities. Option (5) is incorrect because breaking down the cell's membrane would kill the cell.

6. **(5) recognized diseases that viruses caused** (Analysis) The only possible way scientists could have known about viruses before seeing them was by observing their effect on living things—studying the diseases that viruses caused. A virus does not have a nucleus, option (1). Options (2) and (3) could not occur unless scientists could already see viruses. Without seeing viruses, option (4) would be unknown.

7. **(5) All viruses cause disease.** (Analysis) While the passage mentions many viral diseases, it does not state that all viruses cause disease. Options (1), (2), (3), and (4) are incorrect because they are all facts stated in the passage.

GED Mini-Test: Lesson 6 (Pages 80–81)

1. **(3) planets with mountains and valleys** (Comprehension) This is stated in the first paragraph of the passage. Thus, options (1), (2), (4), and (5) are incorrect.

2. **(1) In the future it may be possible to cure the common cold.** (Analysis) This idea underlies all research on cold viruses. It is clear from the passage that option (2) is not true. Options (3) and (4) are not established as completely true. It is not known if all rhinoviruses cause colds, option (5).

3. **(1) A drug to prevent colds may be too risky for so many people to take for such a minor illness.** (Analysis) Because the research focuses on drugs that would prevent colds, some scientists think the research is going in the wrong direction and that focusing on a cure would be better. Option (2) is not supported by the passage. Options (3), (4), and (5) are facts rather than opinions.

4. **(4) disease-fighting substances** (Comprehension) Antibodies are defined in the first paragraph of the passage. Options (1), (2), (3), and (5) are incorrect because they are not definitions of antibodies.

5. **(3) Scientists are studying the blocking of cell receptors as a means of cold prevention.** (Analysis) Option (3) is the only fact. It is stated in the second paragraph of the passage. Options (1) and (2) are opinions. Option (4) is not true. Option (5) is the opposite of what most doctors think, so it is incorrect.

6. **(1) It may help the immune system.** (Comprehension) Some scientists believe vitamin C helps the immune system prevent colds and flus. Options (2), (3), (4), and (5) are incorrect because they refer to curing disease, not preventing disease.

7. **(2) Eat foods high in vitamin C.** (Analysis) If vitamin C helps the immune system, then it would make sense to keep the body's supply of vitamin C high. Option (1) states the opposite. Options (3) and (5) do not make sense because the immune system would need more vitamin C before a disease started in order to fight off the disease. Option (4) is incorrect because these foods are not high in vitamin C.

8. **(3) The immune system resists invading bacteria and viruses.** (Analysis) Option (3) is the only fact. Options (1), (2), and (5) are incorrect because they are all opinions of various scientists. These opinions have not yet been proved. Option (4) is not true.

9. **(2) that the common cold can be prevented or eased with large doses of vitamin C** (Comprehension) The passage states that Pauling proposed that large doses of vitamin C could prevent or reduce the severity of colds. Option (1) is incorrect because that fact had already been established. Options (3) and (4) are the claims of other researchers. Option (5) is not true; Pauling claimed that colds could be prevented, not cured.

Lesson 7

GED Practice: Evaluating Information (Page 83)

1. **(4) Most couples in the United States are fertile.** (Evaluation) Since the passage states that about 20 percent of couples are infertile, it follows that about 80 percent are fertile. Options (1), (2), and (5) are contradicted by the passage. Option (3) is not necessarily true, although peak fertility is an important factor in the timing of having children. However, the trend toward postponing parenthood implies that other factors such as career development, finances, and marital status can enter into such a decision.

2. **(1) In deciding when to have children, couples should take into account that the risk of infertility increases with age.** (Evaluation) Options (2) and (5) are contradicted by the passage. Option (3) is an opinion and is not necessarily true, since many factors affect the timing of having children. Option (4) is not true, since the risk of miscarriage increases with age, regardless of whether or not the couple has had children.

3. **(5) Infertility affects both men and women.** (Analysis) The passage states that infertility affects both sexes equally. Option (1) is an opinion. Options (2) and (4) are not true. Option (3) may be true, but it is not stated in the passage.

4. **(3) more likely to have difficulty producing eggs** (Application) According to the passage, difficulty in producing eggs increases with a woman's age. Options (1), (2), and (4) are incorrect because they describe characteristics of a younger woman rather than an older woman in her forties. Option (5) is incorrect because a woman in her forties has already decided whether to postpone parenthood.

5. **(3) If the twins are of different sexes, then they must be fraternal twins.** (Analysis) The passage states that identical twins are always of the same sex. Thus, twins of different sexes cannot be identical and must be fraternal, making option (3) correct and option (4) incorrect. Option (1) is incorrect because identical twins look extremely similar, but may differ in small ways. Option (2) is incorrect because a set of twins of the same sex could be either identical or fraternal twins. Option (5) is incorrect because nothing in the passage discusses the intelligence or aptitudes of twins.

GED Practice: Mendel and Genetics (Page 85)

1. **(1) He started with purebred plants.** (Evaluation) By starting the experiment with plants that always produced the same characteristics, Mendel made sure that the results of cross-breeding would be reliable. If he had started with hybrid plants, option (2), he would not have been sure why he was getting a mix of traits. If he had selected plants with several contrasting traits, option (3), there would have been so many combinations of characteristics in the offspring that it would have been difficult to keep track of what was going on. Using only one type of plant, options (4) and (5), would have meant that the experiment would not show the results of breeding plants with contrasting traits.

2. **(1) The plants are all hybrids.** (Evaluation) Since the offspring receive a different trait from each parent, they will all be hybrids. Option (2) is not correct because contrasting traits are being bred. Option (3) is not correct because all the offspring had inflated pods, making that the dominant trait. Option (4) is not true; the term hybrid trait is unclear in meaning. Option (5) is not correct because they did not show up in the F_1 generation, so wrinkled pods must be a recessive trait.

3. **(3) a trait that will appear in some purebred and all hybrid offspring** (Analysis) Since a dominant trait is more powerful than a recessive trait, it will appear in all hybrids. It will also appear when two dominant traits are combined in a purebred offspring. Option (1) is incorrect because it leaves out hybrid offspring. Option (2) is incorrect because it leaves out some purebred offspring. Option (4) is incorrect because some offspring will not inherit the dominant trait. Option (5) is incorrect because the dominant trait will always be more powerful when combined with a recessive trait.

4. **(2) Some of the F_2 generation plants showed the recessive trait.** (Evaluation) Although the recessive trait was hidden in their F_1 parents, some of the F_2 plants received two recessive traits from the parents and showed the recessive characteristic. This proved that the recessive trait was carried by

the hybrid F_1 parents even though it did not show. Option (1) does not provide evidence that the recessive trait is present. Option (3) is incorrect because offspring with a dominant trait do not show that the recessive trait was present in the parents. Option (4) is not true; only one in four offspring showed the recessive trait. Option (5) is not true since no F_1 plants showed the recessive traits.

5. **(2) They have characteristics that are easy to identify.** (Comprehension) This is stated in the second paragraph of the passage. Options (1), (3), and (4) are not true. Option (5) is true but was not the reason he selected pea plants.

6. **(2) 1 out of 4** (Comprehension) As the diagram shows, when two hybrids are bred, one out of four offspring will show the recessive trait. The other three will inherit the dominant trait and will show the dominant trait. Options (1), (3), (4), and (5) are incorrect because they are not equal to a chance of 1 out of 4.

GED Review: Lesson 7 (Pages 86–87)

1. **(1) YyTt** (Analysis) The offspring gets YT genes from the female parent and yt genes from the male parent. The resulting genotype is a combination of the two: YyTt. The other options are incorrect because those genotypes cannot be produced by the parents in the question.

2. **(2) All offspring will inherit both recessive traits.** (Evaluation) Since the dominant traits are not present in either of the parents, they cannot show up in any of the offspring, thus eliminating options (1), (3), (4), and (5).

3. **(1) the plant's phenotype** (Evaluation) You could tell only the phenotype because the phenotype is the plant's appearance. You would need to have records from the experiment in order to tell the plant's genotype, because the plant might have some recessive genes that do not show up in the phenotype. You could not tell what genes the plant has with great accuracy just from its appearance, options (2) and (3). You also could not tell what generation it is from just by looking at it, option (4). Option (5) is incorrect because it is impossible to tell what the next generation would be like when you don't know the genotype of the seeds.

4. **(5) 1** (Comprehension) Only one of the 16 genotypes is green with wrinkled pods (yyii). The others all have at least one dominant gene, which would change either the color or the pod shape.

5. **(3) 4** (Comprehension) There are four phenotypes, or appearances, in the diagram. They are yellow and inflated; green and inflated; yellow and wrinkled; green and wrinkled, so options (1), (2), (4), and (5) are incorrect.

6. **(1) always result in a change in the genotype of the offspring** (Analysis) Since the question states that the gene is always passed on to the offspring, it follows that the gene will affect the genotypes of all offspring. Option (3) is therefore eliminated. The new gene may or may not show up in the phenotype, depending on the gene inherited from the female parent, which is unknown. Therefore options (2) and (4) are incorrect. Option (5) is incorrect because the genotype of the offspring would be affected.

GED Mini-Test: Lesson 7 (Pages 88–89)

1. **(4) Adenine is paired with thymine.** (Evaluation) This is the only statement that is always true. Options (2) and (3) are sometimes true. Options (1) and (5) are not true.

2. **(2) It would become longer.** (Analysis) If the spiral were straightened out, the molecule would become longer, not shorter, so option (1) is incorrect. Options (3), (4), and (5) are incorrect because straightening the molecule would make it flat. The other shapes would not result from straightening the helix.

3. **(4) They get some DNA from each parent.** (Analysis) DNA, which transmits hereditary information, must come from both parents. Options (1), (2), and (3) are therefore incorrect. Option (5) is true but does not explain how traits are inherited.

4. **(4) sugar and phosphate** (Comprehension) According to the passage and diagram, sugar and phosphate units alternate on the side pieces of DNA. All other options include at least one nitrogen base, which is not part of the side pieces of DNA.

5. **(3) the extent to which the environment influences characteristics of humans** (Analysis) Since the effect of the environment is not really known, scientists have different

opinions on the extent of its influence. The other options are observable, measurable facts.

6. **(1) There is too much time between generations.** (Comprehension) The human life cycle is fairly long—usually more than 20 years between generations—so to see the results of experiments would take too long. Option (2) is not true. Options (3) and (4) are true, but they have nothing to do with the difficulty of studying generations of humans. Option (5) is a result, not a cause, of the difficulty of studying human generations over time.

7. **(2) use a sample consisting of a large and varied group of people** (Evaluation) To ensure the accuracy of research results, the sample used must be representative of the population as a whole. Therefore, a large and varied group is necessary. Option (1) is too small a sample. Option (3) is not a varied sample. Option (4) is not practical in terms of time and would also not give a large enough sample. Option (5) is not a varied sample.

8. **(2) 30 percent** (Comprehension) Since 30 percent of the people in the general population cannot taste PTC, the likelihood of the next child born not being able to taste PTC is also 30 percent.

Lesson 8
GED Practice: Conclusions and Supporting Statements (Page 91)

1. **(1) The passenger pigeon and great auk were hunted to extinction during the 1800s.** (Analysis) This statement provides supporting evidence in the form of examples of species that over a short period of time became extinct. Options (2), (3), and (5) are true but they do not support the conclusion. Option (4) is not true; whales are still hunted.

2. **(4) Humans will eventually be replaced by another form of life.** (Analysis) Since all species are subject to extinction, it follows that humans are, too. Options (1) and (2) are true but have nothing to do with the general fate of all species. Options (3) and (5) are not true.

GED Practice: Ecosystems (Page 93)

1. **(2) Matter in an ecosystem is being constantly recycled.** (Analysis) This is the generalization that is supported by the other

statements, each of which describes one step in a food chain.

2. **(3) Secondary consumers would have nothing to eat.** (Analysis) This is the immediate effect of the loss of primary consumers, because they are the food for secondary consumers. Option (1) is incorrect; plants would continue to function. Options (2) and (4) are incorrect because the activities of decomposers and tertiary consumers would not be affected immediately. Option (5) is not true; the sun would continue to provide energy.

3. **(3) primary and secondary consumers** (Comprehension) In their role as berry- and seed-eaters, birds are primary consumers (eating plants). In their role as insect-eaters, the birds are secondary consumers (eating animals). Option (1) refers to plants. Options (2) and (4) are only partly correct. Option (5) refers to plants and animals.

4. **(3) secondary consumer** (Comprehension) The crop pests, which feed on plants, are primary consumers. Anything that eats a primary consumer (the crop pest) is a secondary consumer.

5. **(1) All living things are part of an ecosystem.** (Analysis) Although the passage describes what an ecosystem is, it never explicitly states that all living things are part of an ecosystem. It is assumed that the reader understands this. Option (2) is incorrect because humans are part of many ecosystems. Options (3), (4), and (5) are not unstated assumptions because they are clearly stated in the passage or illustration.

6. **(2) to break down dead plants and animals into substances plants can use** (Comprehension) This is stated in the third paragraph of the passage. Option (1) is the role of producers. Option (3) is the role of primary consumers. Option (4) is the role of secondary consumers. Option (5) is the role of the sun.

7. **(1) hawks** (Comprehension) Of the listed organisms, all are primary consumers except the hawk, which is a secondary consumer. Since secondary consumers are farther up the food chain, they are higher-level consumers than the others.

1. **(3) World population remained fairly stable until 1650.** (Analysis) This is the only statement not related to the present rapid growth of world population. The other options all support the conclusion that the population is growing quickly.

2. **(5) decrease in death rate** (Analysis) Option (5) is the only statement which would lead to a rise in the world population. Options (1), (2), (3), and (4) would all slow population growth.

3. **(3) 10** (Comprehension) Since the density in 1990 was 90 and the density in 1650 was 9, 90 ÷ 9 = 10, or a tenfold increase.

4. **(2) Population density is calculated by dividing the number of people living in an area by the amount of land available in the area.** (Analysis) Application of this general rule leads to the conclusion that when there are more people living in the same amount of space, the density increases. Option (1) has nothing to do with population increases. Option (3) is not true; when the death rate is higher than the birth rate, density decreases. Option (4) is true but has nothing to do with increased population density. Option (5) is not true.

5. **(1) It is likely to triple.** (Comprehension) In the last 90 years, the population density tripled; if conditions remain the same, it follows that the density will triple in the next ninety years.

6. **(3) Increase the amount of usable land.** (Analysis) Since the rate of population growth will remain the same, the only way to decrease population density is to spread the population into previously unused areas. Options (1), (2), and (4) have nothing to do with changing the population density of humans. Option (5) would have the effect of increasing population density since there would be less available land.

1. **(5) rapid reproduction and insufficient consumers** (Analysis) The rapid reproduction of rabbits unchecked by sufficient consumers led to the overpopulation of rabbits in Australia. Option (1) is incorrect since it is likely to be a solution to overpopulation. Option (2) may have contributed to the problem, but it was not the main cause. Option (3) is a result of overpopulation. Option (4) is incorrect since too many consumers would prevent the overpopulation of their prey.

2. **(3) Prevent the introduction.** (Comprehension) According to the passage, prevention is the best solution. Option (1) is a solution, but not the best one. Options (2) and (4) are generally beyond human control. Option (5) is incorrect because there is a way to solve these problems, which is stated in option (3).

3. **(3) In stable ecosystems, there is usually at least one consumer that checks another organism's population growth.** (Analysis) Application of this principle leads to the conclusion that introducing a predator may control the organism that is overrunning its new environment. Option (1) is true but has nothing to do with possible solutions to the problem. Option (2) is not true. Option (4) may or may not be true, but the process would take a very long time. Option (5) is a contradiction; if the organism could not find anything to eat, it would not be able to reproduce at a fast rate.

4. **(2) an ecosystem with food and no predators** (Analysis) Since rabbits thrived in Australia, it can be assumed that they found plenty to eat and no animals to fear. Options (1) and (3) are incorrect because without food the rabbits would have starved. Option (4) is incorrect because if there were many meat-eating animals, it is likely that the rabbits would have been eaten. Option (5) cannot be true, since if the ecosystem were similar to Europe's, the rabbit population would not have gotten out of control.

5. **(4) The Introduction of New Species into Ecosystems** (Comprehension) The passage deals generally with what happens when a new species is introduced into an ecosystem. It does not describe stable ecosystems at length, option (1). The example of rabbits in Australia is a supporting detail, option (2). The passage does not say how to prevent the introduction of new species, option (3). It is not primarily about the food chain in stable ecosystems, option (5).

6. **(1) nitric oxide and sulfur dioxide** (Analysis) Nitric oxide reacts with oxygen to form nitrogen dioxide. Nitrogen dioxide and sulfur dioxide react with rainwater to form acid rain. The other options contain gases that do not form acid rain.

UNIT 1

7. **(4) nitric oxide** (Analysis) Car exhaust is one of the main sources of nitric oxide in the atmosphere. When nitric oxide combines with oxygen, it produces nitrogen dioxide. When the amount of nitric oxide from cars is reduced, it follows that the nitrogen dioxide content of the atmosphere would also be reduced. Option (1) is incorrect because nitrogen dioxide is not part of automobile exhaust. Options (2), (3), and (5) are incorrect because they are substances that do not form nitrogen dioxide.

8. **(4) A and B** (Analysis) The passage mentions that both sulfur dioxide and nitric acid combine with water to form acids. Therefore, these two compounds are associated with acid rain. Only option (4) includes both compounds. While carbon monoxide is a pollutant, it is not acid forming.

GED Cumulative Review
Unit 1: Biology (Pages 98–106)

1. **(3) by engulfing them** (Comprehension) The passage states that phagocytes work by surrounding or engulfing bacteria. Option (1) is true of lymphocytes, not phagocytes. Option (2) is incorrect because the phagocytes cannot work until the disease-causing agent is in the body. Options (4) and (5) do not relate to the way phagocytes work.

2. **(2) All white blood cells are the same.** (Evaluation) The passage describes two kinds of white blood cells that fight disease in different ways. Options (1), (2), (4), and (5) are incorrect because they are facts presented in the passage.

3. **(1) have a reduced ability to fight off disease** (Analysis) Someone with HIV is likely to have a reduced number of lymphocytes. Since lymphocytes help fight disease, that person is also likely to have a reduced ability to fight disease. Option (2) is incorrect because fewer lymphocytes means a reduction in antibody production. Option (3) is incorrect because phagocytes aren't necessarily destroyed when lymphocytes are. Option (4) is the opposite of what is likely to occur. Option (5) is incorrect because no mention is made in the passage of a connection between lymphocytes and pulse rate.

4. **(1) A only** (Analysis) Both getting a disease and being given a vaccine start the production of antibodies, Statement A. Statement B is incorrect because a vaccine, under normal circumstances, does not make a person sick. Statement C is incorrect because the respons to a vaccine involves lymphocytes, not macrophages and phagocytes. Thus only option (1) is correct.

5. **(1) More phagocytes and lymphocytes ar needed to fight the infection.** (Analysis) When infectious agents enter the body, the body produces more phagocytes and lymphocytes in order to destroy the infection. Option (2) is incorrect because the body produces phagocytes and lymphocytes. Optio (3) is incorrect because lymphocytes produce antibodies. Option (4) has nothing to do with fighting infection. Option (5) makes no sense; if the body were immune, there would be no infection.

6. **(1) Metamorphosis in the Frog** (Comprehension) The passage and diagram describe the process of metamorphosis, using the frog as an example. Option (2) is too specific. Option (3) is too general, and include animals, such as fish, that do not undergo metamorphosis. Option (4) is also too general, the passage describes metamorphosis only in terms of the frog. Option (5) is not the subject of the paragraph.

7. **(3) Different animal structures are suited to different types of environments.** (Analysis) For example, in showing the change from tadpole to frog, the author shows gill slits, which contain gills, for breathing underwater and legs for moving about on land. The author takes for granted the usefulness of these structures in their environment. Options (1) and (2) are incorrect, since many plants and animals do not undergo metamorphosis. Option (4) may or may not be true, but it does not have anything to do with the process of metamorphosis. Option (5) is not true.

8. **(2) the process by which an immature form changes into a different adult form** (Comprehension) This is the process described in the passage. Option (1) is incorrect because reproduction is a different function from growth. Option (3) is incorrect because it is too general. Option (4) is incorrect because it describes what happens to the mature adult form after metamorphosis. Option (5) refers to respiration, not to metamorphosis.

9. **(2) lungs** (Comprehension) Lungs are structures that are essential to supporting life on land, because without them the animal

could not breathe. The structures in the other options are less vital for land-dwelling animals.

(3) tundra (Comprehension) The areas farthest north are shown by the map key to be tundra. Options (1), (2), (4), and (5) are not as far north as the tundra, option (3).

(3) cacti (Analysis) Of the plants listed, cacti are the only ones that can live in a desert biome. This suggests they would not do well in a tropical rain forest, where it is very wet.

(5) Water in animals' breath is returned to the air. (Evaluation) When animals exhale, they release water vapor into the atmosphere. Option (1) is not true because animals also release water as they breathe. Option (2) is not true; invisible water vapor is found throughout the atmosphere. Option (3) is not true; plants take in water from their roots. Option (4) is not true; the oceans contain most of the water on Earth.

(3) Evaporation from the ocean returns water to the atmosphere. (Analysis) This statement provides evidence by giving an example of water changing form during the water cycle. Options (1) and (2) just restate the conclusion. Options (4) and (5) are true but do not offer the evidence that water is used again and again.

(2) the sun (Analysis) The diagram shows that the sun's heat causes water to evaporate from various places. Options (1), (3), and (4) are incorrect because they are forms of water. Option (5) is also incorrect; the soil serves to store water.

(2) Water conservation is not useful since Earth will never run out of water. (Analysis) Although it is true that water is recycled on Earth, water conservation can be useful because water may run low in particular places. The other options are all facts stated in the passage.

(2) The Human Brain (Comprehension) The passage focuses on the structure of the human brain. It does not describe the entire nervous system, options (1) and (5). It describes more than just the cerebrum, option (3). It describes the human brain, not brains in general, option (4).

(2) vision (Analysis) Since the perception of vision is located in the occipital lobe, a blow to the back of the head is likely to affect it. Options (1) and (4) are located at the side. Option (3) is controlled by the medulla at the base of the brain. Option (5) is controlled in the upper part of the cerebrum.

18. **(5) loss of balance** (Analysis) Since the cerebellum coordinates information from the eyes, inner ears, and muscles to maintain balance, a loss of balance is likely to indicate damage to the cerebellum. Option (1), loss of leg movement, is a specific movement partially controlled by the cerebrum. Options (2), (3), and (4) are likely to be caused by damage to the cerebrum, not the cerebellum.

19. **(4) Motor activity is controlled by the cerebrum and cerebellum.** (Evaluation) Option (1) is partially true, but the cerebrum also needs to be functioning for motor activity to be normal. Option (2) is not true. Option (3) is not likely to be true because the right hemisphere would be able to control at least some speech. Option (5) is contradicted by the passage.

20. **(3) Vestigial structures offer support for the theory of evolution.** (Comprehension) Options (1) and (4) are too specific to summarize the paragraph. Option (2) is not true. Option (5) is incorrect because, by definition, vestigial structures are poorly developed.

21. **(1) Vestigial structures are the remains of organs that were well-developed in common ancestors.** (Analysis) This is a hypothesis that attempts to explain the existence of vestigial structures. It has not been proven. Options (2), (3), (4), and (5) are all facts as presented by the paragraph and diagram.

22. **(1) The appendix of humans is a vestigial organ.** (Evaluation) This is a statement of fact. Option (2) is not likely to be true; it is possible, however, that the ancestors of pythons walked. Option (3) is not true since vestigial organs do not serve an important purpose. Option (4) is not true since the two skeletons are different. Option (5) is not true. Vestigial structures are evidence to support the theory of evolution, but, alone, they do not prove that evolution is fact.

23. **(2) Some animals have a well-developed structure, and others have a corresponding vestigial structure.**

(Analysis) The presence of similar structures in these animals lends support to the idea that they had a common ancestor. Options (1), (3), and (5) are true, but they do not indicate descent from a common ancestor, merely that these organisms have changed over time. Option (4) is not true; the ancestors of porpoises probably had legs.

24. **(4) can give blood to anyone**
(Comprehension) A donor is someone who donates, or gives; thus a universal donor is someone who can give blood to anyone. If you look at the first chart, you can see that type O blood can be given to all other types, option (4). All other options are incorrect.

25. **(3) They could have a transfusion of type A, B, or O blood.** (Analysis) According to the chart, people with type AB blood can receive any of the blood types; thus a shortage of type AB blood would not affect them. They could still receive types A, B, or O, option (3). All other options are incorrect.

26. **(1) Blood Type Frequency in Selected Population Groups** (Comprehension) The chart provides information on the percent of the population that has a particular blood type in various population groups. Option (2) is too general. Options (3) and (4) have nothing to do with the information in the second chart. Option (5) is too specific, since other groups are represented.

27. **(3) Each individual inherits one gene for blood type from each of his or her parents.** (Evaluation) The passage states that a person's blood type depends on two genes inherited from his or her parents. It follows from this that one gene must come from each parent. Option (1) is incorrect because there are more genotypes than blood types. Option (2) is incorrect because there is no AB gene. Options (4) and (5) are not true.

28. **(5) a variety of crop that is not affected by particular chemical plant killers** (Comprehension) This is explained in the first paragraph of the passage. As the passage is about applying herbicides to crops, option (1) is incorrect. No such crop is mentioned. Options (2), (3), and (4) describe crops that are resistant to other types of agricultural problems.

29. **(3) result in herbicides remaining on the crops after harvest** (Analysis) Herbicides

are chemicals that remain in the environment until they break down; therefore they also remain on the plants. Options (1), (2), and (4) are incorrect because the crops are herbicide resistant and would not be affected by the chemical. Option (5) is incorrect because herbicides kill plants, not insects.

30. **(4) Improved cultivation techniques are preferable to herbicides in controlling weeds.** (Analysis) This statement reflects the opinions of some environmental groups. Not everyone shares this point of view. Options (1), (2), (3), and (5) are statements of fact presented in the passage.

31. **(3) Weeds are a problem in large farming areas.** (Analysis) The passage gives both pro-herbicide and anti-herbicide points of view. Both sides agree that weeds must be controlled; they differ as to how. Option (1) is incorrect because the author presents the environmentalists' view that herbicides are not safe. Option (2) is incorrect because the passage indicates some practices that do not require the use of herbicides to grow crops. Options (4) and (5) are not true.

32. **(3) C only** (Analysis) Of the choices listed, Statement C uses only chemicals that are not found in nature. All other options include a method that manipulates nature, but does not add an unnatural substance (Statements B and C).

33. **(4) withstanding the effect of** (Comprehension) An herbicide-resistant crop can withstand the killing effects of the herbicide and live. Option (1), (2), and (3) are meanings for resistant when used in other contents. Option (5) is an incorrect meaning.

34. **(5) sun, grass, rabbit, fox** (Comprehension) The passage describes and the diagram shows the original source of energy as the sun and the final consumer as the fox. Options (1) and (3) are incorrect because they leave out the sun. Options (2) and (4) are incorrect because they list the energy transfer in the wrong order.

35. **(4) appear at the top of the diagram** (Analysis) A predator of the fox would appear above the fox in the diagram. Therefore, option (2) describes the incorrect position. Options (1), (3), and (5) are incorrect because the new predator would be a tertiary (third-order) consumer.

Answers and Explanations

36. (4) The fox population would decrease.
(Analysis) If the rabbit population were
destroyed, the foxes would lose their primary
source of energy and would likely begin to die.
Option (1) is incorrect since the food chain
would need a new primary consumer, not a
producer, to replace the rabbits. Option (2) is
incorrect because foxes are meat eaters.
Option (3) is the opposite of how grass is likely
to be affected. Option (5) is not true because
the food chain would be affected.

**37. (2) An organism that eats only plants
cannot be a secondary consumer.**
(Evaluation) Since producers (or plants) are
always on the bottom level of a food chain,
animals that eat only plants are always
primary consumers. Option (1) is incorrect
since food chains always begin with producers,
which don't feed on other organisms. Option
(3) is incorrect because producers make their
own food. Options (4) and (5) are incorrect
because some consumers eat only plants, some
consumers eat only animals, and some
consumers eat both plants and animals.

UNIT 2: EARTH SCIENCE
Lesson 9
GED Practice: Identifying Implications
(Pages 110–111)

**1. (1) take longer than 225 million years to
make one turn around the center of the
galaxy** (Comprehension) Since our sun takes
225 million years to make one turn around the
galaxy, it follows that a star farther from the
center would take longer, since it has a
greater distance to travel. Therefore options
(2) and (3) are incorrect. Option (4) is incorrect
because heavenly bodies do not change
direction while they are revolving around
another body. Option (5) is incorrect because
all stars are moving.

**2. (4) Its appearance will have changed
slightly.** (Comprehension) Since the
paragraph indicates that the patterns of stars
have changed slightly over thousands of years,
it is reasonable to assume that the patterns
will continue to change slightly. Option (1) is
what the Big Dipper used to look like. Options
(2) and (3) are its present appearance, which
is not likely to remain unchanged. Option (5)
is more than a slight change, and therefore is
not likely to occur.

3. (3) farther from the sun than Earth is
(Comprehension) Since the distance from

Earth to the sun is one astronomical unit, it
follows that a planet more than one
astronomical unit from the sun will be farther
from the sun than Earth is. Options (1) and (2)
are therefore incorrect. Option (4) is incorrect
because a planet farther from the sun than
Earth is likely to receive less, not more, solar
energy than Earth. Option (5) has nothing to
do with distance from the sun.

4. (4) 240 minutes (Analysis) It takes the sun's
light 8 minutes to travel 1 astronomical unit,
so it would take 30×8, or 240 minutes, to
travel 30 astronomical units—the distance
from the sun to Neptune.

GED Practice: The Planet Earth (Page 113)

1. (2) 40 kilometers (Comprehension) The
passage states that the thickness of the crust
is about 40 kilometers under the continents.
Africa is a continent, so the crust beneath it is
about 40 kilometers thick.

**2. (4) changing behavior of seismic waves as
they reach each layer of Earth's interior**
(Comprehension) The passage indicates that
the study of seismic waves led to the conclusion
that Earth has four layers. If the seismic waves
did not change, option (3), scientists would
have concluded that Earth's interior was
basically the same all the way to the core.
Options (1), (2), and (5) are incorrect; they are
evidence that requires direct observation,
which is impossible in Earth's interior.

3. (1) crust (Comprehension) Since the crust
includes Earth's surface, it follows that it has
been explored by people. The other parts of
Earth's interior are out of reach because of
high temperature and pressure. Option (5), all
four layers, is incorrect because only option
(1), the crust, has been explored by humans.

4. (3) iron in the inner and outer cores
(Analysis) Since magnets are often made of
iron, it follows that the iron in Earth's core
would exert magnetic force. The other options
have nothing to do with magnetic substances.

5. (1) vibrations produced by earthquakes
(Comprehension) The passage clearly states
that seismic waves are vibrations produced by
earthquakes. The other options do not
correctly define or describe seismic waves.

**6. (1) It is reasonable to draw scientific
conclusions from indirect evidence.**
(Analysis) The structure of Earth's interior

was figured out by studying the indirect evidence of seismic waves. The author does not indicate that conclusions about Earth's interior are wrong but rather accepts them as reasonable. Option (2) is incorrect; direct evidence is better than indirect evidence. Option (3) is not likely. Option (4) is not true. Option (5) is not supported by the diagram.

7. **(3) travel through the crust and mantle and stop at the outer core** (Application) Since the secondary wave can travel only through solids, it would be stopped only when it reached the liquid (molten) outer core. Since it would be stopped, option (1) is incorrect. Option (2) is incorrect because the wave would not reach the inner core. Options (4) and (5) are incorrect because the wave would travel through both the crust and mantle, which are solid. The passage states that, although parts of the mantle flow like a liquid, it is solid rock.

GED Review: Lesson 9 (Pages 114–115)

1. **(3) The region was once under water.** (Comprehension) Since fossils are most likely to be formed by organisms in or near the water, the best option is (3). Options (1) and (2) have nothing to do with the location of fish. Option (4) is remotely possible, but since mountain streams are usually shallow and rocky, it is unlikely that enough soft sediment would be available to bury the organism quickly. Option (5) does not explain how the fossils may have formed.

2. **(1) human footprints made in concrete before it hardened** (Comprehension) The best option is (1) because it describes evidence of living activity (human footprints) in a substance that hardens and becomes permanent (concrete). Options (2) and (5) are incorrect; a fly is a whole organism and a leaf is a part of an organism; they are not traces. Options (3) and (4) are incorrect; sand and snow do not hold a permanent print.

3. **(5) the bird was buried soon after dying** (Application) The passage says that many dead organisms decay or are eaten before a fossil can form and mentions quick burial as a likely means of fossil preservation. If the bird had been eaten, option (1), it could not form a complete fossil. Option (2) is incorrect because the bird could have died in any number of ways and there is no evidence to support predation. Although option (3) may be true, it is not the most likely option. Option (4) is

incorrect since birds live in many different climates, and there is no evidence that this one necessarily lived in a wet climate.

4. **(4) grooves carved in rock by a glacier** (Application) The passage states that fossils are evidence or remains of living things. Since glaciers aren't living things, they can't leave behind fossils. Options (1), (2), (3), and (5) are all evidence or remains of once living things.

5. **(4) establishing animal behavior** (Comprehension) While scientists can sometimes guess about animal behavior from fossil remains, it is not a primary use and is not mentioned in the passage. All the other options are mentioned as a use of the fossil record.

6. **(3) in the ocean** (Comprehension) The first reference to living things mentions the ocean. Options (1) and (4) are incorrect because they refer to time periods, not places. Options (2) and (5) are not indicated by the time line.

7. **(2) sea-living invertebrates** (Analysis) Options (1), (3), and (4) are incorrect because the time line shows that these organisms appeared after the first fish. Option (5) is incorrect; land plants existed before the first fish, but fish would not have been able to leave the water to eat land plants.

8. **(3) fish, land plants, and dinosaurs** (Comprehension) By the Mesozoic Era fish and land plants had already evolved. Dinosaurs first appeared during the Mesozoic Era. Since these organisms existed, their fossils could occur in rocks of Mesozoic Era. Option (1) is incorrect since many other organisms besides simple ocean organisms had appeared by the Mesozoic Era. Options (2), (4), and (5) are incorrect because horses, primates, and humans didn't appear until after the Mesozoic Era.

9. **(3) The Great Lakes are younger than the Rocky Mountains.** (Evaluation) The time line shows that the Rocky Mountains appeared before the Great Lakes. Option (1) is incorrect; according to the time line, human civilization arose very recently. Option (2) is incorrect; dinosaurs lived during the Mesozoic Era. Option (4) is incorrect; the time line shows that dinosaurs died out about 65 million years ago. Option (5) is incorrect; the first life forms appeared in the ocean.

10. **(3) 160 million years** (Comprehension) The time line is measured in millions of years. Dinosaurs appeared slightly less than 225 million years ago and died out about 65 million years ago. Subtracting 65 from 225 gives 160, which on the time line represents 160 million years. Options (1) and (4) are misreadings of the scale of the time line. Option (2) is incorrect because it represents time passed from the beginning of the time line to the extinction of dinosaurs. Option (5) is incorrect because it is the time from the appearance of dinosaurs to the present.

11. **(1) All organisms evolved from the first living cells.** (Analysis) While most scientists believe this and it is assumed that the reader knows this, the passage does not supply direct evidence that this is true. Options (2), (3), and (5) are shown on the time line. Option (4) can be inferred and supported by the fact that the time line ends with "present" time, under the Cenozoic Era.

GED Mini-Test: Lesson 9 (Pages 116–117)

1. **(1) Temperatures in Earth's interior are high.** (Comprehension) According to the passage, igneous rock is formed from hot liquid rock, and metamorphic rock is formed in the presence of high temperature and pressure. Since both types of rock require high temperatures, which are found in Earth's interior, the correct option is (1). Option (2) contradicts the information presented about metamorphic rock and is also an untrue statement about Earth's interior. Options (3) and (4) do not explain the formation of igneous and metamorphic rocks. Option (5) is untrue; magma hardens slowly beneath Earth's crust.

2. **(2) the slow cooling of molten rock below Earth's surface** (Comprehension) Options (1), (3), and (4) do not contribute to the slow cooling of molten rock, or magma, which is necessary for the formation of large crystals. Option (5) is contradicted by the passage.

3. **(2) become sediments and harden into sedimentary rock** (Analysis) Since sedimentary rock is formed on or near Earth's surface, only option (2) is correct. Options (1), (3), and (4) could be correct if the rock fragments were buried deep in Earth. Option (5) is incorrect because it is sedimentary, not metamorphic, rock that is formed in the ocean.

4. **(4) Metamorphic rock is always formed from igneous, sedimentary, or other metamorphic rock.** (Evaluation) Option (1) is incorrect because igneous rock is formed from magma. Options (2) and (3) are incorrect; sedimentary rock can be formed from both organic and inorganic particles. Option (5) is not true; sometimes molten rock appears on the surface of Earth as lava.

5. **(5) a rock formed from plant remains** (Comprehension) Since plant remains were once alive, a rock formed from plant remains could not be classified as a mineral. (See characteristic **3.**) Options (1), (2), (3), and (4) could all be minerals since they include the basic properties.

6. **(4) high temperatures** (Comprehension) Since smelting is a process that involves heating, one can assume that high temperatures are involved. Option (1) is incorrect; smelting removes impurities. Option (2) might be involved eventually in preparing iron for use, but not in separating the iron from its ore. Option (3) is incorrect; the process requires heating, not cooling. Option (5) is not necessarily a result of the smelting process, but it may appear correct to some who think that smelting has to do with the sense of smell.

7. **(5) value** (Comprehension) A substance's value does not determine whether or not is a mineral. Option (1) is incorrect because minerals must be made of particular elements. Option (2) is incorrect because particles in minerals must be arranged in a pattern. Option (3) is incorrect because a substance must occur naturally on Earth to be considered a mineral. A synthetic substance could not be considered a mineral. Option (4) is incorrect because minerals must be solids.

8. **(4) heating ore to separate a mineral** (Comprehension) According to the last sentence in the passage, this option describes the smelting process. The other options are not mentioned in relation to smelting.

9. **(2) B only** (Analysis) Granite can be made of three or four types of minerals, thus Statement B is true. Statement A is not true; granite is a naturally occurring substance. Statement C is also not true; granite is made of several minerals, so it cannot be called a mineral.

10. **(5) A, B, and C** (Comprehension) The word *pure* indicates that the deposits contain only sulfur, which satisfies the characteristic of particular elements, Statement A. As the deposits were found inside volcanic craters, the deposits are found naturally on Earth, Statement B. The fact that there were *crystalline* deposits indicates that the mineral was a solid, Statement C. Only option (5) includes all three statements.

11. **(4) It was once alive.** (Analysis) A bone was once living tissue and part of a living organism, so it does not fit the definition of a mineral. Option (1) is not true. A bone does contain calcium, option (2), and phosphorus, option (3), but this does not make a bone a mineral. Hardness, option (5) is not part of the definition of a mineral.

Lesson 10
GED Practice: Other Contexts (Page 119)
1. **(1) acid rain wearing away limestone** (Application) When limestone is exposed to acids, a chemical reaction results. Options (2), (3), (4), and (5) are examples of mechanical weathering.

2. **(4) a glass jar full of soup bursts when placed in the freezer** (Application) Since water expands as it freezes, the bursting jar is most similar to the process of mechanical weathering. Option (1) is an example of chemical weathering. Options (2), (3), and (5) are not related to weathering.

3. **(1) A pebble falling downhill breaks as it hits the ground.** (Application) Mechanical weathering is the breaking up of rock without chemical changes, such as what occurs when a falling rock breaks. Options (2), (3), and (5) involve chemical changes. Option (4) involves water changing state, not the breaking up of rock.

4. **(2) inside damp caves** (Application) Acidic water is an agent of chemical weathering. Its action produces the rock formations found in damp caves. Mechanical weathering, not chemical weathering, is likely to occur in the situations described in options (1), (3), and (4). Option (5) is incorrect because water, an agent of both mechanical and chemical weathering, will be scarce during a drought, so weathering is less likely to occur.

5. **(5) a glass jar in a landfill** (Application) The actions mentioned in the passage are least likely to affect a jar. Option (1) would be subject to both chemical and mechanical weathering. Over time, a limestone building, option (2), would be affected by wind and rain. Options (3) and (4) are greatly affected by weathering especially the actions of freezing water.

6. **(3) Weathering on Earth** (Comprehension) The main topic of the paragraph is the effect of weathering on rocks. Options (1), (2), and (4) are all mentioned in relation to weathering and are details of the passage. Option (5) refers to a very minor detail in the passage.

GED Practice: Air and Water (Page 121)
1. **(3) an astronaut** (Application) An astronaut travels above the ozone layer and has no natural protection against the sun's ultraviolet rays. The other options involve people whose occupations do not take them above the ozone layer.

2. **(1) troposphere** (Comprehension) Since the troposphere extends about ten miles up (52,800 feet), the top of Mt. Everest is still well below its upper limit. The other layers of the atmosphere are above the troposphere and are therefore incorrect.

3. **(2) a mountain climber** (Application) As a mountain climber goes higher, the air becomes colder and thinner. Options (1), (4), and (5) are occupations that do not require changes in altitude. Option (3) is incorrect because airline attendants work in a manmade environment, the airplane, in which temperature and air pressure are controlled.

4. **(3) More ultraviolet rays would reach Earth's surface.** (Analysis) Since the ozone layer prevents most ultraviolet rays from reaching the surface of Earth, its destruction would remove a natural barrier. Destruction of the ozone layer would not affect the breathing of oxygen in the troposphere, option (1). Option (2) describes the function of the ozone layer. Option (4) is incorrect because the ozone layer is only part of the stratosphere. Option (5) is incorrect because there would be an effect.

5. **(5) krypton** (Comprehension) The first four options are gases that make up a large portion

Answers and Explanations

of the atmosphere. The passage indicates that krypton is one of the gases present in small amounts.

6. **(1) Gravity holds the atmosphere in place around Earth.** (Analysis) To understand the passage one must know that the atmosphere remains around Earth because of the force of gravity. As the writer does not state or imply it, it is assumed that the reader has this knowledge. Options (2) and (3) are not true. Option (4) is stated in the passage and shown in the diagram. Option (5) is also not true; human beings have been to the moon, which is beyond the mesosphere.

7. **(3) The higher you go in the troposphere, the less oxygen is available.** (Analysis) The runner had difficulty breathing in Denver because it is much higher than Boston, and there is less oxygen. Option (1) makes no sense because neither place has tropical weather. Options (2) and (4) are true but not related to the change in altitude between Boston and Denver. Option (5) is true, but the change in temperature was not the cause of the runner's breathing problem.

GED Review: Lesson 10 (Pages 122–123)

1. **(3) They contain dry air.** (Comprehension) Options (1), (2), (4) and (5) are incorrect because continental air masses do not contain moist air.

2. **(1) maritime polar** (Comprehension) Options (2), (3), (4), and (5) are incorrect because, according to this passage, continental air masses do not tend to cause precipitation. The only other type of air mass that might have caused the snowstorm would be a maritime tropical in winter.

3. **(1) Types of Air Masses** (Comprehension) The passage deals generally with the four different types of air masses. It does not mention what occurs when air masses meet, option (3). Where air masses form, option (2), and the characteristics of continental air masses, option (4), are supporting details of the passage. The passage only covers one of many topics that fall under the broad heading of Air and Water, option (5).

4. **(3) cause weather changes in the contiguous 48 states** (Comprehension) The passage states that changes in weather are caused by air masses and that the contiguous

48 states are affected by air masses that form over northern Canada and the ocean. Option (1) is incorrect because the air mass that forms over Canada would be dry. Option (2) is incorrect because an air mass that forms near Hawaii would be moist. Option (4) is incorrect because an air mass over Canada would be cold. Option (5) is incorrect because the two air masses would bring different types of weather, not just cool, dry weather.

5. **(3) Air masses called tropical originate over tropical seas.** (Evaluation) Since a continental tropical air mass originates over land, all tropical air masses do not originate over tropical seas. Options (1) and (2) explain why the terms maritime and continental are used. Options (4) and (5) are accurate descriptions of air masses.

6. **(2) snowy** (Application) When two such air masses meet, precipitation is the likely result. Snow is the most likely form of precipitation in winter.

7. **(4) they affect the temperature and humidity of the air** (Analysis) It is the change in these two factors that causes the weather to be different. Option (1) is not always true; some air masses bring warm or hot air. Options (2), (3), and (5) are generally true but do not explain why the weather changes.

8. **(5) are most direct at the equator** (Evaluation) If you look at the diagram, you can see that, except at the equator, the sun's rays are spread over a wider area because of the curve in Earth's surface. Therefore, options (1), (2) (3), and (4) are incorrect.

9. **(5) a greater possibility of sunburn** (Application) The diagram shows that the sun's rays are more direct, and therefore more intense, at the equator. Option (3) is incorrect because direct sunlight at the equator produces warmer temperatures. Options (1), (2), and (4) cannot be predicted based on the diagram.

10. **(2) The sun's rays are more concentrated near the equator than near the poles.** (Analysis) This is shown in the diagram. Options (1) and (4) are incorrect because they are not shown in the diagram. Options (3) and (5) might be true, but there is no information about weather patterns in the diagram.

Answers and Explanations

1. **(1) Water vapor in the air condenses.** (Comprehension) The third paragraph explains that this is how clouds form. Option (2) is incorrect because heavy droplets in clouds result in rain. Option (3) is incorrect because water on the surface of Earth evaporates to form water vapor in the air. Option (4) is not related to cloud formation. Option (5) is incorrect because warm air, not cool air, comes from the surface of Earth.

2. **(3) Evaporation and condensation cause precipitation.** (Evaluation) This is the only option that includes all three steps of the water cycle. Options (1), (2), and (5) are only parts of this cycle. Option (4) has the steps in the wrong order.

3. **(3) Water evaporates and then condenses.** (Analysis) Options (1) and (2) are incorrect because the steps are in the wrong order. Option (4) is incorrect because it is water vapor that is carried by the wind. Option (5) is incorrect because once warm air rises, the water vapor condenses.

4. **(2) water running down the bathroom walls after someone takes a hot shower** (Application) Steam condenses on the cooler surfaces of the walls, and drops of water start running down the walls. Option (1) is only a small part of the water cycle. Options (3) and (4) have nothing to do with water. Option (5) is turning water from a solid to a liquid then to a solid again, which is not part of the water cycle.

5. **(2) A very small amount of the water on Earth can be used to meet the needs of living things.** (Evaluation) According to the passage, 97 percent of all water on Earth is ocean water, leaving only 3 percent to meet the needs of most living things. Thus, option (1) is untrue. Options (3), (4), and (5) may or may not be true, but they are not related to the information provided.

6. **(1) 3 percent** (Comprehension) Since undrinkable ocean water accounts for 97 percent of the water on Earth, it follows that only about 3 percent of Earth's water is drinkable.

7. **(2) People sitting near a fireplace feel warm, while people sitting far from the fireplace feel chilly.** (Application) This is correct because heat from the fire is similar to heat from the sun. The most warmth will be provided to things closest to the source of heat. Option (1) is incorrect because ocean water is not heated evenly throughout. Option (3) is incorrect because ocean water is not heated from the bottom up. Option (4) is incorrect because it deals with electrical energy, not radiant energy. Option (5) is incorrect because the passage does not suggest that ocean water is like an insulator.

8. **(1) 35 grams per thousand grams water** (Comprehension) The passage indicates that the ocean's salinity is between 33 and 37 grams per thousand grams water. Therefore, 35 is the only possible answer.

Lesson 11
GED Practice: Fact or Opinion (Page 127)

1. **(2) There are variations in sunspot activity.** (Analysis) This is the only statement that has so far been proved. Option (1) is an opinion that has not been proved. Option (3) is contradicted by the passage. Option (4) is also an opinion. Option (5) does not make sense; sunspots, if they affect North America, would affect the rest of the world also.

2. **(4) Sunspots affect the weather in North America.** (Analysis) This is an opinion, not a proven fact. Options (1), (2), (3), and (5) are all facts.

3. **(5) B and C only** (Comprehension) The passage indicates that periods of drought in North America are shown by rainfall records and tree rings, Statements B and C. Options (1) and (4) are incorrect because they include Statement A, sunspot activity. Although sunspots may affect droughts, they don't indicate droughts. Options (2) and (3) are incorrect because they don't include both rainfall records and tree rings.

4. **(1) data suggesting a correlation between sunspot activity and droughts in Asia** (Evaluation) A correlation between sunspots and drought, a weather condition, supports, though it does not prove, a cause and effect relationship. Option (5) would refute rather than support the opinion. To support the opinion, data correlating sunspots with weather are needed, so options (2) and (4) are incorrect because they don't include both sunspots and weather data. Option (3) is incorrect because tides are not a type of weather.

1. **(3) There is enough oil to last 300 years.** (Analysis) Option (3) is one of two estimates given in the passage. Neither opinion can be proved. Option (1) is a fact because oil is known to be a nonrenewable resource. Options (2) and (4) are incorrect because they are facts. Both energy use and the availability of oil can be measured. Option (5) is also a fact.

2. **(4) Solar energy is a renewable resource.** (Analysis) This information is stated in the third paragraph. Option (1) is an opinion expressed by the author. No data is given to support it. Options (2) and (3) are opinions held by scientists. While citizens and energy conservation are mentioned, option (5) does not appear in the passage.

3. **(3) driving a small, fuel-efficient car** (Application) This would save gasoline, a nonrenewable resource. Option (1) would use more fuel, not less. Option (2) involves conserving water, a renewable resource. Option (4) does not make sense; in warm weather no fuel would be used to heat a home, and added sunlight would just make the building warmer. If air conditioners were in use, this would waste energy. Option (5) involves switching from one nonrenewable resource to another and thus would not help conserve a nonrenewable resource.

4. **(1) Vehicles will eventually be powered by something other than a petroleum product.** (Comprehension) The passage suggests that renewable resources will come to replace nonrenewable resources such as petroleum. Options (2) and (3) are contradicted by the passage. Option (4) makes no sense. Since the supply of oil is limited, it will eventually run out, even if people conserve it. Option (5) is not implied by the passage, which states that at present solar energy is too expensive for widespread use.

5. **(2) The supply would be used more slowly but would eventually run out.** (Analysis) Cutting down on the use of oil will stretch the supply for a longer time, but since the supply is limited, it will eventually run out. Option (1) is the opposite of what happens when a resource is conserved. Option (3) is only partially correct. The supply would be used more slowly, but it would not last forever since it is limited. Option (4) is incorrect because the supply would last longer. Option (5) may be true, but it does not relate to the effect of conservation on supply.

6. **(5) solar energy** (Comprehension) Of the forms of energy mentioned, only solar energy is renewable because there is a constant supply of it from the sun. The other resources are all found on Earth in limited supply.

7. **(4) Conserving oil will postpone the time when supplies run out.** (Evaluation) Option (1) is not true at the present time. Option (2) is incorrect because another shortage could happen, since the supply of gasoline is limited. Option (3) is an opinion about the size of the oil supply. Option (5) may be true, but whatever new supplies are found, they will not be enough to meet long-term energy needs, since the new supplies will be limited also.

8. **(5) petroleum** (Application) Since petroleum is found in deposits on Earth, it would be of most interest to a geologist. Geologists are not primarily concerned with the study of sunlight, ocean water, food, or nuclear energy.

9. **(5) Oil Shortages—Can They Be Avoided?** (Comprehension) The main purpose of the passage is to discuss how shortages of the nonrenewable resource oil can be avoided by using alternate, renewable energy sources. Options (1), (2), (3), and (4) all address only a portion of the issue presented.

10. **(2) using windmills instead of oil-burning power plants to generate electricity** (Application) This idea would replace oil with the energy of wind, which is a renewable resource. All other options are ways to conserve energy resources, not to replace one with another.

GED Review: Lesson 11 (Pages 130–131)

1. **(4) Wind energy can reduce the need for fossil fuels.** (Analysis) This is the most important aspect of wind energy. Option (1) is not true; wind energy is a renewable resource. Option (2) is contradicted by the passage. Option (3) is true, but it is not important. Option (5) may or may not be true, but it is not the most important aspect of wind energy.

2. **(2) how modern wind generators are used** (Comprehension) Modern wind generators are described, but their uses are

not specified. The other options are incorrect because these topics are all covered in the passage.

3. **(4) more reliable** (Comprehension) The passage states that modern wind generators are tough and can withstand storms. Options (1) and (2) are incorrect because the passage makes no mention of size or cost. Options (3) and (5) are incorrect because both are characteristics of earlier wind generators.

4. **(2) powering factories** (Comprehension) All other options are mentioned in the passage as uses of wind power. Only option (2) is not mentioned and is therefore the correct answer.

5. **(3) a need to find more energy sources** (Comprehension) This option is clearly stated in the passage. The other options may be related to an interest in wind energy, but they are not mentioned in the passage.

6. **(3) the unreliability of wind generators** (Analysis) People stopped using wind generators because they didn't always work and thus were unreliable. The need to conserve fossil fuels, option (1), is the cause of new interest in wind generators. Options (2) and (5) did not occur until recently. Option (4) is incorrect since the passage doesn't mention that there was an increase in storms and calm days in the 1940s.

7. **(4) the burning of certain fuels** (Comprehension) The passage states that sulfur is released when coal and oil are burned. Options (1) and (2) are incorrect because oxygen and moisture cannot form acid rain without the burning of certain fuels. Options (3) and (5) are incorrect because they are not related to the formation of acid rain.

8. **(4) Acid rain is formed by sulfur oxides combining with water in the air.** (Analysis) This statement can be supported by information in the first paragraph. Options (1), (2), and (5) are incorrect because they are opinions that are not supported by the passage. Option (3) is not true.

9. **(5) lost their wildlife as result of acid rain** (Comprehension) This is stated in the second paragraph. Option (2) is incorrect because it is a lack of plants and animals that makes the lake look blue. Options (1), (3), and (4) are incorrect because they have nothing to do with information given in the passage.

10. **(3) High levels of acidity can be harmful to living things.** (Comprehension) Since acidic rain can damage or kill plants and animals, you can logically make this assumption. Options (1) and (5) are incorrect because no mention is made of the effect of pure sulfur on living things. Option (2) is incorrect because the only mention of clear, blue water in this passage relates to a lake that has no plants and animals because it has been polluted by acid rain. Option (4) is incorrect because it is the presence of acid in rainwater that can kill plants and animals.

GED Mini-Test: Lesson 11 (Pages 132–133)

1. **(4) Fossil fuels have been and are still of great importance to industry.** (Evaluation) The other options are incorrect because the passage clearly refers to the use of fossil fuels in industry in both the past and the present.

2. **(1) 100% cotton shirt** (Application) This is correct because cotton is a natural fiber. Option (2) is incorrect because cosmetics are produced from petroleum. Option (3) is incorrect because synthetic fibers are produced from petroleum. Options (4) and (5) are incorrect because plastic and gasoline are produced from petroleum.

3. **(2) natural gas were to replace oil as the leading fuel** (Comprehension) The last paragraph of the passage describes natural gas as a "clean-burning" fuel, compared to coal and oil. All other options are incorrect because coal and oil produce more air pollution than natural gas.

4. **(3) formed underground from the remains of plants and animals** (Comprehension) Options (1), (2), and (5) are incorrect because fossil fuels were formed naturally on Earth. Option (4) is incorrect because fossil fuels did not form from pieces of rock.

5. **(4) The use of natural gas does not cause pollution.** (Analysis) While the passage states that natural gas is cleaner burning than coal and oil, it does not say that it is non-polluting. Option (1) is supported by the first paragraph. Option (2) is supported by the second paragraph. Options (3) and (5) are supported by the last two paragraphs.

6. **(3) The last ice age ended about 10,000 years ago.** (Analysis) This statement is one of several facts about ice ages presented in the

first paragraph. The other options are all opinions of scientists about the possible causes of ice ages.

7. **(2) People would move toward the equator.** (Application) The area around the equator would remain the warmest area on Earth. Option (1) is incorrect because the glaciers would be spreading from the South Pole northward into the Southern Hemisphere. Option (3) does not make sense since the glaciers would cover that area. Option (4) is not likely, since people can move toward the equator and many would survive. Option (5) is not related to ice ages, but to seasons.

8. **(2) It would spread northward.** (Analysis) Since Antarctica is located over the South Pole, the spread of its ice cap would be northward into the Southern Hemisphere. Options (1) and (4) are the opposite of what happens during an ice age. Option (3) is incorrect because Antarctica is located over the South Pole. Option (5) contradicts the correct answer, option (2).

9. **(3) What Causes an Ice Age?** (Comprehension) This is a good title because the passage discusses various ideas that have been proposed to explain ice ages, although none of them has been proved. Option (1) is incorrect because we are not in an ice age at present. Option (2) refers to a detail from the passage. Options (4) and (5) are not discussed in the passage.

10. **(4) a decrease in temperatures worldwide** (Evaluation) Since weather becomes colder during an ice age, a drop in temperatures worldwide might signal the start of a new ice age. Options (1), (2), (3), and (5) are more likely to signal the end of an ice age, when increasing temperatures melt glaciers and cause polar ice caps to shrink, thus raising sea levels.

11. **(1) the dust would block the sun's energy, resulting in lower temperatures** (Analysis) Option (1) is the only option that explains how dust could bring on conditions associated with an ice age. There is no evidence given that options (2), (3), (4), and (5) are true.

Lesson 12
GED Practice: Cause and Effect (Pages 134–135)
1. **(3) The beach would get larger.** (Analysis) Since the action of winter storms, with high winds and waves, causes beaches to lose sand, it follows that several mild winters would slow this action. The deposit of sand during the summer would build up the beach. This sand would not be entirely removed during the next winter, so the beach would grow over the years.

2. **(2) Flooding and wind damage are likely to occur.** (Analysis) Barrier islands take the main force of a storm approaching from the sea. Since they are low and made of sand, they are very likely to be damaged by wind and flooding. Although the other options may or may not occur during a hurricane, they are not the major reasons for evacuating people from barrier islands when a bad storm is coming.

3. **(2) A steep face of rock is exposed.** (Analysis) Both normal and reverse faults move rock in such a way that a steep face of rock is created where previously the land had been flat. Option (1) is incorrect because it describes the movement of rock in lateral faults. Option (3) is not indicated in any of the diagrams. Option (4) describes the land before faulting. Option (5) does not describe what happens during a fault. During a fault, rocks break and slide; they do not curve.

4. **(3) formation of mountains** (Analysis) Normal and reverse faults result in the creation of steep rock faces. If this was widespread, the likely result would be a mountainous landscape. Options (1), (2), and (4) do not describe the results of faulting. Option (5) is incorrect because it refers to the climate of an area, not the landscape features.

GED Practice: The Changing Earth (Pages 136–137)
1. **(4) wind** (Analysis) Option (1) is incorrect because it can cause all types of mass wasting. Option (2) is incorrect because it can cause soil creep. Options (3) and (5) are incorrect because they can cause landslides.

2. **(2) soil creep** (Analysis) This is stated in the last paragraph. Option (1) is incorrect because it is the result of mass wasting. Options (3), (4), and (5) are all incorrect because they cause rapid, not gradual, changes in the land.

3. **(5) gravity** (Analysis) No matter what other causes may be involved in mass wasting, gravity is always the basic cause. The other options are also causes, but they are not involved in each case of mass wasting, as gravity is.

4. **(1) the Great Plains** (Application) The Great Plains are least likely to suffer the effects of mass wasting because the landscape is generally flat. Options (2), (3), and (5) are mountainous areas where mass wasting occurs. Option (4), the Grand Canyon, would also be likely to have mass wasting because of the steep slopes.

5. **(3) heavy rain** (Comprehension) The third paragraph states that a mudflow is usually caused by heavy rain. The other options may or may not occur, but they are not the most common cause of a mudflow.

6. **(4) landslide** (Analysis) Since it is a form of rapid mass wasting involving a huge amount of rock, a landslide is likely to cause the most damage to things in its path. Options (1), (2), and (3) are smaller and slower changes that cause less severe results. Option (5) is a landscape feature that results from mass wasting.

7. **(3) The general movement in mass wasting is from high ground to low ground.** (Evaluation) Since the force of gravity pulls things from high places to lower places, all forms of mass wasting follow this pattern. Option (1) is only partially correct; there are other causes of mass wasting. Option (2) is incorrect because rapid mass wasting takes place in mountainous areas. Option (4) is incorrect because heavy rains are not necessary for some forms of mass wasting. Option (5) is incorrect because mass wasting tends to lower mountains, not form them.

8. **(3) sediments piled at the base of a cliff** (Comprehension) According to the passage, a talus slope forms as a result of sediments piling up due to mass wasting. The other options do not describe a talus slope as defined in the passage.

9. **(3) Rapid and Slow Mass Wasting** (Comprehension) The general subject of the passage is the different types of mass wasting. Options (1) and (5) refer to supporting details in the passage. Options (2) and (4) leave out rapid mass wasting.

10. **(2) a road at the base of a steep slope** (Analysis) Damage from mass wasting is most likely to occur at the base of a steep slope where the force of gravity is acting to pull soil and rocks down. Option (1) is incorrect because gravity won't pull rocks up to the crest of a hill. Option (3) is incorrect because a volcano is more likely to be the cause of a landslide than the victim of one. Options (4) and (5) are incorrect because lakes and rivers are only at risk of damage by landslides if they are at the base of steep slopes.

11. **(1) It is not likely to occur during a drought.** (Evaluation) Since earthflows are usually caused by heavy rain, they would be unlikely to occur when there has been little rain. Options (2) and (3) are incorrect since earthflows are examples of slow mass wasting and are therefore slower than rapid mudflows. Option (4) is incorrect because earthflows can occur anywhere there is rain and a slope. Option (5) is incorrect since all mass wasting events eventually produce a talus slope, even though it may take a very long time to form.

12. **(4) rapid mass wasting** (Application) Rocks falling onto a highway are a type of a small landslide which is rapid mass wasting. Option (1) is incorrect because an earth flow is a type of slow mass wasting. Option (2) is incorrect because soil creep does not involve rocks and is the slowest form of mass wasting. Option (3) is incorrect because mudflow is not involved in the situation described. A rockfall does not match the description of slow mass wasting, option (5).

GED Review: Lesson 12 (Pages 138–139)
1. **(2) amount of energy released** (Comprehension) The last paragraph of the passage states that the more energy an earthquake releases, the stronger it is. Options (1), (3), and (4) are incorrect because, while they may be important in other ways, they do not determine the strength of an earthquake. Option (5) may be related to the strength of an earthquake, but this is not mentioned in the passage.

2. **(1) surface waves are the most destructive** (Comprehension) This is correct since it is the surface waves that cause the upheavals in the ground that are so destructive. As the passage does not describe the results of options (2), (3), (4), and (5), you can conclude that they must cause less damage than surface waves. If they caused more damage, that fact would most likely have been mentioned.

Answers and Explanations

3. **(1) the formation of tall mountain peaks**
(Analysis) A glacier wears away rocks, so it
would not make a mountain peak taller. All
other options are effects of a moving glacier.

4. **(3) The edges of the glaciers would melt,
making the glaciers smaller.** (Analysis)
Since glaciers form from the excess snow and
ice that does not melt from season to season, it
follows that unusually warm weather would
cause more melting. This would make the
glacier smaller. Options (1), (2), and (4)
describe what happens when glaciers build
up. Option (5) occurs whether or not the
glacier is getting smaller.

5. **(4) the breaking up of granite by a
jackhammer** (Application) Option (4) is an
example of rock being broken up by humans.
The passage states that erosion is the moving
and wearing away of rock materials by
natural causes. Therefore, options (1), (2), (3),
and (5) are all examples of erosion.

6. **(5) Glacial Erosion** (Comprehension) The
general topic of this passage is erosion caused
by glaciers. Option (1) is too general; the
passage focuses on just one aspect of what
glaciers do. Glaciers are only one of several
agents of erosion, option (2). Options (3) and
(4) are supporting details of the passage.

GED Mini-Test: Lesson 12 (Pages 140–141)
1. **(5) the movement of magma to Earth's
surface** (Comprehension) The key word in
this question is "necessary." All the other
options can be associated with the formation
of certain volcanoes, but only option (5) is a
necessary condition for the formation of all
volcanoes.

2. **(4) the events that cause them to form**
(Comprehension) The article states that
volcanoes are classified according to the type
of eruptions that form them. The other options
are incorrect because, although these factors
may differ in each type of volcano, they are
not the basis for classification.

3. **(3) several quiet eruptions**
(Comprehension) This is stated in the fifth
paragraph of the article. Options (1) and (2)
are incorrect because they form cone-shaped
volcanoes. Options (4) and (5) are incorrect
because they are associated with the
formation of cone-shaped volcanoes.

4. **(2) Lava can be thin and runny.**
(Comprehension) Option (1) is incorrect
because cinder cone volcanoes are formed out
of cinders and rock particles. Option (3) is
incorrect because lava does not flow over a
wide area in an explosive eruption. Options (4)
and (5) are incorrect because lava is magma
that reaches Earth's surface.

5. **(2) when lava flows it is thin and runny**
(Analysis) Since the islands are shield
volcanoes, their lava must be thin and runny.
Options (1) and (3) are not features associated
with shield volcanoes. Option (4) is incorrect
since eruptions still occur on these islands.
Option (5) is incorrect because shield
volcanoes form gently sloping, dome-shaped
mountains.

6. **(5) is a cinder cone volcano**
(Comprehension) The passage states that a
cinder cone volcano has a narrow base and
steep sides, and a shield volcano is dome-
shaped. Therefore, option (3) is incorrect.
Option (1) is incorrect because the volcano
could be either active or dormant. Option (2) is
not true of cinder cone volcanoes. Option (4) is
incorrect because Mt. St. Helens is just one
example of a composite volcano.

7. **(4) Australia** (Comprehension) The map
shows that no major earthquake zone passes
through or near Australia; therefore it is free
of major earthquakes. The other continents all
have areas in an earthquake zone.

8. **(2) western South America** (Application)
The map shows an active zone running along
the west coast of South America. Options (1),
(3), (4) and (5) are incorrect because the zones
shown on the map do not pass through these
areas.

GED Cumulative Review
Unit 2: Earth Science (Pages 142–146)
1. **(5) decreases, then increases, then
decreases, then increases as altitude
increases** (Comprehension) This is correct
because the temperature decreases to -55°C at
the border between the troposphere and
stratosphere; then it increases to 0°C at the
border between the stratosphere and
mesosphere; then it decreases to -100°C at the
top of the mesosphere; finally it reaches
2,000°C at the top of the thermosphere. The
other options are incorrect because they do not
describe the series of increases and decreases
that occur as altitude increases.

2. **(4) It is the layer we live in.** (Evaluation) The troposphere covers Earth's surface, where we live. Options (1), (2), and (3) describe other layers of the atmosphere. Option (5) isn't true of any layer, since the thermosphere is the thickest layer.

3. **(3) They can withstand extremely high temperatures.** (Analysis) This is correct because the temperature in the upper thermosphere ranges from 600°C to 2,000°C. Option (1) is incorrect because the exosphere is much higher than 124 miles. Option (2) is incorrect because the ozone layer is located well below the thermosphere in the stratosphere and mesosphere. Option (4) is incorrect because ice clouds do not form where temperatures are very high. Option (5) is actually true in some cases, but this cannot be inferred from the information given in the diagram.

4. **(3) the mesosphere meets the thermosphere** (Comprehension) The diagram shows that at 50 miles above Earth's surface the mesosphere ends and the thermosphere begins. Options (1), (2), (4), and (5) are not true.

5. **(4) Increased levels of methane cause global warming.** (Analysis) Although there seems to be a relationship between methane levels and climate changes, it has not been proved that increased methane causes global warming. Options (1), (2), (3), and (5) are all facts mentioned in the passage.

6. **(3) The methane level is much higher now than during previous warm periods.** (Analysis) Since there seems to be a relationship between high methane levels and warmer climates, it is reasonable to conclude that the present high methane levels indicate that Earth is in a warming period. Option (1) refers to methane levels in the past. Option (2) is true, but does not indicate the relationship of methane and climate. Option (4), if it were true, would indicate a cooling period rather than a warming period. Option (5) is true, but does not indicate a relationship between methane and climate.

7. **(3) In periods of warmer climate, more methane is in the atmosphere.** (Analysis) This is indicated by the results of the studies mentioned in the passage. Options (1) and (2) are incorrect because no cause and effect relationship has been proved. Option (4) is the opposite of what occurs. Option (5) is incorrect because there is a relationship between methane levels and climate.

8. **(2) During ice ages, the level of methane in the atmosphere increases.** (Evaluation) This is not true because the level of methane decreases during ice ages. The other options are all true according to the passage.

9. **(4) Weathering and erosion can affect all types of rocks.** (Evaluation) The diagram shows that when igneous, sedimentary, and metamorphic rocks are exposed, they are all subject to weathering and erosion. Option (1) is incorrect because metamorphic rocks are also formed from sedimentary rocks. Option (2) is incorrect because sedimentary rocks are formed by pressure. Option (3) is incorrect because igneous rocks are formed from magma. Option (5) is incorrect because heat and pressure cause sedimentary rocks to form metamorphic rocks.

10. **(5) igneous** (Application) The cooling of magma produces basalt, an igneous rock. Option (1) refers to sediments, not rocks. Options (2) and (4) are incorrect because basalt is neither sedimentary nor metamorphic rock. Option (3) is not rock.

11. **(1) The Rock Cycle** (Comprehension) The diagram and information describe the steps in the process by which one type of rock turns into another, which is called the rock cycle. Options (2), (4), and (5) are too specific. Option (3) does not describe the information shown.

12. **(3) C only** (Analysis) An old river bed would contain many sediments that had been deposited by water. Over time, these sediments would form sedimentary rocks, Statement C. Options (1), (4), and (5) are incorrect because sediments do not form igneous rocks, Statement A. Option (2) is incorrect because sediments do not form metamorphic rocks, Statement B. The area might contain some metamorphic rocks that formed from sedimentary rocks, but the sedimentary rocks would be more likely to be seen.

13. **(4) It is not wise to depend only on fossil fuels for energy.** (Analysis) Both short-term shortages, as in the 1970s, and long-term limits on fossil fuel supply indicate a need to develop alternate sources of energy. Therefore, the author does not think we should continue to depend on fossil fuels. Option (1) is

incorrect because the author indicates that seawater may eventually be a useful source of energy. Option (2) is incorrect because nothing in the article indicates the author's opinions about solar energy. Option (3) is incorrect because seawater will never be used up. Option (5) is incorrect because only air-conditioning systems near a supply of cold seawater would be candidates for seawater as a coolant.

14. **(3) a process that uses the difference in temperature between warm and cold seawater to produce electricity** (Comprehension) Ocean thermal energy conversion is defined in the second paragraph of the article. The other options do not explain this process. Options (1), (2), and (4) are not mentioned in the article. Option (5) describes a different process that uses seawater.

15. **(5) Kansas** (Application) Of the five options, only Kansas is located far from the ocean. It would thus be impractical to use seawater in such a location.

16. **(2) Until less electricity is used to pump up seawater than is produced by using seawater, the process will not be practical.** (Comprehension) At present, more electricity is used to pump seawater through the generator than the generator itself produces, causing a net loss in electricity. This obviously is not practical. Option (1) is not likely since the small-scale experiment has yet to produce electricity economically. Option (3) is not true. Option (4) is not true because the article indicates that cooling bills were cut by 75 percent, but that production of electricity was not economical. Option (5) is incorrect because there is no indication that generating electricity from seawater causes pollution.

17. **(5) A and C only** (Analysis) Earth has seasons because of both Statements A and C, Earth's revolution and its inclined axis. Options (1) and (3) are incorrect because they are only part of the cause. Options (2) and (4) are incorrect because rotation, Statement B, causes day and night, not the seasons.

18. **(5) Earth's spinning on its axis** (Comprehension) The passage describes rotation as the spinning of Earth on its axis. Options (1) and (2) are two kinds of revolution. Options (3) and (4) are incorrect because rotation neither causes nor is caused by the seasons.

19. **(2) The northern hemisphere is tilted away from the sun.** (Application) In December it is winter in the northern hemisphere; therefore, we can conclude that the hemisphere is tilted away from the sun. Options (1) and (5) are true in June, not December. Options (3) and (4) are true in spring and autumn.

20. **(1) there would be no seasons** (Application) If Earth revolved as it does now but rotated on an axis that wasn't inclined, every place on Earth would get the same amount of daylight (12 hours) every day. Temperatures would vary with distance from the equator but not with time of year. As a result, there would be global variations in climate but not seasons, so option (2) is incorrect. Option (3) is incorrect because rotation wouldn't change. Option (4) is incorrect because a change would occur. Option (5) is incorrect because revolution wouldn't change.

21. **(4) Different parts of Earth get different amounts of the sun's energy at different times of the year.** (Comprehension) The passage explains that different parts of Earth lean toward the sun at different times of the year. Therefore they get differing amounts of the sun's energy. As a result, option (3) must be incorrect. Options (1) and (2) are incorrect because they include incorrect numbers. Option (5) is incorrect because the southern hemisphere experiences fall on March 21.

UNIT 3: CHEMISTRY
Lesson 13
GED Practice: Other Contexts (Page 151)

1. **(5) a pressure cooker** (Application) A pressure cooker uses the buildup of steam to raise the boiling point of water. The hotter water cooks the foods faster. Options (1) and (3) are appliances that do not need water to cook foods. Options (2) and (4) involve water at temperatures lower than the boiling point.

2. **(1) obtaining drinking water from ocean water** (Application) Ocean water, which contains salts and other minerals, can be distilled to yield pure water for drinking. Options (2) and (3) involve uses of pure water. Although water is boiled for making tea, no water vapor is collected. Option (4) lowers the freezing point; it has nothing to do with removing minerals or other impurities. Option (5) does not involve distillation, since mineral water is sold because of its mineral content.

3. **(2) steel-belted radial tires** (Application) This type of tire has a steel belt embedded in the rubber portion of the tire to give added strength. Thus it is a composite material. Option (1) is a pure substance so it is not a composite and is not correct. Although options (3), (4), and (5) each contain more than one substance, they are not composites because one substance is not embedded in the other for the purpose of combining properties.

4. **(2) it has the properties of two or more materials, one embedded in the other** (Application) Bone consists of elastic protein fibers embedded in calcium phosphate. The calcium adds strength to the bone. The elastic fibers provide flexibility so that the bone does not break easily. Options (1), (3), (4), and (5) are true but each alone is not the reason for bone being a composite material.

5. **(4) a dehumidifier** (Application) A dehumidifier reduces the amount of moisture in the air by cooling the air. As a result the moisture condenses and settles as water drops which are usually collected in a collecting pan. Option (1) would warm, not cool, air. Option (2) may provide comfort but does not take advantage of the principle described. Option (3) would add moisture to the air. Option (5) would make the air cleaner, but it would not affect its moisture content.

GED Practice: Matter (Page 153)

1. **(2) A container of ice cream is left on top of a hot stove.** (Application) This is correct because the solid ice cream would melt into a liquid. Options (1), (3), and (5) are incorrect because changing color, volume, or size does not involve a change of state. Option (4) is incorrect because no change of state occurs when the can of soup is weighed.

2. **(4) A liquid has no definite shape.** (Application) This is correct because liquid cake batter would take the shape of the mold. After the batter is baked, the solid that forms keeps that shape. Options (1), (2), (3), and (5) are not true.

3. **(1) the addition or removal of heat** (Comprehension) According to the passage, heating substances causes them to melt or vaporize. Cooling substances causes them to freeze or condense. All of these changes are changes of state. Options (2), (3), (4), and (5) describe properties of matter, not causes of changes of state.

4. **(2) filling a balloon with helium** (Application) This is an example of one of the properties of gases—expanding to fill the available space in a container. Options (1), (3), (4), and (5) are all examples of matter changing from one state to another.

5. **(1) dew forming on the grass in early morning** (Application) Water vapor in the air condenses as the air cools during the night. Options (2) and (5) are incorrect because they involve melting. Option (3) is incorrect because it involves freezing. Option (4) is incorrect because it involves vaporization.

6. **(4) smelling pollutants released by a nearby factory** (Application) The gases spread out in all directions and can be smelled from a distance. Options (1) and (5) are incorrect because they involve liquids. Options (2) and (3) are incorrect because they involve solids.

7. **(4) no definite shape; definite volume** (Application) Liquids change shape and fill the container they are in, but their volume remains the same regardless of shape. Option (1) describes solids. Option (2) does not describe any of the types of matter. Option (3) describes gases. Option (5), none of the above, is incorrect because there is a correct description, option (4).

8. **(4) Water freezes and vaporizes at different temperatures.** (Application) Water freezes at 0°C and vaporizes at 100°C. Option (1) is incorrect because few substances are found naturally in all three states. Option (2) is incorrect because gases, not liquids, spread out to completely fill their containers. Option (3) is incorrect because some matter is solid and some matter is gas below 100°C. Option (5) is incorrect because liquids are already melted.

GED Review: Lesson 13 (Pages 154–155)

1. **(5) It has the same properties as all other iron atoms.** (Comprehension) Option (5) is the only option that is true. Option (1) is incorrect because the mass of a proton is about 1,800 times greater than that of an electron. Option (2) is incorrect because neutrons have no charge. Electrons, not protons, orbit the nucleus, so option (3) is incorrect. The third paragraph states that iron and copper atoms are different, so option (4) is incorrect.

2. **(1) It breaks down when heated, producing mercury and oxygen.** (Comprehension) This statement shows that substance X is not an element because elements cannot be broken down into other elements. Option (2) is incorrect because nothing stated in the passage refers to the color of an element. Options (3) and (5) are incorrect because elements can react with other substances. Option (4) is incorrect because many elements are solids.

3. **(3) The number of protons in an atom is equal to the number of electrons.** (Analysis) Option (1) is incorrect because the atom would have a positive charge. Option (2) is incorrect because the atom would have a negative charge. Options (4) and (5) are incorrect because neutrons do not have a charge, so they do not affect the charge of an atom.

4. **(4) Atom X has fewer neutrons than atom Y.** (Analysis) This is correct because neutrons and protons have about the same mass—thus extra neutrons in Y could balance the extra protons in X. Options (1) and (2) are incorrect because electrons make up so little of an atom's mass that they could not possibly balance the extra protons. Option (3) would make atom X even heavier. Option (5) is incorrect because atom X would still be heavier by five protons.

5. **(5) the solar system** (Application) The structure of the atom is most similar to the solar system, with the nucleus in the position of the sun and the electrons like the planets orbiting the sun. None of the other options involves objects in orbit around another object.

6. **(3) a hydrogen atom and a chlorine atom sharing a pair of electrons** (Application) This is correct because it describes a covalent bond between hydrogen and chlorine atoms. Option (1) is incorrect because the carbon is still just one element. Options (2), (4), and (5) are incorrect because they describe mixtures.

7. **(3) are present in very few compounds** (Comprehension) If an atom does not bond easily with other atoms, it cannot form many compounds. Option (1) is incorrect because it is clear from the information given that all atoms have electrons. Options (2) and (5) are incorrect because the passage does not indicate that one kind of bond is more likely to form than the other. Option (4) is incorrect because water molecules contain bonds.

8. **(2) Electrons are transferred from one of the atoms to another.** (Comprehension) Since ionic bonds involve the transfer of electrons, and sodium chloride contains ionic bonds, electrons must be transferred in sodium chloride. Option (1) is incorrect because sodium and chlorine are ionically bound. Option (3) is incorrect because covalent, not ionic, bonds involve the sharing of electrons. There is no evidence given to support options (4) and (5).

GED Mini-Test: Lesson 13 (Pages 156–157)
1. **(3) atomic number and properties** (Comprehension) This is stated in the second paragraph. Options (1) and (5) are incorrect because atomic size is not the basis of the periodic table. Options (2) and (4) are incorrect because the number of electrons is not the basis of the periodic table.

2. **(2) neon (Ne), argon (Ar), krypton (Kr)** (Comprehension) This is correct because these elements are all in the same family (or column), group VIIIB. The elements in options (1), (3), (4), and (5) are not all members of the same family. If you selected option (5), you confused elements in the same period (row) with elements in the same group (column).

3. **(3) potassium (K)** (Analysis) According to the passage, in the horizontal rows, or periods, elements are arranged in order of increasing atomic number. The larger the atomic number, the more protons there are in an atom's nucleus. This increases its atomic mass. Of the elements listed, potassium has the fewest protons, 19. Thus potassium has the smallest atomic number.

4. **(4) Elements in group VIB are nonmetals.** (Analysis) Groups run in vertical rows. A heavy zigzag line separates the metals and nonmetals. This zigzag line separates polonium, Po, from the rest of group VIB. Since polonium is to the left of the zigzag line, it is a metal, not a nonmetal. All the other options are supported by the passage or periodic table.

5. **(1) group I** (Application) This element is silvery, like most metals. It causes an explosion when it is dropped into water. This is a violent reaction, which is typical of

UNIT 3

elements in group I. Option (2) is incorrect because there is no mention of a salt. Option (3) is incorrect because there is no description of oxygen-containing compounds. Option (4) is incorrect because there is no mention of acids. Option (5) is incorrect because group VIII elements are nonreactive and would not cause an explosion.

6. **(2) group II** (Application) This element forms Epsom salts. Salts are only mentioned in reference to group II elements. The other options are incorrect because they are not described as forming salts. If you answered option (3), you were misled by the mention of oxygen. However, only one compound was described in the question, and transition elements form more than one compound with oxygen.

7. **(5) group VIII** (Application) Elements in group VIII, inert gases, rarely take part in chemical reactions. Their presence in light bulbs reduces the wear on the filament and makes the bulb last longer. All other options indicate that the elements in them will react to one degree or another.

Lesson 14
GED Practice: Drawing Conclusions (Page 159)
1. **(1) Chemical reactions involve substances changing into other substances.** (Evaluation) Since in chemical reactions you start out with reactants and end up with products, you can conclude that substances are changing. Option (2) is not true. Options (3), (4), and (5) may be true in some cases, but they are not supported by the information in the passage.

2. **(4) CO_2 is a product of the chemical reaction.** (Evaluation) Since CO_2 is on the right side of the arrow, it is a product of the chemical reaction. Option (1) is incorrect because C is a reactant. Options (2) and (3) may be true but are not supported by the information provided. Option (5) is the opposite of the correct answer.

GED Practice: Chemical Reactions (Pages 160–161)
1. **(4) energy needed to start a reaction** (Comprehension) According to the passage, chemical reactions are sometimes started by the application of energy from an outside source, called activation energy. The other options are therefore incorrect.

2. **(4) exploding dynamite** (Application) Exploding dynamite is a reaction in which energy is released, an exothermic reaction. Options (1), (3), and (5) are changes of state, not chemical reactions. Option (2) is an endothermic reaction since heat is absorbed when something is cooked.

3. **(1) Exothermic reactions can be more useful for the energy they release than for their products.** (Evaluation) The purpose of burning fuels, an exothermic reaction, is to release thermal energy for human use. Option (2) is incorrect because endothermic reactions absorb, not release, energy. Option (3) is not true; new bonds can form in exothermic reactions. Option (4) is a change of state, not a chemical reaction. Option (5) is not true, according to the passage.

4. **(1) During the process of rusting, small amounts of thermal energy are released.** (Analysis) Since the release of energy characterizes an exothermic reaction, rusting is an exothermic reaction. Option (2) is not related only to exothermic reactions. Options (3) and (5) are true but do not support the conclusion. Option (4) would support the conclusion that rusting is an endothermic reaction.

5. **(2) Atoms are combining to form molecules.** (Comprehension) When hydrogen atoms and oxygen atoms combine, they form molecules of water, H_2O. Option (1) is incorrect because it describes the process of breaking down a molecule. Option (3) is not true; atoms do not change into other atoms in a chemical reaction. Option (4) is not true; they are undergoing a chemical change. Option (5) is not true; oxygen is a reactant.

6. **(3) It is activation energy.** (Application) Without energy from the sun, photosynthesis would not occur. Options (1) and (2) are incorrect because sunlight is not among the reactants and products described in the item. There is no information given to support options (4) and (5), and they are not true.

7. **(3) the change of one or more substances into a new substance with different properties** (Comprehension) This matches the description of a chemical reaction at the beginning of the passage. Option (1) is incorrect because changes of state do not result in new substances; they merely change

the form of a substance from gas to liquid to solid. Option (2) is also a physical rather than a chemical change. Option (4) may or may not be true of any given reaction. Option (5) is incorrect because size of a substance is not part of the definition of a chemical reaction.

8. **(2) a reaction in which thermal energy is absorbed** (Comprehension) According to the passage, the absorption of thermal energy is part of an endothermic reaction. Options (1) and (3) are incorrect because they contradict the correct definition. Options (4) and (5) are incorrect because they apply to exothermic reactions as well as endothermic reactions.

9. **(2) Hydrogen combines with oxygen to form water.** (Application) Chemical reactions involve the forming of new substances, in this case, water from hydrogen and oxygen. Options (1) and (5) involve physical, not chemical, changes. Options (3) and (4) involve changes in state for water, which are physical changes. Physical changes do not result in new substances.

GED Review: Lesson 14 (Pages 162–163)

1. **(2) The solubility of a gas in liquid decreases as temperature increases.** (Analysis) Options (1), (3), and (5) are true statements, but they do not explain the situation, nor are they all covered in the passage. Option (4) is incorrect because it is an untrue statement.

2. **(5) Stirring causes molecules to move and spread apart more quickly.** (Evaluation) Stirring moves molecules around, causing the rate of solution to increase. Option (1) is incorrect because stirring will not significantly affect the water temperature. Option (2) is incorrect because stirring does not increase the amount of salt that eventually dissolves; it increases the rate at which the salt dissolves. Options (3) and (4) are incorrect because stirring does not change the amount of matter in the container.

3. **(4) the solute** (Application) Since oxygen is dissolved in water, it is a solute. The water and oxygen together are the solution, option (1). The water alone is the solvent, option (2). Option (3) is incorrect since the oxygen is a dissolved gas. Option (5) is wrong because oxygen is dissolved in the liquid water.

4. **(2) It dissolves in water to produce OH⁻ ions.** (Comprehension) This could indicate that the substance is a base. Option (1) is incorrect because acids combine with bases to produce salts. Options (3) and (5) are incorrect because these properties are true if the acid is strong. Option (4) is incorrect because all acids have a pH lower than that of water.

5. **(3) It contains a base.** (Evaluation) This is correct because bases neutralize acids. Option (1) is incorrect because a neutralization reaction produces a salt. Options (2) and (4) are incorrect because they are properties of acids. Option (5) is incorrect because how fast the antacid dissolves does not depend on its ability to neutralize acids.

6. **(4) sulfuric acid, citric acid, pure water, sodium hydroxide** (Comprehension) This is correct because these compounds have been identified as strong acid, weak acid, neutral substance, and strong base, in that order. Options (1), (2), and (3) are not in order. In option (5) the correct order is exactly reversed and reads from highest to lowest.

7. **(3) 7** (Comprehension) This is correct because both salt and water are neutral substances. Options (1) and (2) are incorrect because they are pH values of acids, and options (4) and (5) are incorrect because they are pH values of bases.

8. **(5) a salt** (Application) The passage states that the reaction between an acid and a base produces water and a salt. Options (1), (3), and (4) are incorrect because salts are neutral compounds (pH = 7), not acids. Option (2) is incorrect because a salt is not a base.

GED Mini-Test: Lesson 14 (Pages 164–165)

1. **(1) provide an acid for sodium bicarbonate to react with** (Comprehension) Option (2) is incorrect because sodium bicarbonate breaks down to form carbon dioxide. Options (3) and (4) are incorrect because carbon dioxide is a product of the reaction between sodium bicarbonate and an acid. Option (5) is incorrect because sodium bicarbonate is one of the substances in baking powder to begin with.

2. **(4) It contains an acid.** (Evaluation) This is correct because the passage states that sodium bicarbonate reacts with acids to form

UNIT 3

Answers and Explanations

301

carbon dioxide and water. The other options are incorrect because the passage includes no other conditions that would cause carbon dioxide and water to be produced from sodium bicarbonate.

3. **(2) The Chemistry of Baking Powder** (Comprehension) The passage covers both the chemical composition and reactions associated with baking powder; in other words, it is about chemistry. Options (1) and (5) refer to supporting details of the passage. Option (3) is incorrect because other chemicals common in kitchens besides baking powder are not mentioned. Option (4) is not covered in the passage.

4. **(5) carbon dioxide** (Analysis) This is correct because it is logical that a gas produced would cause the cake to rise. Options (1), (3), and (4) are incorrect because they are not gases, and options (1) and (4) are not produced when sodium bicarbonate reacts. Option (2) is a gas, but there is no mention of oxygen in the passage.

5. **(3) Moisture in the air reacts with the tartrate.** (Analysis) This is correct because tartrate plus water produces acid, which in turn reacts with the sodium bicarbonate in baking powder to release carbon dioxide gas. Option (1) is incorrect because heat causes sodium bicarbonate to break down. Options (2), (4), and (5) are incorrect because no mention is made of reactions involving oxygen.

6. **(1) coke** (Comprehension) Since coke is used up in the process, more must be added to keep it going. Options (2) and (3) are produced again and again, and need not be added. Option (4) makes no sense, since pure iron is the desired product of the reactions. Option (5) is not needed since oxygen is available in the air.

7. **(5) coke and carbon dioxide** (Comprehension) The flow chart shows that coke and carbon dioxide react to produce carbon monoxide. No other steps produce carbon monoxide.

8. **(1) Carbon monoxide reacts with hematite.** (Analysis) The diagram shows that hematite and carbon monoxide react forming iron and carbon dioxide. Option (2) and (3) are incorrect because hematite does not react with coke or carbon dioxide. Option (4) and (5) are incorrect because iron is a product, not a reactant.

9. **(5) provides the oxygen that reacts with coke** (Analysis) Coke reacts with oxygen from air to form carbon dioxide. Option (1) is incorrect because air provides oxygen, not coke. Option (2) is incorrect because no solution forms in this process. Option (3) is incorrect because the passage says that coke burned with air. Option (4) is incorrect because it is carbon monoxide, not air, that reacts with the Fe_2O_3.

Lesson 15
GED Practice: Restating Information (Page 167)
1. **(4) It can be represented by the formula C_3H_8.** (Analysis) The structural formula for propane shows that a propane molecule is made of three atoms of carbon and eight atoms of hydrogen. Option (1) is incorrect because propane contains only carbon and hydrogen. Option (2) is incorrect because propane contains eight atoms of hydrogen. Option (3) is incorrect because propane doesn't contain oxygen. Option (5) is incorrect because propane contains more atoms of hydrogen than carbon.

2. **(5) Ethane has fewer hydrogen atoms than propane.** (Analysis) The structural formula for propane includes eight hydrogen atoms and the diagram of ethane includes six hydrogen atoms. Option (1) is incorrect because propane has three carbon atoms and ethane has two. Option (2) is incorrect because ethane has fewer, not more, hydrogen atoms than propane. Option (3) is incorrect because the formula for ethane is C_2H_6. Option (4) is incorrect because ethane contains different numbers of carbon and hydrogen atoms.

GED Practice: Hydrocarbons (Page 169)
1. **(5) H_2S** (Comprehension) This compound is not an organic compound because it does not contain carbon, and the passage explains that organic compounds contain carbon. Options (1), (2), (3), and (4) are incorrect because they are compounds that contain carbon and thus are organic compounds.

2. **(3) CO_2** (Comprehension) This compound is not a hydrocarbon because it contains oxygen, and the passage explains that hydrocarbons contain only carbon and hydrogen. Options (1), (2), (4), and (5) are incorrect because they are compounds that contain only carbon and hydrogen.

(2) They are both organic compounds and hydrocarbons. (Evaluation) The passage describes the alkane series as the most abundant of the hydrocarbons. Since a hydrocarbon is a special kind of organic compound, the members of the alkane series must be organic compounds also. Option (1) is incorrect because members of the alkane series are organic compounds, not living things. Option (3) is incorrect because the table lists members that are gases and a solid at room temperature. Option (4) is incorrect because the table lists formulas for members having all different numbers of carbon atoms. Option (5) is incorrect because members of the alkane series are made up of only carbon and hydrogen.

4. **(2) Butane boils at a higher temperature than ethane.** (Analysis) The table lists boiling points in order from lowest to highest. The boiling point of butane (−1°C) is higher than that of ethane (−89°C). Option (1) is incorrect because heptane boils at a higher temperature than hexane. Option (3) is incorrect because melting points are not provided. Option (4) is incorrect because, for those series members listed, eicosane contains the most carbon atoms. Option (5) is incorrect because pentane contains five carbon atoms and twelve hydrogen atoms, as compared to four carbon atoms and ten hydrogen atoms for butane.

5. **(1) It is sold in canisters for use in heating.** (Evaluation) This fact is stated in the passage. Option (2) is incorrect because the table reveals that propane has the formula C_3H_8. Option (3) is incorrect because propane contains fewer hydrogen atoms than butane. Option (4) is a fact presented in the passage about pentane, hexane, heptane, and octane, but not about propane. Option (5) is incorrect because propane has a boiling point of −42°C.

6. **(1) C_3H_8** (Application) The fuel that escapes from the container is a gas, and propane, C_3H_8, is a gas at room temperature. Options (2), (3), (4), and (5) are incorrect because these compounds are not gases at room temperature.

7. **(1) It is a liquid at room temperature.** (Comprehension) The table lists hexane as a liquid at room temperature. Options (2) and (4) are incorrect because the formula for hexane is C_6H_{14}. Option (3) is incorrect since the boiling point of hexane is 69°C. Option (5)

is incorrect since hexane contains more hydrogen atoms (14) than carbon atoms (6).

8. **(3) It is a gas at room temperature.** (Evaluation) The table lists octane as a liquid at room temperature, not a gas. Option (1) is incorrect since octane does have a boiling point of 125°C. Option (2) is incorrect since octane along with pentane, hexane, and heptane are found in the gasoline that fuels cars. Option (4) is incorrect because octane's boiling point is higher than that of pentane. Option (5) is incorrect since an octane molecule contains eight carbon atoms and a hexane molecule contains six carbon atoms.

GED Review: Lesson 15 (Pages 170–171)

1. **(4) They are hydrocarbons.** (Evaluation) The passage states that both alkanes and alkenes are hydrocarbon series. Option (1) is true only of alkanes. Option (2) is incorrect because alkanes and alkenes are compounds. Option (3) is incorrect because alkanes and alkenes do not contain calcium. Option (5) is incorrect because alkanes and alkenes contain covalent bonds, not ionic bonds.

2. **(5) Double bonds occur only between the carbon atoms in alkenes.** (Comprehension) The occurrence of double bonds between carbon atoms can be seen in the structural formulas in the table. Options (1), (2), and (4) are not true. Option (3) is incorrect because some alkanes and alkenes do contain the same number of carbon atoms.

3. **(2) C_4H_8** (Comprehension) The structural formula of butene indicates that it consists of four carbon atoms and eight hydrogen atoms. Options (1), (3), (4), and (5) are incorrect since they do not show the correct number of carbon and hydrogen atoms.

4. **(2) has more hydrogen atoms than propene** (Comprehension) Since the chemical formula of propene is C_3H_6, as inferred from its structural formula, propane (C_3H_8) has more hydrogen atoms than propene. Options (1), (3), and (4) are not true. Option (5) is incorrect because temperature is not mentioned in the passage or table.

5. **(4) bonds other than single bonds** (Comprehension) The passage states that unsaturated molecules contain bonds other than single bonds and saturated molecules contain only single bonds. Option (1) is incorrect because both kinds of molecules can

contain hydrogen atoms. Option (2) is only true of saturated molecules. Option (3) is not true because both kinds of molecules contain shared electrons. Option (5) is not true because a molecule cannot contain a reduction reaction, although it may be formed by one.

6. **(1) Saturated hydrocarbons can be produced from unsaturated hydrocarbons through addition reactions.** (Evaluation) The chemical equation shows an addition reaction in which a saturated hydrocarbon is produced from an unsaturated hydrocarbon. Options (2), (3), and (4) are not true. Option (5) is true but is not supported by the information presented.

7. **(1) The product is C_2H_6.** (Evaluation) The product contains two carbon atoms and six hydrogen atoms, so it can be restated as C_2H_6. Option (2) is incorrect since C_2H_6 is the product. Option (3) is incorrect since the product only contains single bonds. Option (4) is incorrect since the only saturated hydrocarbon is the product. Option (5) is incorrect because H_2 is not an unsaturated hydrocarbon.

8. **(3) Double bonding occurs between its carbon atoms.** (Comprehension) The passage states that ethene is an unsaturated hydrocarbon, in which two electrons of one carbon atom are paired with two electrons of another carbon atom to form a double bond. Options (1), (2), (4), and (5) are not supported by the information given and are not true.

GED Mini-Test: Lesson 15 (Pages 172–173)

1. **(2) sugar ferments** (Comprehension) The passage states that ethyl alcohol forms when grain or fruit juice ferments and sugar breaks down. Options (1) and (4) are incorrect since carbon dioxide and grain alcohol (ethyl alcohol) are products of sugar fermenting. Option (3) is incorrect because alcohol has one OH radical and does not take on another one. Option (5) is incorrect because sugar does not lose an OH radical during fermentation.

2. **(1) Grain and fruit juices contain sugar.** (Evaluation) Since the passage states that ethyl alcohol is made by fermenting grain or fruit juices and this process involves breaking down sugar, you can infer that sugar is found in grain and fruit juices. Option (2) is not true because the passage states that radicals stay united during a chemical reaction. Option (3)

is not true because fermentation produces alcohol. Options (4) and (5) are not true.

3. **(3) It contains an OH radical and the elements found in hydrocarbons.** (Application) The passage states that alcohol form when one or more hydrogen atoms in a hydrocarbon are replaced by OH radicals. Thus, alcohols must contain the elements found in hydrocarbons plus OH radicals. Options (1), (2), and (4) are incorrect because many molecules other than alcohols contain carbon, hydrogen, and radicals. Option (5) is not true.

4. **(5) carbon dioxide gas is given off, creating holes in the dough** (Analysis) Since fermentation of sugar produces ethyl alcohol and carbon dioxide gas, the cause of dough rising must have something to do with one of these products. Although option (2) mentions ethyl alcohol, it does not really explain why the dough rises. Option (5) is more reasonable because a gas can expand to form holes in the dough, while liquids expand very little. Options (1) and (3) are not true. Option (4) is not related to the dough's size.

5. **(5) They have different arrangements of atoms.** (Comprehension) The passage states that isomers have the same number and kinds of atoms but different arrangements of atoms and different properties. Therefore, options (1), (2), and (4) are not true. Option (3) is incorrect since two isomers of the hydrocarbon butane are shown.

6. **(3) one carbon atom branches off from the middle carbon atom** (Comprehension) The structural formula shows one carbon atom forming a branched chain in this isomer. Options (1), (4), and (5) are not true, as shown in the diagram. Option (2) is only true of straight-chain butane.

7. **(3) more isomers** (Application) The passage states that the more carbon atoms in a hydrocarbon molecule, the more isomers it can form. Decane has more carbon atoms than pentane, so it is likely to form more isomers. Therefore, options (1), (4), and (5) are incorrect. Option (2), boiling point, cannot be inferred from the information provided.

8. **(1) the straight-chain molecule's less compact arrangement of atoms** (Evaluation) The only factor that can account

for a difference in the way the isomers burn is their only physical difference, a difference in atomic arrangement. Since the isomers don't differ in content, options (2), (3), and (5) are incorrect. Option (4) is incorrect because no mention is made of the branched-chain molecule's higher boiling point.

GED Cumulative Review
Unit 3: Chemistry (Pages 174–176)

1. **(3) gas molecules moving rapidly through less freely-moving liquid molecules** (Analysis) This is correct because gas molecules have more freedom of motion than liquid molecules. Option (1) is incorrect because solid molecules, not gas molecules, move only by vibrating. Option (2) is not a good choice because, although gas molecules could collide with liquid molecules, this would not account for the gas bubbles rising to the top of the liquid. Option (4) is incorrect because no mention is made of forces of attraction between liquids and gases. Option (5) is the reverse of the correct answer.

2. **(4) escape and spread apart** (Application) The passage states that gases will escape from an open container and "disappear." Since their molecules have almost no force of attraction, they will not stay in the tank, option (1), or stay together, option (2). Options (3) and (5) are incorrect because all molecules are constantly in motion.

3. **(5) Molecules of a gas will spread out and fill any container they are in.** (Evaluation) According to the passage, molecules of a gas will move freely and randomly. Thus, they will fill any container in which they are placed. Nothing in the passage supports options (1), (2), (3), and (4).

4. **(1) states of matter and movement of molecules** (Comprehension) This is correct because the passage describes how molecular motion is different for gases, liquids, and solids. Options (2) and (5) are incorrect because no mention of temperature is made in the passage. Options (3) and (4) are incorrect because no mention of molecular size is made.

5. **(2) movement of molecules increases** (Analysis) Because the passage states that molecular motion is greatest for a gas and least for a solid, you can conclude that the movement of molecules must increase as temperature increases. Option (1) is opposite to the correct answer. Options (3) and (4) are opposite to the effects of heating. Option (5) is incorrect because the passage says nothing about how quickly matter changes state.

6. **(5) molecules in solids are held together by forces of attraction** (Application) Rocks are solids, and solids have definite shapes because forces of attraction among their molecules hold them tightly in place. Therefore, option (1) is not true. Options (2) and (4) do not apply to solids. As all molecules are in constant motion, option (3) is not the reason solids have shapes.

7. **(2) a geologist interested in estimating the age of rock samples** (Application) By finding out the amount of radioactive material compared to decayed material in a rock sample, geologists can estimate the age of the rock. The other activities would not make use of radioactive half-life.

8. **(3) After 22,920 years, 1/16 gram of carbon-14 will remain of the original 1 gram.** (Evaluation) The diagram shows that every 5,730 years, half of the carbon-14 has decayed. At 17,190 years, 1/8 gram is left. After another 5,730 years, or 22,920 years altogether, half of 1/8, or 1/16, gram would be left. Option (1) is incorrect because 1/16 gram would be left. Option (2) is incorrect because 1/8 gram remains after 17,190 years. Option (4) is true, but it is not supported by the information provided. Option (5) is incorrect because the passage indicates that the number of protons and neutrons affects the radioactivity of an element.

9. **(4) an unstable nucleus** (Analysis) If a radioactive atom gives off particles until the nucleus is stable, the inference is that an unstable nucleus causes radioactivity. Options (1) and (2) are incorrect because it is the balance between the numbers, not the actual numbers, that causes an atom to be radioactive. Option (3) is not supported by the passage, so it is incorrect. Option (5) is a result of an unstable nucleus, or radioactivity, not a cause, so it is incorrect.

10. **(5) Calcium carbonate is not soluble in water.** (Analysis) The passage states that because calcium carbonate is not soluble in water; it settles out of its solution. Options (1) and (2) are not supported by the passage. Options (3) and (4) are not true.

11. **(4) Calcium chloride and sodium carbonate are soluble in water.** (Analysis) Since calcium chloride and sodium carbonate form solutions with water, they must be soluble in water. Option (1) is a fact stated in the passage. Option (2) is not true. Options (3) and (5) cannot be assumed based on the information presented in the passage.

12. **(2) Sodium chloride is soluble in water.** (Analysis) The passage states that $CaCO_3$ precipitates out because it is not soluble in water. Thus you can conclude that NaCl does not precipitate out because it is soluble in water. Option (1) is incorrect because Na^+ and Cl^- ions form NaCl. Option (3) is incorrect because there is nothing in the passage to indicate how many ions are present. Options (4) and (5) are incorrect because the precipitate is $CaCO_3$, which does not contain any Na^+ ions or Cl^- ions.

13. **(5) Chlorine and sodium** (Analysis) In their outermost energy levels, chlorine has seven electrons and sodium has one, making a total of eight. These two atoms do react with one another. Sodium gives up its one electron to chlorine, forming very stable sodium and chlorine atoms. We know this compound as sodium chloride, or table salt. Options (1), (2), and (3) would all produce unfilled outer energy levels and are not the atoms likely to react most easily. Option (4) includes neon, whose outer energy level is already full, thus it is not likely to react with any atom.

UNIT 4: PHYSICS
Lesson 16
GED Practice: Identifying the Main Idea (Page 181)

1. **(3) How you view motion depends on your frame of reference.** (Comprehension) The general idea of the passage is how frames of reference affect how motion is viewed. Options (1) and (5) are supporting details. Option (2) is implied in the last sentence but is a supporting detail, not the main idea. Option (4) can be true, but it is not the main idea.

2. **(2) Motion Depends on Your Frame of Reference** (Comprehension) The main topic of the passage which makes the best title is the connection between motion and frame of reference. Option (1) is not mentioned in the passage. Option (3) is too general to be the best title. Although trains are mentioned in the supporting details, option (4) is not the subject of the passage. While the passage answers this question, option (5) covers only a detail of the passage.

3. **(4) Two observers have different frames of reference, so their observations of motion differ.** (Comprehension) Option (4) is the only supporting detail listed. Options (1) and (2) are not mentioned in the passage. Options (3) and (5) are not true.

4. **(2) Your frame of reference is the other car which you believe to be motionless; therefore, you must be moving.** (Evaluation) As the other car runs backward, it is farther back in relation to you. If you are assuming that it is stopped, the only explanation is that you are moving forward. Quickly, however, your frame of reference shifts and you realize that the other car has moved. Options (1) and (4) are factors in your first impression, that you are moving, but do not fully explain the situation. Option (3) is untrue because you have not moved. Option (5) is a factor that helps you see that you have not moved—you are still by the sidewalk, not in the intersection—but does not explain the situation.

GED Practice: Moving Objects (Pages 182–183)

1. **(3) 10 meters east** (Analysis) Displacement is a measure of both the distance and direction traveled. Option (3) is the only option that shows the correct distance (10 meters) and direction (north) as shown on the diagram. Option (1) is the distance. Options (2) and (5) are incorrect in terms of length or direction. Option (4) is not true.

2. **(1) 10 meters** (Comprehension) The passage states and the diagram shows that the man traveled a total distance of 10 meters. As a result, option (2) is incorrect. Option (3) is approximately equal to the man's displacement, not his distance. Option (4) is not true, since both distances are 10 meters. The solid arrow showing the man's displacement is shorter than the dotted lines showing his distance, so option (5) is incorrect.

3. **(4) only displacement includes the direction traveled** (Comprehension) Displacement is a measure of both the distance and the direction traveled, whereas distance does not include direction. As a result, options (1), (2), (3), and (5) are not true.

UNIT 4

4. **(2) A and B** (Comprehension) Both statements A and B give information included in the paragraph. Statement C is a generalization, not a supporting detail.

5. **(1) Displacement indicates both the direction and how far an object traveled.** (Comprehension) The main topic of the paragraph is displacement. Option (2) is not true. Options (3) and (4) are supporting details. Option (5) is not mentioned in the passage.

6. **(2) his displacement is zero** (Application) The passage states that when a moving object ends up where it started, it has no displacement. Options (1) and (3) are incorrect because, although the man's starting and ending points are the same, he has still traveled a path that has a length, so his distance traveled is not zero. Option (4) is incorrect because the man's distance traveled, not his displacement, is the length of his circular path. Since the distance is a numerical quantity and displacement includes direction, they cannot be compared directly, so option (5) is incorrect.

7. **(2) 10 meters east** (Application) Displacement is the distance and direction from the starting point to the ending point. After following the path described, the person would be 10 meters east of the starting point. All other options are incorrect calculations of either the distance, the direction, or both.

8. **(5) 60 meters** (Application) The total distance the person traveled equals 30 meters plus 5 meters plus 20 meters plus 5 meters, or 60 meters. All the other options are miscalculations.

GED Review: Lesson 16 (Pages 184–185)

1. **(4) 120 miles** (Comprehension) The first graph shows that the car had traveled a distance of 120 miles after 3 hours time. Therefore, options (1), (2), and (3) are incorrect distance values. Option (5) is a speed, not a distance.

2. **(2) Graphs are one way to describe an object's motion.** (Comprehension) The general topic of the paragraph is the use of graphs to show motion. Options (1) and (5) are supporting details. Option (3) is not true. Option (4) tells where information can be found in the graphs, so it is a supporting detail.

3. **(2) It is constant for 4 hours.** (Evaluation) The second graph shows that the car's speed was 40 miles per hour for all 4 hours. Therefore, options (3), (4), and (5) are not true. Since speed is given in miles per hour, it must be related to time, so option (1) is incorrect.

4. **(5) During the 4 hours graphed, the car made no stops.** (Evaluation) As the second graph shows a constant speed of 40 miles per hour, the car could not have stopped. Option (1) is incorrect because you cannot conclude that all speed is constant just because the speed of the car was constant. Option (2) is incorrect since the fact that speed is given in miles per hour indicates that speed is related to distance. Option (3) is incorrect since it took the car 4 hours to cover 160 miles. Since the car did not slow to a speed of 0 miles per hour after 4 hours, it is unlikely that option (4) is true.

5. **(4) The line would become horizontal at 3 hours.** (Evaluation) The top graph shows the distance the car travels over time. If the car stops moving, the distance does not change, so the line levels off and becomes horizontal. Option (1) is incorrect because a downward turn of the line would indicate a loss of distance. Options (2) and (5) are incorrect because the line would rise more steeply if the car started to move faster, not if it stopped. Option (3) is incorrect because the car would still be at a distance of 120 miles after 3 hours, and the line must continue to show that.

6. **(2) Speed is the distance traveled per unit of time.** (Comprehension) The main idea of the paragraph is the definition of speed. Options (1) and (4) are supporting details. Option (3) is not true. Option (5) is the main idea of the second paragraph.

7. **(1) only velocity describes direction** (Comprehension) Speed describes a rate of motion, whereas velocity describes both rate of motion and the direction an object moves. Therefore, options (2), (3), and (4) are incorrect. Since both velocity and speed describe distance divided by time, option (5) is not true.

8. **(3) 4 kilometers per hour** (Application) Using the equation, speed is calculated as 12 kilometers divided by 3 hours = 4 kilometers per hour. Therefore, options (1) and (5) are incorrect. Option (2) is incorrect for speed and includes the hiker's direction, which is not included in speed. Option (4) is the hiker's velocity.

9. **(5) 1 hour late** (Application) Using the equation to calculate how long the trip will take, time = distance/speed = 400 kilometers divided by 80 kilometers per hour = 5 hours. She will arrive 5 hours after departure, or at 7 P.M., which is 1 hour late. As a result, options (1), (2), (3), and (4) are incorrect.

10. **(2) 46 miles per hour east** (Application) The driver was headed east on Route 3 between 11:00 A.M. and noon. According to the map, the distance is 46 miles, so the driver's speed was 46 miles per hour, and the direction was east. Thus the velocity was 46 miles per hour east. Option (1) gives the correct speed, but the wrong direction. Option (3) gives the incorrect speed and incorrect direction. Option (4) gives the incorrect speed, but the correct direction. Option (5) gives the incorrect speed and no direction.

GED Mini-Test: Lesson 16 (Pages 186–187)

1. **(1) A runner whose speed is decreasing is accelerating.** (Evaluation) Since acceleration is any change in speed, direction, or both, a decreasing speed is acceleration. Since acceleration is the rate of change of velocity, option (2) is not true. Option (3) is not true because a change in direction is acceleration. Option (4) is incorrect because it describes two cars with different velocities, not different accelerations. Option (5) doesn't make sense, since there is an equation for calculating different accelerations.

2. **(4) Acceleration is any change in speed, direction, or both.** (Comprehension) The main idea of the passage is the definition of acceleration. Options (1), (2), (3), and (5) are supporting details.

3. **(5) B and C only** (Application) The passage states that acceleration involves a change in speed, direction, or both. The objects described in Statements B and C are changing their direction or speed, so they are both accelerating. As a result, options (2) and (3) are incorrect. Options (1) and (4) are incorrect because the object in Statement A has a constant velocity. If there is no change in the velocity, there is no acceleration.

4. **(3) 1 meter per second^2** (Application) Using the equation, acceleration = (5 meters per second – 2 meters per second)/3 seconds = 1 meter per second^2. As a result, options (1), (2), (4), and (5) are incorrect.

5. **(4) How you view relative speed depends on the speeds you are used to.** (Comprehension) The main topic of the paragraph is that what seems fast or slow to you depends upon the speeds you are used to. Options (1) and (2) are supporting details. Although option (3) is supported by the paragraph, it does not include the idea that what you are used to influences your definition of speed. Option (5) is not necessarily true, and it is not mentioned in the paragraph.

6. **(2) falcon, race horse, human, caterpilla** (Analysis) The speeds in kilometers per hour mentioned in the paragraph are as follows: falcon, 160; race horse, 70; human, 25; caterpillar, 0.005. Option (2) is the only optio that lists the animals from fastest to slowest. Therefore, options (1), (3), (4), and (5) are incorrect.

7. **(3) a caterpillar** (Application) The speed of a caterpillar is the only speed in the paragraph that is less than that of the sloth. Options (1) (4), and (5) are incorrect since they include animals with speeds faster than that of the sloth. Option (2) is incorrect since the sloth is faster than one of the animals mentioned in the passage.

8. **(4) There is no minimum speed above which all speeds are considered fast.** (Evaluation) Since the paragraph suggests that "fast" is a relative term that depends on what you are used to, there can be no specific speed that is a fast speed. As a result, options (1) and (2) are incorrect. Options (3) and (5) are not true.

9. **(4) the backward "kick" when a soldier fires a rifle** (Application) When the rifle is fired, the gunpowder explodes, sending the bullet out the rifle barrel. This action force causes a reaction that pushes the rifle back, causing a "kick." Because a person is so much larger than a bullet, the kick does not move the person very far. In all the other options, there is an action force: the hot gases push against the rock, the wind pushes against the kite, the force of the bat pushes against the ball, and the swimmer's arm and hand push against the water; all causing a reaction.

Lesson 17

GED Practice: Making Judgments (Page 189)

1. **(5) a bucket of blocks requiring a force of 20N that goes on a shelf 0.1 meter high** (Evaluation) To answer this question, you must figure out the amount of work involved in putting away each toy. Do this by multiplying the weight of the object by the distance it must be lifted. Thus the amount of work involved is 6J for option (1), 6J for option (2), 12J for option (3), 15J for option (4), and 2J for option (5). Putting away the bucket of blocks requires the least amount of work (2J).

2. **(2) Reduce the distance over which the weight is lifted by one-third.** (Evaluation) If the distance is reduced by one-third, then the new distance is two-thirds of the original distance. Using the equation, if work = force × distance, then force × 2/3(distance) = 2/3(work), or a reduction in work by one-third. Tripling the weight, option (2), or tripling the distance, option (5), would triple the work. Reducing the weight by two-thirds, option (3), would reduce the work by two-thirds. Reducing both the weight and distance by one-third, option (4), would reduce the work by five-ninths, because 2/3(force) × 2/3(distance) = 4/9(work)

3. **(4) Your new job requires you to transport heavy supplies in your car.** (Application) Increasing the horsepower of the car's engine will help you carry a heavier load, such as heavy supplies. While adding children to the car, option (5), does increase the load, children are not very heavy, and so the increase in load would be slight. Options (1) and (3) are not related to a car's horsepower. Option (2) would be a good reason to buy a car with a lower-horsepower engine, not a higher-horsepower engine.

GED Practice: Motion (Pages 190–191)

1. **(2) large engine and lightweight body** (Evaluation) The large engine provides a lot of force, and the lightweight body has little mass. This combination makes possible rapid acceleration, which is desirable for a racing car. Options (1), (3), and (5) are incorrect because a small engine would not provide enough force for rapid acceleration. Option (4) is incorrect because the heavy body would decrease the amount of acceleration the large engine could provide.

2. **(4) the force of gravity** (Analysis) Gravity from a celestial body is the most likely force to affect a spacecraft in outer space. Option (1) is incorrect because the spacecraft is not using fuel in outer space. Option (2) might warm the spacecraft, but will not cause a change of direction. Option (3) is incorrect because the force of friction is absent in outer space where there is no matter. Option (5) is incorrect because acceleration would describe a change in direction, but it is not a cause for such a change.

3. **(3) The acceleration of the first ball will be twice that of the second.** (Analysis) According to the equation, force equals mass times acceleration. Acceleration is expressed in units of meters per second^2. Thus, the acceleration of the first ball will be 4 meters per second^2. The second ball's acceleration will be 2 meters per second^2. The remaining options indicate a misuse of the formula.

4. **(5) A car traveling at 40 miles per hour goes around a curve at the same speed.** (Application) This is correct because force is required to change the direction of motion. All the other options are incorrect because they describe either objects at rest or objects continuing in motion in a straight line.

5. **(1) A only** (Application) By changing the force applied to the ball, a pitcher (Statement A) can alter its acceleration, which demonstrates Newton's Second Law of Motion. The other options include Statements B and C, which show inertia, Newton's First Law of Motion.

6. **(2) A package on the seat of a car going 60 miles per hour slides forward when the car stops suddenly.** (Application) This is correct because the package keeps moving forward even though the car stops. It stays in motion. Option (1) is incorrect because it is related to Newton's second law, which is concerned with force and acceleration. Options (3), (4), and (5) are incorrect. While they describe types of motion, these options do not demonstrate an object remaining in motion or at rest (Newton's first law).

7. **(1) Small players can accelerate quickly, while large players can apply force to stop the motion of opponents.** (Evaluation) This explanation is based on Newton's second law. Option (5) is a true statement according

UNIT 4

to Newton's second law, but it does not explain the strategy. Option (2) is not necessarily true. Options (3) and (4) may or may not be true, but they do not explain the strategy.

8. **(4) mass, force, and acceleration** (Comprehension) Newton's Second Law of Motion states that an object (<u>mass</u>) will <u>accelerate</u> in the direction of the <u>force</u> that acts on it. The other options list only two of the three factors or list an incorrect factor.

GED Review: Lesson 17 (Pages 192–193)

1. **(3) a car parked on a hill** (Application) This is an example of potential energy because, if the brake were released, the car would roll down the hill. The other options are all examples of things in motion, which have kinetic energy rather than potential energy.

2. **(2) a turning ferris wheel** (Application) Since the ferris wheel is in motion, it has kinetic energy. The other options are examples of things at rest, which have potential energy rather than kinetic energy.

3. **(5) It has kinetic energy during lifting and potential energy on the table.** (Evaluation) Kinetic energy is the energy of motion, which the rock has while being lifted. Potential energy is the energy of position, which the rock has while sitting on a table. Therefore, option (3) is not true. Since all matter, whether moving or sitting, has energy, options (1) and (4) are not true. Option (2) is not true because the rock gains potential energy when it is placed on the table.

4. **(2) The ball's energy changes form.** (Analysis) The paragraph states that energy is never used up; it only changes form. Therefore, when the ball stops moving, its energy changes form, and option (1) is not true. Option (3) is incorrect because the ball's kinetic energy becomes potential energy. Option (4) is not supported by the information in the paragraph. Option (5) is incorrect because energy is the ability to move or change matter; it is not matter itself.

5. **(1) The cars gain potential energy gradually as they move higher.** (Analysis) The chain that lifts the roller coaster cars transfers energy steadily to the cars. The potential energy increases gradually, not just at the top of the hill, so option (2) is incorrect. The cars move slowly throughout their ride to the top, so their kinetic energy does not

change. Therefore, options (3) and (4) are incorrect. Option (5) is incorrect because energy is transferred from the chain to the cars, not the other way around.

6. **(3) C only** (Application) Potential energy is changed into kinetic energy as something fal and gains speed. At point A, the cars are moving up the hill, so kinetic energy is changing to potential energy. At point B, the cars are at the top of the hill where they hav the maximum potential energy, but this energy does not change into kinetic energy until the cars begin to move down the hill.

7. **(3) Some of the kinetic energy of the falling water changes to heat energy when it hits the bottom of the falls.** (Analysis) The falling water strikes rocks a the base of the falls, causing some of its kinetic energy to be converted into heat energy and raising the temperature of the water at the bottom slightly. Option (1) is incorrect because it is not likely that underwater rocks would give off heat energ Option (2) is incorrect because the amount energy from the sun reaching the base of th falls would be about the same as the amoun reaching the top. Option (4) is the opposite what happens. Option (5) is incorrect because the water gains heat energy; it doe not lose it.

8. **(5) Exercise your whole body to change kinetic energy into heat energy.** (Evaluation) The idea here is to use motion t generate heat. Options (1) and (2) do not generate heat, so they can be eliminated. Options (3), (4), and (5) all involve changing kinetic energy into heat energy, so all are possible. However, the more kinetic energy involved, the more heat energy will be generated. Therefore, it follows that exercisi your whole body will generate the most heat energy, option (5).

9. **(2) popcorn popping** (Application) As popcorn pops, the kernels move and collide with one another. This is most similar to the movement of molecules in a heated substanc Options (1), (3), and (4) are steady, even movements not typical of heated molecules. Option (5) is the opposite of what happens t heated molecule.

10. **(2) Heat leaves your hand and is absorbed by the ice.** (Analysis) Option (1) incorrect because "coldness" is just the

absence of heat, not a substance that can flow. Options (3) and (4) are incorrect because the heat transfer from your hand to the ice causes molecules in your hand to lose energy and molecules in the ice to gain energy. Option (5) is not true.

GED Mini-Test: Lesson 17 (Pages 194–195)

1. **(2) the push of hot gases on a piston** (Comprehension) This is the first step in the process that makes the car move. Option (1) is incorrect because burning is a chemical reaction, not a force, although heat from burning gasoline can produce a force. Option (3) is incorrect because hot gases do not act directly on shafts and gears. Options (4) and (5) are incorrect because they are forces that occur later in the process of moving the car.

2. **(2) exerting pressure** (Comprehension) This is correct because the gases push against the pistons as a result of exploding upon ignition. Option (1) is incorrect because burning the gases would require oxygen rather than release it. Option (3) is incorrect because, although heat is transferred to surrounding substances, this is not what powers the car. Option (4) is incorrect because this is how heat energy not used to power the car is wasted. Option (5) has nothing to do with the gasoline engine in a car.

3. **(4) pushing a grocery cart** (Application) This option is correct because it is the only situation in which you are producing a force that acts on an object and causes it to move. Options (1), (2), and (3) do not involve motion. In option (5), which is tricky, you are not producing the force that is moving the ball—you are just allowing gravity to pull it to Earth.

4. **(2) Heat released from many cars raises the temperature of heavily-traveled streets.** (Analysis) All of the other options could be true—although option (1) sounds a little far-fetched—but they are not based on the information provided.

5. **(4) 15 pounds of effort to raise a 300-pound box** (Evaluation) This is correct because the mechanical advantage is 300/15, or 20. The mechanical advantages of the other options are lower. Option (1) is 12, option (2) is 5, option (3) is 10, and option (5) is 13.

6. **(4) 4 meters high and 12 meters long** (Evaluation) Since you want to raise the box 4

meters, you can immediately eliminate options (1) and (5), because the inclined planes are only 3 meters high. To find the best answer among the remaining options, calculate the mechanical advantage of each inclined plane by dividing the length of the slope by its height. The mechanical advantage of option (2) is 1.5. The mechanical advantage of option (3) is 2. The mechanical advantage of option (4) is 3; thus option (4) is correct.

7. **(2) 12** (Application) To find the mechanical advantage, compare the two forces involved. The resistance of 300 pounds, divided by the effort force of 25 pounds, gives a mechanical advantage of 12. The length of the lever is irrelevant in this problem. All other choices represent a misapplication of the formula or a miscalculation in the formula.

Lesson 18
GED Practice: Cause and Effect (Pages 196–197)

1. **(1) The positively-charged toner is attracted to the negatively-charged areas of the drum.** (Analysis) Because the negatively-charged areas of the drum correspond to the document image, this causes the toner to form the pattern of the image on the drum. Option (2) is incorrect because the image on the drum is an electrical image, not a raised image. Option (3) is incorrect because the document and toner never come in contact with one another. Option (4) is incorrect because electricity, not heat, causes the toner to form the image on the drum. Option (5) is incorrect because the image is not traced; it consists of negatively-charged areas.

2. **(4) A blank sheet of copy paper would result.** (Analysis) Since light would reach all areas of the drum, the negative charge would disappear, leaving nothing for the toner to be attracted to. As a result, the copy would be blank. Option (1) is incorrect because the negative charge would be gone. Option (2) is incorrect because the toner and the document never come in contact. Option (3) is incorrect because no toner has been attracted to the drum; therefore no toner appears on the copy. Option (5) is incorrect because the image of the document did not reach the drum.

3. **(2) more speed for the same amount of fuel energy** (Analysis) If the automobile were streamlined, it would have less drag. This means that it would take less force (fuel energy) to move at a particular speed or

distance. Options (1) and (3) are the opposite of what would happen. Option (4) describes an effect that could occur whether or not the car were streamlined. Option (5) is incorrect because there is an effect, option (2).

4. **(1) decreased speed** (Analysis) Since drag slows down moving objects, increasing drag would decrease an object's speed. Option (2) is the opposite of what would occur. Option (3) is incorrect because increased drag means increased friction, which is likely to create rougher movement. No information is given on rate of airflow, so option (4) is incorrect. Option (5) is incorrect because drag is a kind of friction.

GED Practice: Electricity and Magnetism (Page 199)

1. **(2) The second strip is negatively charged.** (Analysis) This is correct because like charges repel each other. If the second strip were positively charged, option (1), it would be attracted to the first strip. Options (3) and (4) may or may not be true, but they do not explain the effect being described. Option (5) is incorrect because it is positively and negatively charged particles, not atoms, that attract and repel each other.

2. **(3) electron** (Comprehension) According to the passage, electrons have a negative charge. Option (1) is incorrect because protons have a positive charge. Option (2) is incorrect because neutrons have a neutral charge. Option (4) is incorrect because atoms are usually neutral; an ion is a charged particle. Option (5) is incorrect because a field is not a particle.

3. **(3) an area of force** (Comprehension) According to the passage, an electric field is an area of force. The other options are all examples of matter, not force.

4. **(3) C only** (Evaluation) The passage states that a force is exerted on any other charged particle. Therefore, only Statement C, an uncharged particle, would not be affected. Options (1), (2), (4), and (5) are incorrect because each one contains at least one charged particle.

5. **(1) The negative and positive ions will attract each other.** (Analysis) This is true because like charges repel and unlike charges attract. Options (2), (4), and (5) are incorrect because they state the opposite. Option (3) may or may not be true, but it does not answer the question.

6. **(4) force of attraction between protons and electrons** (Comprehension) According to the passage, the attraction between protons and electrons helps hold atoms together. The other options do not explain what holds an atom together.

7. **(2) +1** (Analysis) There is one more proton than there are electrons, so the atom would have a positive charge. The number of neutrons does not matter because neutrons have no charge.

8. **(5) increase their force of attraction** (Analysis) Since the strength of an electric field decreases as distance increases, then the strength of the field must increase as distance decreases. Options (1) and (2) are incorrect because the particles' electric charges would not be affected. Option (3) is not mentioned in the passage. Option (4) is the opposite of the effect that would occur.

GED Review: Lesson 18 (Pages 200–201)

1. **(2) Electrons from the carpet move onto your feet, causing you temporarily to have an electric charge.** (Analysis) This is correct because the situation is similar to the rubbing of a balloon on a sleeve. Options (1) and (3) are incorrect because you, not the carpet, receive the shock—so you must have an electric charge as a result of acquired electrons. Option (4) leaves you out of the action entirely, and option (5) takes the concept of voltage out of context to create a senseless answer.

2. **(1) Protons flowing onto an object cause the object to become positively charged.** (Evaluation) This is correct because no mention is made in the passage of protons being able to move and, in fact, they cannot. Options (2) and (5) are supported by the passage because electric current is pushed through wires by voltage, and a change in voltage would cause a change in current. Option (3) could be supported because both balloons would have a negative charge, and like charges repel each other. Option (4) is supported by the analogy between the flow of electricity and the flow of water.

3. **(1) place the balloons on the wall just before the party begins** (Analysis) This option is correct because this would leave little time for the balloons to lose their negative charge and come loose from the wall. Option (3) would work exactly against this idea.

Options (2), (4), and (5) would not help the balloons stick to the wall.

4. **(2) both make possible the flow of a substance from one place to another** (Comprehension) Voltage pushes electrons through a wire just as water pressure pushes water through a hose. Options (1), (3), and (4) are incorrect because they apply only to voltage. Option (5) is incorrect because voltage is supplied by a battery—and water pressure has nothing to do with powering a battery.

5. **(2) It would be cut in half.** (Analysis) This is correct because the formula $V = I \times R$ shows that lowering voltage by one-half (from 8V to 4V) would lower current similarly as long as resistance stays the same. The other options contradict the correct answer.

6. **(2) a decrease in current** (Analysis) This is correct because as resistance increases, current decreases. Options (1) and (4) are incorrect (this is tricky) because a battery made to deliver eight volts can only deliver eight volts. Options (3) and (5) both refer to an increase in current, and thus contradict the correct answer.

GED Mini-Test: Lesson 18 (Pages 202–203)

1. **(2) picking up pieces of scrap metal on the site and depositing them elsewhere on the site** (Evaluation) This is correct because the electromagnet will gain and lose its magnetism as the current is turned on and off—thus it is ideal for picking up metal objects, and then dropping them again. Option (1) is incorrect because there is no way of knowing whether this machine is equipped to travel distances. Option (5) may or may not be true, depending on the relative strengths of this and other machines on the site. Options (3) and (4) are incorrect because the crane's electromagnet would not cause these effects.

2. **(4) An electric current produces a magnetic field.** (Comprehension) Option (1) is true, but it does not answer the question because it does not say anything specific about electricity. Options (2) and (5) are true, but this passage discusses only the production of a magnetic field from electric current, not the reverse. Option (3) fails to specify that the wire must be conducting an electric current.

3. **(3) The needle is responding to the magnetic field produced by the current in the wire.** (Analysis) Option (1) is incorrect because it does not adequately relate cause and effect. Also, once the current is turned off, the needle will again point northward. Option (5) is incorrect because the magnetism of the compass needle was not produced by the current in the wire. Options (2) and (4) do not explain the situation being described.

4. **(5) Magnetism is related to the movement of electrons.** (Evaluation) The correct option is (5) because a flow of electrons (electric current) produces a magnetic field. Options (2) and (4) are not discussed in the passage. There is nothing in the passage to support options (1) and (3).

5. **(4) illustrated the property of magnetism** (Comprehension) Option (3) is possible, but the discovery of magnetite did much more than just reveal the properties of one metal. Option (2) is incorrect because magnetite is not made of pure iron—it is made of an iron-containing compound. Options (1) and (5) are incorrect because the understanding of poles and artificial magnets came much later.

6. **(3) halfway between the poles** (Analysis) The magnetic field of a bar magnet is strongest around the poles, so it is likely to be weakest at the midpoint, which is the point farthest from each pole. Options (1), (2), (4), and (5) are incorrect because they are positions closer to one of the poles.

7. **(3) Compass needles are magnets.** (Evaluation) Options (1) and (2) are possible but not necessarily true; thus, they are not the best choices. Option (4) is incorrect because any magnet must have a north and south pole. Option (5) is incorrect because it would depend upon how the compass needles were lined up—if the north pole of one needle were near the south pole of the other, they would attract each other.

8. **(4) Earth has a magnetic field** (Comprehension) The magnets must be turning so that one of their poles is pointing to one of Earth's magnetic poles. Option (1) is unlikely. Option (2) is true but does not explain the behavior of magnets on Earth. Option (3) cannot be true of all locations north of a magnet. Option (5) is incorrect because the ice caps are not magnetic.

9. **(4) Keep videotapes away from magnetic fields.** (Analysis) A magnetic field can rearrange the metal bits in the tape, which

would damage or destroy the information stored on the tape. While options (1) and (2) are good advice, they are not related to the explanation of how magnetism changes a recording on videotape. Option (3) is not part of the care instructions for videotapes because ordinary metal objects cannot harm the recording. Option (5) is incorrect because it has no effect on the safety of recordings.

Lesson 19
GED Practice: Drawing Conclusions
(Pages 204–205)

1. **(3) Higher-energy electrons are more likely to occur in an accelerator with a long tunnel than in one with a short tunnel.** (Evaluation) The passage indicates that the longer the tunnel, the greater the acceleration and energy of the particle. Therefore, a particle such as an electron in an accelerator with a long tunnel is likely to have more energy than a particle in an accelerator with a short tunnel. Options (1) and (2) are not supported by the passage since the advantages and disadvantages of the two shapes of accelerators are not discussed. Option (4) is incorrect because the passage does not compare the speeds of protons and electrons. Option (5) is incorrect because the passage says nothing about producing electricity.

2. **(1) A silver pipe is likely to have a lower resistance than a plastic pipe.** (Evaluation) Since conductors allow electric current to flow easily through them, they would also tend to have low resistance. Also, since metals tend to be better conductors than nonmetals, silver would be likely to have a lower resistance than plastic. Option (2) is incorrect because the passage does not mention the effect of temperature or how well a substance conducts electricity. Option (3) is incorrect because plastic is a better insulator then silver. Option (4) is incorrect because a glass tube is likely to have a higher resistance than a copper tube. Option (5) is incorrect because electrons move more readily through metals than through nonmetals.

3. **(1) as electrical wire for a lamp** (Application) Since a conductor allows electrical current to easily flow through it, it would make a good electrical wire. Options (2) and (3) are objects in which insulators are used to prevent electric shock. Options (4) and (5) are also objects for which insulators are more appropriate materials than conductors.

4. **(2) aluminum** (Evaluation) You can infer from the passage that insulators have a higher resistance to the flow of electrons tha[n] conductors. Since aluminum is given as an example of a conductor, it would not have a high resistance. Options (1), (3), (4), and (5) are given as examples of insulators and, thu[s] would have a higher resistance than aluminum.

5. **(3) 24 ohms for a toaster that uses 5 am[ps]** **of current in a 120-volt circuit** (Evaluation) To answer this question, you must substitute the numbers given in each option in the formula for Ohm's law, and see [if] the equation is properly solved. Using optio[n] (3) as an example:

$$24 \text{ ohms} = \frac{120 \text{ volts}}{5 \text{ amps}}$$

Since 120 divided by 5 is 24, option (3) is correct. When you do this calculation for the other options, you will find that they are incorrect. The resistance for option (1) is 3 ohms; for option (2), 1.5 ohms; for option (4), 46 ohms; and for option (5), 70 ohms.

6. **(5) Replace a thin steel wire with a thic[k]** **copper wire.** (Application) If the voltage remains the same, any change that decrease[s] the resistance increases the current. A thin[ner] wire has a higher resistance than a thicker wire, and steel has a higher resistance than copper, so replacing a thin steel wire with a thick copper wire decreases the resistance, which increases the current. Options (1), (2) (3), and (4) all are changes that would increase the resistance, which would decrea[se] the current.

GED Practice: Waves (Pages 206–207)

1. **(3) The depth of the trough of a wave is double the distance from the rest position to the crest.** (Evaluation) The diagram shows, and the passage states, that the depth of the trough of a wave is equal to the distance between the rest position and t[he] crest. The other options are all true and are based on information in the passage.

2. **(4) a disturbance that travels through space or matter** (Comprehension) This definition appears in the first paragraph of the passage. Option (1) is incorrect because not all water movements are waves. Option [(2)] is incorrect because it leaves out space.

Answers and Explanatio[ns]

UNIT 4

Options (3) and (5) are incorrect because they do not mention the transfer of energy.

3. **(1) amplitude** (Application) A surfer would be most interested in the amount of energy a wave has to carry him or her to shore. The passage indicates that the greater the amplitude, the greater the energy. Options (2) and (3) refer to properties of waves that would not be a surfer's main interest. Option (4) is incorrect because all waves are disturbances. Option (5) is not an important factor in surfing.

4. **(4) number of crests that pass a given point and unit of time** (Comprehension) Frequency is defined in the second paragraph of the passage. The other options do not describe frequency.

5. **(1) decreased speed** (Analysis) If both wavelength and frequency decrease, it follows that when you multiply them, the resulting speed will also decrease. Option (2) is incorrect because speed is calculated by multiplying wavelength times frequency. If you change either, the speed will change. If both these figures are decreased, it is not possible for speed to increase, option (3). Options (4) and (5) are incorrect because distance is not determined by these two factors.

6. **(2) divide speed by wavelength** (Analysis) Since speed equals wavelength times frequency, to find frequency, you must divide speed by wavelength. Options (1) and (5) are incorrect because you don't know the frequency and are trying to solve for it. Options (3) and (4) are incorrect because they do not calculate frequency.

7. **(4) 18 meters per second** (Application) To find speed, multiply wavelength by frequency ($3 \times 6 = 18$).

8. **(4) Properties of Waves** (Comprehension) Option (4) is the most general of the options and it covers all the supporting details of the passage. Option (1) is not mentioned in the passage. Option (2) is incorrect because wavelength, frequency, and speed, quantities described in the passage, are not wave parts. Option (3) is incorrect because ocean waves are not the only kinds of waves to which the facts in the passage apply. Option (5) describes supporting details.

9. **(2) B only** (Analysis) The paragraph states that the water is disturbed by an up-and-down movement only. Thus, the boat will bob up and down (Statement B) but will not move any significant distance (Statements A and C), making all other options incorrect.

GED Review: Lesson 19 (Pages 208–209)

1. **(3) an accordion being played** (Application) This is correct because it represents a back-and-forth motion along a straight line. The other options are incorrect because they represent up-and-down motion.

2. **(5) tape deck and speaker system** (Application) This is correct because the sound from the speakers could not travel without air. Option (4) is incorrect because the earphones and wires attached to the cassette player would serve as a medium to transmit sound to your ears. The other options are incorrect because they are not affected by a lack of air.

3. **(2) its molecules are too far apart** (Comprehension) The passage states that solids transmit sound best because their molecules are close together. This implies that a substance whose molecules are far apart would transmit poorly. Options (1) and (3) are incorrect because substances with molecules close together carry sound better than substances with molecules far apart. Option (4) is incorrect because an elastic medium is more effective in carrying sound. Option (5) is incorrect because a gas can be any temperature.

4. **(3) Solids transmit sounds best.** (Application) If you answered option (1), you read the statement too quickly—because there is no such thing as a "sound molecule." Option (2) is incorrect because it does not relate to the information in the passage. Option (4) is not discussed in the passage, and the validity of option (5) cannot be determined from the passage.

5. **(5) Sound waves travel more slowly in cold air than in warm air.** (Evaluation) There is always a time lag between seeing the ball hit and hearing the sound, but in cold weather the difference increases. This is because the speed of sound decreases as air temperature decreases. Options (1) and (2), while plausible, are not related to the subject of the passage. Options (3) and (4) are not true.

UNIT 4

6. **(1) sound that travels through the ground will reach your ears before sound that travels through air** (Analysis) This is correct because sound travels faster through solids than through gases. Option (2) does not explain the expression. Options (3), (4), and (5) are not supported by the information provided.

7. **(4) higher in frequency than radio waves** (Comprehension) The passage states that radio waves are lower in frequency than visible light and ultraviolet waves are higher in frequency than visible light. Option (1) is incorrect because both types of waves are invisible. Option (2) cannot be determined from the information given. (Actually, ultraviolet waves are higher in energy.) Option (3) contradicts the correct answer. Option (5) can be disproved by applying the wave equation given in the introductory passage of the lesson. Even without recalling this information, option (5) would not be the best answer because it cannot be determined directly from the information given.

8. **(1) Air is the only medium through which light can travel.** (Evaluation) This is correct because electromagnetic waves do not need any medium through which to travel. Options (2) and (4) are supported by the fact that light can travel without a medium. Option (3) is true because all electromagnetic waves travel at the same speed in a given medium. Option (5) is supported by the fact that radio waves are invisible.

9. **(2) They travel through a vacuum at 186,282 miles per second.** (Evaluation) All electromagnetic waves travel at the same speed, and light travels through a vacuum at 186,282 miles per second. Therefore, infrared waves, a type of electromagnetic waves, also travel at 186,282 miles per second. Microwave ovens primarily produce microwaves, so option (1) is incorrect. Option (3) is incorrect since all electromagnetic waves travel at the same speed. Option (4) is incorrect because only visible light has frequencies between 400 trillion and 750 trillion Hertz. Option (5) is not true.

10. **(4) radio waves** (Comprehension) The passage states that radio waves are below the frequency of light waves which range from 400 trillion to 750 trillion Hertz. All the other options are above 400 trillion Hertz.

11. **(1) Waves of the Electromagnetic Spectrum** (Comprehension) The passage describes several kinds of waves making up the electromagnetic spectrum. Option (2) is not addressed in the passage. Options (3), (4) and (5) are supporting details.

GED Mini-Test: Lesson 19 (Pages 210–211)

1. **(3) 30°** (Analysis) This is correct because light aimed at an angle of incidence of 30° would be reflected at an angle of 30°, totaling the required 60°. Option (1) is incorrect because the light would be reflected at an angle of 60°, thus hitting a target that would form an angle of 120°. Option (2) is incorrect because the light would hit a target forming an angle of 30°. The light in option (4) would be reflected straight back to the sender. Option (5) is incorrect because an incident angle must be between 0° and 90°.

2. **(4) appear fuzzy and blurred** (Application) Option (1) is incorrect because the light would be reflected randomly in many directions, resulting in a less focused signal. Options (2) and (3) are not supported by the information provided. Option (5) is incorrect because the angle of reflection for each ray will depend upon its angle of incidence.

3. **(4) a mix of all the visible colors** (Comprehension) According to the paragraph, white light contains all the colors. Options (1) and (2) are incorrect because white light contains all the colors, not just one color. Option (3) defines black, not white. Option (5) makes no sense—a rainbow is not white.

4. **(3) There are 17,000 different mixtures of the colors in white light.** (Analysis) Although the rainbow shows seven basic colors, these can be mixed in many combinations, resulting in the huge number of colors we can see. Option (1) is contradicted by the paragraph. Option (2) is true, but it does not explain why we can see so many colors. Options (4) are (5) are not true.

5. **(3) Red light is bent the least.** (Evaluation) Since red light is at the opposite end of the rainbow from violet light, as shown in the diagram, red light must be the least bent of all the colors of light. As a result, options (1) and (5) are incorrect. Neither the passage nor the diagram mention the speed of light, so option (2) is incorrect. Since different colors are bent to different angles in the water drop, option (4) is incorrect.

6. **(5) sunlight bends and separates when it passes through water drops** (Analysis) The paragraph and diagram show that rainbows are caused by the bending and separating of white light in water drops. Option (1) is incorrect because red light has the longest wavelength and violet has the shortest. Option (3) is incorrect because light cannot bend water; light waves bend, or refract, in water. There is nothing in the paragraph or diagram to support option (4). Option (2) is true but is not what causes rainbows to form.

7. **(2) The formation of rainbows is due to refraction only.** (Analysis) In addition to being refracted, the light also reflects off the inside of the drop of water. All other options are supported by the passage either by being stated directly or by implication.

GED Cumulative Review
Unit 4: Physics (Pages 212–213)

1. **(2) increase in size** (Comprehension) This is correct because, if a radioactive atom were to change size, it would get smaller as it releases subatomic particles and energy. Options (1), (3), and (4) are incorrect because during the process of radioactive decay, energy and subatomic particles are released as a radioactive isotope changes into another isotope or element. Option (5) is incorrect because radioactive decay is usually accompanied by the release of gamma rays.

2. **(2) an electric field** (Evaluation) This is correct because alpha particles are positively charged and beta particles are negatively charged. There is no evidence from the information given that any of the other options would have an effect on these particles.

3. **(5) It never took place before the twentieth century.** (Evaluation) This is correct because the passage states that fission reactions can occur naturally, so they must have occurred long ago. For the same reason, option (1) is incorrect. Options (2) and (4) are incorrect because a fission reaction is defined as the splitting of an atomic nucleus in which two smaller nuclei (matter) and energy are released. Option (3) is incorrect because fission reactions are controlled in a nuclear reactor.

4. **(2) contaminating the environment** (Analysis) Options (1), (3), and (4), if they happened, would be short-term effects of an accident at a nuclear power plant. Option (2) is correct because the radioactive material released into the environment would continue to decay for a long time. Option (5) is incorrect because there would be a long-term effect, option (2).

5. **(2) a string of decorating lights** (Application) These are often made such that if one bulb is removed, the whole string goes out. In more important electricity uses such as options (1), (3), (4), and (5), parallel circuits are used to ensure that the whole circuit does not fail if one item on it burns out or is removed.

6. **(2) The current continues in all but one path of the circuit.** (Analysis) Because the other lights and appliances still work after the bulb burns out, this indicates that the circuit must be a parallel circuit. Option (1) would happen if it were a series circuit. Options (3) and (5) are incorrect because blown-out fuses and power shortages have the same effect on both kinds of circuits. Option (4) contradicts the conclusion that the kitchen is on a single parallel circuit.

POSTTEST (Pages 216–234)

1. **(4) in large, flat areas** (Analysis) The area with the most tornadoes—more than 4 per 25,000 square kilometers per year—is the central United States, where the land is flat. The mountainous areas of the United States, near the West and East Coasts, have fewer than 2 tornadoes per 25,000 square kilometers per year; therefore option (1) is incorrect. Option (2) is incorrect because along the seacoasts there are generally fewer than 2 tornadoes, except in the Southeast. Option (3) is incorrect because tornadoes are very rare in most northern areas. Option (5) is incorrect because there are more tornadoes over the land, not over the ocean.

2. **(5) Alaska** (Application) In Alaska during the period covered by this map, there were no tornadoes. Option (1) is incorrect because parts of New England have a relatively high number of tornadoes (for example, 5.1 in Massachusetts). Options (2) and (3) are both incorrect because both states have about 4 tornadoes per 25,000 square kilometers per year. Option (4) is incorrect; the Midwest has more tornadoes than the rest of the country.

3. **(1) potassium nitrate** (Comprehension) If you look at the graph, you can see that potassium nitrate has the steepest line, which indicates the greatest change. At 0°C, 13.3 grams of potassium nitrate dissolve, and at 80°C, 200 grams dissolve. This is the largest change shown, so all the other options are incorrect.

4. **(4) cerium sulfate** (Evaluation) Notice that this line slopes downward. The solubility of cerium sulfate decreases as the temperature increases. Therefore, the behavior of cerium sulfate disproves the idea that all solids become more soluble as the water temperature rises. The other options are incorrect because they support the idea.

5. **(4) releasing laboratory-bred sterile males** (Comprehension) This method is described as being used in the Southwest. Option (1) is incorrect because nothing is mentioned about the current use of chemical insecticides. Option (2) is incorrect because it is too expensive. Options (3) and (5) are incorrect because they involve changing the insects in the wild, not in the laboratory.

6. **(2) Treating cattle individually with chemical insecticides was too expensive.** (Evaluation) It was necessary to find a less costly way to control the screwworm. Option (1) is incorrect because the article does not say that chemical insecticides were hard to obtain; they were just too expensive to use. The article does not support option (3). Option (4) is true but was not the reason stated for deciding to try biological control methods. Option (5) is not true. Biological control methods are generally developed by scientists in well-equipped research laboratories, not on farms.

7. **(5) A, B, and C** (Analysis) The author assumes that it is important to protect an agricultural area. Changing the ecology can help the cattle industry by getting rid of a pest (Statement A). The article does not mention disadvantages because the author assumes they are not very important (Statement B). The author criticizes chemical insecticides in the case of the screwworm mostly because of the cost. The author does not say that chemical insecticides are unsuitable in general (Statement C). Therefore, options (1), (2), (3), and (4) are incorrect since they do not include all the assumptions made by the author.

8. **(2) works best on isolated insect populations** (Evaluation) The sterile-male release method described was successful on the island of Curaçao, which is a small, isolated area. When it was used on the mainland, it was less successful. Option (1) is incorrect because it is difficult to apply the method over a wide area like the southwestern United States. Option (3) is incorrect because it is too general a statement to be supported by the article. In some places, chemical insecticides may work better. Option (4) is incorrect because the article holds that the method was successful. Option (5) is incorrect because the article shows that biological control can wipe out an entire population, thereby ending the problem.

9. **(3) decrease in several generations because many fertilized eggs would be seriously defective and would die** (Evaluation) Males would have sperm that could fertilize the eggs, but the fertilized eggs would be defective. This would lower the number of healthy insects born. Options (1) and (2) are incorrect; eggs would still be fertilized, but they would not develop properly. Option (4) is incorrect because some of the eggs would not produce healthy young; the population would decrease. Option (5) is incorrect because many of the fertilized eggs would be defective, and this would not increase the population.

10. **(2) spaying animals to prevent their reproduction** (Application) Spaying animals and sterilizing male insects reduce the number of offspring the species can produce. Option (1) is incorrect because insecticides directly kill the insects and their eggs. Options (3) and (4) are incorrect because they involve adding a new species, not more of the same species. Option (5) is incorrect because it involves directly killing the pest.

11. **(1) 120/80** (Comprehension) The chart indicates a systolic pressure of 120 and a diastolic pressure of 80, expressed as 120/80. Option (2) is incorrect; it reverses the systolic and diastolic readings. Options (3) and (4) are incorrect; they are not pressures indicated by the chart. Option (5) is incorrect because pressure is expressed as one number over another, not a decimal fraction.

12. **(2) When the heart pumps, blood pressure goes up.** (Analysis) The systolic pressure reading, the higher one, measures

the pressure of blood in the arteries right after the heart pumps. The pumping action forces more blood through the arteries and increases pressure. Option (1) is incorrect because it is the opposite of what happens during pumping action. Option (3) is incorrect because the pumping action of the heart causes changes in blood pressure. Options (4) and (5) are incorrect because when the heart relaxes, blood pressure goes down to the diastolic pressure.

13. **(2) the amplitude of seismic waves at the focus of an earthquake** (Comprehension) The Richter scale measures the amplitude of seismic waves where the earthquake starts. Option (1) is incorrect because the focus of an earthquake is deep in Earth's crust, not on the surface. Option (3) is incorrect because the scale measures amplitude, not direction, of seismic waves. Option (4) is incorrect because the scale does not measure the effects of an earthquake. Option (5) is incorrect because the scale measures intensity, not distance.

14. **(4) the effects of an earthquake on a particular place** (Comprehension) The Mercalli scale rates what an earthquake does. Options (1) and (2) are incorrect since the Mercalli scale measures the effects of an earthquake, not the amplitude of seismic waves. Option (3) is only partly correct. The Mercalli scale is used not only in the area over the focus, but in surrounding areas that feel the earthquake as well. Option (5) is incorrect because the Mercalli scale measures effects, not waves.

15. **(3) had 10 times greater amplitude than they had first estimated** (Analysis) On the Richter scale, an increase of 1 point shows that the seismic waves in the earthquake had ten times greater amplitude; the scientists raised the rating when they realized that there was more energy than they had first thought. Option (1) is incorrect because severity is a judgment, which may be based on the Richter scale ratings, but the precise rating is not based on mere judgment. Options (2) and (4) are incorrect because the rating went up 1 point, not down 1 or 2 points. Option (5) is incorrect because the rating went up by 1 on the scale, which means an increase of ten, not of one hundred.

16. **(4) The earthquake caused less damage in Oakland than in San Jose, so the Mercalli rating in Oakland was lower.**

(Analysis) The Mercalli scale rates the effects of an earthquake in a particular place. Therefore, the same earthquake can have different ratings in the different areas that it affects. Options (1) and (2) are incorrect because the Mercalli scale does not measure amplitude of seismic waves. Option (3) is incorrect because an earthquake can have more than two Mercalli ratings. Option (5) is incorrect because the earthquake caused less damage in Oakland.

17. **(5) Call the poison control center.** (Application) When an overdose of medicine has been taken, the correct first-aid action is to call for advice. There are so many types of medicine that treatments for overdoses vary. Option (1) is incorrect because it is not a treatment for swallowed poison. Options (2), (3), and (4) are treatments for swallowed poison but they are not necessarily appropriate when the poison is a medicine.

18. **(1) Open the doors and windows.** (Application) Since carbon monoxide is a deadly gas, the person who finds the victim must first get fresh air into the area. Otherwise the rescuer might be overcome as well. Options (2) and (4) are not suitable treatments for inhaled poisons. Option (3) should be done after doors and windows are open and after the victim receives artificial respiration, if necessary. Option (5) is part of the first-aid treatment for inhaled poison, but it is the second step after making sure there is fresh air.

19. **(2) removed her blue jeans** (Application) The first emergency action for a poison absorbed through the skin is to remove any clothes that are contaminated. Option (1) is a good idea but not the most important thing to do in the case of a spilled liquid poison. Option (3) is the last step in first aid for poison on the skin. Option (4) is incorrect because it is not a first-aid remedy for any type of poison. Option (5) is incorrect because it is not the first step in treating poison on the skin.

20. **(4) Call the poison control center.** (Application) First aid may have been successful, but to be sure of complete treatment and recovery, the friend should call the local poison control center or other health professionals. Option (1) is incorrect because the eye was washed for the recommended time. The treatment already seems to have been successful. Option (2) is incorrect

because baking soda is not a remedy for poison in the eye. Option (3) is incorrect because the next indicated step is to call for professional help. Option (5) is incorrect because the victim should consult with a health professional.

21. **(2) B only** (Analysis) The chemicals in the dry cell battery may have been used up. The chemical action in a dry cell battery continues even when the switch is off. Therefore, the batteries wear out even though the item has not been used for a while. Statement A is what happens when the circuit is completed in a flashlight with good batteries. It does not explain why this flashlight did not come on. Therefore, options (1) and (4) are incorrect. Statement C is a conclusion about the relative value of the two types of batteries. There is no information in the article supporting this statement. Therefore, options (3) and (5) are incorrect.

22. **(3) An outside electric current restored the chemicals in the battery so that they could produce current again.** (Application) Option (1) is incorrect because it explains why the battery stopped working but not why it resumed working. Option (2) is not true; chemical action continues at a reduced rate. Option (4) is not true; the CD is described as being portable. Option (5) may or may not be true, but it does not explain why the CD player started working again.

23. **(4) The life of the battery is shorter when the flashlight is left on.** (Analysis) When the circuit is complete, a dry cell battery works at current-producing levels, and the chemicals run out faster. Option (1) is incorrect because batteries do not always produce the same amount of current. Option (2) is incorrect because the question does not mention recharging. Option (3) is incorrect because the chemical reaction is faster when the flashlight is on. Option (5) is incorrect because dry cell batteries continue their chemical reaction at a reduced rate when the circuit is broken.

24. **(4) a toy truck** (Application) Batteries are most suited for portable items that cannot be plugged into an outlet. Dry cells are used for smaller toys and machines. Options (1) and (5) are incorrect because they are not portable. Options (2) and (3) also cannot be plugged in while they are operating, so batteries are suitable for them. However, cars and motorized wheelchairs are larger machines that use storage batteries, which can be recharged.

25. **(3) The car's engine generates electricity that recharges the battery as the car runs.** (Analysis) Option (1) is incorrect because the battery is the source of enough current to start the car. Options (2), (4), and (5) are incorrect because car batteries do not need external recharging, so the car would not need to be jump-started.

26. **(3) On June 21, the Northern Hemisphere is tilted toward the sun.** (Evaluation) The diagram shows the top, or northern half, of Earth tilting toward the sun on June 21. Options (1) and (2) are incorrect because there is no information about tides or the moon in the diagram. Option (4) is incorrect because the Northern Hemisphere is tilted toward the sun on that date. Option (5) is not true. It is the tilting of Earth's hemispheres that causes a longer or shorter day. On March 21 and September 21, days and nights of equal length occur because neither the Northern nor the Southern Hemisphere is tilted toward the sun.

27. **(2) The ocean currents in the North Atlantic flow from west to east.** (Application) Because the freighter sails with the current going to England, it makes faster progress in the eastward trip to Liverpool. Option (1) is true but does not explain the difference in the trips. Option (3) is incorrect because the currents flow from west to east in the North Atlantic. Options (4) and (5) do not explain the difference because the freighter does not cross the South Atlantic on either trip.

28. **(3) ice, water, water vapor** (Application) These are three forms of water: solid, liquid, and gas. Option (1) is incorrect because both lumps and grains of sugar are solids; the option provides no gas. Option (2) is incorrect because rock salt and salt crystals are both solids and the option provides no gas; and salt water is a mixture of salt and water, not a form of salt. Option (4) is incorrect because glass and broken glass are both solids, and the option provides no gas. Option (5) is incorrect because a carbonated beverage is not a form of carbon dioxide. It contains bubbles of carbon dioxide gas.

29. **(4) changes in amount of heat** (Analysis) Matter melts and boils at different

temperatures, changing from one state to another. Option (1) is incorrect because a change in chemical makeup would result in an entirely different kind of matter, not another state of matter. Options (2), (3), and (5) may result from a change of state, but they do not cause it.

0. **(4) Another person may pick up the viruses by touching the objects.** (Comprehension) Cold viruses survive for a while on objects and washing the objects gets rid of the viruses. Option (1) is not true. Option (2) is also not true; the viruses survive for up to three hours. Option (3) is incorrect because the person with the cold is already infected. It does not matter if he or she picks up a contaminated object. Option (5) is not true.

31. **(5) Avoid going out in the rain.** (Analysis) According to the article, colds are transmitted when rhinoviruses pass from one person to another, either by contact or by air. The weather does not matter. Preventive measures related to the spread of viruses by contact or air are based on the facts given in the article, so options (1) to (4) are incorrect.

32. **(2) Rhinoviruses may be transferred from your hands to the mucous membranes in your nose.** (Analysis) Washing your hands gets rid of the viruses. Option (1) may be true, but it is not clear that the hands were actually dirty. Option (3) is not true. Rhinoviruses can survive for up to three hours on the skin. Option (4) is true, but it describes transmission of the viruses by air, not by contact with contaminated hands. Option (5) is not true because there is an effect.

33. **(1) Warm air rises and cool air sinks.** (Evaluation) The diagram shows warm air rising. As the warm air becomes cooler, it sinks. Options (2) and (3) are incorrect because they describe the opposite of what actually happens. Option (4) is incorrect because the diagram suggests that the heat of the different types of surfaces influences air movement above them. The truth of option (5) cannot be determined from the diagram. Although the diagram shows a convection cell where land and water meet, there may be other situations in which convection cells occur.

34. **(2) Face inland.** (Application) According to the diagram, the wind is coming off the ocean onto the beach. Facing inland will keep the wind out of your eyes. Option (1) would have the wind coming directly at you. Options (3) and (4) would expose either side of your face to the wind. Option (5) is incorrect because the wind in the diagram is coming from one particular direction.

35. **(1) a stratovolcano** (Application) Mt. St. Helens spewed forth cinders, rock, lava, and ashes, making it a stratovolcano. Option (2) is incorrect because cinder cones are formed without lava flows. Option (3) is incorrect because shield volcanoes are formed primarily by lava flows without cinders and ash. Option (4) is not a type of volcano; all volcanoes contain magma. Option (5) is incorrect because extinct volcanoes do not erupt.

36. **(3) Volcanoes are mountains built from deposits of lava, rock, cinders, or ashes.** (Evaluation) The diagram shows how volcanoes are formed. Option (1) is incorrect because shield volcanoes are not necessarily steep. Option (2) is incorrect because the diagram does not indicate anything about the speed and nature of the eruptions. Option (4) is true, but it is an incorrect answer because the diagram does not show where volcanoes occur. Option (5) is also true, but it is not supported by the diagram.

37. **(3) There must be an equal number of atoms from each element on each side of the equation.** (Analysis) If you examine the equation and the illustration, you will see that before and after the reaction there are four hydrogen atoms, four oxygen atoms, and one carbon atom. They recombine to form different substances, but their number remains the same. Option (1) is incorrect because all reactions do not produce gases. Option (2) is disproved by the information; molecules are said to be made up of atoms. Options (4) and (5) are not supported by the equation given.

38. **(3) mines** (Application) Methane is a hazard in coal mines, where it can cause fire and loss of life. Option (1) is incorrect because people do not come in contact with deposits that are buried deep in Earth. Option (2) is incorrect because in marshes methane tends to bubble up and disperse into the atmosphere. Options (4) and (5) are incorrect because the use of methane is highly controlled in these environments. Therefore, it is less likely to burn accidentally.

Answers and Explanations

39. **(3) the ciliary muscles** (Analysis) These are in position to pull the lens as needed to alter its shape. Options (1), (2), and (5) are not connected to the lens. Option (4) is an opening, not a structure that can control lens shape.

40. **(3) The amount of light entering the eye is changed.** (Analysis) The iris makes the diameter of the pupil larger or smaller, thereby controlling the amount of light that enters the eye. Option (1) is not true. Option (2) is true but is not related to the function of the iris; rather it is related to the position of the optic nerve. Option (4) is true, but the iris does not cause this bulging. Option (5) is not related to the iris.

41. **(5) the source of activation energy** (Application) In this case, the match provides the energy to start coals burning. Option (1) is incorrect because the match is not a property, it is a form of matter. Option (2) is incorrect since the burning of the match is an exothermic reaction, releasing energy. Option (3) is incorrect because the lit match is part of a chemical reaction, not a physical change. Option (4) is incorrect; the resulting forms of matter in this reaction are ashes and gases.

42. **(3) a chemical reaction in which heat energy is absorbed** (Comprehension) Option (1) is incorrect because it defines all chemical reactions, not just endothermic reactions. Option (2) is incorrect because it defines an exothermic reaction. Option (4) is incorrect because it defines activation energy. Option (5) is incorrect because all chemical reactions need activation energy to start.

43. **(3) To the listener, the frequency of the sound waves seems to change.** (Comprehension) As the truck is moving closer, the sound waves seem to have a higher frequency because they take less time to reach the listener. Therefore, the noise of the truck seems higher-pitched when it is coming closer. Options (1) and (2) are incorrect because the noise coming from the truck's engine is actually the same at all times. It only seems to be higher-pitched when it is moving toward you. Option (4) is not indicated by any of the information given. Option (5) is not true.

44. **(2) The Doppler effect can be used to determine whether a source of sound is moving away from or toward someone.** (Evaluation) The faster the source of sound moves toward the observer, the greater the frequency of sound waves detected by the observer. Option (1) is incorrect since the Doppler effect works with other types of wave such as light waves. Nothing in the article suggests that the effect applies only to sound waves. Option (3) is incorrect because the Doppler effect is shown to work with distant sounds. Option (4) is incorrect because the frequency at which sound waves are emitted by the source never changes. It is the frequency at which they are received by the observer that changes. Option (5) is incorrect because nothing in the passage or diagram gives information about wave interference.

45. **(3) steak** (Application) Steak, an animal product, is high in cholesterol. Options (1), (2) (4), and (5) are not animal products and have little or no cholesterol.

46. **(3) builds up on the artery walls and can block the flow of blood to the heart** (Analysis) This is stated in the first paragraph of the article. Option (1) is incorrect because the cholesterol collects in the arteries, not in the heart. Option (2) is incorrect; cholesterol helps produce cell membranes, not destroy them. Options (4) and (5) are not true and are not supported by the article.

47. **(2) the arteries become clogged** (Comprehension) Although hardening of the arteries is a popular term for atherosclerosis, and would seem to imply option (1), a more accurate description of what happens is that the arteries become narrow and clogged. Options (3), (4), and (5) are not characteristics of atherosclerosis.

48. **(2) saturated fat** (Comprehension) This is stated in the third paragraph of the article. The other four types of fat listed are not primary sources of cholesterol in the diet. They are not mentioned in the article.

49. **(3) Most substances expand when heated and contract when cooled.** (Evaluation) Option (1) is incorrect because a few substances such as water expand when cooled. Options (2) and (4) are incorrect because most substances do not contract when heated. Option (5) is incorrect because substances do change in volume when heated or cooled.

50. **(2) Mercury expands when heated.** (Comprehension) Option (1) is true but does not explain why mercury rises in a

POSTTEST

Answers and Explanations

thermometer. Option (3) is not true; mercury expands and does not contract when heated. Option (4) is not possible; heat is not a form of matter and does not take up space. It is a form of energy. Option (5) is also untrue; as with other substances, the glass also expands when heat is added.

51. **(4) A and B only** (Evaluation) When telephone wires expand in the heat, they become longer and sag, Statement A. When glass is suddenly heated, the quick expansion in one portion causes it to break, Statement B. Therefore, options (1) and (2) are correct but incomplete. Statement C is not true; soup, made mostly of water, acts like water when frozen and expands. Therefore, options (3) and (5) are incorrect.

52. **(1) The molecules and atoms of gases are the farthest apart and the most mobile.** (Evaluation) It takes progressively more heat to change matter from solid to liquid to gas. Therefore, it follows that gases have atoms and molecules with the most kinetic energy, moving the fastest and farthest apart. Options (2) and (3) are thus incorrect. Option (4) is also incorrect. If the molecules and atoms always acted in the same manner, the states of matter would not differ. Option (5) is not true; the molecules and atoms of a solid move slowly.

53. **(1) Earth's interior is composed of material much more dense than the crust.** (Analysis) Averaging the greater density of the interior with the lower density of the crust gives Earth's average density. Option (2) is incorrect because if the interior were less dense than the crust, the total density of Earth would have been less than 3 grams per cubic centimeter. Options (3) and (4) are not supported by the diagram. Option (5) is incorrect because a lower density added to the calculation would reduce the final figure and not increase it.

54. **(4) the great pressure on the inner core** (Analysis) The pressure of the upper layers pushes the particles of iron and nickel so close together that they remain solid. Option (1) is incorrect because it suggests that other substances would be in melted or liquid form. The diagram shows the core to be solid and does not list any other substances. No information is given in the diagram about options (2) or (3). Option (5) is incorrect because the composition of the mantle does not affect the state of matter of the inner core.

55. **(1) dairy products** (Comprehension) Dairy products, like many foods, contain little vitamin C. The foods mentioned in options (2), (3), (4), and (5) are described in the article as high in vitamin C.

56. **(5) a fresh orange** (Application) Fresh, uncooked foods are the best sources of vitamin C. Options (1) and (4) are incorrect because these foods are not high in vitamin C. Options (2) and (3) are incorrect because the drying and cooking of these foods decreases their vitamin C content.

57. **(2) More than one egg will be produced.** (Analysis) Fertility drugs increase egg production. Option (1) is incorrect because the fallopian tubes are blocked; they cannot be opened with fertility drugs. Option (3) is incorrect because the woman's blocked fallopian tubes prevent fertilization from occurring naturally. Option (4) is incorrect because giving fertility drugs to the woman has no effect on the man. Option (5) is incorrect because there is no embryo at this point.

58. **(3) They want a child who is genetically their own.** (Evaluation) Because *in vitro* fertilization uses the couple's eggs and sperm, the resulting embryos have their genes. Many couples feel this result is worth the time, stress, and expense of *in vitro* fertilization. Option (1) is true, but successful *in vitro* fertilization also can take a long time. Option (2) is incorrect because the health of a child cannot be guaranteed either by adoption or by *in vitro* fertilization. Options (4) and (5) are not true.

59. **(5) The timing of embryo development and uterus development is off.** (Analysis) There are many chemical and biological changes associated with conception, and if they are not timed right, the embryo will not develop properly. When the egg and reproductive system are separated, the chances of bad timing are increased. Option (1) is incorrect because unfertilized eggs are not transferred. Option (2) is incorrect because defective sperm will not fertilize the egg. Option (3) may occasionally be correct, but the handling of sperm and eggs is strictly regulated to avoid contamination. Option (4) is incorrect because if the sperm are improperly processed, they will not fertilize the egg.

60. **(3) two damaged fallopian tubes** (Analysis) For this woman, there is no way for an egg to

get from the ovary to the uterus. Option (1) is incorrect because unhealthy women are not good candidates for *in vitro* fertilization. Option (2) is incorrect because a woman with non-functioning ovaries cannot produce eggs. Option (4) is incorrect because a woman without a uterus cannot carry an embryo. Option (5) is incorrect because a woman with one functioning fallopian tube can become pregnant naturally.

61. **(1) Ice takes up more space than an equal mass of water.** (Application) The diagram of ice shows more space between molecules than the diagram of water. When water freezes and expands, it exerts more pressure on the glass and breaks it. Option (2) is incorrect because each molecule does not increase in size as the temperature drops. Option (3) is not supported by the information; glass actually contracts when it becomes cold. Options (4) and (5) are not true.

62. **(3) The groups of molecules in water are tightly bound together and must absorb much heat energy before they break apart.** (Analysis) Hydrogen bonds are unusually strong, and they must be broken in order for water vapor to form. Options (1) and (2) are true but do not explain the high boiling point of water. Option (4) is not true; the polarity of water molecules causes them to be attracted to one another. Option (5) is not true.

63. **(2) There are more molecules in 1 cubic centimeter of water than in 1 cubic centimeter of ice.** (Evaluation) Water molecules are closer together in the liquid form, so there would be more molecules in a given volume. Options (1), (4), and (5) are true, but they are incorrect answers because the information says nothing about these properties of water. Option (3) is not true.

64. **(3) circulatory system** (Application) The blood carries substances to all the tissues in the body through the circulatory system. Although the blood circulates through the other systems, it is part of the circulatory system. None of the other systems listed in options (1), (2), (4), and (5) transport substances around the body.

65. **(4) nervous system** (Application) The eyes and ears receive sensory stimuli and pass it on to the brain, which interprets what we see and hear. Options (1), (2), (3), and (5) are incorrect because these systems do not involve seeing and hearing.

66. **(5) reproductive system** (Analysis) If the reproductive system of an individual is not working properly, the individual will still survive. Options (1), (2), (3), and (4) are incorrect because failure of these systems would cause death.

SIMULATED TEST (Pages 236–255)

1. **(4) formation of volcanoes** (Analysis) The map shows a relationship between the boundaries of colliding plates and the locations of volcanoes. Options (1), (2), (3), and (5) are not shown to have any relationship to where plates collide.

2. **(5) western South America** (Application) The map shows a high number of earthquakes and volcanoes along the western coast of this continent. The other options have only a few earthquakes and volcanoes and would not be the best areas to study.

3. **(5) sulfur dioxide** (Analysis) Since sulfur dioxide has the highest density of the gases listed, it also has the highest specific gravity:

$$\frac{2.93}{1.29} = 2.27$$

The other gases all have specific gravities of less than 2.

4. **(1) The densities of air and nitrogen are similar.** (Analysis) Since nitrogen makes up almost 80 percent of air, its density has a great influence on the density of air. Option (2) is not true; at 1.25, nitrogen is less dense than air. Option (3) is true, but it is not related to the proportion of nitrogen in the air. Options (4) and (5) are not true.

5. **(4) from spring to fall** (Comprehension) The article states that ladybugs stop hunting when it gets cold and prey is hard to find. Options (1), (2), and (3) are incorrect because the article implies that ladybugs hunt during the day. Option (5) is incorrect because ladybugs are not active during the winter.

6. **(4) there are varieties of ladybugs that feed on different types of insects** (Analysis) This assumption is made when the author explains that an Australian type of ladybug was imported to California to help

control the cottony cushion scale. If the American ladybugs had hunted this type of scale insect, the Australian variety would not have been necessary. Options (1), (2), and (5) are stated explicitly in the article; therefore, they are not unstated assumptions. Option (3) is not true.

7. **(5) ability to hunt other insects that feed on valuable plants** (Evaluation) People's attitude toward ladybugs is generally positive, because they are beneficial to humans. Options (1), (2), (3), and (4) are not aspects that affect people, so they are not likely to influence the way people view ladybugs.

8. **(3) Many ladybugs are beneficial to humans.** (Evaluation) The article states that many varieties of ladybugs feed on plant-eating insects. The ladybugs help control the destruction of plants that are valuable to humans. Option (1) is incorrect because the article states that many, not all, varieties of ladybugs hunt insects. Option (2) is incorrect because the article describes how the Australian ladybug lays its eggs near the hatchlings' source of food. Option (4) is incorrect because ladybugs take shelter during the winter and resume hunting the next spring. This implies that they survive more than one season and thus longer than two months. Option (5) is incorrect because the article gives no information about the mating habits of ladybugs.

9. **(1) frogs burying themselves in pond bottoms for the winter** (Application) Like ladybugs, frogs hibernate during the winter and become active again in the spring. Options (2), (3), (4), and (5) are other forms of adaptation to cold weather, but they differ from the ladybug's adaptation. Migration, option (2), does not occur; ladybugs take shelter where they are. Changes in color, option (3), protect animals that continue to be active during the snowy winter. Ladybugs do not shed anything during the winter, option (4). They do not grow more protection from the cold, option (5).

10. **(1) A only** (Evaluation) The article states that ladybugs hunt for insects, so if the ladybugs ran out of food it is likely that they would fly away in search of more, Statement A. Options (2) and (4) are incorrect because Statement B is not true. The article refers to other plants as well as citrus trees. Options (3) and (5) are incorrect because statement C is not true.

Ladybugs produce a foul-tasting substance, so birds do not eat ladybugs.

11. **(3) very good condition after one minute of heavy exercise** (Comprehension) The pulse rate of the person in average condition after one minute of moderate exercise is 98 beats per minute. The chart shows that option (1) is 107 beats, option (2) is 102 beats, option (3) is 96 beats, option (4) is 111 beats, and option (5) is 114 beats. Of these, 98 beats is faster than option (3), or 96 beats.

12. **(5) There is a greater difference in the pulse rate between moderate and heavy exercise than between light and moderate exercise.** (Evaluation) For all types of subjects, the jump in pulse rate between moderate and heavy exercise is greater than the jump between light and moderate exercise. Option (1) is incorrect because the chart does not show what happens after more than one minute of exercise. Options (2) and (3) may be true, but they are not supported by the information given. Option (4) is not true; the pulse rate increases from moderate to heavy exercise.

13. **(3) the gravitational pull of the moon** (Comprehension) The first paragraph states that the moon's pull is the primary cause of tides. The sun's gravitational pull, option (2), has some influence but not much compared to the moon. Options (1) and (4) do not affect tides. Option (5) contributes to the movement of high tide around the world, but it is not a cause of tides.

14. **(1) 2 feet** (Comprehension) The typical sea-level change in mid-ocean is stated to be 2 feet. The answer is in the second paragraph of the article. Options (2), (3), (4), and (5) are therefore incorrect.

15. **(5) a current that carries water toward the shore** (Comprehension) When the tide is changing from low to high, the flood current redistributes the water in the direction of the coast, as stated in the third paragraph. Options (1) and (2) are not discussed in the article. Option (3) is incorrect because a flood current does not result in flooding. Option (4) is the definition of an ebb current.

16. **(1) The sun's gravitational pull is added to that of the moon, which increases the height of the tides.** (Analysis) When the moon and sun are in a line on one side of

Earth, their gravitational forces combine and exert more pull on the oceans, increasing the height of the tides. Option (2) is incorrect because if the moon's gravitational pull were weaker, the tides would be lower. Options (3) and (4) are incorrect because the position of the three bodies does not affect rainfall or ice melting on Earth. Option (5) is not true.

17. **(5) none** (Application) The man was vaccinated only three years ago. According to the chart, his immunity should last for 5 to 10 years. Therefore, he needs no further protection, so options (1), (2), (3), and (4) are incorrect.

18. **(2) diphtheria antiserum** (Application) Because it cannot be determined if he is immune, to be safe, he should be given the antiserum. Options (1) and (3) are incorrect because the vaccine will not give him immediate protection. Option (4) is incorrect because after he recovers, he will have his own antibodies and will not need antiserum. Option (5) is incorrect because he needs immediate protection against diphtheria.

19. **(5) none, natural immunity now present** (Application) The article states that since the woman had measles as a child, she has antibodies to fight the disease. Therefore, she needs neither the vaccine nor the antiserum of options (1), (2), (3), or (4).

20. **(2) when they enter school** (Application) To ensure that their protection is constant, children are immunized again when they enter school. This occurs about 4 or 5 years after the last vaccination. Since the immunity lasts from 5 to 10 years, immunizing again after 5 years ensures that protection does not lapse. Option (1) is incorrect because the immunity period is at least 5 years. Options (3) and (4) are incorrect because waiting so long would allow the immunity to wear out. The tetanus and diphtheria vaccines last a maximum of 10 years. Option (5) is incorrect because the diphtheria and tetanus vaccines last only 5 to 10 years. To continue the protection, another immunization would be necessary.

21. **(2) Particles of solids are tightly packed and transmit disturbances quickly.** (Analysis) Gases, on the other hand, have particles that are farther apart. Sound takes longer to pass from particle to particle in a gas. Option (1) may or may not be true in a given situation. Option (3) is not true. Gases transmit disturbances relatively slowly. Option (4) is not true; gases have particles that transmit sound. Option (5) is not necessarily true.

22. **(1) seeing lightning before hearing thunder** (Application) Because light travels faster than sound, lightning is seen before thunder is heard during a thunderstorm. Option (2) is incorrect because the distances are so small that light and sound are perceived at the same time. Option (3) is incorrect because neon signs do not involve sound. Options (4) and (5) are incorrect because they do not compare the speed of light and sound. They involve either light or sound.

23. **(1) The ground transmits sound faster than the air.** (Evaluation) The article indicates that solids (the ground) transmit sound faster than gases (the air). Option (2) is incorrect because it states the opposite. Option (3) is not true; light waves travel more quickly than sound waves. Option (4) is not true because light waves also travel through empty space. Option (5) is untrue because light waves travel through solids and outer space as well.

24. **(4) a hunter hearing hoofbeats by putting an ear to the ground** (Application) Since sound travels faster through a solid, the hunter will hear the hoofbeats sooner through the ground than through the air. Options (1), (2), and (3) are incorrect because they involve transmission of sound through air only. Option (5) is incorrect because the purpose of cupping the ear is to help capture the sound waves traveling through the air.

25. **(3) our ability to see the sun and stars** (Analysis) Sunlight and starlight reach us from outer space. The other options involve the transmission of light waves through matter, which is not outer space.

26. **(3) Mercury is the planet closest to the sun.** (Analysis) Option (1) is not true. Mars, being farther from the sun than Earth, takes longer to travel around the sun. The diagram does not contain enough information to support options (2) and (4). Option (5) is not true. Since the moon revolves around Earth, at times it is farther from the sun than Earth is.

7. (5) faulting and erosion (Application) Faulting exposes older rock layers when a rock mass slips down past several layers of an adjacent rock mass. Erosion exposes older rock layers as layers above them wear away. Options (1) and (4) are incorrect because folding bends the layers but does not break the newest upper layer. Options (2) and (3) are incorrect because they are only partly correct.

8. (1) carbon 14 (Application) The chart indicates that carbon 14 is used to estimate the age of material that was once alive, such as a human bone. Options (2), (3), (4), and (5) all have medical uses.

29. (4) Radioactive substances have many uses. (Evaluation) Option (1) is incorrect because the chart does not give information about the value of radioactive substances. Option (2) is incorrect because uranium 235 is also used in nuclear reactors. Option (3) is incorrect because radioactive substances are used in atomic weapons. Option (5), although true, is incorrect because the chart does not give any information about the origin of radioactive substances.

30. (1) cancerous growths that may cause death if untreated (Comprehension) This definition appears in the first paragraph of the article. Option (2) is incorrect because if the immune system were successful in suppressing the cancerous growth, the growth would not be malignant. Options (3) and (4) are incorrect because malignant tumors are not harmless. Option (5) is incorrect because malignant tumors are cancers; they are not the cause of cancer.

31. (4) being exposed to a high level of radiation (Analysis) Radiation is a known cancer-causing agent. Options (1), (3), and (5) are incorrect because they are practices that lessen the body's intake of artificial substances. Option (2) is incorrect because lack of exercise is not a chemical or physical agent that might cause cancer.

32. (4) Some cancer-causing agents suppress the immune system. (Analysis) People who take drugs to suppress the immune system show a higher number of cancers. This statement, found in the second paragraph, supports the theory that suppression of the immune system is involved in the development of cancer. Options (1), (2), and (3) are true but not related to the role of the immune system. Option (5) is also true, but it deals with a later stage in cancer, not the cause of cancer.

33. (5) erosion by the river (Analysis) As the river gets older, it erodes the sides of its channels and starts to loop from side to side. This process widens its valley. The other options are not related to landscape formation in a river valley.

34. (2) Oxbow lakes are found near old rivers. (Evaluation) Two oxbow lakes are shown in the diagram of the old river. They are created when a meander of the river is cut off from the main stream. Option (1) is incorrect because the diagram does not show how rivers drain. Option (3) is incorrect because no flooding is indicated in the diagrams. Option (4) is incorrect because the diagram of an old river shows a gently sloping valley. Option (5) is incorrect because the diagram of the old river shows no waterfall.

35. (5) thermosphere (Application) The thermosphere is the highest layer shown. It is closest to outer space, and spacecraft would operate very efficiently in its thin air. Options (1), (2), (3), and (4) are all closer to the surface of Earth, where increasing air density would create more friction for a spacecraft.

36. (1) The ozone layer is part of both the stratosphere and the mesosphere. (Comprehension) The diagram shows the ozone layer starting in the upper part of the stratosphere and extending partly into the mesosphere. Option (2) is incorrect because the ozone layer does not reach the thermosphere. Option (3) is incorrect because the troposphere extends to a height of 10 miles. Option (4) is incorrect because the thermosphere extends beyond the mesosphere, which goes up to 50 miles. Option (5) is incorrect because the troposphere is close to Earth's surface, where animals live and breathe.

37. (5) a compound (Application) Water is a combination of two different elements, which makes it a compound. Since water contains more than one type of element or atom, it cannot be an atom, an element, or part of an atom. Thus, options (1), (2), and (3) are incorrect. Option (4) is incorrect because water is a form of matter, not energy.

38. **(1) Elements can be broken down into simpler substances by methods other than chemical reactions.** (Analysis) In the definition of an element, the author states that an element "cannot be broken down into simpler substances by chemical reactions." By specifically mentioning "chemical," the author implies that there are other methods that can break down elements. In fact, nuclear reactions can break down atoms of an element into smaller atoms. Option (2) is incorrect because the information about iron and oxygen is given as an example of a compound. It does not indicate that iron and oxygen are the only elements that combine into compounds. Option (3) is incorrect because it is untrue and because the article does not discuss the states of matter. Option (4) is untrue. Option (5) is incorrect because nothing in the article indicates a greater interest on the part of the author in atoms, elements, or compounds.

39. **(3) rectum** (Analysis) The diagram shows the digestive system ending at the rectum. Options (1) and (2) are incorrect because the liver and the pancreas are in the middle section of the digestive system. Option (4) empties into the rectum. Option (5) is in the middle part of the alimentary canal.

40. **(2) esophagus** (Application) The esophagus passes downward through the chest. When stomach acids irritate the esophagus, the discomfort is felt in the chest. The other organs listed in options (1), (3), (4), and (5) are not in the chest. Discomfort in any of these organs would not be felt in the chest.

41. **(4) running a car engine in a closed garage** (Application) Since carbon monoxide is part of the exhaust, a car engine should not be run in an enclosed area without proper ventilation. Options (1), (2), (3), and (5) are incorrect because they involve using potentially dangerous items in the proper way, which lessens the danger involved.

42. **(5) drowsiness** (Comprehension) According to the paragraph, drowsiness is the first symptom of carbon-monoxide poisoning. Options (1), (2), (3), and (4) are therefore incorrect.

43. **(3) The load moves upward.** (Comprehension) A downward pull on the rope results in the upward movement of the load.

Option (1) is incorrect because the load move Option (2) is incorrect because the load move upward. Option (4) is incorrect because it is the turn of the wheel that helps move the rope. Option (5) is incorrect because the rope does move when you pull on it.

44. **(1) A single, fixed pulley changes the direction in which force must be exerted** (Evaluation) Without a fixed pulley, the effort in lifting a load would be upward. With a fixed pulley, the effort exerted is downward. The pulley changes the direction in which effort must be exerted. Option (2) is incorrect because the single, fixed pulley does change the direction in which effort must be exerted. Option (3) is incorrect because it is easier to pull downward on something with your body weight than it is to lift something. Options (4 and (5) are incorrect because the distance in which the rope is pulled is equal to the distance in which the load is lifted.

45. **(1) respiratory system** (Comprehension) The second paragraph states that respiratory infections are spread by the droplets released through sneezing and coughing. Options (2), (3), (4), and (5) are incorrect because they include areas not infected by airborne pathogens.

46. **(4) A and B** (Analysis) Washing your hands is effective against many respiratory and intestinal pathogens (Statements A and B) because they can be picked up by your hands from sneezes, coughs, or excretions. Options (1) and (2) are incorrect because they are incomplete. Pathogens in the blood (Statement C) generally are spread by insects or other animals that bite and draw blood, not by contaminated hands. Therefore, options (3) and (5) are incorrect.

47. **(1) blood** (Application) Since pathogens are transmitted by means related to where they reside in the host, a pathogen transmitted by an insect bite would affect the blood. The respiratory system, skeleton, digestive system and brain mentioned in options (2), (3), (4), and (5) are not accessible to insect bites.

48. **(2) where it lives in the body** (Comprehension) According to the second paragraph of the article, how the pathogen is spread is related to the place in the body where the pathogen lives. Options (1), (3), (4), and (5) are not relevant.

(4) Cover the lines with material that blocks the electromagnetic fields. (Evaluation) This solution would enable people to continue to use electricity, which is an important source of energy in our society, without moving wires, homes, or businesses. Options (1) and (2) are not practical, since transmission lines are needed where people are located. Option (3) is not a likely solution because it would involve a complete change in the way we live. Option (5) is not only impractical and expensive, but would generate electromagnetic fields anyway.

50. **(5) avoid living near a high-voltage power line** (Application) These lines produce such strong electromagnetic fields, that a person being cautious would try to stay away from them. Option (1) is incorrect; both types of bulbs produce electromagnetic fields. Option (2) is incorrect because magnets produce magnetic fields, not electromagnetic fields. Option (3) is incorrect because the danger it involves is electrocution, not exposure to electromagnetic fields. Option (4) is incorrect because a broken appliance is not working and therefore not producing an electromagnetic field.

51. **(3) Using an electric blanket causes cancer.** (Evaluation) Since the article states clearly that the dangers to health from electromagnetic fields have not yet been proved, it cannot be stated as fact that an electric blanket causes cancer. Options (1), (2), (4), and (5) are all true statements relating to information provided in the article. Note that the key words making option (2) true are "may be." In other words, option (2) states a possibility, not a fact.

52. **(3) Electromagnetic fields cause health problems.** (Evaluation) Although links between certain health conditions and electromagnetic fields have been suggested, so far this relationship has not been proved. Options (1), (2), (4), and (5) are established and proven principles of physics.

53. **(5) water vapor in the air** (Analysis) The water vapor in the air combines with the solid pollutants to form sulfuric acid and nitric acid, which are components of acid rain. Options (1), (2), and (3) are involved in the production or control of air pollutants; they cannot affect pollutants that have been released. Option (4) is incorrect because

although the oceans are polluted by dry deposits and acid rain, they are not involved in the production of wet deposits.

54. **(4) The plants are weakened by the lack of nutrients and harmed by the accumulation of heavy metals.** (Analysis) The diagram shows how the tree is a victim of the action of acidified soil as nutrients are removed and harmful heavy metals are concentrated. Option (1) is incorrect because the diagram indicates that heavy metals are harmful in quantity. Option (2) is incorrect because there are no extra nutrients in the soil. Option (3) is incorrect because the entire plant is weakened, not just the upper part. Option (5) is incorrect because the acidified soil results in weakened plants.

55. **(3) color blindness is related to whether a person is male or female** (Analysis) Color blindness is an inherited characteristic that is linked with sex. Option (1) is not true. Options (2) and (4) are untrue, and they are also unrelated to the distribution of color blindness between the sexes. Option (5) is true under most circumstances, but it is unrelated to the greater incidence of color blindness among men.

56. **(4) railroad engineer** (Application) Since railroad engineers must be able to distinguish red from green on railroad signals, a color-blind person would not be considered for such a position. Options (1), (2), (3), and (5) involve occupations in which the ability to distinguish red from green is not essential.

57. **(4) HIV** (Analysis) The virus HIV is the cause of AIDS. Options (1), (2), and (3) are not causes of AIDS but activities associated with the spread of the AIDS virus. Option (5) involves substances that are produced by the body to fight HIV.

58. **(1) exposure to HIV** (Analysis) HIV antibodies are produced only in response to infection by HIV. Option (2) is incorrect because most transfused blood does not contain HIV. Options (3), (4), and (5) are symptoms of the later stages of AIDS.

59. **(3) A person with HIV can infect others without being aware of it.** (Evaluation) Since the infection is not active during the second stage, which can last for years, many people who assume that they are healthy can

329

unknowingly spread the virus. Option (1) is incorrect because AIDS is spreading into other parts of the population through the sex partners of people in the high-risk groups. Option (2) is incorrect because nothing in the article implies that researchers are near discovery of a cure. Option (4) is incorrect because people do not recover from AIDS. Option (5) is incorrect because intravenous drug users and the sex partners of people in the high-risk groups are also women.

60. **(3) The disease will continue to spread into previously low-risk groups.** (Analysis) Because the sexual contacts of people in the high-risk groups are not limited to other members of the high-risk groups, AIDS is increasingly found in people thought to be at little or no risk. Option (1) may or may not be true. Option (2) is not true; blood is now screened for HIV to make it safe for transfusion. Option (4) has not been true up to now, and nothing indicates that AIDS will become less serious. Option (5) is not true.

61. **(3) pickles** (Application) Vinegar and salt are used to preserve cucumbers, a process that results in pickles. Option (1) is flour containing supplementary minerals and vitamins. Option (2) is milk processed so that the cream is distributed throughout rather than just remaining on the top; the process does not preserve the milk. Option (4) is added to change the taste of food; it is not a food. Option (5) is a product with a supplementary mineral.

62. **(1) yellow food coloring in commercially-prepared baked goods that are made without eggs** (Application) The rich yellow color makes the product look as if it contains eggs. Options (2), (3), (4), and (5) do not affect the appearance of food.

63. **(4) A and B** (Analysis) Since most people no longer grow their own food, food additives are important in preventing the spoiling of food that is transported long distances and stored for long periods (Statement A). In addition, some food additives provide minerals and vitamins that may otherwise be lacking in the diet (Statement B). Options (1) and (2) are incorrect because they are incomplete. Most food additives do not cause disease (Statement C), so options (3) and (5) are incorrect.

64. **(3) Kerosene boils at a higher temperature than gasoline.** (Evaluation) The diagram shows that kerosene boils between 175°C and 325°C, and gasoline boils between 40°C and 174°C. Option (1) is incorrect because the diagram shows that asphalt remains solid in the tower. Option (2) is incorrect because grease is shown as a separate substance made from petroleum. Option (4) is true, but it is not supported by the information provided. Option (5) may be true, but it is not supported by the information provided.

65. **(5) the different temperatures at different heights in the tower** (Analysis) Variations in temperature mean that different substances will boil and condense at different levels, thus separating out. Option (1) is contradicted by the diagram. Option (2) simply causes the petroleum to move, not separate. Option (3) is not true; the process has nothing to do with filters. Option (4) is not correct; the pipes simply transport the substances.

66. **(3) The higher the location in the tower, the lower is the temperature.** (Evaluation) The diagram shows the temperature decreasing as the height increases. Options (1) and (2) are contradicted by the diagram. Options (4) and (5) are not true because some substances remain liquid or solid at all temperatures in the process.

Glossary

acceleration an increase in speed

acid a substance that releases hydrogen ions in a water solution (example: vinegar); pH less than 7.0

activation energy the energy that must be added to start a chemical reaction

adaptation a process that helps an organism survive

adaptive radiation the process by which many species evolve from one species

adrenal gland an endocrine gland that secretes the hormones adrenaline and cortisone

adrenaline a hormone that prepares the body to meet emergencies

air a colorless, odorless, and tasteless mixture of gases; Earth's lower atmosphere

air mass a large body of air that has the same temperature and moisture throughout

alimentary canal the tube that makes up the digestive system

alveoli small air sacs in the lungs at the end of bronchioles

ampere (amp) a measure of the flow of electrons in an electric current

amplitude the distance between the rest position and crest of a wave

anaphase the fourth stage of mitosis, or cell division

angiosperms flowering seed plants (examples: fruit trees and lilies)

antibodies substances produced by the body that fight disease

aorta a large artery that carries oxygen-rich blood from the heart to the body

arterioles small blood vessels that branch from arteries

artery a blood vessel that carries blood away from the heart

atmosphere the layers of gases that surround Earth

atom the smallest particle of an element that has all the properties of that element

atomic mass the number of protons plus neutrons in the nucleus of an element

atomic number the total number of protons in the nucleus of an element

atria the upper chambers of the heart (singular-atrium)

bacilli rod-shaped organisms

base a substance that releases hydroxide ions in a water solution (example: milk of magnesia); pH greater than 7.0

biology the study of living things and how they interact with each other and their environment

biome an ecosystem that covers a large area of the world (example: a desert)

biosphere the thin layer of Earth where life exists

boiling point the temperature at which a liquid changes into a gas

bronchi the two tubes that run from the trachea into each of the lungs

bronchioles tubes branching off bronchi in lungs and ending in alveoli

byproduct a waste material produced during a process (example: oxygen is a byproduct of photosynthesis)

cambium a one-cell-thick layer of growth cells in stems, branches, and roots of woody plants

capillary a tiny blood vessel with walls one cell thick

capsule the thick outer slime layer of a bacterium

carbon monoxide a gas produced when fossil fuels do not burn completely

carbon-oxygen cycle continuous movement of carbon ions between carbon dioxide and sugar and of oxygen ions between water and gaseous oxygen through the processes of photosynthesis and cellular respiration

cell the microscopic unit of matter that makes up all living organisms

cell membrane a thin layer of matter enclosing a cell

cell wall a layer of matter outside the cell membrane that supports and protects plant cells

cellular respiration the chemical process by which living things convert food to energy for their use

cerebellum small part of human brain located below cerebrum at the base of skull; helps control movement; coordinates eyes, inner ears, and muscles to maintain balance

cerebrum largest portion of the human brain, divided into two hemispheres; different areas specialize in different functions

chemical equation the use of formulas and symbols to show what happens in a chemical reaction

chemical formula the representation of an element, ion, molecule, or compound by symbols (letters and numbers) (example: oxygen = O_2, carbon dioxide = CO_2, hydroxide = OH^-)

chemical reaction change in one or more substances to form one or more new substances; change in atoms of a substance; may be exothermic or endothermic

chemistry the study of matter and changes in matter

chlorophyll the green coloring of plants that is needed for photosynthesis

chloroplast the structure in a plant cell that contains chlorophyll; a type of plastid

chromatin the part of a cell's nucleus that contains hereditary information

chromoplast the structure in a plant cell that contains pigments other than chlorophyll; a type of plastid

chromosome a part of a cell that contains hereditary information and is visible during mitosis, or cell division

cinder cone volcano a type of volcano made of cinders and rock particles that forms from explosive eruptions

circuit a complete path in which an electric current flows

climate average weather over a long period of time

cocci bacteria shaped like spheres

composite volcano a type of volcano made of alternating layers of hardened lava and cinders with alternating quiet and violent eruptions

compound a substance formed by the chemical combination of two or more elements in which each loses its identity and the new substance has properties different from these original elements (example: water is a compound of hydrogen and oxygen)

compression the pushing together of molecules in a longitudinal wave

condensation the changing of matter from a gas to a liquid

consumers organisms in a food chain that get their food energy by eating other organisms

continental polar air mass a large body of air originating over land near the poles (example: over northern Canada); cool, dry air

continental tropical air mass a large body of air originating over land near the equator (example: over Mexico); warm, dry air

cortisone a hormone that maintains salt balance

covalent bond a chemical combination of two or more atoms in which electrons are shared

crest the high point of a wave

crust the outer layer of Earth, including Earth's surface

culture in laboratory work, a sterile, pure food medium

cytoplasm the area of the cell (other than the nucleus) that contains other cell structures (called organelles) that carry out the cell's activities

daughter cells the cells produced as a result of mitosis

decomposers in a food chain, organisms that break down dead plants and animals (examples: bacteria and fungi)

denitrification the process by which certain bacteria change nitrates into gaseous nitrogen

density a measure of mass in relation to volume

dicotyledon a flowering plant whose seedling has two leaves (example: tomato)

direct respiration the process by which single-celled organisms exchange gases directly with the environment

displacement distance and direction traveled by an object

distance how far; the length of the path from one point to another

distillation the process of removing dissolved material from a liquid

DNA the molecule that contains hereditary information and controls the activities of each cell; found in chromosomes

dominant trait a trait that will appear in an offspring if a parent contributes it; dominant traits will hide recessive traits

drag the friction created when objects move through air

earthflow the slow, downhill movement of soil and plants

earthquake the shaking and trembling that results from sudden movements of rock deep within Earth

Earth science the study of Earth and the space around Earth

echolocation a process in which an animal locates objects and food by producing a sound that is reflected to the animal

ecosystem a selected area where living and nonliving things interact (example: a swamp)

electric charge a basic property of protons and electrons

electric circuit a continuous unbroken pathway over which electric current can flow

electric current the flow of electrons through a wire

electric field the area of force that surrounds a charged particle

electromagnetic wave a wave that does not need a medium through which to travel (example: a light wave)

electromagnetism the relationship between electricity and magnetism

electron a tiny, negatively-charged particle that revolves around the nucleus of an atom

element a substance that cannot be broken down into simpler substances by chemical means (examples: hydrogen and oxygen)

embryo the early stage of development of a fertilized egg

endocrine system the glands that secrete substances that affect the functions of other parts of the body

endoplasmic reticulum a system of membranes found in the cytoplasm that carries materials throughout a cell

endothermic reaction a chemical reaction that absorbs energy

energy the ability to move matter from one place to another, to change matter from one substance to another, or to change matter from one form to another

environment the surroundings in which an organism lives

epicenter the point on Earth's surface directly above the focus of an earthquake

era a major division of geological time

erosion the gradual wearing away and moving of rock, soil, and sand along Earth's surface

esophagus the tube that connects the mouth and stomach; part of the digestive system

estrogen a hormone that controls the development of secondary sex characteristics in females

evaporation the process of changing a liquid into a gas (example: water to vapor)

evolution an orderly change; usually refers to the development of a species over time

exothermic reaction a chemical reaction that releases energy

external respiration the exchange of gases between the environment and the blood

extinction the disappearance of a species

fault a break in Earth's crust

first law of motion a law developed by Newton stating that objects at rest tend to stay at rest, and objects in motion tend to stay in motion, until they are acted upon by outside forces

flagella whiplike structures that move bacteria through water and other fluids

focus the point under Earth's surface where rocks break and move during an earthquake

food chain the movement of food through an ecosystem

force a push or pull acting on an object (example: friction)

fossil the preserved remains of a once-living thing

fossil fuel a source of energy formed over long periods of time from the remains of plants and animals (example: petroleum)

freezing point the temperature at which a liquid changes to a solid

frequency the number of waves that pass a given point in a given amount of time

friction a force that slows a moving object

galaxy a group of millions or billions of stars (example: the Milky Way)

gamete the sexual reproductive cell formed during meiosis that contains half the chromosomes (i.e., one member of each pair) of the parent cell

gas a form of matter that has no definite shape or volume (example: oxygen)

gene a part of the genetic molecule that determines a particular trait

gene frequency how often a particular gene occurs in a population

genetic code the particular structure of DNA that determines the traits of an organism

genetic drift the chance increase or decrease in the frequency of a particular gene

genetics the study of inherited characteristics

genotype the genes that are inherited

germination the process by which seeds sprout

glacier a large mass of moving ice

gonad a reproductive organ

gravity a force of attraction that exists between any two objects in the universe

gymnosperms nonflowering seed plants (example: pine trees)

half-life the time needed for half the nuclei in a sample of radioactive material to decay into another substance by giving off nuclear particles

heart the major organ of the circulatory system that pumps blood through the system

herbicide a chemical that kills plants

hereditary capable of being passed from a parent to an offspring

Hertz a measure of the frequency of waves

homologous structures body parts from different organisms that have similar structure but perform different functions (example: a bird's wing and a human's arm)

hormone a substance secreted by the endocrine system that affects the function of other parts of the body (example: adrenaline)

host cell a living cell that provides food and energy to another cell

hybrid an organism that has a mixture of dominant and recessive traits

hydrocarbon a special kind of organic compound that contains only the two elements, hydrogen and carbon

hydroxide the OH⁻ ion produced when a base is water

hypothesis a theory considered to be true for the purpose of investigation

ice age a period of thousands of years during which Earth's climate grows colder and the polar ice caps spread north and south

igneous rock a type of rock formed when hot liquid rock cools into crystals (example: granite)

immune system the body's main defense against disease

indirect respiration the process by which many celled organisms exchange gases with the environment

inertia the tendency of an object to keep moving remain at rest

infectious capable of being spread from one organism to another (example: the cold virus is infectious)

inner core the solid iron and nickel center of Earth

insulin a hormone that decreases the level of sugar in the blood

internal respiration the exchange of gases between the blood and the body's cells

interphase the first stage of mitosis, or cell division

ion a charged particle formed from an atom

ionic bond a chemical combination of two or more atoms in which electrons are transferred from one atom to another

isomers two compounds whose molecules have the same number and kind of atoms (and hence, the same chemical formula) but different arrangement of atoms (hence, are different compounds with different properties

isotopes atoms of the same element with different numbers of neutrons

joule (J) a measurement of work

kinetic energy the energy of an object in motion

kingdom one of the five main groups of living things (example: Kingdom Plantae)

landslide a form of rapid mass wasting in which rocks and soil fall quickly down a mountain

va molten rock that breaks through Earth's surface in a volcanic eruption

ucoplast the structure in plant cells that helps change glucose into starch and stores the starch; a type of plastid

ght that part of the electromagnetic spectrum that we can see

quid a form of matter that has definite volume but no definite shape (example: water)

ngitudinal wave a wave that pushes and pulls molecules back and forth parallel to its direction

mphocyte a type of white blood cell that produces antibodies

achine a device that helps people do work by changing the force or distance (or both) involved in a task (example: a lever)

acrophage a type of enlarged phagocyte (white blood cell) that can engulf a hundred bacteria at one time

agma hot liquid rock beneath Earth's surface

agnetic field the area of force that surrounds a magnet

alnutrition a poor state of health that results from an unbalanced diet

antle a layer of Earth below the crust

aritime polar air mass a large body of air originating over the ocean near the poles; cool, moist air

aritime tropical air mass a large body of air originating over the ocean near the equator; warm, moist air

ass amount of matter

ass wasting the downhill movement of rocks and soil caused by gravity

atter anything that has mass and takes up space

echanical advantage the amount of help a particular machine provides

edium the matter through which a wave travels

edulla smallest part of human brain located in brainstem; responsible for control of body organs

eiosis the process in which sexual reproductive cells are formed

elting point the temperature at which a solid changes into a liquid

Mercalli scale a measure from I to XII of the effects of an earthquake on a particular place

meristems areas in seed plants that contain growth cells

mesosphere the layer of Earth's atmosphere above the stratosphere

metamorphic rock a type of rock formed when other rocks are subjected to extreme heat or pressure (example: marble)

metamorphosis the process by which the immature form of an organism turns into a very different adult form (example: caterpillars metamorphose into moths or butterflies)

metaphase the third stage of mitosis, or cell division

mitochondria organelles in a cell's cytoplasm, rod-shaped structures that produce most of the cell's energy

mitosis the process by which a cell divides into two daughter cells identical to the parent cell

mixture a mechanical combination of elements in which each element keeps its own properties (example: air)

molecule the smallest particle of a compound that has all the properties of that compound (example: a water molecule contains two atoms of hydrogen and one atom of oxygen)

monocotyledon a flowering plant whose seedling has one leaf (example: grass)

motion a change in position relative to a fixed object

mudflow a form of rapid mass wasting in which mud slides down a slope

natural selection the idea that individuals having characteristics that help them adapt to their environment are more likely to survive and reproduce

neutral a state in which matter has no electric charge; number of protons equals number of neutrons in an atom; pH equal to 7.0

neutron a particle without a charge in the nucleus of an atom

newton (N) a measure of force

nicotine a poisonous chemical found in tobacco smoke

nitric oxide a gas released by burning gasoline

nitrification a process by which certain soil bacteria convert the nitrogen from decomposing organisms into forms that plants can use

nitrogen fixation a process by which certain bacteria take nitrogen from the atmosphere and combine it with other substances into a form plants can use

nonrenewable resource a resource that cannot be replaced once it is used up (example: coal)

nuclear fission the splitting of an atomic nucleus into two smaller nuclei

nuclear membrane in a cell, the layer of matter that separates the nucleus from the cytoplasm

nucleolus the part of a cell's nucleus that helps make protein

nucleus in biology, the part of the cell that controls cell activities; in chemistry, the small dense core of an atom that consists of protons and neutrons

offspring the direct descendants of an animal or plant

ohm a measure of resistance to the flow of electrons

ore a rock that contains valuable minerals

organ a group of different tissues working together

organ system several organs working together to perform a specific function (example: the digestive system)

organelle a structure in a cell (example: mitochondria)

organic compounds compounds that contain carbon

organic molecules molecules that contain carbon combined with nitrogen, hydrogen, or oxygen, which are the building blocks of all living things

outer core the layer of Earth between the mantle and the inner core

ovaries the female reproductive endocrine glands

oxytocin a hormone that causes uterine contractions during labor

ozone a form of oxygen in the atmosphere that absorbs ultraviolet sunlight

pancreas an endocrine gland that secretes the hormone insulin

parallel circuit an electric circuit in which the current divides and flows in two or more separate paths

parathormone a hormone that regulates the body's use of calcium and phosphorus

parathyroid gland an endocrine gland that secretes a hormone called parathormone

parent cell the cell undergoing mitosis, or cell division

particle accelerator a long, narrow tunnel, charged with electric and magnetic fields, used to accelerate and collide particles in order to release energy and create new particles

pathogen a microorganism that causes disease (example: the AIDS virus)

periodic table an arrangement of the elements according to their properties and atomic number

petroleum oil

pH scale a measurement from 0 to 14 of the strength of an acid or a base

phagocyte a type of white blood cell that fights disease-causing organisms by engulfing them

phenotype in genetics, the appearance of an individual

phloem a type of plant tissue that carries food from the leaves to other parts of the plant

photosynthesis the process by which plants use light energy to make food

physical state the condition of matter with respect to substance or form (for example, shape or volume) which is dependent on temperature and pressure and does not result in a chemical change or reaction; the three physical states matter are solid, liquid, and gas (example: ice water, water vapor); changes in physical state occurs at the freezing (melting) point and boiling (condensation) point

physics the study of matter and energy and how they are related

pituitary an endocrine gland that produces growth hormone, oxytocin, and other hormones

plasmids small structures in bacteria that may contain genetic material

plastids organelles in plant cells; chromoplasts, chloroplasts, and leucoplasts

population density the number of people who live in a specific area

potential energy energy stored in the position of an object at rest

primary consumers in a food chain, animals that eat plants (example: cows)

primary waves the fastest type of seismic waves

producers organisms in a food chain that produce their own food, usually green plants

product a substance formed as a result of a chemical reaction

prophase the second stage of mitosis, or cell division

proton a particle with a positive charge in the nucleus of an atom

pulmonary veins blood vessels that carry oxygen-rich blood from the lungs to the heart

Punnett square a chart used by scientists to predict which traits will be inherited

purebred in genetics, an organism that when bred always produces the same trait

radioactivity the release of energy and matter that results from changes in the nucleus of an atom

rarefaction the spreading apart of molecules in a longitudinal wave

ray a narrow beam

reactant a substance that is an ingredient of a chemical reaction

receptors nerve endings that receive stimuli

recessive trait a trait that does not appear when combined with a dominant trait, and that must be contributed by both parents in order to appear in an offspring; i.e., a trait that appears in the genotype but not in the phenotype

reflection the bouncing of light rays off a surface

reflex an automatic response to a condition in an organism's environment (example: squinting in strong light)

refraction the bending of light rays as they pass from one medium to another

renewable resource a resource that can be replaced (example: trees)

resistance the opposition a material offers to the flow of electrons; in physics, a force that opposes or slows motion (example: the weight of an object)

resources the things organisms need to live, such as water, food, and energy

rhinoviruses a group of viruses that cause most colds

ribosome a part of a cell that has a role in making proteins

Richter scale a measure from 1 to 10 of the amount of energy released by an earthquake

rock cycle the process by which rocks continue to change from one type to another

salinity the amount of salt in ocean water

salt a neutral compound that results from the chemical combination of an acid and a base (example: sodium chloride, or table salt); pH equals 7.0

secondary consumers in a food chain, animals that eat primary consumers (example: lions)

secondary waves seismic waves that can travel through solids but not through liquids or gases

second law of motion a law, developed by Newton, stating that objects will accelerate in the direction of the force that acts upon them; mass and force will affect the rate of acceleration

sedimentary rock a type of rock formed by the hardening of particles of sand, mud, clay, or other sediments (example: sandstone)

seismic waves vibrations caused by movement of rock during an earthquake

semicircular canals structures in the ears that help maintain balance

septum the wall of tissue that separates the right and left sides of the heart

series circuit an electric circuit in which there is only one path for the electric current

shield volcano a type of volcano with quiet lava flows that form a gently sloping mountain made of hardened lava

slime layer the outer covering of a bacterium

soil creep a form of mass wasting in which soil particles gradually move downhill

solid a form of matter that has definite shape and volume (example: brick)

solubility the greatest amount of a solute that will dissolve in a given amount of solvent at a certain temperature

solute the substance being dissolved in a solution (example: salt)

solution a mixture in which two or more substances are dissolved in one another (example: salt water)

solvent the substance doing the dissolving in a solution (example: water)

speciation the development of a new species from an old one

species a group of genetically similar organisms that can mate and produce fertile offspring (example: dogs)

speed distance traveled per unit of time; how quickly an object moved

spindle fibers protein fibers formed during cell division, or mitosis

spirilla corkscrew-shaped bacteria

stomach the part of the alimentary canal where fat begins to be broken down, minerals are dissolved, and bacteria in food are killed by stomach acids

stratosphere the layer of Earth's atmosphere above the troposphere

structural formula diagram using symbols representing the arrangement of atoms in a molecule

sulfur dioxide a gas released by the burning of fossil fuels

sunspots dark spots that appear on the sun's surface

surface waves the slowest type of seismic waves that travel from the focus up to the surface of Earth

synthetic not found in nature

talus slope the rocks and soil that come to rest at the bottom of a mountain or hill as a result of mass wasting

taxonomy the classification of organisms into groups based on evolutionary relationships

telophase the fifth and final stage of mitosis, or cell division

temperature a measure of heat content

tertiary consumers in a food chain, animals that eat secondary consumers

testes the male reproductive endocrine glands

testosterone a hormone that controls the development of secondary sex characteristics in males

thermal energy conversion a process of producing energy, in which the difference in temperature between surface and deep seawater is used to generate electricity

thermodynamics the study of the relationship between heat energy and the energy of motion

thermosphere the uppermost layer of Earth's atmosphere

thymine a nitrogen base that is paired with adenine in DNA

thymosin a hormone that may affect the formation of antibodies in children

thymus an endocrine gland that produces the hormone thymosin

thyroid gland an endocrine gland that produces the hormone thyroxin

thyroxin a hormone that controls how quickly food is converted to energy in cells

trace fossil the evidence or mark of a living thing (example: footprints in rock)

trachea the tube through which air passes from the back of the mouth to the lungs

trait an inherited characteristic of an organism

troposphere the lowest layer of the atmosphere, closest to Earth

trough the low point of a wave

vacuole storage spaces in a cell that contain food or water, or that collect and excrete waste

vaporization the process of adding heat to a liquid in order to change it into a gas

vein a blood vessel that carries blood back to the heart

velocity the distance covered in a specific unit of time

vena cava a large vein that carries oxygen-poor blood into the heart

vent an opening in a volcano

ventricles the lower chambers of the heart

venules small blood vessels that carry blood into the veins

vestigial structure a body structure that is poorly developed or not functioning but that is similar to a well-developed, functioning structure in another organism (example: the vestigial leg bone of some snakes)

virus a single molecule of genetic material surrounded by a coat of protein

volcano the place where lava breaks through Earth's surface

volt a measure of the strength of the source of energy producing an electric current

voltage the source of energy for an electric current

water cycle continuous movement of water from Earth's surface to the air, then back to the surface again

wave a disturbance that travels through space or matter (example: sound waves)

wavelength the distance between the crests of two consecutive waves

weathering the process by which large rocks are broken down into smaller rocks; may be chemical or mechanical

wind moving air

work the result of a force moving an object over a distance

xylem a type of plant tissue that carries water upward from the roots to the stems and leaves

zygote the cell that is produced by the combining of two gametes during sexual reproduction

Index

Telophase, 38
Temperature, 118
Tertiary consumer, 92, 106
Testes, 72
Testosterone, 72
Theory of evolution, 52
Theory of origin of life, 54–55
Thermal energy, 160
Thermal energy conversion, 145
Thermodynamics, 179, 193, 194
Thermosphere, 120, 142
Third Law of Motion, 187
Thymine, 88
Thymosin, 72
Thymus, 72
Thyroid gland, 58–59, 72
Thyroxin, 72
Tides, 240
Time, 185
Topic sentence, 34, 180
Toxin, 76
Trace fossil, 114
Trachea, 47
Trait, 54, 57, 84
Tree surgery, 41
Trees, 41
Trichina worm, 67
Trichinosis, 67
Troposphere, 120, 142
Trough, of wave, 206
TSH hormone, 72
Twins, 83

Undernutrition, 43
Unstated assumption, 66

Vaccine, 98
Vacuole, 36
Valley, erosion of, 139
Vaporization, 152
Vein, 70–71
Velocity, 185
    of wave, 207
Vena cava, 70
Vent, of volcano, 140
Ventricle, 70
Venule, 71
Vestigial structure, 103
Vibration, 242
Virus, 76, 78–79, 80–81
Vitamin C, 81
Volcano, 116, 140–141, 225
Voltage, 200–201
Volts, 200–201

Water
    in Earth's atmosphere, 120,
        122, 124
    in oceans, 125
    in photosynthesis, 40, 44, 49,
        63
    in respiration, 46
    pollutants in, 90
    purification, 51
    in seed germination, 65

Water cycle, 101, 109, 124
Water waves, 207
Watson, James D., 88
Wave, 179, 206–207, 209, 242
    characteristics of, 206–207,
        209
Wavelength, 207
Weather, 122, 127, 133
Weathering, 119, 144
Weight gain during pregnancy,
    43
White light, 211
Wind, 130
Work, measuring, 189, 194, 195

Xylem, 63

Zygote, 39

Answer Sheet

GED Science Test

Name: _____ **Class:** _____ **Date:** _____

○ Pretest   ○ Posttest   ○ Simulated Test

1 ① ② ③ ④ ⑤   12 ① ② ③ ④ ⑤   23 ① ② ③ ④ ⑤   34 ① ② ③ ④ ⑤   45 ① ② ③ ④ ⑤   56 ① ② ③ ④ ⑤

2 ① ② ③ ④ ⑤   13 ① ② ③ ④ ⑤   24 ① ② ③ ④ ⑤   35 ① ② ③ ④ ⑤   46 ① ② ③ ④ ⑤   57 ① ② ③ ④ ⑤

3 ① ② ③ ④ ⑤   14 ① ② ③ ④ ⑤   25 ① ② ③ ④ ⑤   36 ① ② ③ ④ ⑤   47 ① ② ③ ④ ⑤   58 ① ② ③ ④ ⑤

4 ① ② ③ ④ ⑤   15 ① ② ③ ④ ⑤   26 ① ② ③ ④ ⑤   37 ① ② ③ ④ ⑤   48 ① ② ③ ④ ⑤   59 ① ② ③ ④ ⑤

5 ① ② ③ ④ ⑤   16 ① ② ③ ④ ⑤   27 ① ② ③ ④ ⑤   38 ① ② ③ ④ ⑤   49 ① ② ③ ④ ⑤   60 ① ② ③ ④ ⑤

6 ① ② ③ ④ ⑤   17 ① ② ③ ④ ⑤   28 ① ② ③ ④ ⑤   39 ① ② ③ ④ ⑤   50 ① ② ③ ④ ⑤   61 ① ② ③ ④ ⑤

7 ① ② ③ ④ ⑤   18 ① ② ③ ④ ⑤   29 ① ② ③ ④ ⑤   40 ① ② ③ ④ ⑤   51 ① ② ③ ④ ⑤   62 ① ② ③ ④ ⑤

8 ① ② ③ ④ ⑤   19 ① ② ③ ④ ⑤   30 ① ② ③ ④ ⑤   41 ① ② ③ ④ ⑤   52 ① ② ③ ④ ⑤   63 ① ② ③ ④ ⑤

9 ① ② ③ ④ ⑤   20 ① ② ③ ④ ⑤   31 ① ② ③ ④ ⑤   42 ① ② ③ ④ ⑤   53 ① ② ③ ④ ⑤   64 ① ② ③ ④ ⑤

10 ① ② ③ ④ ⑤   21 ① ② ③ ④ ⑤   32 ① ② ③ ④ ⑤   43 ① ② ③ ④ ⑤   54 ① ② ③ ④ ⑤   65 ① ② ③ ④ ⑤

11 ① ② ③ ④ ⑤   22 ① ② ③ ④ ⑤   33 ① ② ③ ④ ⑤   44 ① ② ③ ④ ⑤   55 ① ② ③ ④ ⑤   66 ① ② ③ ④ ⑤

0774